THE KABBALISTIC CULTURE OF EIGHTEENTH-CENTURY PRAGUE

◆

Since the rabbis spoke in riddles and hints,
I will not act as a talebearer and reveal secrets.
What I have written is already enough, and if,
God forbid, this was a mistake may th
good Lord atone for me.

EZEKIEL LANDAU
Tsiyun lenefesh ḥayah, Pesaḥim 56a
(Prague, 1783)

Why do you gaze upon the heavens?
Is it not enough to know your course on earth?
Why do you engage in kabbalah?
It is exceedingly deep; who can find it out?
The righteous walk in its ways, but the sinner
shall stumble in them.

A Dialogue Between the Years 5560–5561
(Prague, 1800), anonymous work

[The author] increased understanding of the
[kabbalistic Lurianic work] *Mishnat ḥasidim*, which
until now has been like the writings of sealed
books, since it is written in an extremely abbreviated
manner . . . Also, until this time no one has looked
at the [classic Lurianic] *Ets ḥayim*, whose ways
are hidden . . . When his book . . . is published,
those who are fearful of the word of God
should jump to buy this book.

EZEKIEL LANDAU
approbation (1744)

THE LITTMAN LIBRARY OF
JEWISH CIVILIZATION

Dedicated to the memory of
LOUIS THOMAS SIDNEY LITTMAN
who founded the Littman Library for the love of God
and as an act of charity in memory of his father
JOSEPH AARON LITTMAN
and to the memory of
ROBERT JOSEPH LITTMAN
who continued what his father Louis had begun
יהא זכרם ברוך

Get wisdom, get understanding:
Forsake her not and she shall preserve thee
PROV. 4: 5

THE KABBALISTIC CULTURE OF EIGHTEENTH-CENTURY PRAGUE

◆

Ezekiel Landau (the 'Noda Biyehudah') and his Contemporaries

◆

SHARON FLATTO

London
The Littman Library of Jewish Civilization
in association with Liverpool University Press

The Littman Library of Jewish Civilization
Registered office: 4th floor, 7–10 Chandos Street, London W1G 9DQ

in association with Liverpool University Press
4 Cambridge Street, Liverpool L69 7ZU, UK
www.liverpooluniversitypress.co.uk/littman

Managing Editor: Connie Webber

Distributed in North America by
Oxford University Press Inc., 198 Madison Avenue,
New York, NY 10016, USA

First published in hardback 2010
First published in paperback 2015

Catalogue records for this book are available from the
British Library and the Library of Congress

ISBN 978-1-906764-79-1

Publishing co-ordinator: Janet Moth
Copy-editing: Lindsey Taylor-Guthartz
Proof-reading: Agnes Erdos
Index: Christine Headley
Designed by Pete Russell, Faringdon, Oxon.
Typeset by Hope Services (Abingdon) Ltd

Printed and bound in Great Britain by
CPI Group (UK) Ltd., Croydon, CR0 4YY

In memory of my mother

DR ZEHAVA FLATTO

ZIKHRONAH LIVRAKHAH

whose guidance, tireless devotion, and insatiable pursuit of knowledge served as a constant source of inspiration

Her mouth was full of wisdom,
her tongue with the teaching of kindness.
She rose before daybreak to provide
for her household.

And in honour of my father

DR LEOPOLD FLATTO

who gave me the love of learning necessary to begin this project and the ongoing support required to complete it

Acknowledgements

NUMEROUS PEOPLE deserve thanks for helping me at various stages of my research and writing.

This study began as a doctoral thesis at Yale University, under the guidance of my advisers David Ruderman and Paula Hyman. Professor Ruderman introduced me to the delights and subtleties of early modern Jewish history; Professor Hyman taught me about the fascinating complexities of modern Jewish history. Both continue to serve as models in their rare combination of uncompromised academic rigour with steadfast dedication to teaching.

From the moment Professor Elliot Wolfson (who eventually joined my dissertation committee) told me that he could not comment on my research findings until he saw the actual 'texts', I knew I had met the scholar who could guide me through the difficult kabbalistic terrain required for this project. He has done so with incredible generosity, enthusiasm, and support. I am greatly indebted to him.

After completing my Ph.D., I was fortunate to receive a postdoctoral fellowship at Brown University. My colleagues there (particularly Lynn Davidman and Saul Olyan) not only encouraged me to publish this book but provided me with a supportive environment in which to work. At Brooklyn College, my academic home, I have had the privilege of working in a vibrant atmosphere with wonderful colleagues and students. I am especially grateful to the chair of my department, Sara Reguer, a friend and a colleague, and to Jonathan Helfand, who has frequently offered me sage advice. Other Brooklyn College colleagues who deserve special mention are Sid Leiman, Robert Shapiro, Herbert Druks, and David Berger.

Over the years, many other colleagues have shared their knowledge of Jewish history and other fields with me, influencing my thinking and sharpening my arguments. Among these I especially thank my 'library friends' at the Jewish Theological Seminary—Seth Schwartz and Arnold Franklin—with whom I have spent countless hours 'shmoozing' and fine-tuning specific points; Elisheva Carlebach, who gave me indispensable advice about choosing this project; Moshe Idel, who encouraged me to pursue this topic at its initial stages; Daniel Abrams, who introduced me to many of the treasures of the Scholem library and to various thirteenth-century kabbalistic manuscripts; and Jay Berkovitz, Edward Fram, and Yehudah Mirsky, who offered valuable comments. I am also grateful to the editors at the Littman Library, Connie Webber, Lindsey Taylor-Guthartz, and Janet Moth, who have done a great deal to enhance this manuscript through their excellent editorial work.

The research for this book was conducted in many libraries and archival collections in the United States, Europe, and Israel. I wish to thank the staff who have helped me at each of these institutions. In the United States, they include the Jewish Theological Seminary of America, Columbia University, Harvard University, the New York Public Library, and the Leo Baeck Institute. I am particularly grateful to the research librarians at the Jewish Theological Seminary, Yisrael Dubitsky and Jeremy Meyerowitz, who have assisted me with numerous bibliographical queries. Jerry Weiss deserves a special thanks for making his eighteenth-century rare book collection available. I am indebted to the archivists and librarians at the following institutions in Prague: the Státní Židovské Muzeum (State Jewish Museum); the Státní ústřední archiv (Central State Archives), the Municipal Archives, and the National Library of the Czech Republic. I am also grateful to the following institutions in Israel for allowing me to make use of their collections containing important Prague materials: the Jewish National and University Library, the Central Archives for the History of the Jewish People, and the Schocken Library.

'without flour there is no Torah'
(MISHNAH *Avot* 3: 17)

Much of the research and travel for this book was made possible by financial assistance from various fellowships and institutions. I have received grants from the Leo Baeck Institute, the DAAD (Deutscher Akademischer Austausch Dienst), the Yale University Dissertation Fellowship, the National Foundation for Jewish Culture, the Memorial Foundation for Jewish Culture, and the PSC–CUNY Research Award. I am extremely grateful for their generous assistance. I also thank the Whiting Foundation for its teaching prize, which enabled me to take a semester's sabbatical in order to complete this book.

'Either friendship or death'
(BT *Ta'anit* 23*a*)

During the course of this often lonely project, I was blessed with the support of extraordinary friends. David Chasman read through my entire dissertation and was the first fan of this project. Thanks to his tremendous generosity, there was hardly an idea in the dissertation that I did not discuss with him. My friends Nehama Edinger, Rebecca Darshan, and Hadassah Segal have constantly provided me with encouragement, sound advice, and laughter, and are probably too tired of hearing about this book to ever read it. I also thank Seth Aronson, Chana Stiefel, Suzanne Kling, Miryam Segal, Lawrence Horwitz, and Miriam Bloom for their many years of friendship and kindness.

My greatest debt is owed to my family, who have nurtured me in every way possible. They have particularly enhanced this work, which combines the world of Torah learning with critical academic scholarship. My brother David Flatto, who is a rabbi, lawyer, and Judaic studies scholar, helped with his extensive knowledge of rabbinics, his lawyerly ability to evaluate an argument, his creativity, and his gift for seeing the larger picture. I was blessed to grow up in a home with parents who treasured the mind and spirit. Their deep appreciation for history, Judaic studies, and the arts inspired me to pursue a career in European history and Judaic studies. My father, a brilliant, unassuming mathematician and *talmid ḥakham*, taught me early on the importance of precision, clarity of thought, pursuit of excellence, and the value of the life-long study of rabbinic texts. My mother—a genuine Renaissance woman—was interested in everything from history to art, Bible to economics, Hebrew language to travel, all of which gave me a richer understanding of many of the subjects addressed in this study. Above all, she loved nothing more than family, rigorous scholarship, and a good book. I cannot even begin to imagine all the *naches* she would have had from seeing this book published.

I also thank my beloved husband Ysoscher Katz, whose hero for many years—even before we met—was the Noda Biyehudah. He has helped me improve the book with his tremendous knowledge of rabbinic texts as well as with his incisive comments. I also thank him for creating a home with me that is filled with warmth, children, academic scholarship, and Torah. Our children Avi and Gavriel—'with whom God has favoured' us (Gen. 33: 5)—deserve credit for forcing me to remember that there is a world outside of eighteenth-century Prague.

New York, 2009 SHARON FLATTO

Contents

Note on Transliteration and Conventions Used in the Text

THE transliteration of Hebrew in this book reflects consideration of the type of book it is, in terms of its content, purpose, and readership. The system adopted therefore reflects a broad approach to transcription, rather than the narrower approaches found in the *Encyclopaedia Judaica* or other systems developed for text-based or linguistic studies. The aim has been to reflect the pronunciation prescribed for modern Hebrew, rather than the spelling or Hebrew word structure, and to do so using conventions that are generally familiar to the English-speaking reader.

In accordance with this approach, no attempt is made to indicate the distinctions between *alef* and *ayin*, *tet* and *taf*, *kaf* and *kuf*, *sin* and *samekh*, since these are not relevant to pronunciation; likewise, the *dagesh* is not indicated except where it affects pronunciation. Following the principle of using conventions familiar to the majority of readers, however, transcriptions that are well established have been retained even when they are not fully consistent with the transliteration system adopted. On similar grounds, the *tsadi* is rendered by 'tz' in such familiar words as barmitzvah, mitzvot, and so on. Likewise, the distinction between *ḥet* and *khaf* has been retained, using *ḥ* for the former and *kh* for the latter; the associated forms are generally familiar to readers, even if the distinction is not actually borne out in pronunciation, and for the same reason the final *heh* is indicated too. As in Hebrew, no capital letters are used, except that an initial capital has been retained in transliterating titles of published works (for example, *Shulḥan arukh*).

Since no distinction is made between *alef* and *ayin*, they are indicated by an apostrophe only in intervocalic positions where a failure to do so could lead an English-speaking reader to pronounce the vowel-cluster as a diphthong—as, for example, in *ha'ir*—or otherwise mispronounce the word.

The *sheva na* is indicated by an *e*—*perikat ol*, *reshut*—except, again, when established convention dictates otherwise.

The *yod* is represented by *i* when it occurs as a vowel (*bereshit*), by *y* when it occurs as a consonant (*yesodot*), and by *yi* when it occurs as both (*yisra'el*).

Names have generally been left in their familiar forms, even when this is inconsistent with the overall system.

Introduction

KABBALAH was both venerated and feared in eighteenth-century Prague. Some Jews maintained that it contained essential truths that must be disseminated. Others viewed it as a sacred mystical system that had to be restricted. Kabbalistic concepts, always controversial, were both incorporated into numerous prayer books and banned from study in certain Prague circles. Even more remarkable, however, is the profound inner struggle visible in the teachings and pronouncements of Prague's traditional leaders. Many of the city's rabbinic authorities and communal figures simultaneously concealed and disclosed mystical traditions. Promoters of kabbalah emerged from a broad swath of Prague's society, including the rabbinic elite, the community's laity, and sectarian groups, which threatened to undermine rabbinic Judaism. Caught in a web of tentative and tense interrelationships and harbouring a range of attitudes towards kabbalistic study and practice, these believers often had to veil their kabbalistic secrets in order to advance them.

This book describes the multi-layered mystical rabbinic culture of eighteenth-century Prague.[1] It reveals the largely overlooked prominence of kabbalah in traditional life, particularly in the biography and writings of one of the towering figures of Ashkenazi (east and central European) Jewry, Ezekiel Landau (1713–93), Prague's chief rabbi from 1754 to 1793. In exploring the deep roots of mysticism in this eighteenth-century capital of rabbinic culture, it sheds light on a central aspect of the life and world-view of a large number of early modern Ashkenazi Jews.

Certain themes and methodological assumptions surface throughout the book. (A description of the book's sections is appended at the end of the introduction.) Among its main themes are the neglect of Prague's rabbinic culture; the importance of Prague as a meeting ground between East and West; the centrality of kabbalah for Prague Jews and its persistence over the *longue durée*; the tremendous influence of Landau in Prague; and the hitherto unnoticed importance of kabbalistic ideas in Landau's thinking and their dissemination in many of his Prague writings, albeit at times obliquely as a result of his complex

[1] Throughout this book I use the phrase 'rabbinic culture' in a broad sense to denote traditional Jewish culture that was informed by classical rabbinic texts, elite rabbinic learning, and talmudic and halakhic (Jewish legal) norms and practices.

relationship with emerging mystical and modernizing trends. After addressing these themes the book charts and analyses the wide range of kabbalistic materials that Landau and Prague Jews drew upon, and explores this phenomenon in the light of earlier scholarly discussions of the range of mystical sources that influenced seventeenth- and eighteenth-century Ashkenazi Jews. Another of my aims is to frame this project within the context of various developments in contemporary Jewish studies. This book builds on, but also amends and revises, recent influential scholarly contributions in the areas of central and east European Jewish history, hasidism, Haskalah (the Jewish Enlightenment), and kabbalah. It thus contributes to the broader fields of early modern Jewish history, Jewish mysticism, and the cultural-anthropological study of the modernization and acculturation of traditional communities.

Background

Despite the pre-eminence of Prague's eighteenth-century Jewish community and its rich kabbalistic and halakhic traditions, there has been little scholarship on the city's Jewish culture during this transitional period because of erroneous assumptions made by scholars with an anti-traditional bias. These scholars maintained that the authority of the central European rabbinate and the vibrancy of traditional Jewish communities waned during the latter half of the eighteenth century.[2] In fact, however, the rabbinic culture and leadership of Prague's Jewish community, one of the largest and most prestigious in the world at this time,[3] flourished, and arguably reached its peak, during this era. As a result of these misconceptions, the history of Prague's eighteenth-century rabbinate, as well as its impact on numerous Ashkenazi Jewish communities, has been neglected.[4]

A survey of the historical works on Habsburg Jews during this period highlights their focus on the incipient modernization of the minority of late eighteenth-century Jewry, and their oversight of its prevailingly traditional society. Emblematic of this trend is Ruth Kestenberg-Gladstein's magisterial *Neuere Geschichte der Juden in den böhmischen Ländern*, which examines this transitional age for Bohemian Jewry, stressing primarily Prague's Haskalah along with the

[2] See e.g. Yosef Hayim Yerushalmi's foreword to Carlebach, *Pursuit of Heresy*, p. xii.

[3] At least 10,000 Jews resided in Prague during this era. See Kestenberg-Gladstein, *Neuere Geschichte*, 1, 2, 29; ead., 'Chapters in the History of Czech Jewry' (Heb.), 32; Kieval, 'Autonomy and Interdependence', 76. Only Amsterdam and Salonica seem to have had larger Jewish populations. See Kieval, 'The Lands Between', 50 n. 18.

[4] See Abramsky, 'Crisis of Authority', 13; Twersky, 'Opening Remarks: Major Trends in Modern Jewish History'.

relatively small number of elite Jews who modernized, but not its rabbinic culture.[5] Kestenberg-Gladstein, like most scholars of Habsburg Jewry, neglects the wealth of historical material contained in the vast number of eighteenth-century rabbinic writings, including sermons, responsa, commentaries, and polemical treatises, replete with information on Prague's rabbinic authorities, values, and institutions.[6] While some scholars, such as William McCagg in his *History of Habsburg Jews*, openly acknowledge that they pay more attention 'to the assimilationist elite than to the broad traditionalist masses of Jewry', others do so less explicitly.[7]

By focusing on the small group of eighteenth-century Prague Jews who became involved in the Haskalah or who assimilated, and by ignoring the nature of the traditional milieu, these studies present a skewed portrait of this period of Prague Jewish history, actually dominated by rabbinic culture. In addition to distorting the importance of the prevailing traditional society, this omission hampers scholarship's understanding of the maskilim (advocates of Jewish Enlightenment) and assimilationists, who both emerged from this traditional society and responded to it. This book seeks to redress this imbalance by examining the factors that allowed Prague Jewry's traditional life to persist during the eighteenth century and by documenting its continued vitality. It focuses on Prague's major rabbinic figures and institutions, and extensively analyses the spiritual, and especially kabbalistic, trends that shaped and animated Prague's traditional Jewish culture.

Notwithstanding initial inroads of various modernizing and potentially subversive mystical movements, which were soon to weaken Prague's traditional authority, and despite Habsburg emperor Joseph II's (1741–90) official abolition of the Jewish community's autonomy through his 1781 Toleranzpatent (Edict of Toleration), Prague's Jewish community continued to thrive during the latter half of the eighteenth century. Slow socio-economic transformation, a powerful rabbinate, and unrelenting antisemitism contributed to the continued existence of Prague's traditional society. This book demonstrates that Prague's late eighteenth-century rabbinate was more influential, more conservative, and less open to modernization and the Haskalah than has been recognized (see especially Part I below). Even with numerous changes legislated by the Habsburg state, the main rabbinic institutions, such as the Jewish high court, talmudic

5 See Samet, review of Kestenberg-Gladstein, *Neuere Geschichte* (Heb.).

6 There are a few studies on Ezekiel Landau that do give more weight to selected rabbinic materials. However, these works are primarily hagiographic and do not critically examine Landau's life and writings. See Kamelhar, *Mofet hador*; Gelman, *The Noda Biyehudah and his Teaching* (Heb.).

7 McCagg, *History of Habsburg Jews*, 48. See also Kestenberg-Gladstein, *Neuere Geschichte*, 38. She asserts that her book focuses on the cultural changes which affected only a small segment of Prague Jewry in the wake of Joseph II's 1781 Toleranzpatent.

academies, and traditional elementary schools, functioned and retained their influence throughout Landau's tenure. During the late eighteenth century Prague was also home to over fifty prominent rabbinic scholars and judges, who have been almost entirely overlooked. Furthermore, Landau's sermons, which span his Prague career, are replete with criticisms of Prague Jews' minor ritual lapses, suggesting that this community largely continued to live within the framework of halakhah.[8] Prague's vibrant rabbinic culture during the latter half of the eighteenth century stands out in comparison to west European Jewish centres such as Berlin, where several scholars have dated the incipient decline of traditional values and practices to the early eighteenth century.[9]

Between East and West

A more nuanced depiction of Prague's rabbinic culture during this transitional age requires a reassessment of its place within the matrix of East and West. Most studies of this period focus either on the modernization of west European Jewry or on the traditional life of east European Jewish society,[10] while the culture of central European Jews, and specifically that of Prague, has been largely neglected. Gershon Hundert's *The Jews in Poland–Lithuania during the Eighteenth Century* laments that Jewish historiography has not concentrated enough on the areas where most Jews lived.[11] This oversight has included the vast Jewish population of central Europe, and particularly its largest centre, Prague. Moreover, the few extant studies that do address Prague Jews during this era investigate only their interaction with the West, ignoring the enormous impact of east European trends on Prague's culture and society. Situated at the crossroads of Europe, Prague was inevitably affected by immigrants, students, merchants, and travellers from both eastern and western Europe. Several of its prominent rabbinic authorities, including Mordecai ben Abraham Jaffe (*c.*1535–1612,

[8] This view is also expressed by Saperstein in his '*Your Voice Like a Ram's Horn*', 145–6. Jacob Katz, however, contends that the halakhic observance of Prague Jews declined significantly during the 1780s. See Katz, *Out of the Ghetto*, 146–7.

[9] See e.g. Shohet, *Changing Eras* (Heb.), where he points to the significant deviance found during this period. Steven Lowenstein, *Berlin Jewish Community*, however, dates the decline of Berlin's traditional Jewish culture to the last decades of the 18th c. Even with this later date, west European Jews witnessed an earlier and more intense decline of traditional culture than occurred in Prague.

[10] On recent important works on Jewish life and culture in eastern and western Europe during this transitional era see Hundert, *Jews in Poland–Lithuania*; Bartal, *Jews of Eastern Europe*; Rosman, 'Innovative Tradition'; Wodzinski, *Haskalah and Hasidism in the Kingdom of Poland*; Feiner, *Jewish Enlightenment*.

[11] *Jews in Poland–Lithuania*, 1, 233. He, however, is primarily referring to Jews in east European lands.

commonly called the Levush), Ephraim Solomon of Luntshitz (1550–1619, popularly referred to as the Keli Yakar), Isaiah Horowitz (*c.*1565–1630, also known as the Shelah), and Jonathan Eybeschütz (*c.*1690–1764), were educated in eastern Europe.[12] Landau too spent the first forty years of his life studying in educational institutions and serving in rabbinic posts in various districts of Poland. At the same time, because of Prague's position as a geographical and cultural nexus, some of its traditional mores were challenged by nascent groups emerging in eastern and western Europe during the latter half of the eighteenth century: the Frankists and new hasidim in nearby eastern Europe and the maskilim in neighbouring Prussia. This book expands the limited scholarship on central Europe, and demonstrates that while Prague's culture was shaped from both directions, its primary influence was actually the East.[13] It was especially affected by east European Jewry's emphasis on *pilpul* (casuistic or dialectical talmudic study), its absorption of eclectic kabbalistic teachings, and its embrace of the mystical and ascetic ideals of the old-style hasidim (pietists).[14]

In studies on Poland and Lithuania, Gershon Hundert and Moshe Rosman have emphasized the popularity of kabbalah in the daily practices and beliefs of eighteenth-century Polish and Lithuanian Jews. Both have shown that, during this period, kabbalah became an integral aspect of the 'grammar' of many east European Jews' religious, literary, and popular expression.[15] Nevertheless, several scholars have observed that even more work remains to be done on the story of kabbalah's widespread dissemination among the masses during this era.[16] This careful study of Prague's eighteenth-century rabbinic sources and institutions continues along these lines by uncovering the centrality of kabbalah for a large segment of eighteenth-century Prague Jews. In this process, vital cultural similarities between east and central European Jewry emerge.

Prague Jews' *Mentalité*

In reconstructing the primary role of kabbalah in the development of the *mentalité* and religious psychology of Jews living in eighteenth-century Prague, this study draws on the methodology of scholars of the French Annales school and historians affiliated with this group, such as Marc Bloch, Lucien Febvre, and

12 Still, quite a few of Prague's intellectual elite looked towards the West, and members of its intelligentsia, such as Herz Homberg (1749–1841) and Baruch Jeitteles (1762–1813), spent time in Berlin.

13 Although Western influences made inroads into Prague during the end of the 18th c. (see Part I), they only became a driving force during the first half of the 19th c.

14 On the old-style hasidim in 18th-c. Poland and Galicia, see Rosman, *Founder of Hasidism*, 27–41; Dinur, 'Origins of Hasidism'; Jacobs, *Hasidic Prayer*, 8.

15 See Rosman, 'Innovative Tradition', 548–52, 560; Hundert, *Jews in Poland–Lithuania*, 119, 159.

16 See e.g. Hubka, 'The "Zohar" and the Polish Synagogue', 184.

Fernand Braudel.[17] Heeding Braudel's arguments, this book examines the ideas that remained widespread among Prague Jews over the *longue durée* of the eighteenth and early nineteenth centuries, instead of focusing solely on 'the history of events', an approach which often exaggerates the revolutionary nature of specific political changes.[18] The world-view that emerges from this longitudinal perspective is one suffused with mystical values. A wide range of kabbalistic doctrines permeated the beliefs, fears, and desires of Prague's Jews despite the dramatic political events and changes that occurred during the late eighteenth century.

Close study of late eighteenth-century Prague sources reveals that the world of Prague Jews at the onset of the Enlightenment and in the years following the promulgation of the Toleranzpatent is one replete with demons, angels, and transmigrated souls.[19] This was a culture in which many believed, for example, that the emission of semen 'in vain' created demons whose atonement required public and private kabbalistic rituals. Among the scores of kabbalistic tropes that were prominent in the rites and beliefs of Prague Jews were the notions that both the Shekhinah (literally 'God's presence') and the divine sparks, exiled since Adam's fall, needed to be redeemed. Undoubtedly, there was a great disparity in the level of comprehension of the complex kabbalistic concepts that served as the underpinning of these motifs. Both the elite and the laity, however, accepted their core doctrines. Consequently, an array of kabbalistic symbols appeared in diverse eighteenth- and early nineteenth-century Prague works, ranging from intricate talmudic commentaries to more popular polemical and liturgical writings.

Kabbalistic prayers and customs appear in almost every standard prayer book published in Prague during Landau's career in the city. These invaluable guardians of kabbalistic traditions and rituals have been virtually untouched by historians.[20] Remarkably, many include extra-liturgical kabbalistic texts, such as the liturgy for the monthly kabbalistic fast-day intended for both men and women, Yom Kippur Katan (Minor Day of Atonement), and texts for *tikun shovavim* (restorations for the 'ill bred': penances atoning for demons created

[17] See e.g. Bloch, *Rois thaumaturges*; id., *Société féodale*; Febvre, *Problème de l'incroyance au XVIe siècle*; Braudel, *Méditerranée et le monde méditerranéen á l'époque de Philippe II*; id., 'Histoire et sciences sociales'; Lefebvre, *Grande Peur de* 1789. For a discussion of both the Annales group and journal, see Burke, *The French Historical Revolution*; Huppert, 'Annales Experiment'.

[18] The history of 'events' was also scorned by earlier scholars. See e.g. Durkheim, 'Préface', p. v.

[19] I should be careful to stress that I am depicting general trends. Clearly, there was a range of beliefs, not homogeneity of opinions, among Prague Jews.

[20] Prague Jews either observed these rituals or, at the very least, were regularly exposed to them.

through emission of semen).[21] Numerous liturgical works incorporate other mystical prayers from the kabbalistic Lurianic and *musar* (ethical-mystical) literature. Assorted kabbalistic pamphlets, some only recently discovered, were also published in Prague during the eighteenth century. Among these are several *tikun ḥatsot* (midnight vigil) prayer books, Lurianic liturgical treatises, and prayers recited by mourners and the sick. Other works of this type were confiscated by censors and burned by the Inquisition, making an exact survey of this material nearly impossible.[22] Nevertheless, the extensive record of eclectic kabbalistic liturgical treatises indicates their wide use in Prague.

Beyond describing the pervasiveness of kabbalistic phrases and doctrines in the writings and rituals of Prague Jews, this book follows the call of various cultural anthropologists by attempting to provide a 'thick description' of the meaning that kabbalistic terms and practices had for members of Prague's Jewish community, thereby providing a window into the spiritual world of Prague Jews.[23] For them, kabbalah was not just a theoretical system but a way of construing meaning. To use the terms of the cultural anthropologist Clifford Geertz, for Prague Jews kabbalistic symbols were as much a *description of* the world as they were *concepts for ordering* the world and their experiences of it.[24] For example, the daily and yearly cycle of a large portion of Prague's Jewish community was organized by kabbalistic tenets: midnight was seen as an auspicious time for lamenting for the Shekhinah, as was the eve of the new moon. Numerous Prague Jews believed that the final redemption would only occur when the kabbalistic goals of restoring the Shekhinah and the divine sparks were fulfilled. As I will show, a large number of kabbalistic motifs also shaped Prague Jews' understanding of basic religious concepts, such as the nature of evil, the soul, and divine providence. Kabbalistic notions likewise motivated normative religious practices. Their halakhic observances, in accordance with kabbalistic

21 The *tikun shovavim* penances, which were often accompanied by fast-days, were recited during six winter weeks when the weekly Torah portions 'Shemot', 'Va'era', 'Bo', 'Beshalakh', 'Yitro', 'Mishpatim', 'Terumah', and 'Tetsaveh' were read. The acronym of the Hebrew names of these portions form the name *shovavim t't*, which is the name of this rite. The liturgical text for this kabbalistic ritual was frequently, although not always explicitly, filled with kabbalistic symbolism. On this ritual, see Horowitz, *Shenei luḥot haberit* (*Shelah*), 306*b*. For a discussion of this rite, see Scholem, *On the Kabbalah and its Symbolism*, 156–7; Hallamish, *Kabbalah in Liturgy, Halakhah and Customs* (Heb.), 567–94.

22 For example, a list of Hebrew books from Prague and other areas of Bohemia burnt in 1715, *Catalogus Librorum Hebraicorum privatim combustorum*, includes forty-nine talmudic and kabbalistic works. See Putík, 'Prague Jewish Community'.

23 See Clifford Geertz's classic essays in his *Interpretation of Cultures* and *Local Knowledge*. See also Rosman, 'Prolegomenon to the Study of Jewish Cultural History'.

24 See Geertz, 'Religion as a Cultural System', in his *Interpretation of Cultures*, esp. p. 123. For critiques of this and other ideas of Geertz, see Frankenberry and Penner (eds.), *Language, Truth, and Religious Belief*, 218–45 ('Geertz's Longlasting Moods, Motivations and Metaphysical Conceptions').

beliefs, were infused with mystical meaning, stimulating them to pay painstaking attention to the commandments' most minute details. In short, kabbalah, intertwined with halakhah, comprised a totalizing framework through which many Prague Jews engaged with the world.

Ezekiel Landau: Prague's Rabbi, Jurist, and Political Leader

Given Landau's central role in Prague, any effort to understand the rabbinic and kabbalistic outlook of its Jewish community has to focus on his life and writings. As chief rabbi and head of both the Jewish court (*beit din*) and a major talmudic academy in a city that boasted one of the largest European Jewish populations, a distinguished rabbinic tradition, and scores of prominent scholars, Landau held a position of great distinction. His official status, recognized by the Habsburg government, made him Prague Jewry's supreme authority for judicial, religious, and political affairs. Surprisingly, no one has written a critical account of either his life and works or the impact he had on Prague's Jewish community.

Landau's primary contributions were to Jewish legal scholarship and the defence of traditional Judaism, which makes his efforts at popularizing kabbalah all the more intriguing. In order to appreciate the significance of his kabbalistic involvement and teachings, it is necessary to recognize his wide-ranging influence.

His extraordinary mastery of the entire corpus of classical Jewish texts enabled him to play a pivotal role in shaping normative rabbinic law. His counsel in halakhic and communal matters was sought by a wide spectrum of rabbinic leaders, scholars, and laity.[25] As a result, he composed over 850 responsa, addressing almost every facet of Jewish law. These responsa were published in a monumental two-volume collection, the *Noda biyehudah* ('Known in Judah'), in Prague in 1776 and 1811 respectively.[26] This collection is so well known that Landau is commonly referred to as the Noda Biyehudah. The lasting impact of his legal rulings and analysis is best demonstrated by the enduring authority

[25] Although most of Landau's responsa are addressed to rabbinic scholars, Jacob Landau recounts that his father answered all queries, regardless of the correspondent's position within the Jewish community. See J. Landau, *Divrei yedidot*, 34.

[26] The first volume of the *Noda biyehudah* was published by Landau, the second by his son Samuel. These volumes are traditionally referred to as *Kama* (first) and *Tinyana* (second), and references below are to *NB Kama* and *NB Tinyana*. One of the reasons that Landau decided to publish his responsa was that many of his earlier responsa had been stolen during a house fire in 1775. See J. Landau, *Divrei yedidot*, 33. While Landau named the *Noda biyehudah* in honour of his father, Judah Landau, the meaning 'known in Judah', or among the Jews, was certainly also intended. Each volume is divided according to the four areas of law dealt with in the four volumes of the classic Jewish legal codes, Jacob ben Asher's *Arba'ah turim* (or simply *Tur*) and Joseph Karo's *Shulḥan arukh*: 'Oraḥ ḥayim' (OḤ), 'Yoreh de'ah' (YD), 'Even ha'ezer' (EH), and 'Ḥoshen mishpat' (ḤM).

of this work, and also by the popular reception of his talmudic commentary, the *Tselaḥ*, both of which have become part of the standard rabbinic canon.[27]

In addition, Landau's extensive writings include numerous sermons delivered at Prague's nine synagogues,[28] a gloss, *Dagul merevavah* ('Pre-eminent among Ten Thousand')[29] on the classic legal code *Shulḥan arukh*, as well as recently discovered glosses on Hayim Vital's (1542–1620) kabbalistic texts,[30] *Derekh ets ḥayim* and *Peri ets ḥayim*.[31] Recognizing Landau's astounding legal erudition and authority, the Habsburg monarchs Maria Theresa (1717–80) and Joseph II also consulted with him on matters relating to Jewish law and public policy.[32] Landau's proposals, some of which are found in tracts and responsa composed especially for these occasions, were often adopted by the monarchs.[33]

Throughout his career, Landau had tremendous influence on Jews in various parts of the world and was accordingly often referred to as the 'Rabbi of the

[27] The *Tselaḥ* is an acronym for *Tsiyun lenefesh ḥayah*, meaning, 'A Guidepost for the Living Soul'. The title is a play on words: *ḥayah*, meaning 'living', is also the name of Landau's mother, to whom he dedicates his commentary. The commentary covers many talmudic tractates. The first volume, on tractate *Pesaḥim*, was published in 1783 in Prague. In two responsa, Landau mentions that he is preparing it for publication (see *NB Tinyana*, 'ḤM', no. 6, 8 Sept. 1783; 'EH', no. 59, 25 Sept. 1783). The second and third volumes of the *Tselaḥ*, on tractates *Berakhot* and *Beitsah*, were published by his third son, Israel, in 1791 and 1799 respectively. The *Tselaḥ* on tractates *Shabat*, *Eruvin*, *Yoma*, *Sukah*, *Rosh hashanah*, *Ta'anit*, *Megilah*, and *Ḥagigah* was first published in Warsaw in 1879; the *Tselaḥ* on *Zevaḥim*, *Menaḥot*, and *Ḥulin* was first published in Warsaw in 1891; and the *Tselaḥ* on *Nezikin* was first published in Jerusalem in 1959. The entire *Tselaḥ*, which includes commentaries on additional tractates, was published in four volumes as *Tselaḥ hashalem* in 1995. Since this is the most comprehensive edition, the citations and page numbers from the *Tselaḥ* that appear in this book refer to this edition.

[28] A large number of these are found in the collections *Ahavat tsiyon* ('The Love of Zion') and *Derushei hatselaḥ* ('Sermons of the *Tselaḥ*'). In Prague in 1827, Samuel Landau published *Ahavat tsiyon*, a partial compilation of his father's Prague homilies, and *Doresh letsiyon*, a collection of his father's Yampol homilies. Ezekiel Landau's *Derushei hatselaḥ*, another collection of his Prague homilies, was published in Warsaw: although the title page of its first edition records that it was published in 1886, the Hebrew date indicates that it was published in 1884.

[29] Israel Landau published *Dagul merevavah* in Prague in 1794, a year after his father's death. The title of this work is based on a phrase in S. of S. 5: 10.

[30] Hayim Vital was the chief formulator of the kabbalistic teachings of Isaac Luria, often referred to as the Lurianic kabbalah. Most of his magnum opus, the *Ets ḥayim* ('The Tree of Life'), was composed between 1573 and 1576. During the 17th c., the Ashkenazi kabbalist Meir Poppers produced a recension of Vital's writings which became extremely popular in Europe. Poppers divided this work into three parts: *Derekh ets ḥayim* ('The Way of the Tree of Life'), *Peri ets ḥayim* ('The Fruit of the Tree of Life'), and *Nof ets ḥayim* ('A Branch of the Tree of Life'). These works are discussed in greater detail in Chapter 9.

[31] Most of the printed editions and manuscripts that we have of Landau's works are quite reliable. First, most of his published writings were printed in Prague during his lifetime or by his sons, Samuel and Israel, shortly after his death. In addition, many of his extant manuscripts were either handwritten by him or contain his signature.

[32] Best known among these were questions concerning the establishment of Prague's Jewish Normalschule (modern elementary school) in 1782, and Joseph II's proposal to impose civil marriage laws in 1783.

[33] See e.g. Landau's *Ḥukei ha'ishut* ('Laws of Marriage').

entire Diaspora'.[34] He played a decisive role in many of the seminal intra-communal controversies plaguing eighteenth-century Jewry. Records of his interventions survive in scattered sources, including letters to other leaders, sermons, and rabbinic writings. These are collected and analysed for the first time in this study.[35] Best known among the communal controversies that Landau refereed is the dispute between the two towering Ashkenazi rabbinic figures, Jacob Emden (1697–1776) and Jonathan Eybeschütz,[36] concerning mystical amulets written by Eybeschütz, and their alleged connection to the Sabbatian heresy. Had it not been for Landau, this dispute might have split Ashkenazi Jewry. Another cause célèbre in which Landau intervened was the disputed 1766 Cleves *get* (bill of divorce).[37] His validation of this divorce writ and the inclusion of his lengthy letter addressing this matter in a work entitled *Or hayashar* stirred the wrath of Frankfurt's rabbinic leaders.[38] As a result, Frankfurt's court decreed that no Landau family member could hold a rabbinic seat in Frankfurt for the next three generations. Even more dramatically, perhaps, Landau's well-known sermons and diplomatic letters against the Berlin Haskalah made him a notorious figure to many radical maskilim.[39] Landau's harsh critiques of both the maskilic educator Naphtali Herz Wessely (1725–1805) and the 'father of the Haskalah' Moses Mendelssohn (1729–86) had widespread repercussions and were frequently cited in traditional and maskilic circles.

Landau's legal responsa, which often dealt with issues pertaining to the incursion of modernity upon Ashkenazi Jewish communities, had a permanent

[34] This honorific epithet is found in the headings of many of Landau's approbations. See also Spitz, *Zikhron elazar*, 3; Sofer, 'Eulogy for Landau', delivered 26 Dec. 1793, printed in his *Derashot ḥatam sofer*, i. 103*b*. Landau's responsa and other writings, which were sent all over Europe, also reached and influenced cities in the Ottoman empire and Israel.

[35] Some of these letters have only recently surfaced in the collection of Landau's writings purchased several years ago by the Karlin-Stolin hasidim.

[36] On Landau's attitude towards Eybeschütz, see Leiman, 'When a Rabbi Is Accused of Heresy', 179–94; Graetz, 'Ezechiel Landau's Gesuch an Maria Theresia gegen Jonathan Eibeschütz'; Lieben, 'Zur Charakteristik des Verhältnisses zwischen Rabbi Jecheskel Landau und Rabbi Jonathan Eibenschitz'.

[37] The controversy engendered by this *get* was one of the major rabbinic disputes of the 18th c. It hinged on the validity of the divorce given by Isaac b. Eliezer Neiberg to Leah the daughter of Jacob Guenzhausen, in 1766 in the city of Cleves, shortly after they were married. The bridegroom's father claimed that the divorce was brought about by the machinations of the bride's relatives. Subsequently, the Frankfurt *beit din* and other rabbinic authorities invalidated the *get*, declaring that the bridegroom was not of sound mind at the time of the divorce. The Cleves rabbis, however, upheld the validity of the divorce, and received the support of most of the influential rabbis of the era, including Landau.

[38] For Landau's intricate legal discussion of this issue (dated 27 Tamuz 5527 (24 July 1767)), see Aaron Simeon of Copenhagen's collection of letters supporting this divorce writ, *Or hayashar*, 55–64. See also Landau's remarks in *Derushei hatselaḥ*, sermon 28, 43*b*.

[39] On Landau's response to the Haskalah, see Part I.

influence on the praxis of Ashkenazi Jews in both eastern and western Europe. Decisively responding to a wide range of issues that arose during this transitional era, his bold decisions informed almost all late eighteenth-century and subsequent discussions of these matters, often stirring vehement debates. Illustrative of such cases are Landau's granting permission for men to shave under certain circumstances on intermediate festival days;[40] his consent to the performance of autopsies in specific situations;[41] his discussion of the permissibility of eating sturgeon;[42] and his prohibition on the use of the recently introduced gadget, the umbrella, on the sabbath.[43] His harsh responsa pertaining to hasidism, the nascent mystical movement in eastern Europe, also had an enormous impact on Ashkenazi culture, informing the attitude of many of his contemporaries towards this pietistic movement. Landau's tremendous stature meant that recipients of his critiques, including various hasidic masters, often felt the need to respond to—and ironically even at times to internalize—them.

Landau's influence continued long after his death in 1793.[44] Over the next several years, a number of diverse eulogies were published in his memory, attesting to the broad spectrum of his admirers in both eastern and central Europe, spanning from the most strictly orthodox rabbis to moderate maskilim and early reformers.[45]

40 On the controversy stirred by this, see *NB Kama*, 'OḤ', no. 13; *NB Tinyana*, 'OḤ', nos. 99–101. See also Benayahu, *Shaving on the Intermediate Festival Days* (Heb.), esp. 20–9, 139–68; Samet, 'Halakhah and Reform' (Heb.), 10–22.

41 *NB Tinyana*, 'YD', no. 210.

42 The sturgeon does not conform to the standard criteria identifying a fish as kosher, for although it has scales they are extremely hard to separate from the body. For Landau's responsa on this topic, see *NB Tinyana*, 'YD', no. 28. For Samuel Landau's discussion of his father's responsum on this issue, see ibid., nos. 29 and 30, and S. Landau, *Shivat tsiyon*, no. 29. For more rabbinic literature discussing this responsum of Landau's see the Makhon Leyerushalayim edition of the *Noda biyehudah* (Jerusalem, 1990) ad loc. Landau's responsum on this topic also engendered much discussion and writing among the early reformers. See e.g. Aaron Chorin's pamphlets *Imrei no'am* and *Shiryon kaskasim*, where he argues that, like his teacher Landau, he deems the sturgeon to have scales and accordingly to be a kosher fish. For a discussion of this halakhic controversy and other 18th-c. rabbinic writings on this issue that have recently surfaced, see Heshel, 'Additional Documents on the Sturgeon Controversy of 1798' (Heb.).

43 See *NB Tinyana*, 'OḤ', no. 30. Although the umbrella is an ancient invention, its use only became common in Europe during the last decades of the 18th c. See Crawford, *History of the Umbrella*. Another atypical topic discussed in Landau's responsa is hunting. See *NB Tinyana*, 'YD', no. 10. Since this issue is so rare in the responsa literature, one may speculate that it arose as a result of the increased wealth and acculturation of individual Jews during this period.

44 Landau died on 17 Iyar 5553 (29 April 1793).

45 See e.g. the following eulogies: Karpeles, *Derush lehesped even haot yeḥezkel lemofet*; Fleckeles, *Olat ḥodesh hashelishi*, sermon 17, 71*a*–78*a*; Triebitsch, *Goren ha'atad*, 7*a*–14*b*; Karlburg, *Divrei avel al mot hagaon yeḥezkel landa halevi*, 2*a*–15*a*; Zunz, *Hespeda yekara deshakhbi*; the maskil Baruch Jeitteles, *Emek habakhah*; id., *Megilat eikhah al mot yeḥezkel*; the maskil Joseph Ha'efrati of Tropplowitz, *Alon bakhut*; R. Eleazar Low (also called the Shemen Roke'ah), *Sama deḥayei*, sermon 17, 41*b*–44*a*; Deitsch, *Kol bokhim*, published at the end of his *Divrei yosef*, 3–14. Moses Sofer also discusses Landau's death in a eulogy delivered in Dresnitz, Moravia, on 26 Dec. 1793, published in *Derashot ḥatam sofer*, i. 103*b*.

His legacy was carried on, to a certain extent, by his children, grandchildren, and students. Many of his pupils served in distinguished rabbinic and communal posts throughout Europe, where they often spread his teachings. To evaluate the scope of Landau's contributions, my research mines the Hebrew and Yiddish works of his sons, Jacob (*c.*1745–1822), Samuel (1750–1834), and Israel (1758–1829), German Habsburg governmental records, archival sources from Prague's Jewish community, and the writings of Landau's students, especially those of his chief disciple, Eleazar Fleckeles (1754–1826).[46]

Landau's Kabbalistic Proclivities and their Interplay with Prague's Mystical Culture

Landau's writings and teachings have continued to shape halakhah and rabbinic thought to the present day. His dominant legacy is that of a rigid and austere legal authority who staunchly opposed esoteric studies and practices.[47] This image largely derives from Landau's repeated protestations that he refrained from all esoteric matters, as well as his vocal opposition to the nascent mystical hasidic movement. My work challenges this widely held conception.

In fact, Landau's public discomfort with esotericism must be understood in the context of his staunch resistance to emerging mystical and modernizing trends. Underlying his reluctance to discuss kabbalah, even while he is promoting its central ideals, are several factors. First, he deemed it necessary to advance traditional learning given the recent shift in Prague Jewry's educational priorities that resulted from state-mandated secular education and the Enlightenment.[48] He was also extremely concerned about the strong sectarian Sabbatian and Frankist presence in Prague.[49] His objection to the Sabbatians' and Frankists' use of kabbalah was a function of his broader denunciation of these mystical groups, who based a large portion of their antinomian practices on kabbalistic ideas. Landau's frequent harsh condemnation of the Sabbatians and Frankists reflects his contention that

[46] Since methodological issues arise when one uses any one genre or author in order to document historical events and/or cultural trends, my study employs evidence found in diverse genres and works. On the critical use of sermons and responsa as historical sources, see Soloveitchik, *Responsa as a Historical Source* (Heb.); Saperstein, *Jewish Preaching*, 1–103; Gries, 'Between History and Literature' (Heb.), 113–22.

[47] The most recent scholar to uphold the view that Landau did not engage in esoteric matters is Benny Brown. See his discussion of Landau's theology in Halbertal, Kurzweil, and Sagi (eds.), *On Faith* (Heb.), 406–10.

[48] Joseph II's Normalschulen and the maskilic emphasis on secular education challenged the Ashkenazi rabbinic ideal of focusing almost exclusively on talmudic studies.

[49] Although Frankism was a more radical manifestation of Sabbatianism, in his denunciation of these sectarians Landau, like most Jews, does not distinguish between the Sabbatians and the Frankists. See Scholem, *Kabbalah*, 290.

they were an even greater threat to traditional Judaism than either the Habsburg state or the maskilim. Finally, he felt threatened by the increasing success of hasidism and its mass popularization of kabbalistic secrets. Ironically, his denunciation of these groups further masks his involvement with kabbalah and his dissemination of its teachings.

Notwithstanding his oft-repeated assertion that he did not 'delve into esoteric matters', my research exposes the centrality of kabbalah for Landau, its integration into his halakhic world-view, and its frequent incorporation into his writings and public addresses.[50] Seminal kabbalistic notions, such as the exiled Shekhinah, *gilgul neshamot* (the transmigration of souls), the *sefirot* (the ten aspects, or potencies, of the Divine), and the theurgical role of the commandments, are pivotal to Landau's thought, informing his hermeneutical approach to the Torah and aggadah (rabbinic legends and homiletic passages). The redemption of both the divine sparks and the Shekhinah is the prism through which he views the goals of religious activity. Remarkably, he makes extensive use of kabbalistic terms, such as *tikun* (mending or restoration), *sefirot*, *kelipot* (shells; demonic forces), and *devekut* (cleaving to or achieving a mystical union with God) in almost every one of his Prague homilies. In these sermons, he both builds on mystical concepts known to Prague Jews and introduces them to less familiar ones.[51] Beyond his use of basic mystical terms, various recondite kabbalistic comments in his sermons, commentaries, and, especially, in his recently found glosses on Hayim Vital's *Derekh ets ḥayim* and *Peri ets ḥayim*, highlight his deep engagement in kabbalistic speculation.[52]

Due to the length of his illustrious Prague career and his consequent influence over several generations of its inhabitants, the rabbinic and kabbalistic teachings and practices of Landau and his colleagues often converge with those of Prague Jews at large. Landau's charismatic and authoritative leadership enabled him to play an exceptionally significant role in directing and sustaining the culture of Prague's Jewish community. At the same time, his writings were

[50] All genres of Landau's work, albeit to a varying extent, include both technical legal discussions and kabbalistic teachings. His synthesis of these subjects is best exemplified by his Prague homilies, in which he frequently weaves kabbalistic and halakhic concepts together.

[51] Landau's homilies probably also popularized kabbalistic ideas among those who could not read them in the Hebrew or Aramaic original, particularly uneducated men and women.

[52] Conventional scholarship dates the emergence of kabbalah, in contradistinction to early Jewish mysticism, to late 12th-c. Provence and 13th-c. Catalonia. In this period, mystical writings first discussed the theosophical aspects of God, known as the *sefirot*. See Scholem, *Origins of the Kabbalah*; Idel, *Kabbalah*, 251. Since zoharic, Cordoverian, and Lurianic sources contain both theosophical-theurgical and ecstatic-mystical elements, I use both 'kabbalah' and 'mysticism' in my discussion of these texts. Since both aspects are likewise found in Landau's works, I also use these two terms in my examination of his thought and writings.

informed by and reacted to existing cultural mores in the city. As a result Landau, who devoted much of his career to shaping the practices and values of his community, regularly tailored his works to their needs and outlook.[53] What is especially captivating about the writings of both Landau and other figures in eighteenth-century Prague is that, in the terms of the French cultural historian Roger Chartier, they often reveal the convergence of cultural and religious values that were 'shared' by the elite and the laity.[54]

In this vein, kabbalah influenced some popular rites promoted by Landau and observed by Prague Jews, even as he moderated them in accordance with his fear of various challenges posed to traditional Judaism in Prague. In several homilies, he recommends that his congregants continue to conduct the nightly kabbalistic *tikun ḥatsot* vigil and that they adopt other practices espoused by Safed kabbalists. In repeated sermons, he stresses that specific nomian (halakhic) and anomian techniques as well as proper intentions during prayer lead to the kabbalistic goal of elevating the Shekhinah and the loftiest mystical ideal of *devekut*. Landau even seems to have been active in compiling a 1786 Prague prayer book *Tikun nefesh* ('Restoration of the Soul'), which is replete with kabbalistic concepts and liturgical texts. This work, with Landau's name on its title page, was reprinted in Prague several times. Nevertheless, his public comments on various kabbalistic customs, such as the recitation of the *leshem yiḥud* formula,[55] a practice he himself endorsed on occasion, are frequently much more guarded even in his Prague writings. In his responsa, he often rejects such practices.

What emerges, then, is that although Landau uses kabbalistic motifs in all genres of his work, they are given different weight and meaning depending on where they are used.[56] His Prague sermons are laced with kabbalistic images, as

[53] Some Annales scholars also wrote about influential historical figures in order to portray the relationship between these personalities and the groups they were addressing. See e.g. Febvre, *Destin: Martin Luther*.

[54] Of course, as noted above, each of these groups frequently had a different degree of understanding of the kabbalistic ideas underlying these texts. Roger Chartier and other scholars, such as Sara Nalle and Carlo Ginzburg, have researched how various texts were read and their ideas shared, to varying degrees, by the elite and the workers and merchants in early modern Europe. See e.g. Cavallo and Chartier (eds.), *History of Reading in the West*; Chartier, 'Reading Matter and "Popular" Reading'; Nalle, 'Literacy and Culture in Early Modern Castile'; Ginzburg, *The Cheese and the Worms*.

[55] The formula announces that the purpose (*leshem*) of the ritual being performed or the prayer being recited is to achieve the unification (*yiḥud*) of the godhead.

[56] Landau's use of identical kabbalistic motifs in a wide range of writings therefore cannot be attributed to the specific content, purpose, or intended audience of any individual source. (To be sure, however, he does give certain ideas different weight in different sources.) His various works also occasionally refer to each other, indicating that he consciously employed similar themes in diverse writings. See e.g. *Tselaḥ*, *Ber.* 4*b* (p. 16), where he refers to multiple types of repentance that he discussed in a Prague sermon. These ideas indeed appear in *Derushei hatselaḥ*, sermon 3, 6*b*.

are his glosses on aggadic material in the *Tselaḥ*. In his responsa, however, his discussion of kabbalistic matters is extremely restrained, and at times even dismissive.[57] Yet even there his veneration for kabbalah surfaces 'between the lines' in certain queries. An explanation for this discrepancy is that his homilies and Talmud commentaries were primarily directed at a Prague audience who were acquainted with and admired kabbalah.[58] In contrast, in his responsa, which were addressed to a broader and more diverse audience, Landau felt uncomfortable revealing kabbalistic ideas, fearing that they would reach places where they were unknown, and that they might be rejected or misused. In addition, in his halakhic writings he was especially careful to observe the traditional Ashkenazi hierarchy of giving halakhah precedence over all other disciplines, including kabbalah.

Prague's Eclectic Mystical Canon

Beyond demonstrating the pervasiveness of mysticism in Prague's rabbinic society, this book aims to provide a comprehensive reconstruction of the nature of this mystical world. In the course of analysing the kabbalistic texts and tenets that influenced Landau and Prague Jews, this study charts the diverse kabbalistic schools that were dominant in eighteenth-century east European rabbinic circles. By tracing the eclectic kabbalistic sources that permeated Prague's Jewish culture, this work employs the approach advocated by Moshe Idel in *Hasidism: Between Ecstasy and Magic*, which calls for a 'panoramic' analysis of early hasidic writings that takes into account the wide array of mystical sources, in addition to Lurianic kabbalah, that shaped hasidism.[59] Idel demonstrates that the mystical sources of the teachings of numerous eighteenth-century hasidic masters were more eclectic than previously depicted.[60] However, despite Idel's advocacy of a

[57] For example, in his commentaries and sermons Landau is willing to discuss the concept of *gilgul*, while in his responsa he is extremely reluctant to refer to this topic (see Part IV below). This is also true concerning his willingness to discuss the aggadah and the esoteric secrets that he believed it housed (see Part II).

[58] By contrast, Landau's sermons from his tenure in Yampol, *Doresh letsiyon*, contain almost no kabbalistic references. The reason for this requires further research into the nature of the Yampol community and Landau's career there.

[59] See Idel, *Hasidism*, 9–17. It should be noted that, although Lurianic kabbalah was the dominant kabbalistic school in the 17th and early 18th cc., several scholars, such as Bracha Sack and Isaiah Tishby, have demonstrated that Cordoverian kabbalah was also influential during this era. See Sack, 'Influence of Cordovero on Seventeenth-Century Jewish Thought'; Tishby, 'Confrontation between Lurianic Kabbalah and Cordoverian Kabbalah' (Heb.).

[60] Idel asserts that the authoritative status of Lurianic kabbalah declined during the middle of the 18th c., allowing other trends of kabbalah, such as the ecstatic, to gain popularity. See Idel, *Hasidism*, 31, 33; id., 'Perceptions of Kabbalah', 67–8.

panoramic analysis of the influential kabbalistic works during this period and his application of this approach to early hasidic texts, he does not apply this analysis to works of non-hasidic rabbinic leaders of the era.[61]

In Part III I extend the panoramic approach to the writings of eminent non-hasidic eighteenth-century Prague rabbis, most prominently Landau, highlighting the centrality in both Landau's works and numerous other Prague sources of a wide range of kabbalistic materials. Emphasis is placed on the Zohar (The Book of Splendour), a classic work of Jewish mysticism written primarily during the thirteenth century, and on later kabbalistic doctrines developed in sixteenth-century Safed, especially those of Moses Cordovero (1522–70) and Isaac Luria (the Ari; 1534–72).[62] Many of Prague's rabbinic and liturgical writings draw on ideas from these and other kabbalistic works, exhibiting a unique blend of rabbinic and mystical motifs, and this is explored in Part IV. This study is the first to document the role of disparate and even competing systems of medieval and early modern kabbalah in the culture of a major Jewish community and the works of a distinguished eighteenth-century rabbi.[63]

Landau's writings reveal that he seldom engaged in original kabbalistic speculation. This actually highlights the sincerity of his belief in kabbalah. For him, as for most kabbalists, the goal is to study, practise, and transmit kabbalistic teachings, not to alter them. His view of kabbalah as ancient lore leads him to disseminate its teachings with integrity and with as little of his own 'contributions' as possible. While modern scholars' interest in the 'novelty' of a thinker's kabbalistic writings is a worthwhile academic pursuit, it is not a helpful measuring stick for evaluating kabbalah's role for a specific thinker or for his milieu. Despite Landau's fidelity to older kabbalistic texts, his kabbalistic discussions do display creativity however. On various occasions, his syncretic manner of blending together and juxtaposing ideas from different periods and diverse kabbalistic schools is highly original.

[61] However, he does suggest that a few non-hasidic 18th-c. rabbinic authorities also relied on a variety of kabbalistic sources. My work on Landau shows this to be true.

[62] Most scholars claim that the Zohar was primarily written during the last decades of the 13th c. by a group of kabbalists in Castile. Moses Cordovero, who wrote numerous works including a commentary on the Zohar, was one of the most influential kabbalists in Safed. Isaac Luria studied briefly in Safed with Moses Cordovero. The influence of the Zohar and of Cordoverian and Lurianic kabbalah on 18th-c. Ashkenazi culture in general and on Landau's writings in particular is discussed in great detail in Part III.

[63] Much work has been done by scholars such as Tishby, Sack, Wolfson, Idel, and Liebes on the combinations of earlier kabbalistic systems in the later kabbalistic writings of figures who were not leading halakhic authorities. See e.g. Idel, *Hasidism*; Tishby, 'Confrontation between Lurianic Kabbalah and Cordoverian Kabbalah' (Heb.). There are also several important studies on leading 18th-c. rabbinic figures. See e.g. Schachter, 'Rabbi Jacob Emden', and Etkes, *Unique in his Generation* (Heb.). These studies, however, either ignore or treat marginally the synthesis of kabbalistic systems in the writings of these rabbis.

Both the lack of critical biographies on Prague's prominent eighteenth-century rabbis and historians' neglect of the majority of their writings have contributed to scholarship's oversight of the significance of a broad range of kabbalistic texts in eighteenth-century Prague. An array of the city's rabbinic, liturgical, and other texts exhibits Prague Jews' familiarity with eclectic kabbalistic sources and doctrines. In Landau's sermons and commentaries, he often prefaces his discussions of concepts from the Zohar, *musar* treatises,[64] and Lurianic literature with the assertion that these kabbalistic notions 'are already well known'.[65] He also employs zoharic, Lurianic, and Cordoverian motifs as a means of rebuking and inspiring change in the praxis of Prague Jews, demonstrating his belief that members of his community valued these teachings.

The Broader Context

Because of the prominence of both Prague's Jewish community and Landau, this study forces us to revisit certain general assumptions and historical theories about eighteenth-century Jewish society and culture. The undocumented impact of several kabbalistic schools on Landau and Prague Jews necessitates a re-examination of kabbalah's overall influence. Further, it calls for the reassessment of kabbalah's evolution, accounting for the coexistence of several kabbalistic systems in eighteenth-century Jewish thought. The documentation of the diverse kabbalistic sources that affected central and east European Jews also reinforces Isaiah Tishby's, Bracha Sack's, and Moshe Idel's challenge of the older scholarly theory that the almost exclusive reign of Lurianic kabbalah set the stage for the proliferation of Sabbatianism and hasidism.[66]

The writings of Landau, an eminent opponent of hasidism, or mitnaged, ironically demonstrate that many of the ideals conventionally ascribed to the new hasidic movement then emerging in eastern Europe were prevalent in eighteenth-century traditional rabbinic society at large.[67] This discovery forces us to reassess non-hasidic rabbinic culture, the novelty of hasidism in general, and the nature of

[64] The genre of kabbalistic-ethical *musar* treatises was first cultivated by Cordovero and his disciples in 16th-c. Safed.

[65] See e.g. Landau, *Derushei hatselaḥ*, sermon 25, 39*b*; id., *Tselaḥ*, *Ber.* 9*b*; id., *Ahavat tsiyon*, sermon 1, for the first day of *Seliḥot* prayers (1756), 2*a*, and sermon 4, 6*b*.

[66] See Sack, *Orchard Guard* (Heb.); Idel, *Hasidism*. For a more detailed discussion, see Part II below.

[67] Although some scholars use the term 'mitnaged' to designate only those individuals who used political means to oppose hasidism, I, like many others, use the term more broadly to refer to Ashkenazi Jews with wide influence who opposed hasidism publicly. For a broad use of this term, see e.g. Dubnow, *History of Hasidism* (Heb.), 3. Landau probably did not oppose the hasidim in person since there were no new hasidim in Prague. He did, however, denounce them in all genres of his published works.

the rabbinic opposition to this nascent movement.[68] Scholarship has been misled by the explicit polemical claims of the opponents of hasidism that great matters of principle separated them from the hasidim.[69] This book aims to present a nuanced portrait of the relationship between the early mystical hasidic movement and the culture of non-hasidic traditional Ashkenazi Jews.[70]

Until now, most of the sparse scholarship on eighteenth-century non-hasidic culture has been devoted solely to centres into which hasidism penetrated, such as Vilna and Shklov. Scholars have tended to focus on the rabbinic opposition to hasidism and the culture that was championed in these places, especially the teachings of Elijah, the Gaon of Vilna (1720–97) and his disciples.[71] This narrow focus has contributed to scholars' inattention to the diverse landscape of eighteenth-century rabbinic society.[72] It has also led to the neglect of many of the prominent centres of eighteenth-century Jewry, including Frankfurt, Metz, and Prague.[73]

This book is one of the first attempts to redress these oversights. In particular, it exposes the tremendous impact of east European rabbinic and kabbalistic traditions on Prague's traditional culture and specifically on its pre-eminent rabbinic authority, Ezekiel Landau. This careful examination explores the rabbinic institutions, writings, and values as well as the kabbalistic schools, practices, and doctrines which, at the onset of modernity, were paramount for Prague Jews and Landau. It accordingly offers a more complete portrayal of rabbinic culture during the last years that it thrived in one of the most important centres of European Jewry.

*

[68] This study also begs the question as to how these kabbalistic ideals disappeared so rapidly from non-hasidic circles.

[69] Precisely because the differences between the new hasidim and the mitnagedim were not that great on many issues during this formative period for both camps, the polemics between them were all the more vicious. To borrow Freud's phrase, this is a classic example of 'the narcissism of small differences'.

[70] On this topic, see my article, '*Hasidim* and *Mitnaggedim*'.

[71] A subsidiary issue in my work highlights that there is more to the philosophy of the mitnagedim, and certainly to the broader category of non-hasidic Ashkenazi culture, than the teachings of the Gaon of Vilna and his disciples. Relatively few works address 18th-c. non-hasidic rabbinic culture in general and the leaders who opposed hasidism in particular. Nevertheless, there are several important books on the religious and social background of various 18th- and 19th-c. mitnagedim, especially the Gaon of Vilna and his disciples. See Etkes, *Unique in his Generation* (Heb.); A. Nadler, *Faith of the Mithnagdim*; B. Z. Katz, *Rabbinate, Hasidism, Haskalah* (Heb.); Avivi, *Kabalat hagerah*; Lamm, *Torah Lishmah*.

[72] Other biases, such as scholarship's distorted emphasis on incipient modernization (as discussed earlier), have also led to the neglect of the diverse landscape of 18th-c. traditional Jewish society.

[73] There are, however, certain notable exceptions. See e.g. Berkovitz, *Rites and Passages*, where he addresses various aspects of the 18th-c. Jewish community of Metz.

The Structure of the Book

Part I provides an overview of the history and inner workings of the eighteenth-century Jewish community of Prague. This section focuses on the efflorescence of Prague's rabbinic culture during the latter half of the century despite Joseph II's Toleranzpatent, which officially abolished the Jewish community's autonomy. It chronicles the continued importance of halakhah and kabbalah within this culture, and surveys Prague's largely overlooked talmudic academies, Jewish court system, and numerous rabbinic scholars. The wide political and religious influence of Ezekiel Landau is specifically charted and analysed. The final chapter identifies various trends and developments which threatened Prague's traditional culture during the last decades of the century, including the Haskalah, the increasing centralization of the Habsburg state, and Sabbatianism. The unique responses of Prague's rabbinate to these challenges are examined.

Part II explores the role of kabbalah in Landau's thought, writings, and even his halakhic reasoning. His education in Poland, his observance of various mystical customs, and his eclectic works all reflect his intense involvement with this esoteric lore. The irony of Landau's frequent claim that he does not engage in kabbalah, which often prefaces his kabbalistic remarks, is noted and investigated. Finally, this section reveals the various factors underlying his reluctance to discuss kabbalah publicly.

Part III identifies the specific kabbalistic schools, sources, and trends that Landau and other eighteenth-century Prague rabbis employ in their diverse writings. In particular, it focuses on Landau's appropriation of tenets which originate in zoharic, Cordoverian, Lurianic, and other kabbalistic 'schools'. This section also demonstrates that although he is primarily a transmitter of earlier mystical traditions, he occasionally uses and combines terms and concepts unique to a particular kabbalistic school in an original and daring manner.

Part IV offers a thematic analysis of the major mystical tenets found in Landau's works and in numerous other eclectic Prague sources. Unlike the kabbalistic ideas discussed in Part III, these teachings are common to many schools, and cannot therefore be traced to an individual kabbalistic school with certainty. In addition, this section shows both Landau's syncretic use of kabbalistic, rabbinic, and philosophical texts and the interweaving of ideas from different genres in the world-view and writings of many Prague and other Ashkenazi Jews. This section's close study of the prominent mystical doctrines that shaped the *mentalité* of Prague's rabbinic elite as well as that of its laity highlights the widespread importance of this lore in eighteenth-century Prague.

PART I

JEWISH CULTURE IN EIGHTEENTH-CENTURY PRAGUE

ONE

Prague's Jewish Community

PRAGUE'S LOCATION at the heart of Europe, with Poland and Hungary to the east, and France, Saxony, Bavaria, and other German states to the west, placed it at the crossroads between eastern and western Europe and made it a centre for cross-cultural encounters. At the intersection of numerous trade routes, Prague was a cosmopolitan city, a nexus of cultural and intellectual exchange. The Italian, German, and Spanish nobility who maintained residences there contributed to the city's cultural life, as did the merchants who passed through.[1] During the latter half of the eighteenth century, Prague was one of Europe's most vibrant cities whose numerous religious and cultural institutions attracted Europe's intelligentsia. This period saw a flourishing of the sciences and the humanities as well as various religious movements. As the capital of Bohemia and the city with the second largest population in the Habsburg empire,[2] Prague played a pivotal role in shaping eighteenth-century Habsburg history and culture.[3]

For centuries, the city was known for the architecture, influence, and cultural and religious activity of its numerous institutions.[4] Often called the city of a hundred spires, Prague housed sundry churches and monasteries. Its famed castle, which was sometimes used by government officials, stood on a hillside overlooking the Old Town below, where the Jesuit Clementinum and the medieval Charles University were situated. Eighteenth-century Prague was also an artistic centre. Theatre and opera gradually made their way from the elite

[1] On the encounters between various nationalities and cultures in Prague, see Demetz, *Prague in Black and Gold*, 237–40; Kieval, 'The Lands Between', 44.

[2] See Ingrao, *Habsburg Monarchy*, 214; Demetz, *Prague in Black and Gold*, 245.

[3] For histories of the 18th-c. Habsburg empire in general and the Bohemian Crown land in particular, see Kerner, *Bohemia in the Eighteenth Century*; Hantsch, *Die Geschichte Österreichs*; Mikoletzky, *Österreich: Das grosse 18. Jahrhundert*; Winter, *Frühaufklärung*; id., *Barock, Absolutismus, und Aufklärung in der Donaumonarchie*; Macartney, *Habsburg Empire*; Wangermann, *Austrian Achievement*; Kann, *History of the Habsburg Empire*; Hassenpflug-Elzholz, *Böhmen und die böhmischen Stände*; Kann and Zdenek, *Peoples of the Eastern Habsburg Lands*; Hoensch, *Geschichte Böhmens*; Evans, 'Habsburg Monarchy and Bohemia'; Ingrao, *Habsburg Monarchy*; id. (ed.), *State and Society in Early Modern Austria*.

[4] On the history and institutions of Prague, see Schuerer, *Prag*; Svoboda, *Prague*; Landisch, *Praha*; Burian, *Prag die Altstadt/Prague the Old Town*; Demetz, *Prague in Black and Gold*.

town palaces to the public venues which began to appear at this time. The famous Nostitz theatre opened in 1783, and hosted the première of Mozart's *Don Giovanni* in 1787.[5] The first coffee houses were also established in Prague during the eighteenth century.[6] All these new institutions fostered novel forms of sociability and cultural interaction.

While the cultural landscape of Prague was becoming more open, central Europe was in turmoil and Habsburg policies remained intolerant of non-Catholics and foreigners. For most of the mid-eighteenth century, the empire was embroiled in a series of wars in which it incurred great financial loss and which caused great suffering to its people. In 1740, after the death of the Habsburg emperor Charles VI (1685–1740), his daughter Maria Theresa ascended the throne.[7] Empress Maria Theresa, whom the historian Charles Ingrao labelled as the last Baroque Habsburg monarch,[8] wielded great power on account of her strong charisma and her absolutist claim to the divine right of kings.

Shortly after her accession, the new king of Prussia, Frederick II, seized Lower Silesia from the Habsburg empire.[9] France, Spain, and Prussia united against Maria Theresa, supporting Charles Albert, the prince-elector of Bavaria, in his claim to the Habsburg throne.[10] In 1741 the Bohemian Estates recognized Charles Albert as king of Bohemia, and from November 1741 to January 1743, Franco-Bohemian forces besieged Prague.[11] On 1 November 1744 the Prussian army briefly occupied Prague for a second time.[12] The War of Austrian Succession lasted for eight years, ending in 1748. Austria emerged with many casualties, much lost territory, and deep economic losses.

[5] On opera and theatre in 18th-c. Prague, see Schuerer, *Prag*, 267–95; Mörike, *Mozart auf der Reise nach Prag*; Seifert, *Mozart v Praze/Mozart in Prague*; Demetz, *Prague in Black and Gold*, 240, 254–9, 262–5.

[6] Prague's first coffee house, which was located in the Old Town, opened in 1713.

[7] Charles VI was emperor from 1711 to 1740. On Maria Theresa, see von Arneth, *Geschichte Maria Theresia's*; McGill, *Maria Theresa*; Macartney, *Maria Theresa and the House of Austria*; Roider (ed.), *Maria Theresa*; Crankshaw, *Maria Theresa*. On Maria Theresa's succession to the throne, see Ingrao, 'Pragmatic Sanction and the Theresian Succession'.

[8] Ingrao, *Habsburg Monarchy*, 169. Ingrao claims that although Maria Theresa instituted many reforms most of them did not introduce anything 'conceptually new'.

[9] Frederick II reigned from 1740 to 1786.

[10] On the War of Austrian Succession, see Pick, *Empress Maria Theresa*; Ingrao, *Habsburg Monarchy*, 152–99; Roider (ed.), *Maria Theresa*; Kerner, *Bohemia in the Eighteenth Century*.

[11] The siege was followed by Maria Theresa's May 1743 coronation in Prague. Although Charles Albert reigned as a rival emperor from 1742 to 1745, after his death in 1745 his son supported Maria Theresa.

[12] This Prussian siege of Prague was over by the end of November 1744. As the Prussians departed, Prague's populace pillaged the Jewish Town, and killed thirteen Jews.

Maria Theresa, a staunch Catholic, harboured a particular antipathy for the Jews.[13] She accused them of spying for Frederick II, providing economic aid to the Prussians during the 1744 siege of Prague, and supporting Charles Albert's bid for the monarchy. Despite a continuous Jewish presence in Prague for nearly a thousand years,[14] on 18 December 1744, after the Austrians liberated Prague from the Prussians, Maria Theresa ordered the expulsion of Prague Jewry and pledged that the Jews would eventually be expelled from all of Bohemia. Although this complete expulsion never occurred, in March 1745 Prague's Jews were banished from the city.[15]

After much pressure from the city council, the guilds, and the Bohemian estates and chancellery, all of whom were financially dependent on the Jewish community, as well as an international effort on the part of influential court Jews, Maria Theresa rescinded the expulsion order in the summer of 1748.[16] This, however, was accompanied by the imposition of an exorbitant 'toleration' tax. The Jews' taxes, which had always been disproportionately high compared to those of their Christian neighbours, now increased almost threefold.[17] The toleration tax was subsequently increased every five years, and was only repealed in 1846.[18]

When the Jews returned in 1748 many became impoverished as a result of these taxes and other discriminatory regulations.[19] In numerous sermons Prague's chief rabbi Ezekiel Landau lamented the exorbitant taxation and other

[13] On Maria Theresa's antisemitism, see Crankshaw, *Maria Theresa*, 313; Ingrao, *Habsburg Monarchy*, 170; Kann, *History of the Habsburg Empire*, 189–90.

[14] The first account of Jewish life in Bohemia dates from the 10th c. See Kieval, 'The Lands Between', 23. On the history and communities of the Jews in Bohemia and particularly in Prague, see Kestenberg-Gladstein, 'Chapters in the History of Czech Jewry' (Heb.), 11–82; Mahler, *History of Modern Jewry*, 241–68; id., *History of the Jewish People* (Heb.), ii. 207–45; Gold (ed.), *Die Juden und Judengemeinden Böhmens*; Kieval, 'Autonomy and Interdependence'; id., 'The Lands Between', 23–52; McCagg, *History of Habsburg Jews*; Sadek, 'La Chronique hébraïque de l'histoire des juifs pragois'; Abeles Iggers (ed.), *Jews of Bohemia and Moravia*; Brosche, 'Das Ghetto von Prag'; Vilímková, *Prague Ghetto*.

[15] On the Jews' expulsion from Prague, see M. Breuer, 'Early Modern Period', 153–4; Demetz, *Prague in Black and Gold*, 246; Kieval, 'The Lands Between', 34.

[16] See Mevorakh, 'Jewish Diplomatic Activities to Prevent the Expulsion of Jews from Bohemia and Moravia' (Heb.); M. Breuer, 'Early Modern Period', 153–4.

[17] To 204,000 gulden per annum.

[18] On the exorbitant taxes imposed on Prague Jews and on Jews in the Habsburg empire in general, see Putík, 'Prague Jewish Community', 11–14; Kestenberg-Gladstein, *Neuere Geschichte*, 79, 82; Mahler, *History of Modern Jewry*, 246–50, 254; Parík, *Jewish Town of Prague*, 11. In addition to the set amount of taxes imposed on the Jews, until 1808 they paid a special 'perdon' tax on meat, wine, and other commodities. During Maria Theresa's reign the general population's taxes were doubled. On her general tax reforms see Ingrao, *Habsburg Monarchy*, 161–4.

[19] For example, in 1748 and 1760 the government decreed that Jews should wear yellow pieces of cloth and that the men should sport beards. See Deutsch and Ochser, 'Prague', 164. In addition, old discriminatory laws remained in place.

hardships that the Jews experienced under Maria Theresa's rule.[20] A letter from the Frankfurt archives reveals that in 1759 he even expressed an interest in leaving Prague to become Frankfurt's chief rabbi because he could no longer watch Prague's Jews suffer under this financial burden.[21] His main disciple Eleazar Fleckeles in fact left Prague for several years because the steep taxes had reduced him to poverty.[22]

Peace did not last long in the Austrian empire. In August 1756 Prussia launched what became the Seven Years War.[23] In a major shift of alliance, Prussia joined with Great Britain and invaded Saxony, a de facto declaration of war on the anti-Prussian coalition which now comprised Austria, France, and Russia. The war, which lasted from 1756 to 1763, left Frederick II victorious and in control of Silesia. Austria again suffered significant casualties.

Prague was particularly affected by the Seven Years War. Shortly after its outbreak Landau composed a prayer for the welfare of the imperial government and its army, to be recited twice daily in Prague's synagogues.[24] Later that year, on 22 December 1756, he issued a ban of excommunication against any Jew aiding the Prussians.[25] When the Prussians laid siege to Prague in the spring of 1757 Landau again demonstrated not only his patriotism but also his commitment to the Jewish community by declining an opportunity to flee the city.[26] He remained with his community, and encouraged them to defend Prague alongside

[20] See Landau, *Derushei hatselaḥ*, sermon 8 for Shabat Teshuvah (the sabbath preceding Yom Kippur), 16*a*, where he bemoans the fact that no other Jewish community has to pay taxes as high as Prague Jews do to the 'kind' Empress Maria Theresa. He complains, 'has such an exorbitant tax been seen [imposed] in any other country? But our queen . . . she is not cruel by nature. In fact, she is full of grace and mercy.' Landau's praise for the empress should not be taken too literally. For various other remarks of Landau's regarding hardships experienced under her rule, see e.g. *Derushei hatselaḥ*, sermon 37, for Shabat Hagadol (the sabbath before Passover), 50*b*; sermon 23 for the Ten Days of Repentance, 35*a*–*b*; sermon 28, for Shabat Teshuvah, 43*b*; sermon 30, for the Ten Days of Repentance, 45*a*; sermon 38, for Shabat Hagadol, 51*b*–52*a*. See also Landau, *Ahavat tsiyon*: sermon 1 (1756), 2*b*; sermon 2, for the first day of *Seliḥot* prayers (1761), 4*a*; sermon 8, for the eve of the new month of Shevat (1 Jan. 1775), 12*b*.

[21] 'Letter of R. Levi Panta of Prague', dated 30 Jan. 1759, found in the archival documents of the Frankfurt am Main Jewish community, *Sefunot*, 8/4 (1990), 105–6. Panta was a judge in the Prague Jewish community.

[22] See Fleckeles, introduction to *Olat ḥodesh*.

[23] On the Seven Years War see Ingrao, *Habsburg Monarchy*, 172–7.

[24] Landau, *Prayer for Maria Theresa's Good Fortune in War*. Prague Jews began to recite this German prayer on 5 Sept. 1756. A Hebrew translation of this prayer is found in Kamelhar, *Mofet hador*, 31–2. See Klemperer, 'Rabbis of Prague', 59.

[25] This ban, issued in the Altneu synagogue, was printed in a German-language pamphlet together with Landau's *Prayer for Maria Theresa's Good Fortune in War*. See Klemperer, 'Rabbis of Prague', 59. A Hebrew copy of this ban appears in Kamelhar, *Mofet hador*, 32–5.

[26] See Jacob Landau, *Divrei yedidot*, 33 and Landau's Hebrew eulogy for Maria Theresa, *Derush hesped*, 5*b*. On incipient patriotism during this period, see Saperstein, 'War and Patriotism in Sermons to Central European Jews'.

the city's other residents.[27] In June 1757, after the siege ended,[28] Prague Jewry offered prayers of thanksgiving in a special service conducted in the Altneuschul (Old-New Synagogue).[29] The remainder of Maria Theresa's individual reign as well as the period of her co-regency (1765–80) with her son Joseph II were more peaceful.[30] During this period, the political condition of Prague's inhabitants, including its Jews, remained largely unchanged.

The size, location, and stature of Prague's Jewish community made it the political, economic, and religious centre of Habsburg Jews during the eighteenth century.[31] The community's leaders often decided affairs that affected all of Bohemian Jewry.[32] Prague's liminal position also enabled it to influence Jewish communities in both eastern and western Europe. During the eighteenth century, Prague's Jewish community was one of the largest in the world.[33] According to the 1754 government census, 30,000 Jews resided in Bohemia. Since it is likely that many Jews deliberately avoided this census,[34] most scholars put this figure at roughly 40,000, with 10,000 to 11,000 residing in Prague.[35] Prague's Jewish population was thus significantly larger than any of the nearby west or east European centres of Jewish culture: Berlin (*c.*2,000), Frankfurt (*c.*3,000), Vienna (*c.*3,000), and Brody (*c.*7,000).[36]

[27] Jacob Landau, *Divrei yedidot*, 33. Jacob, Landau's son, reports that during the Prussian siege of 1757 the Jews assisted in quelling the city fires, and that his father helped the community's poor.

[28] The Prussian defeat at Kolin on 18 June 1757 caused them to end their siege of Prague, which had begun in May of that year. On the battle of Kolin and the Prussian siege of Prague, see Asprey, *Frederick the Great*, 445–58.

[29] Muneles, *Bibliographical Survey of Jewish Prague*, 80, item 266.

[30] When Maria Theresa's husband Francis Stephen died in 1765, Joseph II became co-regent with his mother.

[31] For a discussion of various aspects of Jewish life in this important Jewish centre during the 17th and 18th cc., see Putík, 'Prague Jewish Community'; id., 'Prague Jews and Judah Hasid'.

[32] Kieval, 'The Lands Between', 36. During the 18th c. most Bohemian Jews were scattered in over 800 small towns and villages. See Kestenberg-Gladstein, *Neuere Geschichte*, 3; ead., 'Chapters in the History of Czech Jewry' (Heb.), 19; Kieval, 'Autonomy and Interdependence', 76.

[33] Kestenberg-Gladstein, *Neuere Geschichte*, 29; ead., 'Chapters in the History of Czech Jewry', 32; Kieval, 'The Lands Between', 34.

[34] Many Jews probably did not participate in the census because of the government's restrictive population laws. See p. 31 below. It is also possible that some Prague Jews avoided the census for religious reasons: on the biblical critique of taking censuses see 2 Sam. 24. On modern rabbis' hesitation to participate in a census see e.g. Waldenberg, *Tsits eli'ezer*, vii, no. 3, which offers an extensive discussion about the contemporary census. See also Weinberg, *Seridei esh*, i, no. 140.

[35] See Herman, 'Evolution of the Jewish Population of Bohemia and Moravia'; Kestenberg-Gladstein, *Neuere Geschichte*, 1–3; McCagg, *A History of Habsburg Jews*, 12. See also Kestenberg-Gladstein, 'The 1724 Census' (Heb.).

[36] M. Breuer, 'Early Modern Period', 151; Demetz, *Prague in Black and Gold*, 250; Kestenberg-Gladstein, *Neuere Geschichte*, 29 n. 125. Although the largest number of Jews (hundreds of thousands) lived in Poland and Lithuania during the 18th c., Jewish settlement there tended to be more decentralized than in other parts of Europe. Brody was the largest Jewish settlement in eastern Europe. See Mahler, *Statistics about Jews in Former Poland* (Yid.); Rosman, 'Innovative Tradition', 519–20; Hundert, *Jews in Poland–Lithuania*, esp. 21–31, 71.

Prague's Jewish Town, or ghetto, which stood on the right bank of the Moldau (Vltava) River, was one of the city's five administrative units.[37] It bordered the centre of Prague's crowded Altstadt (Old Town), home to Prague's main marketplace, numerous churches, Charles University, coffee houses, and theatres. By the first decades of the eighteenth century,[38] Jews comprised half the population of the Old Town and over a quarter of the city's entire populace.[39] The location of the Jewish community, as well as its size, made it integral to the general fabric of Prague's economic and cultural life. The 1729 census reveals that about half of Prague's Jews were merchants, involved in all aspects of the city's commerce. The remaining Jews were mostly artisans or public servants.[40] Unlike many Jewish communities, Prague had a wide range of skilled Jewish artisans. Although the Jewish guilds in the city primarily catered to other Jews, they also had a non-Jewish clientele.[41] By virtue of the community's economic importance, the wealth and intellectual achievement of some of its members, and its numerous prestigious institutions, Prague was frequently hailed as a 'city and mother in Israel',[42] and the 'capital of the Jewish Diaspora'.[43]

Like most medieval and early modern Jewish communities, the Prague Jewish *kehilah* (community) was a distinct self-governing body for a large part of the eighteenth century, with political, legal, and religious autonomy. One of its primary tasks was to assess and collect taxes owed by its members. The *kehilah* also maintained an independent judicial system, established educational institutions,

[37] Until 1784 Prague was divided into the five administrative units of the Old and the New Towns, Vyšehrad, Hradčany, and the Jewish Town.

[38] Between 1705 and 1754 Prague had around 40,000 inhabitants.

[39] Although a separate administrative unit and surrounded by a wall, in many ways Prague's ghetto was considered part of the old town. See Drábek, 'Die Juden in den böhmischen Ländern', 127; Placht, *Lidnatost a spoločenská skladba českého státu v 16–18 století* , 310, 320; Kieval, 'The Lands Between', 31; McCagg, *History of Habsburg Jews*, 11. On the overpopulation of Prague's Jewish Town, see J. Jeitteles, *Benei hane'urim*.

[40] According to Kestenberg-Gladstein's analysis of the 1729 census records 49.9% of the heads of Prague Jewish households were merchants, 27.5% were artisans, and 22.5% were 'servants'. The 'servants' category included the 198 employees of the Jewish community, sixty to seventy Prague Jews who worked in the 'free professions', such as medicine, pharmacy, and midwifery, and domestic servants. See Kestenberg-Gladstein, *Neuere Geschichte*, 12–14; ead., 'Chapters in the History of Czech Jewry' (Heb.), 23–4. Putík argues that Kestenberg-Gladstein's broad use of the 'servants' category, in which she includes both public appointees and unskilled workers, is misleading. For the alternative categories used by Putík to classify the occupations of Prague Jews, see Putík, 'Prague Jews and Judah Hasid', pt. 1, 90–102

[41] Kestenberg-Gladstein, *Neuere Geschichte*, 372. On the history of Prague's Jewish guilds, see Kieval, 'Autonomy and Interdependence', 82–3.

[42] See e.g. Landau's *hitnatselut* (a disclaimer often found at the beginning of rabbinic books stating that their use of the term *akum* (idolater) does not refer to contemporary Christians) for *Tselaḥ* on *Pesaḥim*. See also Kestenberg-Gladstein, 'Chapters in the History of Czech Jewry' (Heb.), 32; Buxbaum, 'Introduction: Rabbi Bezalel Ranschburg' (Heb.), 34. During this period, Prague was also referred to as the 'metropolitan of Israel'.

[43] Landau, *Derushei hatselaḥ*, sermon 8, 16*a*.

and organized social welfare associations, known as *ḥevrot*.[44] Among their many functions, these *ḥevrot* ministered to the sick and needy, buried the dead, and attended to other religious and social needs.[45]

Prague's autonomous Jewish body was the largest and oldest in Bohemia. Technically, the heads of this distinguished administrative body were the *Ältesten*, the *ziknei ha'edah* (community elders). In reality, however, the community's administration was often run by a smaller group of three to five *parnasim*, elders selected from the economic and social elite. This group rotated their jobs each month and accordingly were called *parnasei ḥodesh* (monthly elders). Their main duties were to assess and collect taxes, most of which were remitted to the monarchy, and to act as the Jewish community's representatives to the state. It seems that the *Primator*, or *Primas*, who presided over the *Judenstadt* (Jewish town), served as the head of the *parnasim*.[46] The most famous eighteenth-century *primators* were Israel Frankel (1712–91) and Löbl Duschenes.[47] On official occasions, a communal senate of about twenty-four members, known as the *edah* (assembly), consisting of *Ältesten*, *ketsinim* (wealthy communal officers), and scholars, was convened.[48] Prague's Jewish community employed approximately 200 individuals. These included the chief rabbi, sixty-three schoolteachers, and a gravedigger.[49]

The *kehilah* also oversaw many of Prague Jewry's major institutions. Among these were the sixteenth-century Jewish town hall, rebuilt between 1763 and 1765,[50] and the ghetto's hospital.[51] The *kehilah* also administered some of Prague's yeshivas (talmudic academies) as well as its traditional elementary

[44] See Kieval, 'Autonomy and Interdependence', 55–6, 84; Kestenberg-Gladstein, 'Chapters in the History of Czech Jewry' (Heb.), 30.

[45] Numerous *ḥevrot* (societies) are mentioned in the archives of the State Jewish Museum and in inscriptions on Prague tombstones. These include: the Society for Clothing the Naked, the Society for the Needs of Children, the Society for the Care of Women in Childbirth, and the Society for Ransoming Prisoners. Various associations were affiliated with synagogues, such as the Association for Reciting Psalms and the Society of Those who Say Special Morning Prayers. Societies were also established for the study of classic religious works. Prague's Hevrah Kadishah (Burial Society), which was founded in 1564, was a powerful institution in the Prague ghetto. See Goldberg, *Crossing the Jabbok*; Muneles, 'From the Archives of the State Jewish Museum', 100–7.

[46] On the history and composition of Prague's internal Jewish government, see Kestenberg-Gladstein, *Neuere Geschichte*, 23–4; ead., 'Chapters in the History of Czech Jewry' (Heb.), 29–30; Putík, 'Prague Jews and Judah Hasid', pt. 1, 52–66.

[47] See Kestenberg-Gladstein, *Neuere Geschichte*, 141; McCagg, *History of Habsburg Jews*, 67.

[48] The *edah* was comprised of communal elders, wealthy *Schutzjuden*, and scholars.

[49] Among these communal employees were sixty-one male schoolteachers, two female schoolteachers, and lower court judges. See Kestenberg-Gladstein, *Neuere Geschichte*, 13, 24; ead., 'Chapters in the History of Czech Jewry' (Heb.), 24, 30.

[50] The Jewish town hall, built by the financier and court Jew Mordecai Maisel, is first referred to in documents from 1541. See Parík, *Jewish Town of Prague*, 8, 36–7, 39.

[51] The ghetto hospital was a public building. See Vilímková, *Prague Ghetto*, 38; Demetz, *Prague in Black and Gold*, 247.

school, or *ḥeder*,[52] which focused on talmudic study and provided instruction in Hebrew reading and Bible. The Jewish court, or *beit din*, whose members were probably appointed by the *primator* or the *parnasim* and whose jurisdiction was honoured by the state judiciary, was one of the *kehilah*'s central institutions. It had civil and criminal legal authority over disputes between members of the Jewish community and complaints of Christians against Jews.[53] In addition to the *ḥeder* and *beit din*, the *kehilah* also maintained Jewish cemeteries: the old Jewish cemetery, which was used until 1787, and the cemetery at Olšany, which became the community's main cemetery after 1787.[54]

Eighteenth-century Prague was also home to nine large synagogues administered by the *kehilah*, as well as various smaller ones.[55] These were the Altschul, dating from the twelfth or thirteenth century, the thirteenth-century Altneuschul, the oldest extant synagogue in Europe; the sixteenth-century Pinkas, High, Neuschul, and Maisel synagogues as well as the Klaus synagogue, the largest in the ghetto; and finally the seventeenth-century Grosserhof (Great Court) and Zigeuner synagogues.[56] Most of these synagogues had a women's gallery.[57]

[52] Some of Prague's yeshivas were privately funded. During the 18th c. Prague had at least one *ḥeder*. On Landau's appeal to contribute to this *ḥeder*, see *Derushei hatselaḥ*, sermon 1, for the first day of *Seliḥot* prayers, 5*a*–*b*. For a brief discussion of Jewish education in Prague during the late 17th and early 18th cc., see Putík, 'Prague Jews and Judah Hasid', pt. 1, 103–4.

[53] Adler, 'Das älteste Judicial-Protokoll des jüdischen Gemeinde-Archives in Prag 1682', 217; Kestenberg-Gladstein, *Neuere Geschichte*, 24, 66–7. The complaints of Jews against Christians were tried in the city court.

[54] The tombstones of the old Jewish cemetery date from 1439 to 1787. In 1787 Joseph II closed the overcrowded cemetery for sanitary reasons, and Prague Jews were subsequently buried at the Olšany cemetery, which had been established during an epidemic in 1680. Many members of the Landau family, as well as Fleckeles and numerous other Prague scholars, are buried in this cemetery, which was in use until 1890. On the old Jewish cemetery, see Parík, *Jewish Town of Prague*, 60–71; Vilímková, *Prague Ghetto*, 143–83; Muneles, *Epitaphs from the Ancient Jewish Cemetery of Prague* (Heb.); Greenblatt, 'The Shapes of Memory'. On the old cemetery at Olšany, see Parík, *Jewish Town of Prague*, 82–4. These cemeteries were maintained by Prague's Hevrah Kadishah. See Muneles, 'From the Archives of the State Jewish Museum', 101.

[55] Various 18th-c. sources indicate that there were nine large synagogues and many smaller ones in Prague. A traveller who passed through Prague in 1719 wrote that Prague's Jewish Town had twenty streets and nine synagogues. See *Israelietische Letterbode*, 10 (Amsterdam, 1884–5), 161. In a sermon delivered on 16 Elul 5540 (16 Sept. 1780), printed in Fleckeles, *Olat ḥodesh*, 69*a*, Fleckeles asserts that Prague has 'nine large, magnificently built synagogues as well as countless small ones'. In Landau's 1786 approbation for Tsevi Hirsh of Vaidoslav's *Erets tsevi* (dated 18 Adar II 5546; 18 Mar. 1786) he writes that during the author's stay in Prague he managed to preach in all nine synagogues.

[56] The Altneu, Pinkas, High, Maisel, and Klaus synagogues are still standing. The Altneu synagogue was founded around 1270. Its women's gallery, however, was only added in the 18th c. The Pinkas synagogue was built around the early 14th c., and rebuilt in 1535. The High Synagogue was built *c.*1568, the Maisel synagogue in 1592, and the Grosserhof synagogue *c.*1627. On Prague's synagogues, see Vilímková, *Prague Ghetto*, 103–38; Parík, *Jewish Town of Prague*, 20–35, 42–57.

[57] According to halakhah a quorum of ten men (*minyan*) is required for public prayer. All the indications suggest that in the 18th c. women also attended synagogue.

The celebrated rabbis and preachers of eighteenth-century Prague, such as Ezekiel and Samuel Landau, Eleazar Fleckeles, and Zerah Eidlitz (*c.*1725–80) were affiliated to these synagogues, where they preached to both men and women.[58] Alongside these established institutions, there was also a proliferation of small *minyanim* (prayer quorums) held in private homes,[59] against which Landau and others repeatedly railed.[60]

Despite Prague Jewry's autonomy and numerous institutions, the government imposed various restrictions on Bohemian Jewry as a whole. The harshest of these were the Familiantengesetze promulgated by Charles VI in 1726 and 1727, which remained in effect until 1848.[61] These laws limited the number of Jewish families who could reside in Bohemia to the number dwelling there in 1726: 8,541 in all of Bohemia and 2,335 families specifically in Prague. In order to maintain this demographic status quo, the Familiantengesetze permitted only the eldest son of each family to marry and raise a family in Bohemia.[62] All other children either had to emigrate or remain single. The Habsburg state also barred Jewish settlement in locales which did not have a Jewish community before 1726. Even in those areas where they were allowed to settle, the Jews were only permitted to purchase homes that had been 'Jewish houses' before 1726.

The Familiantengesetze devastated the Jews both socially and economically. The size of the community was effectively frozen. Further, since Habsburg law required any individual who wished to engage in business to own his home, the restriction on Jewish home ownership curtailed involvement in trade. Consequently, 1726 marked the beginning of a period of economic decline for

58 Only a few of Landau's sermons mention where they were delivered. These homilies, published in *Ahavat tsiyon*, were given in the Maisel and Great Court synagogues. Headings in *Ahavat tsiyon* indicate that Samuel Landau preached at both the Klaus and Maisel synagogues. For the many synagogues where Fleckeles and Eidlitz preached, see Fleckeles, *Olat ḥodesh*, and Eidlitz, *Or layesharim*. Although these rabbis affiliated with and preached in most of Prague's synagogues, it seems that each had his favourite.

59 For example, in 1782 a private synagogue, or prayer room, was established in the house of the Mosheles family. These private prayer quorums required a special permit from the emperor. See Vilímková, *Prague Ghetto*, 137.

60 See *Derushei hatselaḥ*, sermon 3, for the Ten Days of Repentance, 7*a*. Here, Landau laments that 'in our great sins' many small *minyanim* have proliferated in Prague. He exclaims that he would like to abolish all those that have not received the necessary legal permits. See also ibid., sermon 22, for the Ten Days of Repentance, 33*a*; sermon 24, for Shabat Teshuvah, 38*a*.

61 The Familiantengesetze limited the Jewish population in Bohemia, Moravia, and Silesia. On the Familiantengesetze, see Kestenberg-Gladstein, *Neuere Geschichte*, 1–2; Kieval, 'The Lands Between', 34; McCagg, *History of Habsburg Jews*, 12, 71.

62 Even the eldest son could only marry after the death of his father. The autonomy of the Jewish community was also affected by these laws. Voting privileges in the *kehilah* were extended only to the oldest sons of families with a *Familiennummer*.

Bohemian Jewry, the brunt of which was borne by the lower classes.[63] In various responsa, Prague's rabbinic leaders refer to the hardships imposed by the Familiantengesetze,[64] whose restrictions, while limiting Prague's Jewish population, preserved the state's tax revenues by maintaining the annual payment for which the Jewish community was liable. Due to the weakness of the early eighteenth-century Habsburg state, however, these laws did not entirely impede the community's growth: in time, there came to be many more Jewish families than the Familiantengesetze permitted. These families were appropriately nicknamed by the Jews the *überzähligen Familien*, or 'excess families'.

During the latter half of the eighteenth century, trade restrictions, onerous tax burdens, and the devastating fire of 1754 caused a further decline in the financial state of Prague's Jewish community.[65] The rift between Prague's wealthy Jews and the community's poor majority steadily widened.[66] In numerous homilies from this era, Prague preachers lament this increasing poverty.[67] Landau poignantly describes it as being more pronounced than the poverty he had witnessed in any other place.[68]

Class structure in eighteenth-century Bohemian society was determined by land ownership; Jews, who were neither permitted to own land nor allowed to purchase Christian homes, developed their own means of class differentiation.[69] They acquired status through the ownership of a *Judenhaus* (Jewish house). Only *Hausjuden* (home owners), or *ba'alei batim*, received the privileged status of *Schutzjuden* (protected Jews), who were allowed to engage in trade, obliged to

[63] Kestenberg-Gladstein, 'Chapters in the History of Czech Jewry' (Heb.), 18–19, 25; id., *Neuere Geschichte*, 16–17, 353, 356.

[64] Landau refers to the Familiantengesetze in several responsa. See *NB Tinyana*, 'OḤ', no. 8; 'ḤM', no. 41. See also Fleckeles, *Teshuvah me'ahavah*, i, nos. 109, 112.

[65] Prague archival records show that the economic situation of the Jews declined between 1702 and 1771. See Muneles, 'From the Archives of the State Jewish Museum', 106–7. See also Kestenberg-Gladstein, *Neuere Geschichte*, 32, 372; Vilímková, *Prague Ghetto*, 37–8, 79, 134, 138. On the various hardships endured by the Jewish community, see also *Ahavat tsiyon*, sermon 1, 2*a*.

[66] Kestenberg-Gladstein, *Neuere Geschichte*, 14–15. On the gap between rich and poor in Prague's Jewish community in the wake of the Jews' return in 1748, see Vilímková, *Prague Ghetto*, 79. During the late 17th and early 18th cc. a huge gap had already come to exist between rich and poor Jews in Prague. See Putík, 'Prague Jews and Judah Hasid', pt. 1, 84–9.

[67] See *Derushei hatselaḥ*, sermon 3, 7*b*; sermon 9 (5 Oct. 1769), 17*a*, in which Landau asserts that the humiliation and poverty of Prague's Jews 'increases yearly due to dwindling resources and income. All types of businesses, even those permitted to non-Jews, are off limits for Jews.' See also *Derushei hatselaḥ*, sermon 19, for the Ten Days of Repentance, 30*a*; sermon 28, 43*b*; sermon 38, 51*b*–52*a*. See also *Ahavat tsiyon*, sermon 1, 2*b* and sermon 8, 12*b*, in which Landau bewails the fact that Prague Jews have become so poor that many do not even have winter coats to wear. See also Eidlitz, *Or layesharim*, 38*b*, 22*b*.

[68] In particular, Landau states, in *Ahavat tsiyon*, sermon 1, 2*b*, that he witnessed poverty in Prague that he had not been accustomed to during the first half of his life in Poland.

[69] Kestenberg-Gladstein points out that marriages between Bohemian Jews of different classes were the exception. See 'Chapters in the History of Czech Jewry' (Heb.), 25, 28.

pay taxes, and permitted to have a family. This class division also affected the structure of the Jews' autonomy. Only *ba'alei batim* could choose the community's representatives and serve as communal elders.[70] Employees of the Jewish community, such as the chief rabbi and the rabbinic court judges, usually lived in houses owned by the community and were not given permanent residence rights. They were considered *publike Bediente* (public servants), who were generally provided with accommodation and a salary, and were allowed to reside in Prague as long as they worked in the city. Unlike the *Schutzjuden*, their eldest sons were not automatically granted the right to live in Prague with a family.[71]

The restriction of Jewish residence to 'Jewish houses' created a concrete separation between the Jews and Christians in Prague until the middle of the nineteenth century. The Jews generally had to live in the Judenstadt, which was separated from the Altstadt by a gated wall.[72] Jews were also barred from various public spaces, such as the university library and the theatre, during most of the eighteenth century.[73] Nevertheless, there was frequent contact between Jews and Christians. The ghetto gates were only closed at night. During the day Jews could walk freely through the rest of the city. Some of their houses and synagogues were across the road from Christian homes or afforded views of the numerous churches and convents in the vicinity. Jews could not help but have contact with their Christian neighbours.

Cultural, social, and economic interaction took place between Prague's Jews and Christians during the latter half of the eighteenth century.[74] Several sermons attest to Prague Jewry's participation in the city's cultural activities. Despite the city magistrate's prohibition on Jews attending the theatre, Landau laments, in a 1762 homily, that many Prague Jews go to the theatres and desire non-Jewish

[70] See Kestenberg-Gladstein, 'The House as a Feature of the Feudal-Estate Character of Pre-Emancipation Jewry' (Heb.); ead., *Neuere Geschichte*, 16–18, 21–2, 24, 378. More recently, Alexandr Putík has argued that other Jews also paid taxes and had the right to vote. He maintains, however, that in certain areas the *Hausjuden* did enjoy special privileges. See Putík, 'Prague Jews and Judah Hasid', pt. 1, 78–9.

[71] It seems that the rabbis had the status of *überzähligen Familien.*

[72] In general, Jews could not live outside the ghetto gates, which were only finally destroyed in 1822. In addition, from 1727 to 1848 the practice of Jews purchasing Christian houses stopped almost completely. See Vilímková, *Prague Ghetto*, 40; Kestenberg-Gladstein, *Neuere Geschichte*, 11–12, 112–13.

[73] For example, Jews were not permitted to attend the Market-Hall theatre, which was opened in Prague around 1740. When the theatre could not sell out its shows it applied to the city magistrate to let Jews attend, but its request was regularly denied. Jews were not officially permitted to attend the theatre until 1781.

[74] Some aspects of this interaction are discussed in Kestenberg-Gladstein, *Neuere Geschichte*, 95–155, Saperstein, *'Your Voice Like a Ram's Horn'*, 130–3, 140–2, and Abeles Iggers (ed.), *The Jews of Bohemia and Moravia*. Putik chronicles the grimmer consequences of Prague's Jews and Christians living in such close proximity (i.e. robberies and murders of Jews); it also increased the likelihood of conversion. See Putík, 'Prague Jewish Community', 15–42.

pleasures.[75] In another sermon, he rebukes them for 'running to' comedies and operas.[76] As early as 1650 the archbishop of Prague, Cardinal Arnošt Harrach, allowed Prague's Jewish musicians to play at Christian weddings and banquets.[77] Jewish musicians and singers were employed in Prague well into the latter half of the eighteenth century.[78] Landau admonishes Prague Jews who play or listen to the violin, organ, or harp, declaring that such joy is prohibited in the Exile.[79] The Jews whom Landau criticizes here were probably also taking pleasure in music performed by Prague's Christian musicians.

Prague's taverns, coffee houses, and even private homes provided places where the city's Jews and Christians could socialize. Although Prague Jews spoke *böhmische Judendeutsch*, Yiddish with Czech expressions, among themselves, they communicated in German with their non-Jewish neighbours.[80] The interaction between Christians and Jews figures prominently in several of Landau's responsa. In one responsum he avers that he would like to ban Jews from drinking in non-Jewish coffee houses. This practice, however, was too entrenched to be rooted out.[81] In a 1768 Prague homily, the popular preacher Zerah Eidlitz condemns Prague Jews for routinely frequenting taverns and coffee houses.[82] This complaint is echoed in a sermon of Landau's.[83] Landau also censures his community for eating in non-Jewish homes.[84] The extent of casual interaction between Jews and non-Jews is apparent in both Fleckeles' and Landau's criticism of Prague Jews for technical violations arising from their use of non-Jews to perform certain prohibited tasks on the sabbath.[85] In a 1783 sermon, Fleckeles

---

[75] See *Ahavat tsiyon*, sermon 3, for the Prague Charitable Works Society (Hebrew year 5522; 1761 or 1762), 5b.   [76] *Derushei hatselaḥ*, sermon 23, 36a.

[77] Central State Archives, Prague, no. NM-P1–7/5. See Vilímková, *Prague Ghetto*, 76, 79. The Jewish community, like the population at large, had its own professional musicians with their own guild.

[78] On the Jewish musicians and singers in 18th-c. Prague, see Nettl, 'Bemerkungen zur jüdischen Musik- und Theatergeschichte in Böhmen'; Kestenberg-Gladstein, *Neuere Geschichte*, 31; Putík, 'Prague Jews and Judah Hasid', pt. 1, 96.

[79] *Derushei hatselaḥ*, sermon 23, 36a, and sermon 30, 45b–46a, in which Landau observes that, 'from the day our Temple was destroyed, all song and happiness were prohibited. Yet, in our great sins, all day and all night the voices of singers and the playing of harps and violins are always heard in the markets and streets . . . Further, all meals are filled with sensuous love songs.'

[80] Kestenberg-Gladstein, *Neuere Geschichte*, 164, 358; id., 'Chapters in the History of Czech Jewry' (Heb.), 40, 74 n. 6 (relating to ch. 2). Only later, however, did Czech Jews refer to their Yiddish dialect as *böhmische Judendeutsch*.   [81] *NB Kama*, 'YD', no. 36.

[82] Eidlitz, *Or layesharim*, 79b. See also ibid. 36b, 86b.   [83] See *Derushei hatselaḥ*, sermon 23, 36a.

[84] Ibid., sermon 30, 46a.

[85] See *Derushei hatselaḥ*, sermon 23, 35b, where Landau censures Prague Jews' practice of asking non-Jews to open up a fish if it died on the sabbath. Elsewhere, he criticizes Prague Jews for violating the sabbath by having non-Jews warm up their milk and coffee for them. See *Derushei hatselaḥ*, sermon 36 for Shabat Hagadol, 49b. On the history of the halakhic concept of a non-Jew who performs acts for Jews, which are forbidden for Jews on the sabbath, see J. Katz, *The Shabbes Goy*.

further reproaches Prague Jews' habit of visiting non-Jewish homes on the sabbath in order to have hot coffee, punch, or hot chocolate.[86]

Nevertheless, the city's Jews and Christians primarily interacted in the economic sphere. Many Jews sold their merchandise in the Old Town market square. In fact the Jewish section of this square, the Tandlmarkt, was situated close to the church of St Gallus. Jews also bought various foods, such as marmalade, from non-Jewish shops,[87] and often provided financial services, most prominently moneylending, to non-Jews.[88] On occasion, they employed non-Jews, principally as builders, contractors, and household help.[89] Both Jews and Christians used each other's artisans,[90] and Landau reproaches his community for baking bread and pies in the ovens of non-Jewish bakers and for patronizing non-Jewish tailors. Their reliance on these tailors, he claims, leads to the Jews' frequent violation of the biblical prohibition on wearing *sha'atnez*, clothes that combine wool and linen.[91] Eighteenth-century Christian masons were employed by Jews in order to carve tombstones in Prague's Old Jewish Cemetery.

Despite the strong economic and social ties between the two communities, Prague's Jews were constantly reminded, by their leaders' words, by antisemitic acts, and by government decrees, of their precarious position in the Habsburg state. Prague's rabbis repeatedly warned the community of the antisemitic sentiments of many Habsburg subjects. The Jews were also the object of violence, robbery, and assault.[92] Landau's sermons occasionally refer to this hostility:[93] in one homily he asserts that the Jews' enemies constantly conspire to vilify them in the eyes of the empress and her ministers.[94] In an attempt to mitigate

[86] Fleckeles, *Olat ḥodesh*, 'Derush milei dishemaya', 3, 26 Elul 5543 (23 Sept. 1783), 30*b*.

[87] Landau criticizes Prague Jews for regularly buying a variety of marmalade from non-Jews. See *Derushei hatselaḥ*, sermon 23, 36*a*.

[88] On Landau's discussion of Prague Jews' economic interaction with non-Jews, see e.g. *Ahavat tsiyon*, sermon 8, 12*a*; *Derushei hatselaḥ*, sermon 22, for the Ten Days of Repentance, 33*b*, and sermon 36, 49*b*.

[89] See e.g. *NB Kama*, 'Oraḥ ḥayim', no. 12. Landau's sermons also repeatedly address Jews who have non-Jewish domestic employees. See e.g. *Derushei hatselaḥ*, sermon 4 for Shabat Shuvah (*c*.1757), 8*b*.

[90] On the employment of both Jewish and Christian artisans by Jews and Christians, see Vilímková, *Prague Ghetto*, 146; Demetz, *Prague in Black and Gold*, 250–1.

[91] This prohibition appears in Lev. 19: 19 and Deut. 22: 11. On Landau's critique of Prague Jews for purchasing threads from non-Jews and for going to non-Jewish tailors, see *Derushei hatselaḥ*, sermon 8, 15*b*, where he exclaims that Prague's Jewish court has already issued a decree against local Jews' practice of patronizing non-Jewish tailors. See also *Derushei hatselaḥ*, sermon 22, 33*b*. On his rebuke of Prague Jews for baking in the ovens of non-Jewish bakers, see *Derushei hatselaḥ*, sermon 37, 51*a*.

[92] On the hostile relations between Jews and Christians in Prague during the 17th and 18th cc., see Carlebach, *The Death of Simon Abeles*; Putík, 'Prague Jewish Community', 20–6.

[93] See e.g. *Derushei hatselaḥ*, sermon 30, 45*a*, and sermon 39 for Shabat Hagadol (1782), 53*a*; *Ahavat tsiyon*, sermon 8, 12*a*.

[94] *Derushei hatselaḥ*, sermon 19, 29*b*.

the situation, Prague rabbis frequently declared their loyalty to the monarchy and pleaded for the Jews' continued protection.[95] Although Landau usually praised government officials, a homily in which he complains that Jews are despised by rulers who seek their destruction belies his commonly expressed gratitude to the government.[96] Various responsa, sermons, and government documents reveal that the Catholic authorities were indeed suspicious of the Jews and were constantly placing restrictions on their autonomy.[97] For example, Maria Theresa introduced a requirement that Jews must receive government permission to issue bans.[98] Ironically, in 1780 Landau had to apply for a government licence to deliver his eulogy for Maria Theresa.[99]

One of the most severe restrictions which the Habsburg government imposed on Jewish cultural life was the censorship of Hebrew works.[100] From the beginning of Maria Theresa's reign the state began to strengthen its censorship system, and by 1751 it had established a censorship commission.[101] All books brought into Prague during this period needed a permit.[102]

During the latter half of the eighteenth century, the two Christian Hebraists who served as the official censors and translators of Hebrew works in Prague were Father Leopold Tirsch (d. 1788), the author of several books on Hebrew

[95] This theme is often reiterated in the approbations of Prague's rabbis and in their *hitnatseluyot*, or apologetic statements, found in the prefaces of many of their works. These *hitnatseluyot* were usually written to appease Prague's Hebrew censors. See e.g. Landau's *hitnatselut* for *NB Kama*; his approbation for Eisenstadt's *Or haganuz*, dated 5 Tamuz 5526 (12 June 1766); his approbation for *Maḥzor keminhag polin fiham umehrin*, pt. 2; and his approbation for Zahlin's *Hadarat eliyahu*. See also Samuel Landau's comments in *NB Kama*, 'YD', no. 1. On Landau's request for the Habsburg governments' protection of the Jews, see for example his 1767 prayer on the occasion of Maria Theresa's recovery.

[96] *Derushei hatselaḥ*, sermon 30, 45*a*. On the complexity of Landau's attitude towards the state, see Hess, 'Rabbi Ezekiel Landau' (Heb.), 243–56.

[97] For an examination of the government's suspicions of the Jews, see e.g. its query to Landau whether it is permissible under Jewish law to swear falsely on an invalid Torah scroll. See *NB Kama*, 'YD', no. 71.

[98] See Hess, 'Rabbi Ezekiel Landau' (Heb.), 245, 249. For instance, Landau states that he waited for government permission to issue his 1756 ban against traitors. See the copy of the ban in Kamelhar, *Mofet hador*, 33.

[99] See Landau, *Derush hesped*, 46, 6*b*. Landau delivered his eulogy for Maria Theresa on 10 Dec. 1780. A Hebrew text of the eulogy was published a few weeks later. Shortly afterwards, two German translations were published. For a discussion of this eulogy, see Saperstein, 'In Praise of an Anti-Jewish Empress'.

[100] On the censorship of Hebrew books in Bohemia and particularly in Prague, see Kisch, 'Die Zensur jüdischer Bücher in Böhmen'; S. H. Lieben, 'Beiträge zur Geschichte der Zensur hebräischer Drucke in Prag'; Putík, 'Prague Jewish Community', 28–37.

[101] Although Joseph II relaxed the state's censorship system, the state still banned books against Catholicism and the government in 1781. See Ingrao, *Habsburg Monarchy*, 166, 170, 198; Demetz, *Prague in Black and Gold*, 252; McCagg, *History of Habsburg Jews*, 47.

[102] The enforcement of this rule is apparent in Landau's approbations. See e.g. his approbation for Eisenstadt's *Or haganuz*, where he notes that he has not seen the book in question since a permit is required to import books into Prague.

and Yiddish,[103] and Karl Fischer (1755–1844), who was appointed censor in 1788.[104] Both interacted with Prague's Jewish leaders. For example, in two responsa Landau and Fleckeles addressed questions from Tirsch and Fischer respectively concerning the humiliating *more judaico*, or Jewish oath, required for Jewish testimony to a court.[105] As the librarian of Prague University, Fischer was the first non-clergyman to hold the position of Hebrew censor in Prague. During his years as censor, he was in close contact with Fleckeles and several other Prague rabbis and intellectuals,[106] such as Bezalel Ranschburg (1762–1820) and Baruch Jeitteles (1762–1813). A study of their correspondence, which includes New Year greetings, legal queries, and many other social and official letters, reveals the warm relationships that developed between Fischer and these scholars, at times extending beyond the professional realm.[107]

With the knowledge that their writings would be subject to the censor, rabbinic authors in Prague largely concealed their criticisms of non-Jews, and apologetically explained disparaging rabbinic statements concerning them. In Landau's sermons and responsa, he uses the name 'Ishmael', which normally connotes Muslims or Arabs, as a code word for Christians.[108] The meaning of the term is clear from his observation that he and his congregation are currently in the *galut yishma'elit* (exile in Muslim or Arab lands),[109] and when he refers, as does Fleckeles, to facts that are unique to the Habsburg empire, such as the Familiantengesetze, in the context of his discussion of this exile.[110] Strikingly, Landau never uses the terms *galut notsrit* or *romit* (exile in Christian, or Roman, lands); by contrast, he mentions the unbearable hardships of the *galut yishma'elit*

[103] Among censor Tirsch's writings are: *Handlexikon der Jüdischdeutschen Sprache*, *Grammatica Hebraea*, and the German translation of Landau's eulogy for Maria Theresa. See Muneles, *Bibliographical Survey of Jewish Prague*, 84, item 286 and 96 item 331; Saperstein, 'In Praise of an Anti-Jewish Empress', 20.

[104] On Karl Fisher, see Cermanová, 'Karl Fischer I'; ead., 'Karl Fischer II'; ead. and Marek, *Between the Christian and Jewish Worlds*. Kestenberg-Gladstein claims that Karl Fischer was of Jewish extraction. See 'Chapters in the History of Czech Jewry', 76 n. 42.

[105] See *NB Kama*, 'YD', no. 71. On Karl Fischer's enquiry as to the gravity of Jews' oaths to non-Jews, see Fleckeles, *Teshuvah me'ahavah*, i, no. 26.

[106] On the friendship between Fleckeles and Fischer, see S. H. Lieben, 'Rabbi Eleasar Fleckeles'; Žáček, 'Zwei Beiträge zur Geschichte des Frankismus in den böhmischen Ländern', 371; Kisch, 'Die Zensur jüdischer Bücher in Böhmen', 469. On Fischer's contact with members of the Prague Gesellschaft Junger Hebräer and with other Jewish intellectuals in Prague, see Kestenberg-Gladstein, *Neuere Geschichte*, 199, 234.

[107] Most of these letters remain unpublished.

[108] On Landau's use of this term in his sermons, see n. 111 below. On his use of this term in his responsa, see, for example, his responsum to Fleckeles, printed in Fleckeles, *Teshuvah me'ahavah*, i, no. 112. For a discussion of Landau's use of code words for Christianity in his responsa, see Hess, 'Rabbi Ezekiel Landau' (Heb.), 24 n. 16, 255. On Fleckeles' use of the code word *yishma'el*, see, for example, Fleckeles, *Teshuvah me'ahavah*, i, no. 35.

[109] See e.g. *Derushei hatselaḥ*, sermon for Passover, 59*a*, and sermon 25 for the Ten Days of Repentance, 39*a*.

[110] See Fleckeles, *Teshuvah me'ahavah*, i, nos. 109, 112.

in almost every sermon.[111] Landau and other Prague rabbis chose the term 'Ishmael' to avoid the wrath not only of the Catholic censors but also of the antisemitic Habsburg subjects in Prague. In the same vein, in numerous *hitnatseluyot* (apologetic prefatory remarks that appear in many Hebrew printed works),[112] approbations,[113] and sermons,[114] Landau, like most eighteenth-century Prague rabbis, stresses that the Christians of his day do not fall under the rubric of the idol-worshippers discussed in rabbinic literature, and as such must be dealt with honestly and respectfully.

Landau's accommodation of the censor, as well as his awareness of the precarious state of the Prague Jewish community, is poignantly expressed in his comments concerning apostates. In one homily he asserts that once a Jew leaves the community and is lost among 'the wicked Ishmaelites', Jews are no longer obliged to reproach him, as they would be to rebuke a member of their own community.[115] This harsh ruling, proclaiming that an apostate who has undergone public conversion is no longer part of the Jewish community, must be viewed in the light of Habsburg legislation that prohibited a convert's renunciation of Christianity so long as he or she remained in Habsburg lands.[116] Landau's jibe against the 'wicked Ishmaelites', which he assumed would escape the censor's eye, was probably a reaction to this legislation and symptomatic of his fear that the number of those converting might increase.

Aside from restrictive censorship, the latter half of the eighteenth century witnessed the deterioration of Hebrew printing in Prague, which had been one of the most prominent centres of Hebrew printing during the sixteenth century, as well as an important Yiddish printing centre during the seventeenth

[111] See e.g. *Derushei hatselah*, sermon 6 for Shabat Teshuvah, 13*b*; sermon 15 for Shabat Teshuvah, 25*b*; sermon 21 for Kol Nidrei (eve of Yom Kippur), 32*a*; sermon 22, 34*a*; sermon 24, 37*a*, 38*a*; sermon 26, for Kol Nidrei, 41*a*; sermon 27, 41*b*; sermon 28, 43*a*; sermon 37, 50*b*; sermon 38, 51*b*; sermon 40 for Shabat Hagadol, 54*a*. Both the context and content of many of these statements, such as their references to the abject poverty of and the exorbitant taxes levied upon the Jews as well as to the workers in the Bohemian villages, indicate that Landau is referring to the Christians in the Habsburg lands.

[112] See e.g. Landau, *hitnatselut*, in *Tselah, Pes.*; id., *moda'ah rabah* ('an important proclamation'), in *Tselah, Ber.*; id., *hitnatselut*, in *NB Kama*.

[113] See, for example, Landau's approbation for *Mahzor keminhag polin fiham umehrin*, pt. 2. Unlike the approbations which he wrote before living in Prague, Landau's Prague approbations are often written on the condition that the works to which he lends his endorsement be uncritical of the Jews' countrymen. See e.g. Landau's approbations for Kadish, *Ma'amar kadishin*, Eisenstadt's *Or haganuz*, and *Mahzor keminhag polin fiham umehrin*, pt. 1.

[114] See *Ahavat tsiyon*, sermon 8, 12*a*.

[115] *Derushei hatselah*, sermon 24, 37*a*. For a discussion of Landau's statement here, see J. Katz, *Exclusiveness and Tolerance*, 150.

[116] In general, Landau was lenient with converts to Christianity who wanted to return to Judaism so long as they had not renounced Judaism publicly and voluntarily. See *NB Tinyana*, 'EH', nos. 24, 142, and 144; Wind, *Rabbi Ezekiel Landau* (Heb.), 77.

century.[117] By 1786, however, the city's last two Hebrew printing houses were sold to non-Jews.[118]

Although the eighteenth century was a period of great uncertainty for Prague Jews, it was a time of growth. Over the century they were subjected to political turmoil engendered by the War of Austrian Succession, the Seven Years War, and a three-year expulsion. When they returned in 1748 they were faced with an almost threefold tax increase as well as the harsh Familiantengesetze limiting both their numbers and areas of residence. Yet despite these adverse conditions and further antisemitic legislation Prague Jews participated in the cultural life of this thriving Habsburg city, and interacted with their Christian neighbours in the social and economic spheres. Thanks to its size, intellectual achievements, and the wealth of some of its members, Prague's Jewish community also had a decisive influence on eighteenth-century Bohemian Jewry at large. In particular, Maria Theresa's reign was a period of efflorescence for Prague's rabbinic culture.

117 On Hebrew and Yiddish printing in Prague, see Freimann, 'Die hebräischen Druckereien in Prag'; Friedberg, *History of Hebrew Printing in the Towns of Central Europe* (Heb.); Kestenberg-Gladstein, *Neuere Geschichte*, 147–8; Kieval, 'Autonomy and Interdependence', 61–5.

118 Landau's third son, Israel, worked as a Hebrew printer for one of the non-Jewish printing houses in Prague. On the government's 1782 proposal to aid Prague's ailing Hebrew publishing industry, see Kestenberg-Gladstein, *Neuere Geschichte*, 147 n. 5.

TWO

Prague's Rabbinic Culture: Halakhah and Kabbalah

FROM THE FOURTEENTH CENTURY on, Prague was a major centre of rabbinic leadership and talmudic study. Many of Europe's most prominent rabbis held positions in the city.[1] Spanning the fourteenth century to Prague's 'Golden Age', during the reign of the eccentric Habsburg Emperor Rudolf II (1552–1612), this distinguished group included the kabbalist and poet Avigdor Kara (d. 1439), the composer of the well-known elegy *Et kol hatela'ah* (written to commemorate Prague Jews' suffering during the terrible 1389 riots), as well as the famed Judah Loew ben Bezalel (*c.*1525–1609), commonly referred to as the Maharal. The Maharal was a prolific and influential author, best known for his unique approach to the aggadah (rabbinic legends and homiletic passages), ethics, Jewish philosophy and mysticism. He also advocated various educational reforms, befriended the astronomer Tycho Brahe, and, according to Jewish folklore, created a golem. Sharing an interest in the occult with Rudolf II, who held his court in Prague during the Maharal's lifetime, he was granted a meeting with the emperor in 1592.[2] In that year, Mordecai ben Abraham Jaffe (*c.*1535–1612), another important Prague-born talmudist and kabbalist, succeeded the Maharal in his office of *av beit din* (head of the Jewish court). Jaffe is often called the Levush, after his ten works (the *Levushim*) on Joseph Karo's legal writings and other halakhic, scientific, philosophical, and kabbalistic subjects.[3]

During the late sixteenth, seventeenth, and eighteenth centuries, Prague's rabbinic reputation continued to grow. At this time, Prague's leading rabbis included Ephraim Solomon of Luntshitz (1550–1619), popularly referred to as the Keli Yakar after the title of his widely used Pentateuch commentary. Luntshitz is also known for his original sermons, published in an array of books.[4]

[1] For a survey of the major rabbinic figures who lived in Prague, see Klemperer, 'Rabbis of Prague'. In addition to this general survey, many of these figures have been studied individually. See e.g. Bokser, *The Maharal*; Sherwin, *Mystical Theology and Social Dissent*; Davis, *Yom-Tov Lipmann Heller*.

[2] Nevertheless, the exact reason for this meeting remains unknown. On Rudolf's II interest in the occult and his reign in Prague, see the important work of Evans, *Rudolf II and his World*.

[3] On Jaffe, see Kaplan, 'Rationalism and Rabbinic Culture in Sixteenth-Century Eastern Europe'.

[4] Ephraim of Luntshitz was the chief rabbi of Prague during the 1610s; see Levin, 'Seeing with Both Eyes'.

Isaiah Horowitz (*c.*1565–1630), who penned the influential ethical-mystical *musar* treatise *Shenei luḥot haberit* (Two Tablets of the Covenant), often referred to by its acronym, the *Shelah*, also served as a rabbi in the city.[5] Other seventeenth-century leaders of Prague's Jewish community included Chief Rabbi Yom-Tov Lipmann Heller (1579–1654), best known for his popular Mishnah commentary the *Tosefot yom tov* and his autobiography *Megilat eivah*,[6] and Aaron Simon Spira (1600–79), a renowned talmudist. Although they have been largely neglected by scholarship, eighteenth-century Prague also boasted numerous renowned rabbinic figures. Among them are Abraham Broda (d. 1717), the director of a large yeshiva,[7] David Oppenheim (1664–1736), a scholar and famed book collector, Netanel Tsevi Weil (1687–1769), who headed a Prague yeshiva until the Jews' expulsion in 1745;[8] and Jacob Wiener Hamburger (d. 1753), the author of the talmudic commentary *Kol kol ya'akov*. The dominant rabbinic figure in Prague during the early decades of the century was Jonathan Eybeschütz, one of the greatest eighteenth-century talmudists and kabbalists, who was later accused of espousing heretical Sabbatian beliefs.[9]

The city also enjoyed a long tradition of Jewish mysticism, kabbalistic study, and the publication of important kabbalistic works. From the fourteenth century on, many of its rabbinic authorities were deeply immersed in Jewish mysticism.[10] Some of Prague's kabbalists also held non-rabbinic positions, such as the physician Shabetai Sheftel Horowitz (*c.*1561–1619), a nephew of Isaiah Horowitz, who wrote the well-known kabbalistic works *Shefa tal* and *Nishmat shabetai halevi*, both of which were influenced by Cordoverian kabbalah.[11]

The seventeenth century saw the publication of numerous other kabbalistic books in Prague, many of which were dedicated to popularizing classical kabbalistic texts and ideas. Among these were various aids to the study of the

[5] Isaiah Horowitz was born in Prague and taught there from 1614 to 1621. Horowitz's exhaustive *musar* treatise provides kabbalistic explanations for many halakhic practices. On Horowitz and the *Shenei luḥot haberit*, see Krassen's introduction to Isaiah Horowitz, *Generations of Adam*, 1–38; Piekarz, *Beginning of Hasidism* (Heb.), esp. 209–15, 228–30, 309–13, 387–90; Wolfson, 'Influence of Luria on the Shelah' (Heb.).

[6] Yom Tov Lipmann Heller was the chief rabbi of Prague from 1627 to 1631. On this fascinating figure, see the excellent biography by Davis, *Yom-Tov Lipmann Heller*.

[7] Abraham Broda directed his Prague yeshiva from 1693 to 1709.

[8] On the large number of rabbis in Prague during the late 17th and early 18th cc., see Putík, 'Prague Jews and Judah Hasid', pt. 1, 97, 103–4.

[9] On Eybeschütz, see Zinz, *Gedulat yonatan*; Greenwald, *Rabbi Jonathan Eybeschütz* (Heb.); Perlmuter, *Rabbi Jonathan Eybeschütz and his Relationship with Sabbatianism* (Heb.).

[10] Among them were a large number of the rabbis listed in the opening paragraphs: Avigdor Kara, Judah Loew b. Bezalel, Isaiah Horowitz, Yom Tov Lipmann Heller, Aaron Spira, Meir Fischels (Bumsla), Jonathan Eybeschütz, and Zerah Eidlitz. For a survey of most of these rabbis' involvement with kabbalah see Klemperer, 'Rabbis of Prague' (1950), 49, 53, 62, 146; (1951), 62.

[11] On Shabetai Horowitz, who was born and died in Prague, see Sack, *Orchard Guard* (Heb.).

Zohar, such as Issachar Ber ben Petahiah Moses' introduction to the Zohar, *Pitḥei yah* (Prague, 1609), as well as his zoharic explanations and glossaries *Mekor ḥokhmah* (Prague, 1610) and *Imrei binah* (Prague, 1610). In 1610 another important kabbalistic treatise, *Sefer hakaneh*,[12] a product of Byzantine kabbalah, was published for the first time in Prague by the local kabbalist Eleazar ben Abraham Perles-Altschul (*c.*1577–1639),[13] who added a commentary and explanations, *Keneh binah keneh ḥokhmah*, in order to make the work accessible to a wider audience. Prague's publishing output during this period included other classical mystical and kabbalistic texts, such as *Sefer yetsirah* (1624), the first systematic Hebrew mystical book, and *Tomer devorah* (1621), Cordovero's popular *musar* treatise. In the following decades additional works introducing students to basic kabbalistic teachings were published, including Reuben Hoeshke of Prague's *Yalkut re'uveni* (1660), a widely used anthology of kabbalistic aggadah, and *Gilgulei neshamot* (1688), a treatise on transmigration by the Italian kabbalist Menahem Azariah da Fano (1548–1620).[14]

Particularly noteworthy are several books published in Prague that focused on the intertwining of halakhah and kabbalah and the importance of kabbalistic rites. Among these are Issachar Ber's *Yesh sakhar* (1609), examining halakhic teachings found in the Zohar, and a work entitled *Shulḥan arukh* (1660), attributed to Luria, that draws on the works of Hayim Vital. The latter is the first published work devoted to Lurianic customs and rituals.[15]

Numerous kabbalistic prayer books, and prayer books with kabbalistic texts, were also published in Prague during the seventeenth and eighteenth centuries. *Sha'arei tsiyon*, a popular Lurianic prayer book by Nathan Nata Hannover (d. 1683), incorporated manifold kabbalistic texts, including *tikun ḥatsot*, Yom Kippur Katan, and *tikunim* for the Seventh of Adar, Shavuot, and Hoshanah Rabbah.[16] Its widespread use is attested to by its frequent reprinting in Prague (1682, 1688, and 1692). In 1704 another Lurianic prayer book, *Derekh ḥayim*, was published in the city. Many of the kabbalistic texts recorded in these and other

[12] *Sefer hakaneh*, attributed to the family of the illustrious tannaitic figure, R. Nehunyah ben Hakaneh, was probably written around the end of the fourteenth century. It contains an introduction to kabbalah.

[13] Though member of Prague's intelligentsia in this period, Perles-Altschul did not have an official rabbinic position. He collected, transcribed and published various Cordoverian, Lurianic and other kabbalistic works. See Reiner, 'Biography of an Agent of Culture'.

[14] Other kabbalistic works published in Prague during the 17th and 18th cc. include Reuben Katz's *Oneg shabat* (1700).

[15] This Lurianic book is based on the work of the 17-c. kabbalist Jacob Tsemah (d. after 1665). It is similar to Tsemah's book on Lurianic customs, *Nagid umetsaveh* (Amsterdam, 1712).

[16] Over forty editions of *Sha'arei tsiyon* were published during the 18th c. On the widespread use of this prayer book, see Hundert, *Jews in Poland–Lithuania*, 130.

works, such as the penitential rite of *tikun shovevim*, were subsequently republished in the majority of eighteenth-century and numerous early nineteenth-century Prague prayer books.[17] Various late seventeenth-, eighteenth-, and early nineteenth-century Prague prayer books also explicitly incorporate kabbalistic prayers and customs established or endorsed by the Ari (Isaac Luria) and the Shelah (Isaiah Horowitz).[18]

Kabbalistic liturgical pamphlets devoted to specific occasions were also frequently published in Prague. Specific Lurianic prayer pamphlets for the sabbath (*tikunei shabat*) and for the holidays of Shavuot and Hoshanah Rabbah, as well as kabbalistic texts for Yom Kippur Katan, were regularly printed and reprinted in Prague during the late seventeenth and first decades of the eighteenth century.[19] Several late eighteenth-century kabbalistic pamphlets, including various editions of the nightly *tikun ḥatsot* (1767, 1782, and 1787) vigil, *tikun shovevim*, and a *tikun ḥatsot* for the seventh of Adar, have also recently surfaced. Indicating the wider use of the latter work, its title page states that the observance of this kabbalistic rite is the custom of Israel.[20]

[17] See e.g. *Sidur: tefilot mekol hashanah*, published by the grandchildren of Judah Bak (Prague, 1713); *Maḥzor*, published by Yehudah Lipmann and his brothers (Prague, 1756 or 1757), ii. 24*b*, 76*a*–80*b*; *Maḥzor*, published by Bezalel b. Samuel Fleckeles and Samuel b. Leizer Bahur (Prague, 1782), ii. 76*a*–80*b*; *Seliḥot*, published by Bokh and Katz (Prague, 1784), 109*b*–110*a*; *Seliḥot*, another edition published by Bokh and Katz (Prague, 1784), 150*a*–*b* (this second edition was published slightly later; it includes corrections mentioned in the errata of the first edition); *Maḥzor*, Elfenwangerfehen publishers (Prague, 1798), ii. 101*b*–106*b*; *Seliḥot*, published by Moses Landau (Prague, 1836), 287*b*. On the inclusion of kabbalistic texts in late 17th-c. Prague liturgical works, see *Seder shomerim laboker*, published by the grandchildren of Moshe Katz (Prague, 1692); *Seder shomerim laboker*, published by the children of Judah Bak (Prague, 1696). In my survey of extant 17th-c. Prague liturgical works (those that I had access to), I found fewer kabbalistic texts in liturgical works printed during the first half of that century. Nevertheless, they do appear. See e.g. *Seliḥot* (Prague, 1605), 120*b*; *Shomerim laboker* (Prague, 1617, 1650).

[18] e.g. the book of *Seliḥot*, published by Moses Landau (Prague, 1836), 186*a*, states that it is customary that all community members receive lashes at synagogue on the eve of Yom Kippur. It continues to explain that Luria only insisted that four lashes be given, corresponding to the four letters of the Tetragrammaton. See also *Maḥzor* (Prague, 1757), i. 126*a*, and ii. 24*b*; *Maḥzor*, published by Bezalel b. Samuel Fleckeles and Samuel b. Leizer Bahur (Prague, 1782), i. 126*a*; *Maḥzor*, published by Moses Landau (Prague, 1835), i.

[19] Lurianic prayer pamphlets containing *tikunei shabat*, *tikunim* for Shavuot and Hoshanah Rabbah, and Lurianic *teḥinot* were published in Prague in 1650, 1651, 1657, 1662, 1673, 1675, 1685, 1690, 1691, 1692, 1700, 1702, 1703, 1705, 1709, 1713, and 1719. Yom Kippur Katan pamphlets were published there in 1666, 1692, 1702, 1707, and 1713. It is interesting to note that while there are many extant *tikunei shabat* and Yom Kippur Katan pamphlets from the late 17th and early 18th cc., few such pamphlets are available from the second half of the 18th c. Whether they were published and did not survive, or whether they were not published at all because of the fear of being considered Sabbatian, or for other reasons, is difficult to ascertain.

[20] This *tikun* pamphlet for 7 Adar was published in 1787 by Prague's Hevrah Kadishah (Burial Society). 7 Adar is the day on which Moses' death is traditionally commemorated; consequently, in many early modern Jewish communities, the Hevrah Kadishah held its annual dinner on this date.

Other sources similarly point to the continued popularity of various kabbalistic texts and rituals in Prague during the last decades of the eighteenth century. The cover page of a 1794 Prague *tikun shovevim* pamphlet attests that, although this text had been republished in Prague on several occasions during recent years, there were no longer any copies available for purchase.[21] A considerable number of Prague Jews continued to observe this prayer rite—and perhaps even its accompanying fast days—in order to atone for demons created through nocturnal emissions and onanism.

Remarkably, a range of Yiddish kabbalistic liturgical pamphlets and books relating stories about various kabbalists were also published in Prague.[22] Yiddish translations of several Yom Kippur Katan and Lurianic *teḥinot* pamphlets appeared during the last decades of the seventeenth and first decades of the eighteenth century (1692, 1702, 1709, and 1713).[23] Another Prague pamphlet, *Ma'aneh lashon*, containing kabbalistically informed prayers for cemetery visits, was translated into Yiddish and published in Prague in 1708. The publication of these liturgical works in the vernacular shows that these kabbalistic prayers were also meant to be recited by the masses, even those not versed in Hebrew.

Prague's rabbis and communal leaders, many of whom were kabbalists or appreciated kabbalah, also endorsed the wider community's observance of kabbalistic customs. A salient example is found in the 'odd' practice observed in the Altneuschul, and probably in all Prague synagogues, of reciting Psalm 92 (*Mizmor shir leyom hashabat*) twice on Friday evenings. This custom derives from Lurianic kabbalah and is promoted in both Luria's prayer book and Vital's *Peri ets ḥayim*. It seems that 'Prague was the only community in all of Europe' to observe this kabbalistic tradition rigorously.[24]

[21] See *Seder tikun shovevim* (Prague, 1794). The printer states that he therefore decided to print a third edition of this liturgical pamphlet.

[22] See e.g. *Fun tsvay maysim* ('Two Miraculous Tales'), stories related to Luria, and *Ein mekhtig sheyn mayse* ('A Mightily Beautiful Tale'), a story about the kabbalist R. Adam Ba'al Shem.

[23] Yom Kippur Katan pamphlets with Yiddish translations were published in Prague in 1692, 1702, and 1713. A Lurianic *teḥinot* pamphlet with a Yiddish translation was published in Prague in 1709.

[24] On this custom, see Sperber, *Customs of Israel* (Heb.), iv. 1–7. The surviving observance of this custom is mentioned in a responsum of Aaron Epstein, published in 1933. I would like to thank Yisrael Dubitsky for showing me this source. Another possible reason for the repetition of this psalm (although Sperber rejects this suggestion) is that for many years it had been the custom of the Altneu synagogue, and perhaps all Prague synagogues, to recite the 'Welcoming of the Sabbath' service accompanied by instruments. Therefore, it is possible that the congregants recited the 'Praise of the Sabbath' psalm twice in order to ensure that this psalm, which officially marks the beginning of the sabbath, was recited at least once without instruments, since there is a rabbinic injunction against playing instruments on the sabbath. Like Sperber, however, I do not believe that this was the main reason for this Prague custom; rather, its origin was kabbalistic. On the practice of playing instruments at the Altneu synagogue on Friday evenings, see Ellenson, 'Disputed Precedent', in his *After Emancipation*, 121–38. I would like to thank David Ellenson, my neighbour, for giving me a copy of this article.

Many of Prague's eighteenth- and early nineteenth-century liturgical treatises also promoted ascetic rituals promoted by medieval and early modern Jewish mystics. These include flagellation, fasting, the donning of sackcloth and ashes, the removal of shoes, intense wailing, and self-imposed isolation.[25] Prague's liturgical works and various eighteenth-century rabbinic writings demonstrate that these customs were observed in the city, particularly on the eve of various holidays, suggesting that the rabbinic authorities endorsed these practices.

Strikingly, eighteenth-century Jewish communal leaders in Prague occasionally supported non-kabbalistic works and rites by explaining their kabbalistic significance. In this vein, Prague's Jewish high court gave its approbation for a Pentateuch devoted to correct grammar and cantillation published in the city in 1779.[26] The high court judges explained that a major reason to buy the book was that it dealt with matters alluding to lofty 'secrets above' and kabbalistic goals. 'He who reads and chants the [biblical] text correctly brings about [the kabbalistic ideal of] *tikun* (restoration) . . . while he who reads it incorrectly . . . contributes to the destruction of the supernal house above.'[27] This text and other Prague sources reveal the prominence of essential kabbalistic doctrines for Prague's rabbinic leaders and their belief that these notions would sway Prague Jews.

The pre-eminence of Prague's eighteenth-century rabbinate, which included some of the most distinguished talmudists and kabbalists, afforded it influence not only in Prague but throughout Bohemia. Realizing the extent of this power, during the latter half of the eighteenth century the Habsburg monarchy recognized Prague's chief rabbi as the leading religious authority of Bohemian Jewry.[28]

At the same time, state-imposed innovations challenged Prague's traditional rabbinic culture during the last decades of the eighteenth century. In the

[25] These practices are often recommended for the eves of Rosh Hashanah and Yom Kippur. See e.g. *Maḥzor*, published by Yehudah Lipmann and his brothers (Prague, 1756 or 1757), i. 125*b*, 126*b*; *Maḥzor*, published by Bezalel b. Samuel Fleckeles and Samuel b. Leizer Bahur (Prague, 1782), i. 126*b*, 128*b*; *Maḥzor*, published by Sebastian Diesbach (Prague, 1804), i. 76*b*–77*a*; *Maḥzor*, published by Moses Landau (Prague, 1833), 1; *Maḥzor* for the entire year, published by Moses Landau (Prague, 1834), 1*b*–2*b*; *Maḥzor* for the first day of Rosh Hashanah, published by Moses Landau (Prague, 1834), 1; *Maḥzor* , published by Moses Landau (Prague, 1835), 1; *Seliḥot*, published by Moses Landau (Prague, 1836) 121*b*–122*a*, 186*a*.

[26] Approbation for the revised version of the Pentateuch of Isaac Premesla, originally published in Amsterdam in 1754 and republished in Prague in 1779, under the supervision of Zerah Eidlitz. The approbation is dated 14 Elul 5539 (26 Aug. 1779) and signed by Ezekiel Landau, who probably composed it, and by all the other judges on Prague's Jewish high court: Judah Leib Kasovitz, Salomon Emerich (Gumperz), Moshe Ginsburg Shapira, Josef Lieberles, and Levi Panta.

[27] Ibid.

[28] Kieval, 'The Lands Between', 36, 38. In *c.*1749, six years before Landau assumed the position of chief rabbi of Prague, the state recognized the holder of this post as Bohemian Jewry's highest religious leader.

Habsburg empire, external legislation precipitated political, cultural, and social change for the Jews.[29] With Maria Theresa's death in 1780, her son Joseph II was able to advance his programme of legal reforms.[30] An enlightened absolutist, he wished to continue the unification of political authority in his empire, which until then had been largely split among local principalities, the nobility, and the Church.[31] His attempt to continue his mother's work of centralizing the state, as well as his enlightened ideals, led him to grant religious toleration to his Protestant and Greek Orthodox subjects in October 1781, and to abolish serfdom in Bohemia a month later. Also central to Joseph's reforms was his granting of religious toleration to the Jews.[32]

Joseph II's edicts concerning the Jews, which spanned the 1780s, began with his Toleranzpatent for Bohemia issued on 19 October 1781.[33] The Toleranzpatent attempted to restructure the political, religious, and economic life of Prague Jewry. It officially abolished the Jewish community's autonomy and allowed the Jews greater participation in commerce and the trades, in order to make them more 'useful to the state'.[34] In time, the abolition of communal autonomy transformed Prague's rabbinic leadership from communal officials to religious functionaries.

Several historians claim that the Toleranzpatent marks the beginning of the modernization of Bohemian Jewry, characterized by political and cultural transformation.[35] The edict eliminated many intentionally humiliating symbols and

[29] See Silber, 'Historical Experience of German Jewry and its Impact on Haskalah and Reform in Hungary', 110; Kieval, 'Autonomy and Interdependence', 85; id., 'The Lands Between', 48. This stands in contrast to west European countries, where the Jews' cultural transformation and fight for political and social acceptance were largely internally driven.

[30] On Joseph II, see Bernard, *Joseph II*; Beales, *Joseph II: In the Shadow of Maria Theresa*; id., 'The False Joseph II'; Blanning, *Joseph II.*

[31] On the relationship between the Enlightenment and Joseph II's reforms, see Blanning, *Joseph II and Enlightened Despotism*; Beales, 'Was Joseph II an Enlightened Despot?'; Ingrao, *Habsburg Monarchy*, 182, 184, 199, 218.

[32] Blanning, *Joseph II*, 72–6, 106–7; Demetz, *Prague in Black and Gold*, 248; Kieval, 'Caution's Progress', 80. Joseph II nevertheless proclaimed Catholicism the official state religion.

[33] On Joseph II's Toleranzpatent, see Kestenberg-Gladstein, *Neuere Geschichte*, 34–66; Kieval, 'Autonomy and Interdependence', 85–8; id., 'Caution's Progress', 79–81; id., 'The Lands Between', 41–2; J. Katz, *Out of the Ghetto*, 161–6; Bernard, 'Joseph II and the Jews', 101–19; Pribram (ed.), *Urkunden und Akten zur Geschichte der Juden in Wien*, i. 494–500; Singer, 'Zur Geschichte der Toleranzpatente in den Sudetenländern'; Dubin, *Port Jews of Habsburg Trieste*.

[34] Declaration of Joseph II, 1 Oct. 1781, in Pribram, *Urkunden und Akten zur Geschichte der Juden in Wien*, 476. Cited and trans. in Kieval, 'Autonomy and Interdependence', 84, and id., 'The Lands Between', 41.

[35] On the limited economic effect of the Toleranzpatent for the majority of Jews, see Kestenberg-Gladstein, *Neuere Geschichte*, 38, 65–6; Kieval, 'Caution's Progress', 80, and id., 'Autonomy and Interdependence', 84–90.

restrictions previously imposed on Jews,[36] such as the required 'Jewish' clothing and badges, as well as the decree obliging men to sport beards. It revoked the *Leibmaut* (body tax) that Jews paid when travelling, opened institutions of higher learning to them, and permitted them to partake of various forms of public entertainment, such as the theatre. It also allowed them to build their own factories and to work in non-Jewish ones. In 1784 Joseph II issued the Sprachgesetz (language law), mandating that all Jewish communal business and public records, which had been kept in Yiddish or Hebrew, be kept in German. Throughout the 1780s Joseph issued additional ordinances designed to make the Jews more useful to the state. His reforms attempted to eliminate distinctively Jewish behaviour and to erode the Jewish community's organizational structure,[37] and were most effective in the cultural sphere. They furthered Enlightenment goals through legislation, and effected changes which challenged traditional Jewish society.

Despite the Toleranzpatent and related legislation, various policies and social factors helped preserve the pre-Enlightenment structure of Prague's Jewish community until the nineteenth century. The government's half-way measures, which neither removed the restrictions imposed by the 1726–7 Familiantengesetze nor rescinded all special Jewish taxes,[38] still discriminated against Jews and did not completely dissolve the Jewish community's unique character.[39] Even Joseph II's cultural reforms affected only a small group of upper-class Jews. The lives of the middle- and lower-class majority remained largely unchanged.

Persistent antisemitism also led to the failure of Joseph II's attempts at complete acculturation of the Jews. The prejudices of a range of Catholic Church and government officials were too powerful to be undone by legislation. Christian leaders of all denominations mocked Joseph as the 'Emperor of the Jews', and many ignored his Toleranzpatent, as far as they could.[40] Numerous antisemitic pamphlets concerning his granting of toleration to Habsburg Jews

[36] See *Derushei hatselah*, sermon 39, 53*a*. In this 1782 sermon, delivered several months after Joseph II's promulgation of the Toleranzpatent for Bohemia, Landau remarks that Joseph had kindly removed all 'symbols of slavery' that had been imposed upon the Jews.

[37] For instance, in order to encourage the acculturation of the Jews, Joseph II decreed in 1787 that they adopt German first and family names.

[38] See Kestenberg-Gladstein, 'Chapters in the History of Czech Jewry', 35. The Toleranzpatent opens with the declaration that it does not annul the population and residence restrictions imposed on the Jews.

[39] Habsburg Jews were not permitted to own land until 1841, and their special tax was first revoked in 1846. Only after the revolution of 1848 were their residence and marriage restrictions removed. See Kieval, *Making of Czech Jewry*, 6.

[40] See Ingrao, *Habsburg Monarchy*, 199; Kestenberg-Gladstein, *Neuere Geschichte*, 85, 387.

appeared during the 1780s.[41] Despite his official abolition of Jewish autonomy, the prejudices and legal restrictions that remained helped maintain the traditional social and economic structure of Jewish society in Prague's ghetto (where most Prague Jews had to reside until 1848) throughout the eighteenth century.

A poignant example of the continued segregation of Prague's Jews and Christians even after the issuing of the Toleranzpatent can be found in an introduction written by Israel Landau in 1793 in which he extols the virtues of the Prague University library.[42] The censor, Karl Fischer, granted two Jews, Israel and another maskil, Meir Fischer (1788–1858), permission to use the library.[43] Israel explains that the library is a rare place where individuals of different religions can sit together without feeling threatened, alluding to the strong animosity that existed between the two communities. No other Jews, however, were afforded this privilege.

Besides the persistent social prejudices and economic framework which ensured the continuity of Prague Jewry's traditional social structure, the plethora of late eighteenth-century rabbinic scholars continued to strengthen its traditional rabbinic culture. Although some historians claim that rabbinic influence declined sharply during the latter half of the eighteenth century,[44] Prague's rabbinic leaders retained their authority through the first few decades of the nineteenth century.[45] This era was actually the heyday of the city's rabbinic culture and leadership. Many eighteenth-century rabbinic sources reflect the self-consciousness of Prague's rabbis about the particularly high level of intellectual productivity during this period. In a responsum written during his Prague career Landau asserts that the city 'consistently produced the leading rabbis of the generation'.[46] Fleckeles similarly depicts eighteenth-century Prague as a beautiful city 'filled with sages and scribes'.[47]

[41] These included the following pamphlets: Ignaz Klingler, *Ueber die Unnütz und Schädlichkeit der Jüden im Königreiche Böheim und Mähren* (Prague, 1782); id., *Ueber die Unnütz und Schädlichkeit der Jüden im Königreiche Böheim, Mähren und Oesterreich* (Prague, 1782); anon., *Ueber die Schädlichkeit der Juden in Böhmen*.

[42] This introduction is found in Landau's republication of Abraham Farissol's *Igeret orḥot olam* in Prague in 1793. Israel Landau published three texts in this anthology: Abraham Farissol's *Igeret orḥot olam*, first published in Ferrara in 1524; Abraham ibn Ezra's *Yesod morah*, first published in Constantinople in 1530; and Moses Maimonides' *Igeret teiman*, first published in Hanau in 1629. Nonetheless, this anthology is usually referred to as *Igeret orḥot olam*. For a discussion of this introduction, see Kestenberg-Gladstein, *Neuere Geschichte*, 149–53; ead., 'Chapters in the History of Czech Jewry', 39–40.

[43] They received this permission in about 1790.

[44] See Abramsky, 'Crisis of Authority', 13–21; Yerushalmi, foreword to *Pursuit of Heresy*, p. xii.

[45] As pointed out in the Introduction, the flourishing of Prague's rabbinate during this era stands out in comparison to the position of the rabbinate in west European cities.

[46] *NB Tinyana*, 'EH', no. 116. See also the letter of Landau's appointment to the Prague rabbinate, in Kamelhar, *Mofet hador*, 18.

[47] Fleckeles, *Olat ḥodesh hashelishi*, sermon 2, dated 5 Elul 5547 (19 Aug. 1787), 9*a*.

Notwithstanding Prague's numerous illustrious rabbis, it was largely the scholarship and accomplishments of Ezekiel Landau that made it the most distinguished Jewish community in central Europe during the latter half of the eighteenth century. After leaving his rabbinic post in the Polish city of Yampol, where he had served for nearly ten years (1745–54), Landau became the *Oberrabbiner* (chief rabbi) of Prague from 1754 to 1793. Internal rabbinic strife related to the controversy between Jonathan Eybeschütz and Jacob Emden,[48] which had already divided much of eighteenth-century Jewry, as well as other factors, had left Prague without a chief rabbi since 1736.[49] Although at first Landau's rabbinic authority was challenged by several eminent Eybeschütz supporters, including Rabbi Meir Fischels (Bumsla) (1703–69), Ephraim Wehli, and Zerah Eidlitz,[50] who had advocated Eybeschütz's appointment as Prague's chief rabbi, Landau was soon widely accepted as the unchallenged spiritual leader of Bohemian Jewry.[51] During his early years, Landau helped rebuild Prague's Jewish community after its various major catastrophes, including the siege and looting of Prague from 1741 to 1743 and again in 1744, the Jews' expulsion between 1745 and 1748, and the great fire of 1754.[52] His efforts helped to re-establish Prague as one of the most vibrant rabbinic and educational centres of European Jewry.

As Prague's chief rabbi, Landau was the supreme authority of the Jewish community's religious, judicial, and political affairs. In addition to serving as the *av beit din*, the head of the Jewish rabbinic court, he directed a higher academy for talmudic learning, which became an acclaimed centre for Jewish studies. Both Landau's responsa and Fleckeles' writings reveal Landau's communal responsibilities and busy schedule.[53] Every morning he taught at the academy, and during the afternoon he headed the Jewish court and dealt with administrative and

[48] Jacob Emden of Altona-Hamburg accused Eybeschütz, a leading 18th-c. rabbinic authority, of espousing Sabbatian beliefs. For a discussion of the Emden–Eybeschütz controversy, see Cohen, *Jacob Emden*, 118–242; Liebes, *Messianism of Rabbi Jacob Emden* (Heb.); Schachter, 'Rabbi Jacob Emden', 390–498.

[49] This position had been vacant since the death of David Oppenheim in 1736.

[50] Eidlitz was brought up and educated by Eybeschütz. See Eidlitz's eulogy for him in *Or layesharim*.

[51] There are many folk-tales which recount the opposition of Eybeschütz's supporters to the appointment of Landau as chief rabbi. However, most of these tales also describe the waning of this opposition and the wide acceptance of Landau's authority as soon as the breadth of his rabbinic knowledge was recognized. See Klein, 'Zuschrift', 526, 541; J. Jeiteles in *Bikurei ha'itim*, 10 (1829), 75; Kamelhar, *Mofet hador*, 22–4; Klemperer, 'Rabbis of Prague' (1951), 56–7.

[52] On the many catastrophes that had been visited upon Prague Jewry, see Landau, *Ahavat tsiyon*, sermon 1, 1756, 2*a*.

[53] Landau's responsibilities as chief rabbi are also enumerated in the letter of his appointment to the Prague rabbinate. See the copy of this letter in Kamelhar, *Mofet hador*, 18–19.

communal affairs.[54] His early mornings and his evenings were devoted to answering legal queries from correspondents throughout Europe.[55]

Although he was a strong advocate of tradition, at the end of his career Landau accommodated several Habsburg reforms. Joseph II's Toleranzpatent for Bohemia required all children to obtain a secular education and large communities to establish government-supervised Normalschulen (modern elementary schools). Instead of denouncing this project entirely, Landau assisted in the shaping and establishment of Prague's Normalschule for Jewish children, even composing a prayer for its opening on 2 May 2 1782.[56] During the initial planning stages of the school's curriculum, the government-appointed overseer of Prague's Normalschule, the priest Ferdinand Kindermann Ritter von Schulstein, consulted Landau and implemented many of his proposals.[57] Landau's requests to review all curricular materials and to limit the school's hours were honoured.[58] In this way he ensured that only children aged from 11 to 13 attended the Normalschule, and then only from 5 to 7 p.m., leaving the majority of the school day and most of a child's school years for Jewish studies.[59] In a similar spirit, he supported the conscription of Jewish recruits to the Austrian military in 1788, when Joseph became the first European ruler to enlist Jewish soldiers.[60] In May 1789 Landau delivered a patriotic speech to these

[54] *NB Kama*, 'YD', no. 38. See also Fleckeles, *Olat ḥodesh hashelishi*, sermon 17 ('Eulogy for Ezekiel Landau', dated 18 Iyar 5553; 30 Apr. 1793), 72*a*.

[55] See *NB Tinyana*, 'OḤ', nos. 34, 87.

[56] See Landau, *Prayer for the Opening of the Normalschule in the Jewish Quarter* (Heb.). A 1782 sermon already hints at Landau's suspicions that the Normalschule's teachers will not only teach writing, grammar, arithmetic, and ethics but will also try to undermine traditional Judaism. See *Derushei hatselaḥ*, sermon 39, 54*a*. On the state-mandated Normalschule for Jewish children in Prague and on Landau's central role in shaping it, see Wiener, *Nachricht von dem Ursprunge und Fortgange der deutschen jüdischen Hauptschule zu Prag*; Wanniczek, *Geschichte der prager Haupt-, Trivial- und Mädchenschule der Israeliten*, 9–11, 13; Kestenberg-Gladstein, *Neuere Geschichte*, 41–50; Singer, 'Zur Geschichte der Toleranzpatente in den Sudetenländern', 264–69; Kieval, 'Caution's Progress', 90–1; id., 'Autonomy and Interdependence', 86–7; Silber, 'Historical Experience of German Jewry', 110–11.

[57] See Kieval, 'Autonomy and Interdependence', 88; Kestenberg-Gladstein, *Neuere Geschichte*, 44–5; Silber, 'Historical Experience of German Jewry', 111. On Ferdinand Kindermann, see Winter, *Ferdinand Kindermann Ritter von Schulstein*.

[58] Landau inspected and signed every page of the textbook that was published for Prague's Jewish Normalschule. See Kestenberg-Gladstein, 'Chapters in the History of Czech Jewry', 74 n. 3. The girls' Normalschule opened in 1785.

[59] While children attended the Normalschule only from 5 to 7 p.m. in the winter, there was an additional session from 10 to 12 a.m. in the summer. Landau ensured that only technical skills, and no Jewish subjects, were taught at the Normalschule during his period. See Wanniczek, *Geschichte der prager Haupt-, Trivial- und Mädchenschule der Israeliten*, 14, 15.

[60] See Klemperer, 'Rabbis of Prague' (1951), 70; Kieval, 'The Lands Between', 42. Later, however, Landau orchestrated efforts to have the Crown rescind this draft. In 1790, a group led by his son Samuel petitioned Emperor Leopold to stop the Jews' conscription. See Kestenberg-Gladstein, *Neuere Geschichte*, 339–40; McCagg, *History of Habsburg Jews*, 68. Klemperer asserts that as early as 1788 Landau sent a group to petition Joseph II to cancel this draft.

conscripts, expressing his hope that they would remain faithful to their religion and loyal to the Habsburg government.[61] His authority and diplomatic skills made him instrumental both in facilitating the acceptance of these innovations by Prague Jews and in persuading government officials to moderate them, mitigating their threat to traditional Judaism.[62]

Aware of Landau's vast erudition and impressive standing, the state often consulted him on other legal and political innovations and adopted his suggestions. In the wake of Joseph's 1783 decree that civil marital and divorce laws applied to all his subjects, Landau was called on to identify conflicts between civil and Jewish marital law. In 1785 he wrote a pamphlet on Jewish matrimonial law in German.[63] He made a plea for Jews to be allowed to adhere to their traditional laws. The monarchy granted his request. During Landau's career government officials also sought his counsel on other Jewish legal matters, such as the permissibility of delayed burial, a highly contested issue among Jewish leaders during the 1770s, and technicalities concerning the Jewish oath.[64]

The government's respect for Landau and his interaction with various Habsburg monarchs is further illustrated by other sources and events. In 1776, four years after Austria's annexation of Galicia during the first partition of Poland, Maria Theresa offered Landau the opportunity to serve as Galicia's government-appointed chief rabbi. At the behest of Prague's Jews, he declined the position and remained in Prague.[65] Austria's monarchs also paid homage to Landau by holding occasional meetings with him.[66] In turn, he composed an array of patriotic sermons and prayers in honour of the Habsburg monarchs Maria Theresa,

[61] Landau, 'Sermon to the First Jewish Recruits to the Austrian Military'. This first-hand account of Landau's 12 May 1789 speech is also published in Kestenberg-Gladstein, *Neuere Geschichte*, 70–2 and Kamelhar, *Mofet hador*, 81–3.

[62] Prague Jewry's acceptance of the Normalschule in 1782, for example, was largely due to Landau's endorsement of the school. Only six years earlier, in 1776, Maria Theresa's attempt to establish a Normalinstitut for Prague's Jewish community was opposed by Prague Jewry's leaders. See Wanniczek, *Geschichte der prager Haupt-, Trivial- und Mädchenschule der Israeliten*, 15; Kestenberg-Gladstein, *Neuere Geschichte*, 41–2, 50; Kieval, 'Caution's Progress', 89.

[63] Ezekiel Landau, *Ḥukei ha'ishut* ('Marital Laws'). For a Hebrew translation of this German pamphlet, entitled *Ḥukei ha'ishut al pi dat mosheh vehatalmud* ('Marital Laws According to the Law of Moses and the Talmud'), see Gelman, *The Noda Biyehudah and his Teaching* (Heb.), 135–49.

[64] On Landau's responsum to government officials concerning the Jewish oath, see *NB Kama*, 'YD', no. 71. But the government did not always listen to Landau. For example, in 1784 the Austrian government asked him for the Jewish view on delayed internment, but rejected his reply opposing this practice. Both Landau's response and a sharp critique of it by the Berlin maskil Dr Marcus Herz were published in *Hame'asef* in 1786, and in a German-language appendix to *Hame'asef* in 1787. A Hebrew translation of Herz's critique was published in *Hame'asef* in 1789. On this matter, see Klemperer, 'Rabbis of Prague' (1951), 68–9; J. Katz, *Out of the Ghetto*, 150.

[65] See *NB Tinyana*, 'OḤ', no. 36. On this appointment, see also Kamelhar, *Mofet hador*, 69–71.

[66] Maria Theresa met Landau on two occasions, and was impressed by him. See Kestenberg-Gladstein, *Neuere Geschichte*, 44 n. 36.

Joseph II, and Leopold II (1747–92). Among these are a prayer for Maria Theresa's recovery from an illness (1767),[67] *Derush hesped* (a eulogy for the empress, 1780), *Shevaḥ vehoda'ah* (a sermon to mark Joseph II's military victory at Belgrade, 1789), and *Krönungslied und Gebet* (a prayer for Leopold II's coronation, 1791).

Notwithstanding Landau's important political role, his main accomplishments were in Jewish scholarship and the defence of traditional Judaism. In Prague, he had a great impact on his community through his sermons, speeches delivered on special occasions, and eulogies.[68] A large number of these, frequently delivered in one of Prague's many synagogues, are found in the collections *Ahavat tsiyon* (The Love of Zion) and *Derushei hatselaḥ* (Sermons of the Tselah, i.e. Ezekiel Landau).[69] Landau also held sway over the Jews of Prague and throughout the Ashkenazi world through his monumental responsa collection, the *Noda biyehudah*, and his acclaimed talmudic commentary *Tsiyun lenefesh ḥayah* (*Tselaḥ*) (A Guidepost for the Living Soul). The latter is a commentary on various talmudic tractates, initially intended for his students. In addition, he composed *Dagul merevavah*, a significant commentary on the legal code *Shulḥan arukh*. Landau's diverse works were widely used and often republished. The scope of his influence is also testified to by the value attached to his approbations, which for decades were sought to promote a broad spectrum of books published throughout Europe.[70] The range of his writings and his powerful position made him one of the towering rabbinic authorities and intellectual leaders of the era.

Landau's creativity in the area of Jewish law has had an enduring impact on rabbinic jurisprudence. Already during his lifetime he was renowned for his ingenious ability to conceptualize and occasionally reinterpret complex concepts and aspects of Jewish law and ritual. He was one of the rare rabbinic authorities

[67] Landau, *Prayer for the Healing of Maria Theresa*. Shortly afterwards, he composed a prayer of thanksgiving for Maria Theresa's recovery.

[68] Landau's homilies often illustrate how he mediated between rabbinic paradigms and the realities of Jewish life in Prague.

[69] Although the letter of Landau's appointment to the Prague rabbinate stated that he was only responsible for delivering two sermons a year, on the sabbaths before Yom Kippur and Passover (Shabat Teshuvah and Shabat Hagadol) (see the letter in Kamelhar, *Mofet hador*, 19), he preached more frequently, composing homilies for the following occasions: the first day of the penitential month of Elul, the eve of Rosh Hashanah, Rosh Hashanah, the Ten Days of Repentance, the fast-day of Gedaliah, Kol Nidrei, Hanukah, the eve of the new moon of Shevat, Passover, Shavuot, and for Prague's Gemilut Hasadim association. Since Landau's rebuke in his sermons is often directed at the specific practices of different groups within the community, it seems that he delivered them to Prague Jewry at large. The Prague judge R. Levi Panta (d. 1782) attests to Landau's frequent preaching in Prague, sometimes as often as 'two and three times a month', as well as to his homiletical talents. See 'Letters from the Archives of the *Kehilah* of Frankfurt', 105 (R. Levi Panta's letter is dated 2 Shevat 5519; 30 Jan. 1759). For another first-hand account of Landau's talent as a preacher, see Klemperer, 'Rabbis of Prague' (1951), 58 n. 10.

[70] During Landau's career, he gave 67 approbations. On the role of approbations during the 18th c., see Reiner, 'Wealth, Social Position and the Study of Torah' (Heb.).

who applied his legal and conceptual genius to *pesak*, adjudicating matters of halakhah. His innovative positions on complex issues of law revolutionized the traditional understanding of seminal legal issues and set the agenda for many of the debates on these matters up until the present day. Among the groundbreaking rulings recorded in his responsa, Prague court decisions, and other communal writings are those concerning menstrual purity (*nidah*) and the applicability of the concept of agency (*sheliḥut*) in cases involving a transgression.[71] His halakhic and talmudic commentaries similarly include pioneering halakhic discussions and decisions. Best known among these are his distinctive methods of measuring items necessary for ritual purposes and the possibilities and limits of men and women fulfilling ritual obligations for one another (*arvut*).[72] Landau's daring legal verdicts were often the result of his disregard for the opinions of later rabbinic authorities (the *aḥaronim*, authorities from the fifteenth century onwards). On occasion he was even willing to argue with the opinions of medieval rabbinic jurists (*rishonim*)[73]—a phenomenon that is uncommon among other leading *aḥaronim*.[74] His bold rulings and teachings were not merely spread by his own writings but also by his numerous students.[75]

During his tenure as Prague's chief rabbi the city housed several prestigious rabbinic academies. Landau's yeshiva was the most famous and successful, attracting students from diverse European communities,[76] who came to study

[71] For Landau's discussion of *nidah*, see e.g. *NB Kama*, 'YD', no. 55. His reinterpretation of the agency concept led him to invalidate a divorce writ given by a messenger to a woman against her will. His adjudication on this matter caused a huge uproar, stirring much halakhic debate, and occasionally slipping into personal acrimony among his family members. See *NB Kama*, 'EH', nos. 75–82; *NB Tinyana*, 'EH', no. 112.

[72] For Landau's discussion of measurements for ritual purposes, see *Tselaḥ*, *Pes.* 116*b* (p. 345). For his discussion of *arvut*, see *Dagul merevavah*, 'OḤ', no. 271; id. *Tselaḥ*, *Ber.* 20*b* (pp. 81–4).

[73] For a recent discussion of the periodization of the *rishonim* and *aḥaronim*, see Yuval, 'Rishonim and Aharonim, *Antiqui et Moderni*' (Heb.). For a discussion of Landau's views of the status of medieval and later rabbinic authorities, see Hess, 'Rabbi Ezekiel Landau' (Heb.). It should be noted that, while Hess's discussions of Landau's responsa are often helpful, Hess's categorization of the early and later *rishonim* is at times confused and misleading. In addition, Hess fails to note that, while Landau does indeed have tremendous respect for the early *rishonim*, he does occasionally disagree with them.

[74] One notable exception is Elijah, the Gaon of Vilna (the Gra). Both he and Landau would, on occasion, disagree with the opinions of the *rishonim*. However, Landau's strong endorsement of the method of *pilpul* is in sharp contrast with the Vilna Gaon's rejection of it. In fact, Landau's Talmud commentary, the *Tselaḥ*, is often viewed as a classic example of the *pilpul* style. On Landau's masterful use of the *pilpul* method, see Dimitrovsky, 'On the *Pilpul* Style' (Heb.). On the Vilna Gaon's approach to rabbinic texts, see Harris, *How Do We Know This?*, 235–9.

[75] Landau frequently corresponded with his students long after they had left his yeshiva. In fact, he sent 116 responsa to forty of his former students. See e.g. *NB Kama*, 'YD', no. 18; *NB Tinyana*, 'YD', no. 13. See also Hess, 'Rabbi Ezekiel Landau' (Heb.), 295.

[76] See Klein, 'Zuschrift an Herrn Moses Mendelson in Hamburg', 541; Kamelhar, *Mofet hador*, 24; Klemperer, 'Rabbis of Prague' (1951), 57.

especially with him.[77] Various eighteenth- and nineteenth-century sources report that during the many years that Landau headed the yeshiva, it was attended by thousands of students. Even if these numbers are inflated, a large number of students did flock to his academy. A certain Dr Klein, who had attended the yeshiva from 1829 to 1832, recounts that because of the academy's increasing enrolment it eventually outgrew Landau's home and was first moved into the large Klaus synagogue and from there to the court in front of the synagogue.[78] In his eulogy for Landau, Fleckeles, who had studied at Landau's yeshiva for ten years,[79] relates that Landau taught four different daily Talmud and Codes classes to four groups of students.[80] Landau also remarks, in a responsum, that every Friday he taught his pupils a section from the Pentateuch along with the commentary of Rashi.[81]

Many of Landau's students became influential communal and rabbinic leaders in Prague and in other European communities at the turn of the century. Among the most famous of these pupils were Eleazar Fleckeles, who headed the Prague court after Landau; Bezalel Ranschburg, a talmudic scholar and teacher;[82] and Baruch Jeitteles, a leader of Prague's Haskalah,[83] who was the son of the physician Jonas Jeitteles (1735–1806), 'the father of Prague's Haskalah' and a longstanding friend of Landau.[84] Other prominent students included Abraham Danzig (1748–1820), a rabbinic judge in Vilna;[85] Aaron Chorin (1766–1844), a pioneer of early Reform Judaism in Hungary; Peter Beer (1758–1838), a Bohemian maskil, historian, and teacher at Prague's Normalschule;[86] Naphtali Herz Homberg (1749–1841), also a teacher at the Normalschule, a radical advocate of religious reform, and a member of Mendelssohn's maskilic circle in

[77] On Landau's devotion to teaching, see e.g. *NB Kama*, 'YD', no. 15; ibid., 'OḤ', no. 18; *NB Tinyana*, 'OḤ', no. 139; ibid., 'ḤM', no. 46.

[78] Klein, 'Zuschrift an Herrn Moses Mendelson in Hamburg', 524, 541; Kamelhar, *Mofet hador*, 24. On Fleckeles' report that Landau had thousands of students over the course of his sixty-year career, several hundred of whom became teachers and judges, see Fleckeles, *Olat ḥodesh hashelishi*, sermon 17, 71*b*.

[79] Fleckeles studied at Landau's yeshiva between the ages of 14 and 24. See Spitz, *Zikhron elazar*, 3–4.

[80] Fleckeles, *Olat ḥodesh hashelishi*, sermon 17, 72*a*.

[81] *NB Kama*, 'YD', no. 7.

[82] On Bezalel Ranschburg, see Buxbaum, 'Introduction: Rabbi Bezalel Ranschburg' (Heb.). Although Ranschburg was primarily a student of R. Judah Leib Fischels, he was also a student of Landau's. See ibid. 27, 29–30, 36.

[83] On Baruch Jeitteles, see Kestenberg-Gladstein, *Neuere Geschichte*, esp. 125–46, 253–9. See also Jeitteles' eulogy for Landau, *Emek habakhah*.

[84] On Jonas Jeitteles, see Kestenberg-Gladstein, *Neuere Geschichte*, 118–24; ead., 'Chapters in the History of the Jews in Czech Lands', 36.

[85] Abraham Danzig wrote the well-known halakhic work *Ḥayei adam*.

[86] Peter Beer studied at Landau's yeshiva between the ages of 14 and 18 and taught at Prague's Normalschule from 1811 until his death. On Beer, see Hecht, *Ein jüdischer Aufklärer in Böhmen*; Brenner, 'Between Haskalah and Kabbalah'. On Aaron Chorin, see McCagg, *History of Habsburg Jews*, 127–8.

Berlin;[87] and Moses Kunitz (1774–1837), a Hungarian maskil and scholar of kabbalah.[88] Landau's second son, Samuel, who also studied at the yeshiva, was an eminent rabbinic scholar. Like his father, he composed numerous responsa, which were published in the collection *Shivat tsiyon* (Return to Zion).[89] When Landau fell ill in 1783, Samuel took responsibility for the daily affairs of the yeshiva,[90] and after his father's death in 1793 he officially assumed the academy's directorship.

Meir Fischels (Bumsla) was the director, or *rosh yeshivah*, of the other large and prestigious Prague yeshiva.[91] Fischels had studied under Eybeschütz, who had himself established and headed a yeshiva in Prague.[92] An extremely wealthy man, Fischels financed his own academy, which he directed for forty years. During this lengthy tenure, he had numerous students. From 1753 to 1769 he also served as the *rosh beit din*, the second most important judge in the Prague Jewish court system.[93] Although most of Fischels's writings were burned during the 1754 fire, many of his teachings were preserved in the works of his students and colleagues.[94] Despite initial tension between Fischels—a supporter of Eybeschütz—and Landau, the relationship between the two grew warmer over

[87] On Herz Homberg, see Hecht, 'Clash of Maskilim'; Kestenberg-Gladstein, *Neuere Geschichte*, 56–64; Mahler, *A History of Modern Jewry*, 260–1; McCagg, *History of Habsburg Jews*, 70–1, 111–12; Altmann, *Moses Mendelssohn*, esp. 359–60.

[88] On Moses Kunitz, see Fahn, 'Rabbi Moses Kunitz' (Heb.). Other distinguished students of Landau include Baruch b. Bezalel Brandeis (1755–1825), a preacher in Prague, who wrote *Leshon ḥakhamim*; Beer Pereles (1734–1806), a judge in Prague's lower court (see Landau's responsum to Pereles in *NB Tinyana*, 'ḤM', no. 1); David Deutsch (1756–1831), the author of *Ohel david*; and Wolf Mayer (1778–1850), who became the first Hebrew and Bible teacher at Prague's Normalschule in 1809. On Mayer, see Nosek, 'Jewish Hebrew Studies in the Czech Lands'. For a partial list of Landau's students, see Kamelhar, *Mofet hador*, 26–7. Extended critical studies of all these transitional figures, who were students of Landau, still remain a desideratum since they have largely been ignored by scholarship.

[89] Some of Samuel Landau's responsa are published in his father's responsa collection, the *Noda biyehudah*.

[90] Landau writes that he fell ill while he was involved in the printing of the last chapters of his commentary on *Pesaḥim*, which was published in 1783. See his epilogue to the *Tselaḥ*, *Pes.*, 349. See also *NB Tinyana*, 'EH', no. 20, and 'ḤM', no. 46.

[91] On Meir Fischels, see Buxbaum, 'Rabbis Meir and Leib Fischels' (Heb.); id., 'Introduction: Rabbi Bezalel Ranschburg', 26 n. 6.

[92] Eybeschütz headed his yeshiva until he left Prague in 1741. During his tenure in Prague from 1715 to 1741 he had numerous students. See Landau, 'Eulogy for Jonathan Eybeschütz' (Heb.) in his *Derushei hatselaḥ*, 46*b*. On Eybeschütz's roles as educator, judge, and preacher in Prague, see Carlebach, *Pursuit of Heresy*, 177; Kamelhar, *Mofet hador*, 16; Wind, *Rabbi Ezekiel Landau* (Heb.), 30–1.

[93] Meir Fischels became the *rosh beit din* of Prague's Jewish court after the death in 1753 of its former *rosh beit din*, Jacob Wiener Hamburger. The complex hierarchy of the Prague Jewish court system is discussed below.

[94] Meir Fischels's teachings and responsa are found in the works of his son, R. Judah Leib Fischels, as well as in those of Fleckeles, Bacharach, Ranschburg, and Landau. See e.g. *NB Kama*, 'YD', nos. 36, 81, 82 and 88.

time and eventually they became in-laws.[95] Landau praises Fischels in his responsa,[96] and upon Fischels's death in 1769 Landau delivered a powerful eulogy for him. After Fischels's passing, his son, Judah Leib Fischels (b. *c.*1732), became the yeshiva's director, a post he held for nearly forty years, until his death in 1808.[97]

There are many parallels in the family histories of Meir Fischels and Ezekiel Landau.[98] Both of these outstanding talmudists were succeeded in their post of *rosh yeshivah* by their sons, and both had sons active in Prague's Haskalah. Fischels's son Moses Fischer (1759–1833)[99] belonged in his early years to a maskilic Prague group, the Gesellschaft der jungen Hebraeer (Society of Young Hebrews), and subscribed to the leading Haskalah journal, *Hame'asef*.[100] He later took a rabbinic post in Vienna. His son, Meir or Marcus Fischer, was a prolific author of German and Hebrew historical works.[101] Landau's sons and grandsons were similarly involved, to varying degrees, in maskilic circles. His eldest son, Jacob, a talmudic scholar and wealthy Brody merchant, associated with maskilim in Galicia. Samuel Landau, like Moses Fischer, joined the Gesellschaft der jungen Hebraeer in his youth and in later years subscribed to *Hame'asef*.[102] Landau's third son, Israel, worked from around 1782 as a Hebrew printer in a Christian printing house in Prague. He was also influential in Prague's early Haskalah.[103] Landau's grandson, Moses Landau (1788–1852), headed Prague's Jewish community, and established a Hebrew press in the city, which published various maskilic writings.[104] Moses was also actively involved in

[95] Landau refers to Meir Fischels (Bumsla) as his in-law. See e.g. *Tselaḥ, Ber.* 35*a* (p. 131); *Tselaḥ, Ber.* 9*b* (p. 36), *corrigenda*. On the relationship between Landau and Fischels, see Kestenberg-Gladstein, *Neuere Geschichte*, 275 n. 195; Klemperer, 'Rabbis of Prague' (1951), 56.

[96] See *NB Kama*, 'YD', nos. 72 and 82.

[97] On Judah Leib Fischels, see Buxbaum, 'Rabbis Meir and Leib Fischels' (Heb.); id., 'Introduction: Rabbi Bezalel Ranschburg' (Heb.), 27 n. 15. Fischels also had many students in Prague.

[98] On these two families, see Kestenberg-Gladstein, *Neuere Geschichte*, esp. 125–7, 146–7, 275–6; Lamed, 'Ezekiel Ben Judah Landau (his sons)'; Y. Horowitz, 'Meir ben Ephraim Fischels'; Lamed, 'Fischer'.

[99] The name Fischels was changed to Fischer after Joseph II's mandate that Jews must adopt German family names. See Buxbaum, 'Introduction: Rabbi Bezalel Ranschburg' (Heb.), 26 n. 6.

[100] Kestenberg-Gladstein, *Neuere Geschichte*, 125, 275, 335 n. 14; Lamed, 'Fischer', col. 1318. Moses Fischer also supported Mendelssohn's translation and even corresponded with him regarding the project. See Altmann, *Moses Mendelssohn*, 408.

[101] On Meir Fischer, see Kestenberg-Gladstein, 'Chapters in the History of Czech Jewry', 44; ead., *Neuere Geschichte*, 275–83.

[102] Lamed, 'Ezekiel Ben Judah Landau (his Sons)', col. 1390. On Samuel Landau's and Moses Fischer's halakhic correspondence and discussions, see *NB Tinyana*, 'OḤ', nos. 57 and 112; ibid., 'ḤM', epilogue.

[103] In his youth, Israel studied in Brody with the talmudist and early maskil Israel Zamosc (*c.*1700–72), who had previously taught Mendelssohn in Berlin.

[104] On Moses Landau, see Kestenberg-Gladstein, *Neuere Geschichte*, esp. 249–52.

other maskilic projects, such as editing and contributing to *Bikurei ha'itim*, a Hebrew literary annual which continued the tradition of *Hame'asef*.[105] Within two generations each of these families produced leaders of Prague Jewry's progressive intellectual elite, a testimony to the rapid acculturation that penetrated even the city's most illustrious rabbinic dynasties.

Besides the two large yeshivas, there were numerous *batei midrash*, or *Studiehäuser* in Prague. Rich businessmen would often establish a *beit midrash* in a section of their home, and then grant certain scholars the privilege of teaching and living there with an accompanying stipend. Association with a *beit midrash* made the scholar eligible for the prized *Lehrlizenz* (teaching licence) and the status of official communal employee. Since most scholars did not reside in government-designated 'Jewish houses' and were therefore unable to engage in trade, their affiliation with a *beit midrash* afforded them both a residence and the ability to earn a living. Among the many *batei midrash* in Prague were those of Samuel Lucka (1720–92), where the distinguished rabbi Bezalel Ranschburg studied after his marriage;[106] the study houses of Joachim Edler Popper and of the *Primator* (president of the *Judenstadt*) Israel Frankel, both of which engaged Fleckeles in a rabbinic post;[107] the *beit midrash* of Baruch Jeitteles, a former student of Landau;[108] and the *beit midrash* of Simon Kuh (d. 1773), which supported the eminent Prague judges Michael Bachrach (1730–1801) and Jacob Ginzburg (1743–1815).[109]

Another communal institution overseen by the rabbinate was the Jewish court, invested with both legislative and executive authority. It adjudicated cases on the basis of Jewish law and had the ability to enforce laws that were binding on the community. For these reasons, the Jewish community officially barred Jews from taking their cases to non-Jewish courts.[110] The community's judicial system was comprised of two courts: the *Groeschelbethdin* (literally 'penny court'), or lower court, and the *Obergericht*, or high court.

Twelve jurists served on the lower court. Receiving a small but regular salary, these lower court judges would hear any minor case from members of the community. This court convened every day between afternoon and evening prayer services.

105 Landau was involved with *Bikurei ha'itim* during the 1820s. When it was discontinued in 1832 he published a few volumes of the scholarly journal *Kerem ḥemed*, which in some respects replaced *Bikurei ha'itim*.

106 See Buxbaum, 'Introduction: Rabbi Bezalel Ranschburg' (Heb.), 33.

107 Spitz, *Zikhron elazar*, 16.

108 The *Zylinder* hat, which symbolized progressive education, was worn at Baruch Jeitteles's *beit midrash* and at Samuel Landau's yeshiva. See Kestenberg-Gladstein, *Neuere Geschichte*, 360 n. 49.

109 Ibid. 139–41. Another *beit midrash* in Prague was that of Matthathias Neugröschel. See Landau's approbation for Neugröschel's *Be'er sheva*, dated 20 Heshvan 5535 (25 Oct. 1774), in which he states that while Neugröschel was in Prague there were always students in his *beit midrash*.

110 Wind, 'Ezekiel Landau' (Heb.), 94; Kestenberg-Gladstein, *Neuere Geschichte*, 15 n. 63, 24.

Appeals for cases tried at the lower court and cases of matrimonial law were adjudicated in the high court.[111] This court normally comprised five subordinate jurists, ranked in order of their authority, and the *av beit din*, or chief justice, all of whom were chosen from the most illustrious of Prague's rabbis. These *Oberjuristen* were given the honorific titles *morei shavah* (teachers of religious matters) and *Appellanten* (members of the court of appeals).[112] Some of the five judge's posts were occasionally left vacant. Governmental consent was required to promote judges within the ranks of the high court. The *rosh beit din*, or president of the court, was the most important of the five ranked judges, while Prague's chief rabbi served as the *av beit din*, his status being superior to that of the five ranked judges. The *av beit din* directed the high court and was the only member to receive a regular salary.[113]

Although it enjoyed considerable autonomy, the Jewish court occasionally faced challenges from within the community. In some sermons Landau complains of Prague Jews who ignore the *beit din* and undermine the authority of Jewish law.[114] He particularly rails against the community's neglect of the courts' specific decrees, such as those prohibiting the employment of married female servants and the wearing of coloured shoes.[115] In addition, despite a communal law that barred Jews from bringing their cases to non-Jewish courts, Prague Jews, especially the richer ones, occasionally went to these courts, where a speedy trial was more readily available.[116] While these examples are significant, they do not entirely negate the importance of Prague's eighteenth-century *beit din*. Disregard for the authority of the Jewish court is a common theme in rabbinic homilies, and Landau's complaints are probably overstated and not an accurate historical portrayal. Indeed, until the end of the eighteenth century a large number of the cases between Prague's Jews were brought before the *beit din*. It appears that the cases tried in non-Jewish courts remained in the minority.[117]

111 On the Jewish high and low courts in Prague, see Klemperer, 'Rabbis of Prague' (1951), 76–7; Vilímková, *Prague Ghetto*, 58.

112 In Hebrew, these rabbis were referred to as רבני דמו״ש, an acronym for *dayan morei shavah*. On the use of this title in Prague, see Lieberman, *Tent of Rachel* (Heb.), i. 474.

113 The income of Prague's chief rabbi was high, but he was dependent on the community for his salary. Nonetheless, Landau wielded great authority in Prague. See Kestenberg-Gladstein, *Neuere Geschichte*, 18, 24, 25.

114 See *Derushei hatselah*, sermon 8, 16*a*, sermon 22, 33*b*.

115 Ibid., sermon 1, 4*a*, in which Landau asserts that *more than two years have passed* since the Prague Jewish court issued a decree against the wearing of coloured shoes. Such an ordinance, banning many luxuries, including coloured shoes, was promulgated by Landau and Prague's Jewish court during the week of the portion of 'Ki tetse', 5527 (Sept. 1767). This sermon can therefore be dated to *c.*1770. On the 1767 sumptuary laws issued in Prague, see below.

116 Kestenberg-Gladstein, *Neuere Geschichte*, 15 n. 63.

117 There are indications, however, that Jews may have been more likely to take complex cases to non-Jewish courts. It should be noted that the volume of Landau's responsa dealing with monetary

Among the important functions of the Jewish court was the issuing of *takanot*, ordinances,[118] which dealt with various communal matters such as the harsh taxes imposed on Jews and the promulgation of various sumptuary and alimentary laws.[119] One of the most famous of these ordinances was decreed in 1767, imposing numerous restrictions on the type of celebrations held by different classes of Prague Jews.[120] Based on the level of taxes individuals paid, it determined how many guests they could invite, when musicians could play, and what kinds of meat, fish, hot beverages, and alcohol could be served. Interestingly, rather than minimizing class distinctions, these laws highlighted them.[121] In addition, these ordinances also prohibited Jews from donning ostentatious dress, specifically powdered wigs and silk scarves. Women were also forbidden to wear gloves, green hats, or expensive dresses outside the ghetto. A commission was appointed to fine or even incarcerate individuals violating these orders.[122]

In 1784 Joseph II restricted the Jewish court's authority, abolishing its judicial autonomy in both civil and criminal matters. These powers were transferred to the city's civil courts. Jewish courts retained their authority only over religious affairs, making the Jews' penny court redundant and leading to its dissolution.[123]

matters, 'Ḥoshen Mishpat', contains the fewest queries. This phenomenon also occurs in the responsa collections of various other influential late 18th-c. and 19th-c. *posekim* (halakhic authorities), such as the Hatam Sofer and Avnei Nezer (R. Abraham Bornstein, 1839–1910). The relative brevity of these volumes may indicate that during this period central and east European Jews did not routinely turn to their rabbinic authorities and courts concerning complex monetary matters.

118 These were often issued by the rabbinic court in conjunction with other communal leaders, including the *parnasim*.

119 For example, in 1652, 1654, 1662, and 1702 the Prague Jewish community issued *takanot* concerning meat taxes and other matters. On the history and use of sumptuary laws, see Hunt, *Governance of the Consuming Passions*; Hundert, *Jews in Poland–Lithuania*, 87–95; Berkovitz, 'Social and Religious Controls in Pre-Revolutionary France'; id., *Rites and Passages*, esp. 39–51; Roth, 'Sumptuary Laws of the Community of Carpentras'; Bonfil, *Jewish Life in Renaissance Italy*, esp. 104–11.

120 These Yiddish ordinances are published in Jerold Weiss, *Zion Hamtzuyenes*, 121–30. They also appear in Hebrew translation in Kamelhar, *Mofet hador*, 37–9.

121 Of course, these laws were probably intended to ensure that the wealthy—those who threw the most lavish parties—paid the appropriate taxes due to the community. In addition, although rabbinic literature emphasizes the importance of minimizing the difference in expenditure between rich and poor (see e.g. BT *MK* 27*a*–*b*), 18th-c. society worked hard to maintain visible markers distinguishing individuals of different economic and social ranks. See Hundert, *Jews in Poland–Lithuania*, 91–3; Hunt, *Governance of the Consuming Passions*, 108–41; Berkovitz, *Rites and Passages*, 45–7. For example, during the 17th and 18th cc., the seating plan in Prague's Pinkas synagogue was determined according to its members' economic and social standing. For a discussion of this phenomenon, see Davis, *Yom-Tov Lipmann Heller*, 7.

122 While it is true that these *takanot* were not always observed—as noted above—the fact that the court felt at liberty to issue such detailed ordinances suggests the tremendous control that the state afforded it over the minutiae of Prague Jews' behaviour.

123 See Klemperer, 'Rabbis of Prague' (1951), 77; Kestenberg-Gladstein, *Neuere Geschichte*, 66–7.

Although this transfer of legal authority was only one aspect of Joseph II's centralization of Prague's legal system, which was unified under a central magistrate at this time,[124] for the city's Jews this diminishing of rabbinic influence was significant.

The rabbinic high court, however, continued to function into the nineteenth century, adjudicating religious matters according to the principles of Jewish law. During this period, the *Oberjuristen* retained their titles and a great measure of their authority. Nonetheless, the position of *av beit din* was abolished after Landau's death in 1793. Several years earlier, in May 1790, a group led by Landau's son Samuel petitioned the new emperor Leopold II to reinstate the full authority of the Jewish court. Their petition was declined. Samuel, with a group of Prague elders, petitioned the newly inaugurated emperor Francis II (1768–1835) on this matter once more in 1792, and was rebuffed again.[125] Nevertheless, the religious authority of the Jewish court remained more or less intact.

During Landau's Prague career many of the city's most prominent rabbis served as judges on the high court. (Until now, scholarship on Habsburg Jewry has not provided a comprehensive list of these rabbis.) Shortly before Landau's arrival in Prague, Meir Fischels became the *rosh beit din*. During Landau's early years in Prague, the judges on the high court, other than Fischels, were Isaac Wolf Austerlitz (d. 1762), a student of Eybeschütz, Asher Anshil Oizers (d. 1765), a pupil of Abraham Broda, Judah Leib Kasovitz (d. 1782), another supporter of Eybeschütz,[126] and Moses Ginsburg Shapira (d. 1783), who died en route to Israel.[127] By 1767 the two vacancies created on the court by the deaths of Austerlitz and Oizers[128] had been filled by Solomon Zalman Emerich (Gumpel) (1713–94), the author of numerous rabbinic works, and Joseph

[124] Demetz, *Prague in Black and Gold*, 254. The four towns of Prague, the Old, the New, Vyšehrad, and Hradčany, along with their legal systems, were united on 12 Feb. 1784. Although it was a separate administrative unit, the Jewish ghetto was often considered a part of the Old Town.

[125] See McCagg, *History of Habsburg Jews*, 68; Adler, 'Das älteste Judicial-Protokoll', 219; Mahler, *History of Modern Jewry*, 258–9; Klemperer, 'Rabbis of Prague' (1951), 77. These petitions had initially been spurred by opposition to those of the Jewish Bohemian *Landesprimator*, Joachim Popper, and reform-minded Jews, which asked the government to give the religious court less authority.

[126] Both Isaac Wolf Austerlitz and Judah Leib Kasovitz signed a letter supporting Eybeschütz in 1752. See Eybeschütz, *Luḥot edut*, 11.

[127] Notably, the following Prague high court judges were signatories of the 9 Feb. 1756 approbation for *Me'il tsedakah*: Ezekiel Landau, Judah Leib Kasovitz, Wolf Austerlitz, Meir Fischel Bumsla, and Asher Anshil Ozrish. It is possible that the judge Moses Ginsburg Shapira was away when this approbation was signed.

[128] Landau delivered eulogies for both of these judges. His eulogy for Isaac Wolf Austerlitz, delivered on 28 Mar. 1762, is recorded in a manuscript of one of Landau's students. It was recently published: see *Kerem shelomoh*, 7 (1991), 6–8. His eulogy for Asher Anshel Oizers, dated 10 Feb. 1765, is included in *Ahavat tsiyon*, sermon 6, 9*b*–11*a*.

Lieberles (d. 1780).[129] Following Fischels's death in 1769, Levi Panta (d. 1782) joined the court, and the acclaimed talmudist Judah Leib Kasovitz became *rosh beit din*.[130] In 1780 Michael Bachrach resigned his position at the penny court, and later that year assumed the post left vacant in the high court by Lieberles' death. In about 1782, after Kasovitz's death, Emerich became the *rosh beit din*.[131] During this period, the death of Panta and the departure of Shapira opened other positions on the court.[132] Shortly thereafter, Jacob Ginzburg was appointed as the high court's third judge, and in 1783 Fleckeles, returning from four years in Moravia,[133] became the court's fifth-ranked judge.[134]

Since no chief rabbi, and therefore also no *av beit din*, was chosen after Landau's death, the members of Prague's high court served not only as jurists but also as the community's de facto religious leaders. Emerich was the *rosh beit din*, or head rabbi, and the other ranked judges, in descending order, were Bachrach, Jacob Ginzburg, and Fleckeles.[135] At this point, Samuel Landau made his desire to be appointed as the fourth-ranked judge clear, but was rebuffed.[136] In response, he raised the issue of the conflict between Bachrach's and Ginzburg's positions on the court and their free residence in apartments

[129] These facts are based on a number of approbations as well as the 1767 Prague *takanot* against luxuries. The signatories of these *takanot* were *av beit din* Ezekiel Landau and members of the *beit din*: Meir Fischel Bumsla, Judah Leib Kasovitz, Solomon Zalman Emerich, Moses Ginsburg Shapira, and Joseph Lieberles.

[130] See e.g. the following list of Prague high court judges who signed a *te'udat ḥaver*, a certificate conferring the title of rabbinic scholar, on 14 Tamuz 5534 (23 June 1774): Ezekiel Landau, Judah Leib Kasovitz, Solomon Zalman Gumpel Emerich, Moses Shapira, Joseph Lieberles, and Levi Panta. The certificate is published in P. Nadler (ed.), *Sefer ginzei yehudah*, 58. See also ibid. 59 for another *te'udat ḥaver*, from 1778, with the same signatories. See also Landau's references to Judah Leib Kasovitz as Prague's *rosh beit din* in *NB Kama*, 'YD', no. 58 and *Tselaḥ*, *Pes.* 76*b* (p. 288).

[131] Judah Leib Kasovitz died in Sept. 1782. See *Gal-ed*, no. 119. *Gal-ed* contains 170 tombstone inscriptions from the old Jewish cemetery of Prague, collected and published by Koppelmann Lieben.

[132] Levi Panta died in Jan. 1782. See *Gal-ed*, no. 115. Landau's unpublished eulogy for Panta is housed in the Jewish Theological Seminary in New York. An unpublished letter by the wife of Moses Ginsburg Shapira places his death, in Sidon, on 3 Adar I 5543 (5 Feb. 1783).

[133] Fleckeles served as a rabbi in Kojetin, Moravia from 1779 to 1783.

[134] See e.g. the high court judges who signed the approbation for *Sefer she'iltot* on 15 Kislev 5546 (17 Nov. 1785). It includes all the *Oberjuristen* of that time: Landau, Bachrach, Jacob Ginzburg, and Fleckeles.

[135] S. H. Lieben, 'Rabbi Eleasar Fleckeles', 13; Kestenberg-Gladstein, *Neuere Geschichte*, 141–2; Klemperer, 'Rabbis of Prague' (1951), 75, 77. At this time, Fleckeles was the fifth-ranked judge and the position of fourth-ranked judge was left vacant.

[136] During Landau's lifetime he attempted to secure Samuel an appointment to the high court. See Klein, 'Zuschrift an Herrn Moses Mendelson in Hamburg', 542. While Dr Klein asserts that Landau was unsuccessful in this endeavour because of Samuel's previous bankruptcy, Kestenberg-Gladstein claims that it was because of Samuel's maskilic past. See Kestenberg-Gladstein, *Neuere Geschichte*, 142 n. 146.

established by Simon Kuh, which were explicitly meant for scholars not employed by the community.[137] Ginzburg consequently resigned from the court. After Emerich died in 1794, Bachrach assumed the post of *rosh beit din*, Fleckeles became the court's second-ranked judge, and Samuel Landau was appointed the third-ranked judge. Upon Bachrach's death in 1801, Fleckeles became *rosh beit din*, and retained this position until his death in 1826. At that time, Samuel Landau finally attained the post he had desired for so long. He remained *rosh beit din* until his death in 1834.[138]

Numerous other distinguished rabbinic *Unterjuristen* (lower-court judges), talmudic scholars, authors, and educated members of the laity resided in Prague during the latter half of the eighteenth century. Some served in an official rabbinic capacity. The most outstanding members of this group were Zerah Eidlitz, a prominent Talmud teacher and preacher in Prague;[139] Isaiah Wiener (1726–98), the author of the halakhic work *Bigdei yesha*;[140] Ephraim Wehli (d. 1787), an expert on the halakhic writings of Moses Maimonides (1138–1204);[141] Eleazar Karpeles (d. 1832), an acclaimed rabbinic scholar;[142] and Abraham ben Yom-Tov Bondi (d. 1786) and his son Nehemiah Feivel Bondi (1762–1831), both of whom wrote halakhic and talmudic treatises.[143]

Despite legal restrictions, persistent antisemitism, and state-imposed changes, which affected the Jewish community of Prague, the latter half of the eighteenth century witnessed the flourishing of Prague's rabbinic culture. Heir to a long and rich halakhic and mystical tradition, Prague enjoyed its heyday of rabbinic scholarship during this era. Its acclaimed yeshivas, its renowned court

137 Samuel's complaint was published in both *Hame'asef* and *Ha'orev* (Vienna, 1795), which latter publication was attributed by some scholars, such as Lieben and Kestenberg-Gladstein, to Baruch Jeitteles. On this incident, see Klemperer, 'Rabbis of Prague' (1951), 75–6; S. H. Lieben, 'Rabbi Eleasar Fleckeles', 14 n. 1.

138 Klemperer, 'Rabbis of Prague' (1951), 79–81; S. H. Lieben, 'Rabbi Eleasar Fleckeles', 15, 17.

139 On Landau's praise of Eidlitz, see his approbation for Eidlitz's *Or layesharim*. On Eidlitz see also Klein, 'Zuschrift an Herrn Moses Mendelson in Hamburg', 524–5.

140 Both Landau and Judah Leib Kasovitz, Prague's *rosh beit din*, wrote approbations for *Bigdei yesha*.

141 See Fleckeles, *Olat ḥodesh hashelishi*, sermon 2 ('Eulogy for Ephraim Wehli', dated 5 Elul 5547 (19 Aug. 1787), 9*a*. On Wehli, see also Klein, 'Zuschrift an Herrn Moses Mendelson in Hamburg', 541; Kamelhar, *Mofet hador*, 22–3.

142 Both Landau and his son Samuel sent responsa to Eleazar Karpeles. See e.g. *NB Tinyana*, 'OḤ', nos. 1, 53; Samuel Landau, *Shivat tsiyon*, nos. 47, 54. See also Karpeles' eulogy for Landau, *Derush lehesped even ha'ot yeḥezkel lemofet*.

143 The Bondis were a prominent scholarly family in Prague. Abraham Bondi wrote *Zera avraham*, which was published by Nehemiah, the author of *Torat neḥemyah*. Among the other well-known scholars in Prague were Moses Cohen-Rofe, an eminent talmudist; Jacob Judah Ausch, a judge on Prague's lower court; Salman Koreff, a renowned talmudist; and Samuel Leib Kauder (1766–1838), who wrote responsa and talmudic novellae. On Kauder, see Buxbaum, 'Introduction: Rabbi Bezalel Ranschburg' (Heb.), 38–9; Klemperer, 'Rabbis of Prague' (1951), 81.

system, its distinguished scholars, and the numerous rabbinic works written and published in the city all made it a centre of Jewish scholarship. The rabbinic leadership, which boasted some of the towering rabbinic figures of the generation, attracted students and scholars from all over Europe. Nevertheless, notwithstanding this 'golden era', incipient stages of modernization, state-imposed legislation, and trends within the Jewish community that were gaining momentum during the late eighteenth century began to threaten the city's rabbinic culture. By the beginning of the nineteenth century these trends, some of which were rooted in kabbalah, began to undermine the Prague rabbinate.

THREE

Mystical and Modernizing Trends: Prague's Rabbinic Culture Threatened

Cultural Changes Imposed by the State

It is impossible to overstate the importance of the state in the transformation of Prague's traditional Jewish society, particularly its embrace of German culture. Joseph II's systematic policy of Germanization reshaped several of the central community institutions. State-imposed secular education forced the rabbinic authorities to modify the curriculum offered to Prague's Jewish youth. Because of the traditional rabbinic assertion of the primacy of Torah, which often precluded the study of extra-talmudic subjects, secular disciplines were usually excluded from formal studies of Ashkenazi students.[1] Joseph II's state-mandated Normalschulen, whose curriculum included German, mathematics, geography, and morality, challenged this rabbinic ideal.[2] After the opening of Prague's Jewish Normalschule in 1782, the rabbinate allowed secular subjects to be introduced into the curriculum. This innovation diminished the hours devoted to talmudic learning, and gave pupils basic tools to advance in secular disciplines, especially in Germanic studies.

The Enlightenment, Haskalah, and Maskilim

Compounding the changes imposed by the state, internal forces challenged the prevailing educational, religious, and social norms of the traditional Jewish community. In the 1770s the Jewish Enlightenment, or Haskalah, centred in Berlin, began to emerge in central Europe. Like the absolutist Habsburg monarchy, the maskilim, enlightened Jewish exponents of change, advocated the reorientation

[1] On the traditional rabbinate's educational priorities as well as its attitudes towards the study of subjects other than Talmud and halakhah, see J. Katz, 'Halakhah and Kabbalah', 33–63; Twersky, 'Law and Spirituality in the Seventeenth Century'; id., 'Religion and Law'.

[2] Kieval, 'Autonomy and Interdependence', 86, 89; id., 'The Lands Between', 44. Although the Normalschulen were state-mandated, the government allowed parents to provide secular education through other means. Many Prague Jews avoided the Normalschule by hiring tutors for their children's secular education.

of many of the Jewish community's basic priorities and institutions.[3] According to Haskalah scholar Shmuel Feiner, the maskilim produced the first modern Jewish ideology of transition.[4] The main goals of the predominantly liberal and rationalist maskilim were the recognition of the value of secular studies, more openness to the surrounding society, and the acculturation of Jews, primarily through knowledge of the vernacular. The Prague maskilim, along with other acculturating Jews, stressed the importance of secular education, frequently at the expense of talmudic studies, which they sometimes derided. They promoted the integration of secular disciplines, particularly philosophy, into the Jewish world-view. Consequently, they often supported the Habsburg state's educational and cultural reforms, which they viewed as serving their own goals.

The most common form of religious expression among the various eighteenth-century European Enlightenment movements was deism. Although European deism assumed varied forms, they possessed some common characteristics. Most deists and advocates of Enlightenment believed in a transcendent Creator who could not change the immutable laws of nature and had no control over the fate of individuals. Adopting the Enlightenment's veneration of reason and critical thought, the deists applied them not only to science and philosophy but also to theology. Many of them maintained that natural law and religious truth could only be derived through reason, and opposed any religion based on divine revelation. French deists, like Voltaire and Diderot, who occasionally skirted the borders of atheism, generally took a particularly harsh stance against revealed religion and the authority of its leaders. German deists, however, influenced by both English deism and German pietism, were largely swayed by the teachings of Christian Wolff (1679–1754), who attempted to reconcile deism and Christianity. Some German deists believed that there was a direct correspondence between natural and biblical law.[5]

The early German maskilim were influenced by the less radical ideas of various German and English deists, but by the 1790s the Haskalah in Germany had become more radicalized, launching vituperative attacks against both revealed

[3] For general works on the Enlightenment, see Porter, *Enlightenment*; Porter and Teich (eds.), *Enlightenment in National Context*. On the Jewish Enlightenment in Berlin and Prague and rabbinic responses to it, see Feiner, *Jewish Enlightenment*; id., *Haskalah and History*; id., 'Early Haskalah in the Eighteenth Century'; Feiner and Bartal (eds.), *Varieties of Haskalah* (Heb.); Feiner and Sorkin (eds.), *New Perspectives on the Haskalah*; Sorkin, *Moses Mendelssohn and the Religious Enlightenment*; B. Z. Katz, *Rabbinate, Hasidism, Haskalah* (Heb.); Altmann, *Moses Mendelssohn*; M. Graetz, 'Jewish Enlightenment'; Pelli, *Age of Haskalah*; Kestenberg-Gladstein, *Neuere Geschichte*, 29, 96, 115–331; ead., 'National Character of the Prague Haskalah' (Heb.); Kieval, 'Caution's Progress', 81–91.

[4] Feiner, 'Towards a Historical Definition of the Haskalah', in Feiner and Sorkin (eds.), *New Perspectives on the Haskalah*, 184–219.

[5] See Woloch, *Eighteenth-Century Europe*, 238; Pelli, *Age of Haskalah*, 8–11, 13–16, 18; J. Katz, *Out of the Ghetto*, 97–8.

religion and rabbinic authority.[6] Several Prague maskilim, such as Landau's students Herz Homberg and Baruch Jeitteles, spent time in Berlin during the 1770s and 1780s and were directly influenced by the Haskalah movement there.[7] Other Prague Jews were indirectly affected by the Berlin Haskalah as well as by other trends of Enlightenment and deism, which became popular in the Habsburg empire.

Many notions spawned by the Enlightenment influenced leading church officials, government leaders, and educational institutions in the Habsburg empire.[8] As part of Maria Theresa's programme of state centralization, the government reformed and secularized various universities in accordance with Enlightenment principles. Reforms intended to reflect German notions of natural law espoused by philosophers such as Christian Wolff were instituted in the theology, law, and philosophy faculties of Prague's university.[9] Joseph II extended the enlightened educational and religious reforms initiated during his mother's reign. Enlightenment ideas among Habsburg officials and at the university—open to Jews in 1781 and only a few streets from the Jewish quarter—seem to have influenced the ghetto's inhabitants.

There is evidence of more radical deistic and atheistic tendencies in Bohemia from the 1770s to the 1790s. While Habsburg officials advanced Enlightenment teachings of German rationalists such as Wolff, the government restricted and persecuted radical forms of deism in the empire. In the 1770s government authorities, in an attempt to limit the spread of radical deism, initiated new censorship rules, designed to restrict the importation of atheistic works into Bohemia. During Joseph II's reign, in the 1780s, the government exposed a group of Bohemian deists and other individual deists, all of whom were severely punished.[10] Curiously, despite the precarious position of deism in Bohemia, a 1791 address by Moses Weiner (d. 1814), who served in various capacities

[6] M. Graetz, 'Jewish Enlightenment', 344–54; Pelli, *Age of Haskalah*, 18–23, 28–32, 47; Lowenstein, *Berlin Jewish Community*, 5, 95–103.

[7] See Altmann, *Moses Mendelssohn*, 359–60; Kestenberg-Gladstein, *Neuere Geschichte*, 126; M. Graetz, 'Jewish Enlightenment', 344; McCagg, *History of Habsburg Jews*, 111.

[8] Enlightenment ideas were already advocated by several of Maria Theresa's ministers who had studied at German universities, where they were introduced to the rationalist teachings of Christian Wolff. In addition, during her reign, the Italian Catholic reformer, Lodovico Antonio Muratori, who endorsed secular knowledge, and conceptions of natural law that were rooted in the German Enlightenment, also had a strong influence on Habsburg church officials and Habsburg cultural reform. See Ingrao, *Habsburg Monarchy*, 165–7, 170, 184.

[9] Similar reforms were instituted at the university in Vienna. During Maria Theresa's reign the government also began to remove Jesuit and other religious influences from the universities.

[10] Schaller, *Kurzgefasste Geschichte der kais. kön. Bücherzensur*, 9; Demetz, *Prague in Black and Gold*, 248–9; J. Katz, *Out of the Ghetto*, 147. Blanning, *Joseph II*, 75.

at Prague's Normalschule, including its directorship, manifests radical deistic tendencies.[11]

An examination of Landau's Prague homilies and talmudic glosses also reveals the prevalence of deism in Prague. In these writings he repeatedly censures the deists or 'the philosophers of his day' for ascribing everything to natural law. He complains that 'the heretics, who believe in nature and deny providence, have increased in our generation'.[12] In one homily he refers to one of these groups as 'the philosophers who are now called "materialists"'.[13] He also attacks these groups for denying God's ability to alter natural law, perform miracles, and grant reward or mete out punishment.[14] In ridicule of them, he points out that although 'out of shame they do admit that the world has a Creator', they claim that 'He has abandoned it'.[15] He further criticizes contemporary philosophical sects for renouncing the divine revelation of the Written and Oral Torah and for mocking these sacred works.[16] In response to the deistic tendencies of Jews and non-Jews alike, Landau frequently stresses the themes of divine providence, miracles, and reward and punishment.

Two of Landau's homilies containing scathing attacks against the deists can be dated to the 1770s and 1780s.[17] The first is from *c.*1775, as we can tell from its reference to the Bohemian peasant revolt, which occurred during that year.[18] In it he enumerates various types of philosophers who deny providence and

[11] Weiner was a teacher at the Normalschule from 1782 to 1812, and its director from 1812 to 1814. On Weiner, see Kestenberg-Gladstein, *Neuere Geschichte*, 46, 55–6, 206.

[12] *Derushei hatselaḥ*, sermon 25, 38*b*. Here he elaborates that there are different contemporary groups who all espouse these heretical beliefs. See also id., *Tselaḥ*, *Ber.* 28*b* (p. 109); *Derushei hatselaḥ*, sermon 13, for the first day of *seliḥot* prayers, 22*a*, and sermon for Shabat Hagadol, 55*b*.

[13] *Derushei hatselaḥ*, sermon 25, 38*b*. This group of philosophers, he explains, believes neither in creation *ex nihilo* nor in the immortality of the soul.

[14] See ibid., sermon for Passover, 58*a*–*b*, and sermon 25, 40*a*; id., *Tselaḥ*, *Ber.* 28*b*.

[15] *Derushei hatselaḥ*, sermon for Passover, 58*a*. See also ibid., sermon 25, 39*b*–40*a*.

[16] Ibid., sermon 25, 40*a*, and sermon 14 for the Ten Days of Repentance, 24*a*–*b*.

[17] Unlike many of Landau's sermons that cannot be dated, since they are neither in chronological order nor reveal information about the particular years during which they were delivered, these two sermons can be dated on the basis of the historical events they discuss. Jacob Katz largely bases his argument concerning the increasing popularity of deistic thought and the neglect of halakhah among Ashkenazi Jewry during the 1780s on Landau's and Fleckeles' sermons from this period. See J. Katz, *Out of the Ghetto*, 146–7. Although a few of Landau's sermons from these years do reveal these tendencies, Katz's proof is weakened by the fact that other sermons where Landau addresses these themes are hard to date. Due to this and other factors, the spread of these trends is difficult to date definitively. In my opinion, Landau's sermons and other contemporary sources indicate that by and large Prague Jews continued to adhere to halakhah during this period. See my discussion in the Introduction.

[18] *Derushei hatselaḥ*, sermon for Shabat Hagadol, 55*b*. On the peasant revolt, see Trebitsch, *Korot ha'itim*, para. 42, on the year 1775. See also Ingrao, *Habsburg Monarchy*, 186.

pronounces all of them heretics;[19] in particular, he condemns Prague Jews, stating that 'in the Jewish street, those who lack all knowledge but have read a bit from these [secular] books, speak against providence and faith and belittle the revealed Torah'.[20] These themes resurface in a homily delivered about seven years later, in 1782,[21] in which his harsh polemic against the deists again indicates his perception of an urgent need to refute these 'heretical' beliefs.

Responding to the deists and maskilim, Landau refutes the popular belief in reason, 'objective' enquiry, and philosophy, and defends the centrality of faith in Judaism. In a 1782 sermon he stresses that faith is 'the basis of all' and 'the root of the Torah'. His polemic against the deists accentuates the limits of reason and the futility of applying critical-scientific methodology to theology.[22] He mocks contemporary theologians, pointing out that what one Jewish or gentile theologian 'proves' the next disproves.[23] He points to the absurdity of the assertion that man can attain knowledge of metaphysical matters through scientific and philosophical enquiry since these methods are inadequate to comprehend even the natural world or man's soul.[24] Strikingly, Landau, a great supporter of the medieval halakhic giant Maimonides, criticizes some of his classical philosophical investigations, heavily influenced by Aristotelianism, for the same reason.[25] He often conflates his critique of the ancient Greek philosophers, particularly 'Aristotle and his cohorts', with his censure of the rationalist beliefs of contemporary 'heretical' philosophical sects, who were influenced by ancient Greek concepts.[26]

Like many Jewish thinkers who have listed the principles of faith in response to perceived internal and external threats,[27] Landau enumerates tenets of faith in

[19] *Derushei hatselah*, sermon for Shabat Hagadol, 57*a*. He exclaims that there is a range of opinions among the philosophers as to the precise role, if any, of providence. All, he asserts, however, ultimately heretically maintain that nature is the dominant force.

[20] Ibid. 55*b*.

[21] Ibid., sermon 39, 53*b*. In this homily, delivered on the sabbath before Passover, Landau refers to the recently issued Toleranzpatent. Since Joseph II promulgated the Toleranzpatent for Bohemia in Oct. 1781, we can date this sermon to the sabbath preceding Passover on 23 Mar. 1782. Once again Landau laments that various heretical sects have arisen among the Jews. In response, he stresses that the entire corpus of Oral Law is as sacred as the Ten Commandments, which were accepted by some deists as the equivalent of natural law.

[22] See *Derushei hatselah*, sermon 39, 53*b*. Landau conveys similar sentiments in his talmudic commentary. See *Tselah*, *Ber.* 28*b* (pp. 109–10), where he warns his readers against any philosophical enquiry since many individuals from the 'philosophical sect' deny the essential doctrines of Judaism.

[23] See *Derushei hatselah*, sermon 39, 53*b*.

[24] See e.g. ibid., sermon 25, 40*a*.

[25] See *Ahavat tsiyon*, sermon 3, 4*b*.

[26] See e.g. *Derushei hatselah*, sermon for Passover, 58*a*; sermon 39, 53*b*; sermon 28, 42*a*; sermon 36 for Shabat Hagadol, 49*a*.

[27] See e.g. Isaac Abrabanel's critique of Maimonides' and other Jewish philosophers' listing of principles of faith: Abrabanel, *Rosh amanah*, ch. 23, 136–41; Schechter, 'Dogmas of Judaism' in his *Studies in Judaism*, 147–81; Neumark, *Toledot ha'ikarim beyisra'el*, ii, 130–1.

reaction to the challenges that Deism and the radical Haskalah posed to traditional Judaism. In light of his repeated depictions of contemporary 'philosophical' views, his list of principles, embedded within some of his sermons and commentaries, while espousing age-old doctrines, such as the centrality of God's continual providence over individuals and the world after Creation, divine reward and retribution, God's ability to perform miracles, and the revelation and authority of the Written and Oral Torah, is clearly polemical.[28]

Landau's resistance to the application of rationalism to theology is apparent in his position on probing *ta'amei hamitsvot*, the underlying rationale for the commandments. In response to early maskilim, who frequently offered a rational basis for the commandments in order to reconcile them with Enlightenment ideas,[29] he dismisses this endeavour, reiterating his view that the commandments are based on faith, not reason. He often bolsters this position by repeating the rabbinic dictum that one should not delve into the reasons for the commandments.[30] Landau's stance concerning *ta'amei hamitsvot* is also, in part, a reaction to the more radical maskilim's use of *ta'amei hamitsvot* as a vehicle to undermine the authoritative status of the commandments. These maskilim argued that since the commandments are merely a means to righteousness, they could be eliminated if alternative means to this end are found.[31] Other radical maskilim, echoing deistic sentiments, rhetorically asked why an almighty God, who has no will or wants, would care whether people observe the commandments.[32] Partly in response to the tendency of maskilim to engage in *ta'amei hamitsvot*, and despite his own frequent remarks on the kabbalistic functions of the commandments, Landau routinely insists that one should not delve into the commandments' rationale.

Fear of the *maskilim* also contributed to Landau's and other Prague rabbis' strong defence of the aggadah. In a 1783 Prague sermon, his student Fleckeles rebukes the Berlin maskilim as heretics who violate the commandments, asserting that they 'despise the *agadot*'.[33] Fleckeles' jibe is in accord with various maskilic sources, particularly *Hame'asef*, the leading journal and mouthpiece of the Berlin

[28] See e.g. *Derushei hatselah*, sermon for Passover, 58*b*, and sermon 39, 53*b*. His repeated listing of these principles demonstrates his fear that some Prague Jews had renounced even the most basic tenets of traditional Judaism.

[29] See e.g. Mendelssohn, *Jerusalem*, 99, 128. For a discussion of this development, see Pelli, *Age of Haskalah*, 26–7, 43.

[30] See e.g. *Derushei hatselah*, sermon 39, 53*b*.

[31] See e.g. Levison, *Tokhahat megilah*, 9*b*; Berlin, *Besamim rosh*, no. 251 (pp. 77*a*–*b*). On Levison see Ruderman, *Jewish Thought and Scientific Discovery*, 332–70.

[32] On this maskilic claim see e.g. Fleckeles, *Olat hodesh hasheni*, sermon 3 (Days of Repentance, 1783), 56*a*. Landau also addresses this issue and discusses the kabbalistic function of the commandments in *Ahavat tsiyon*, sermon 2 (1761), 3*a*–*b*; *Derushei hatselah*, sermon 39, 53*b*.

[33] Fleckeles, *Olat hodesh hasheni*, sermon 3, 56*a*–*b*. Fleckeles also laments that they scorn the esoteric secrets.

Haskalah, which mock the irrationality of the aggadah.[34] In Landau's introduction to his Talmud commentary on *Berakhot*, published in 1791, he defends the aggadah, which, he writes, is harshly disparaged 'by the *asafsuf* (riffraff) in our midst', who 'chirp like unclean birds'.[35] His use of the biblical term *asafsuf*[36] is a pun on and a reference to the maskilic journal *Hame'asef*.[37] Both Landau's discussion of the significance of the aggadah and his allusions to the esoteric truths contained in *agadot* are, in part, aspects of his wider defence of rabbinic Judaism against the rationalist critiques of the maskilim and deists.

Landau also emerged as a leading critic of maskilic projects and innovations in the religio-cultural and political spheres. His major controversies with maskilim were occasioned by the publication of a few influential maskilic works in the early 1780s. The first of these controversies was spurred by the writings and ideas of Moses Mendelssohn, the leader of the Berlin Haskalah. Mendelssohn, whose philosophical thought was largely influenced by Gottfried Leibnitz and Christian Wolff, attempted to reconcile philosophy and Judaism. He also advocated curbing the rabbis' coercive powers.[38]

Besides his numerous philosophical writings, Mendelssohn produced a German translation of the Pentateuch, which disseminated some Enlightenment ideas and played an important role in various maskilic cultural initiatives.[39] This High German translation along with its multi-authored Hebrew commentary, the *Biur* (meaning: explanation, clarification), was entitled *Netivot hashalom*.[40] Its publication was announced in 1778, and completed in 1783.[41] Many of the contributors to the *Biur*, such as Naphtali Herz Wessely, Herz Homberg, and Solomon Dubno (1738–1813), became central figures in the early Haskalah.

Although certain scholars, such as Moshe Samet, contend that 'Landau did not oppose the Haskalah *at all* [my italics]', or that, at the very least, his attitude

34 This theme appears repeatedly in *Hame'asef* during the 1780s.

35 *Tselaḥ*, short introd.

36 See Num. 11: 4.

37 The first three volumes of *Hame'asef* were published between 1784 and 1786. By 1785, the list of *numeranten* (subscribers) for *Hame'asef* already included twelve Prague Jews.

38 On his discussion about limiting the coercive powers of religious authorities, particularly their right to excommunicate, see e.g. Mendelssohn, *Jerusalem*, 73–4.

39 On Mendelssohn's Bible translation project, see Altmann, *Moses Mendelssohn*, esp. 368–83; Sorkin, *Moses Mendelssohn and the Religious Enlightenment*, 53–89; M. Graetz, 'Jewish Enlightenment', 304–12; Lowenstein, 'Readership of Mendelssohn's Bible Translation'; E. Breuer, *Limits of Enlightenment*.

40 The translation was written in a sophisticated German in Hebrew characters. The goal of the *Biur* was to offer a literal reading of the Pentateuch which was in line with Enlightenment views.

41 The prospectus for *Netivot hashalom*, entitled *Alim literufah*, was circulated in 1778, and its first volume, Genesis, was published in 1780. See Lowenstein, 'Readership of Mendelssohn's Bible Translation', 180.

towards the Haskalah, Mendelssohn, and *Netivot hashalom* was more moderate than portrayed by previous historians,[42] such as Heinrich Graetz,[43] numerous sources indicate otherwise. A private collection of Landau's writings, found in Russian archives and only recently made public, as well as other contemporary documents, reveal that he both opposed the Haskalah and censured Mendelssohn and his Bible translation more vehemently than depicted in recent scholarship.[44]

While Landau never mentions Mendelssohn in his sermons, he refers to him in various approbations, personal letters, and in his talmudic commentary. The earliest source in which he discusses Mendelssohn is a letter, found in a Russian archival collection, dated to the Hebrew month of Sivan (May–June) 1782. It is addressed to the chief rabbi of Berlin, Tsevi Hirschel Lewin,[45] and expresses Landau's response to Mendelssohn's call for rabbinic leaders to rescind their executive authority to issue the ban,[46] exclaiming that all the accusations that have been levelled against Mendelssohn are justified and that 'he has neither a part in the God of Israel nor his Torah'.[47] He then denounces Mendelssohn as an apostate, heretic, and informer.[48] If he could verify that Mendelssohn had indeed published these ideas, Landau continues, he would admonish all Jews to separate from Mendelssohn and his circle. Moshe Samet and Alexander Altmann argue that this letter must be a forgery since it is 'not in accord' with

42 See Samet, 'Mendelssohn, Wessely, and the Rabbis of their Time' (Heb.), 254.

43 See H. Graetz, *History of the Jews*, ed. Löwy, v. 417; Kestenberg-Gladstein, *Neuere Geschichte*, 87, 127; Klein, 'Zuschrift an Herrn Moses Mendelson in Hamburg', 541.

44 The Karlin-Stolin hasidim purchased these previously unknown writings of Ezekiel and Samuel Landau several years ago. The Institute of Microfilmed Hebrew Manuscripts at the Hebrew University in Jerusalem recently acquired microfilms of this collection. Some of the letters written by Ezekiel Landau concerning the Berlin maskilim have been published in the Karlin-Stolin journal *Kovets beit aharon veyisra'el*: see issues 8/1 (43) (1992); 8/2 (44) and 8/3 (45) (1993). This collection contains additional letters by Landau relating to this subject that still await publication. For a brief discussion of Landau's and other leaders' responses to Wessely in this periodical, see Heshel, 'Opinions of the Rabbinic Leaders of the Generation' (Heb.). Although Heshel's piece is informative, one needs to bear in mind that this journal is an organ of the Karliner hasidim, and does not offer a critical-historical view.

45 See *Kovets beit aharon veyisra'el*, 8/3 (1993), 123–5.

46 This call by Mendelssohn was cited about a month earlier in Naphtali Herz Wessely's pamphlet *Rav tov leveit yisra'el*. These ideas also appear in Mendelssohn's introduction to Manasseh ben Israel's *Vindiciae judaeorum*, which he translated into German and published in Berlin in 1782. See Heshel, 'Opinions of the Rabbinic Leaders of the Generation' (Heb.); Altmann, *Moses Mendelssohn*, 463–74, 485.

47 *Kovets beit aharon veyisra'el*, 8/3 (1993), 123–5. This citation is from a handwritten copy of the letter that Landau made for his own records.

48 Landau also calls Mendelssohn *oto ha'ish* (lit. 'that [evil] man'), a term usually used in rabbinic literature as a derogatory epithet referring to Jesus. See e.g. Jacob ben Moses Moellin (Maharil), *Sefer maharil*, 'Likutim', 103 (p. 637). Landau may be using this term to mock Mendelssohn's close contact with Christian intellectuals and ideas.

everything else that is known about Landau.[49] The letter is admittedly sharp in tone, but certainly in line with Landau's other critiques of Mendelssohn and various maskilim.

Landau's first reference to Mendelssohn's Bible translation appears in his commentary on *Berakhot*, probably written by 1783.[50] In a gloss in this commentary, he remarks on an enigmatic statement of the medieval commentator Rashi that one should not accustom one's children to study too much Bible, since this discipline is enticing. Landau explains that

> The *apikorsim* [heretics] also study Bible for the sake of knowing its language in the same way as they study other languages . . . [This is] especially [worrying] in our time, when the German Bible translation [i.e. that of Mendelssohn] has become widespread.[51] It attracts people to read the books of the gentiles in order to become fluent in their language. Therefore he [Rashi] warned against this [study of Bible].[52]

His words clearly reflect contemporary threats facing traditional rabbinic culture. He is particularly troubled by the new trend among the 'heretics', who despite their denial of the divinity of the Torah, study and teach Bible as literature. His reservations about Bible study are twofold: his concern that heretical teachers knowledgeable in Bible will lead students astray, and his fear that the use of Mendelssohn's Bible translation will cause children to study German books.[53]

In his preface to this talmudic commentary Landau similarly condemns the increasing trespasses occurring in his generation as a result of this voluntary translation of the Bible. Recounting a rabbinic legend that the world was darkened for three days when the Jews were forced to produce the Septuagint, a Greek translation of the Bible, during the Ptolemaic period, he laments the further darkened state of the world now that the 'plague' of translation

[49] See Samet, 'Mendelssohn, Wessely and the Rabbis of their Time', 252 n. 109; Altmann, *Moses Mendelssohn*, 835 n. 84. Interestingly, Samet admits that he cannot prove from the letter itself that it is a forgery. On this letter, see also Heshel, 'Opinions of the Rabbinic Leaders of the Generation', 122 n. 16.

[50] Although the *Tselaḥ* on *Ber.* was published in 1791, it seems to have been written by 1783, the year in which Mendelssohn's *Netivot hashalom* was completed. See Landau's epilogue to the *Tselaḥ* on *Pes.*, 349, where he explains that, although he had intended to publish his glosses on tractates *Ber.*, *Beits.*, and *Pes.* together, after falling ill he only had the strength to publish one tractate. He chose to publish *Pes.*, which he was studying with his students at the time. Landau's gloss on *Pes.* was published in 1783. On Landau's reaction to Mendelssohn's translation, see M. Graetz, 'Jewish Enlightenment', 307–8; Altmann, *Moses Mendelssohn*, 382–3, 397–8, 486–7; Samet, 'Mendelssohn, Wessely and the Rabbis of their Time' (Heb.), 242–3.

[51] During this period the expression *targum ashkenazi* (lit. German translation) which Landau uses in this passage is almost always a reference to Mendelssohn's Bible translation.

[52] *Tselaḥ*, *Ber.* 28*b* (p. 110). This text is also translated, albeit somewhat differently, in Altmann, *Moses Mendelssohn*, 486–7.

[53] *Tselaḥ*, *Ber.* 28*b*. On Mendelssohn's pedagogical goals for his Pentateuch translation, see Altmann, *Moses Mendelssohn*, 369–70, 381.

has spread voluntarily.[54] In a 1783 homily, replete with rebuke against the decreasing knowledge of Hebrew and the increasing number of biblical translations, Fleckeles cites Landau's criticism concerning contemporary biblical translations,[55] which was later published in the *Tselaḥ*.

Fleckeles' censure of Mendelssohn's translation in autumn 1783 is the first public repudiation of the translation in Prague.[56] Fleckeles insinuates that although biblical translations are occasionally permitted as aids for the masses, this does not apply to Mendelssohn's translation, since its highly complex language is itself inaccessible to the general readership. He also denounces the translation's methodology, stating that rather than employing traditional rabbinic exegesis, it only uses ideas which accord with universalistic notions.[57]

After two years of silence on the matter, in a 1785 approbation for another German Pentateuch translation, Landau again criticizes Mendelssohn's work.[58] Whether he had finally resigned himself to the necessity of translations in his day or had opposed only Mendelssohn's translation is difficult to assess. In his approbation for Sussmann Glogau's Pentateuch,[59] Landau asserts that he prefers this literal translation to Mendelssohn's, since the latter 'forces the young to spend their time reading gentile books in order to become familiar with refined German so that they can later study the translation'. He continues that 'our Torah is thereby reduced to a handmaiden to the German tongue'.[60] The other signatories of this significant approbation were the High Court judges Bachrach, Jacob Ginzburg, and Fleckeles. Prague's rabbinical court thereby took a unified stance against using Mendelssohn's translation to educate Jewish children, because of the curricular changes it would introduce.

[54] *Tselaḥ*, *Ber.*, preface. Landau's legend is perhaps based on a similar anecdote found in tractate *Soferim* 1: 7.

[55] Fleckeles, *Olat ḥodesh hasheni*, sermon 1 for the Days of Repentance (1783), 13*a*–*b*, 16*a*–*b*.

[56] In *Sendschreiben an die deutschen Juden*, published in an appendix to *Hame'asef* in 1788, David Friedländer responded to Fleckeles' criticism of Mendelssohn's translation. On Fleckeles' condemnation of Mendelssohn's translation, see J. Katz, *Out of the Ghetto*, 149–50; Altmann, *Moses Mendelssohn*, 487.

[57] Fleckeles, *Olat ḥodesh hasheni*, sermon 1, 16*a*–*b*.

[58] Landau's approbation, dated 13 Tamuz 5545 (21 June 1785) for Sussmann Glogau's translation, *Torah veḥamesh megilot im perush ashkenazi*. This approbation was later published in *Hame'asef* (1786), 142–4.

[59] Although the editor of *Hame'asef* doubted Landau's authorship of this approbation, I see no reason to question it, even though many scholars, such as Altmann, Katz, and Samet, have done so. See Altmann, *Moses Mendelssohn*, 821 n. 106; J. Katz, *Out of the Ghetto*, 247 n. 25; Samet, 'Mendelssohn, Wessely, and the Rabbis of their Time' (Heb.), 243.

[60] Landau's approbation for Sussmann Glogau's translation, *Torah veḥamesh megilot*. Landau laments the fact that the availability of Mendelssohn's translation meant that students master neither the Hebrew meaning of biblical words nor the main teachings of the Torah. An English translation of much of this approbation is found in Altmann, *Moses Mendelssohn*, 382–3. My translation is largely based on Altmann's.

About half a year later, Landau reiterated his reservations concerning Mendelssohn's translation, in an approbation for another work competing with Mendelssohn's Bible project: Solomon Dubno's independent edition of the Pentateuch.[61] In 1780, Dubno, who had originally collaborated on Mendelssohn's Pentateuch,[62] disassociated himself from the project. While working with Mendelssohn in 1779, Dubno had asked Landau for a recommendation for Mendelssohn's *Netivot hashalom*. In Landau's 1786 approbation for Dubno's work, he explains that he had declined Dubno's earlier request to endorse Mendelssohn's project because he had worried that Mendelssohn's *targum ashkenazi* (German translation) 'would prove a stumbling block to Jewish children and lead to the neglect of Torah study'.[63] As early as 1779, he feared that the pedagogical use of Mendelssohn's translation would undermine the status of Jewish studies.

Despite Landau's harsh denunciation of Mendelssohn and his reservations concerning his translation, he did not ban *Netivot hashalom*, as asserted by several scholars.[64] The Prague grammarian, Avigdor Levi (d. 1810),[65] relates that in about 1781 he informed Mendelssohn that, despite rumours to the contrary, Prague's chief rabbi had rebuffed those individuals who wanted him to ban Mendelssohn's translation.[66] The Prague maskil Judah Jeitteles (1773–1838), in the preface to his *Introduction to the Aramaic Language*, cites Landau's son Jacob's attestation that his father had defended Mendelssohn against the rabbis who wanted him to denounce the translation.[67] In addition, Samuel Landau was among the first ten subscribers to the first edition of Mendelssohn's *Netivot*

[61] Dubno's Pentateuch project was never completed and Landau's approbation for it was only published later by the Dutch maskil Gabriel Polak in *Ben gorni*, 44. See Samet, 'Mendelssohn, Wessely, and the Rabbis of their Time' (Heb.), 243.

[62] Dubno wrote the prospectus for *Netivot hashalom* in 1778, in collaboration with Mendelssohn, as well as the *Biur* on Genesis. See M. Graetz, 'Jewish Enlightenment', 304–6.

[63] Cited and trans. by Altmann in *Moses Mendelssohn*, 382.

[64] The scholar N. Brüll, for example, had originally asserted that Landau banned *Netivot hashalom*. See Altmann, *Moses Mendelssohn*, 823–4 n. 80. See also Samet, 'Mendelssohn, Wessely, and the Rabbis of their Time' (Heb.), 240.

[65] Interestingly, on 28 Mar. 1783 Landau gave an approbation for a grammatical work, *Davar tov*, by Avigdor Levi, a friend and supporter of Mendelssohn's, who lived in Prague. On Avigdor Levi, see Altmann, *Moses Mendelssohn*, 367–8.

[66] Levi added this note to his reproduction of Mendelssohn's 1781 letter to him. In this letter Mendelssohn wrote that he had heard rumours that Landau had banned the translation. The note was first published in Mendelssohn, *Letters of Rabbi Moses Dessau* (Heb.; published by Levi), 11. See Altmann, *Moses Mendelssohn*, 396–7; Samet, 'Mendelssohn, Wessely, and the Rabbis of their Time' (Heb.), 240–1.

[67] J. Jeitteles, *Introduction to the Aramaic Language* (Heb.), 3*a*–*b*. Samuel Landau showed Judah Jeitteles these remarks of his brother Jacob, which were handwritten in the margins of Jacob's manuscript of *Divrei yedidot*. Some of Judah Jeitteles' introduction is translated in Altmann, *Moses Mendelssohn*, 398.

hashalom, published in 1783, indicating that this work was not under the ban.[68]

Without a ban in place and with the increasing Germanization of Prague Jewry, Mendelssohn's translation gained popularity in Prague, particularly among the younger generation. In March 1783, before Mendelssohn's project was even completed, he wrote to the overseer of Prague's Normalschule, the priest Ferdinand Kindermann, that his translation had 'been welcomed also in Prague'. He suggested that his translation could be sold to Prague students. 'Maybe the local primary school also has a bookstore at its service . . . I think that a considerable sale [of the book] can be expected in your locality.'[69] In December 1784, Kindermann replied that he had received the invaluable translation. It seems that Kindermann endorsed Mendelssohn's translation for use in Prague's Jewish Normalschule. Surprisingly, by 1816, despite his late father's opposition to the translation, Samuel Landau was advocating that parents use Mendelssohn's translation to teach their children Torah and correct German.[70] Other rabbinic educators in Prague during the first decades of the nineteenth century, such as Nahum Trebitsch (1779–1842), also recommended the use of Mendelssohn's translation.[71] From 1833 to 1837, Landau's grandson, Moses Landau, published a twenty-volume edition of the Bible in Prague, which included both Mendelssohn's German translation and the *Biur*[72]—clearly a far cry from his grandfather's vehement opposition to the use of this maskilic translation and commentary several decades earlier.

The second public controversy between Landau and the maskilim centred on Naphtali Herz Wessely's pamphlet *Divrei shalom ve'emet* (Berlin, 1782).[73] Wessely, a contributor to Mendelssohn's translation project and active in the

[68] See Klein, 'Zuschrift an Herrn Moses Mendelson in Hamburg', 541; Hildesheimer, 'Moses Mendelssohn in Nineteenth-Century Rabbinical Literature', 24, 26; Kestenberg-Gladstein, 'Chapters in the History of Czech Jewry', 37. Landau's son Israel subscribed to the edition of *Netivot hashalom* published in Prague in 1801.

[69] Mendelssohn, *Gesammelte Schriften*, v. 611–13, trans. by Altmann in *Moses Mendelssohn*, 487–8.

[70] Samuel Landau, *Ahavat tsiyon*, sermon 12, for the eve of the new month of Shevat 5576 (30 Jan. 1816), 19*a*. He recommends that when a child reaches 6 or 7 his parents should study the Hebrew Pentateuch with him along with the German translation as found in the Pentateuch editions published in Berlin, Vienna, and Prague. In this way, Samuel writes, he will master a grammatically correct German, 'which is necessary in our lands'. It is almost certain that he is advocating the use of Mendelssohn's translation here, which was published in Berlin in 1783, in Vienna in 1808, and in Prague in 1801 and 1807.

[71] Hildesheimer, 'Moses Mendelssohn in Nineteenth-Century Rabbinical Literature', 18.

[72] See Nosek, 'Jewish Hebrew Studies in the Czech Lands', 38.

[73] On Wessely's *Divrei shalom ve'emet* and the controversy it stirred, see Feiner, *Jewish Enlightenment*, 87–104; E. Breuer, 'Naphtali Herz Wessely', 27–47; Eliav, *Jewish Education in Germany* (Heb.), 39–51; Altmann, *Moses Mendelssohn*, 477–86; Samet, 'Mendelssohn, Wessely, and the Rabbis of their Time' (Heb.), 244–57.

Berlin Haskalah, published this pamphlet shortly after the issuing of Joseph II's Toleranzpatent.[74] *Divrei shalom ve'emet* supported the Toleranzpatent's educational reforms and harshly criticized the traditional rabbinic curriculum. In this treatise, Wessely argues that *torat ha'adam* (the law of man), an expression he uses to designate all secular studies, is a necessary prerequisite to the study of divine law. He harshly condemns talmudic scholars who are ignorant of the law of man and states that they are of no value to society. Only gifted pupils, he further asserts, should pursue talmudic studies. These proposed educational reforms were obviously unacceptable to most rabbinic authorities. The publication of this treatise solidified rabbinic opposition to the Berlin Haskalah, which the rabbis now publicly denounced. Thanks to Landau's charisma and authority, he soon emerged as the leader in the polemic against Wessely.

Care must be taken to describe the nature of Landau's opposition accurately. Notwithstanding the claims of recent scholars,[75] he was not categorically opposed to secular studies. He himself had some knowledge of mathematics, history, and various scientific fields.[76] In his responsa he occasionally employs scientific knowledge, and frequently relies on the expertise of scientists and doctors for his legal rulings.[77] His son Jacob recounts in a short biography of his father that Landau 'greatly enjoyed the company of scientists'.[78] In both his responsa and talmudic commentaries, Landau uses critical methods in his analysis of the Talmud and its medieval commentaries. He often examines variant texts and occasionally explains the views of different authors and sources by considering their historical contexts.[79] He also suggests textual emendations on the basis of his logical analysis or perception of scribal or printing errors.[80] Besides using critical methods and secular materials, he also gave numerous approbations for

[74] *Divrei shalom ve'emet* was probably published in Jan. 1782. Landau had already received a copy of it on the eve of the new month of Shevat, 16 Jan. 1782. See the letter cited in n. 88 below. Several previous studies, which were unaware of this letter, place the publication of *Divrei shalom ve'emet* later in the year. See Altmann, *Moses Mendelssohn*, 478, 833 n. 28.

[75] See e.g. Ellenson, *Rabbi Esriel Hildesheimer*, 11.

[76] See e.g. Jacob Landau, *Divrei yedidot*, 32; Ezekiel Landau, *Tselaḥ*, *Ber.* 10*a* (p. 38), and 34*a* (pp. 128–9); *Pes.* 94*a* (p. 325); id., *NB Tinyana*, 'EH', no. 81, and 'YD', no. 28.

[77] See e.g. *NB Kama*, 'YD', nos. 46, 55, 58, and 'EH', no. 69; *NB Tinyana*, 'YD', no. 21. On Landau's respect for doctors and scientists, see Hess, 'Rabbi Ezekiel Landau' (Heb.), 117–19.

[78] Jacob Landau, *Divrei yedidot*, 32. Of course, Jacob, who himself became a maskil and valued such cross-cultural exchanges, may have exaggerated the extent of his father's interest in science and other secular subjects.

[79] See *Tselaḥ*, *Ber.* 34*a* (pp. 128–9), and 58*b* (p. 216); *NB Kama*, 'EH', no. 26, and 'YD', no. 1; *NB Tinyana*, 'OḤ', no. 113.

[80] See e.g. *Tselaḥ*: *Pes.* 2*a* (p. 2); *Ber.* 3*b* (p. 12); *Ber.* 17*a* (p. 69); *NB Kama*, 'OḤ', no. 21; *NB Tinyana*: 'OḤ', nos. 54, 57; 'ḤM', no. 8; 'EH', no. 76. See also Hess, 'Rabbi Ezekiel Landau' (Heb.), 126–35. It should be noted, however, that such textual emendations can be found in earlier rabbinic works as well. See e.g. the writings of the Maharshal (R. Solomon b. Jehiel Luria, 1510–73) and Tosafot.

books of grammar, history, geography, Jewish philosophy, mathematics, and the natural sciences.[81]

Nevertheless, Wessely's proposed educational reform would have given priority to secular studies over religious studies, and this was unacceptable to Landau. Although several years earlier he had endorsed Wessely's *Yein levanon*, a commentary on the mishnaic tractate *Pirkei avot*,[82] now, on 23 March 1782, Shabat Hagadol (the sabbath before Passover), he strongly censured Wessely and his recently published *Divrei shalom ve'emet*.[83] In this sermon, Landau rails:

> I have seen an inverted world. How can one envy the study of Torah, when an *evil man* [my italics] has arisen from our people and brazenly asserted that the Torah is not at all important, that an animal carcass is worth more than talmudic scholars, that etiquette is more important than the Torah?[84]

The 'evil man' in this passage refers to Wessely. The declarations to which Landau alludes are barbs against talmudic scholars found in *Divrei shalom ve'emet*.[85] Although he is quick to denounce Wessely's educational values, he takes care to praise Joseph II's educational initiatives, stressing the importance of knowing etiquette and a grammatically correct German. In contrast to Wessely, however, he emphasizes that this knowledge is important merely for utilitarian purposes. The primary focus of study must be Torah. Landau continues to warn Prague Jews to read only those German books which specifically aid them in learning the German language, and not philosophical works.[86]

Aside from publicly condemning Wessely in his Prague sermons,[87] Landau also advocated the denunciation of Wessely in various letters to European

[81] See e.g. Landau's approbations for Jonah ben Elijah Landsofer, *Me'il tsedakah*; Hayim ben Moses Shek, *Yad hayim*; Isaac Satanow, *Siftei renanot*; Avigdor Levi ben Simhah Glogau, *Devar tov*; Baruch Shikh, *Keneh hamidah*; Elijah ben Hayim Hakohen Hekhim, *Shevilei derakia*; Gedaliah ben Solomon Lipschitz, *Ets shatul: [perush al] sefer ikarim*; Ashkenazi, *Sefer hababur*. Notwithstanding his approbations for these books, Landau is often critical of involvement in secular disciplines. See e.g. *Tselah, Ber.* 28*b* (p. 109).

[82] Landau gave his approbation for Wessely's *Yein levanon* on 12 July 1771. In this approbation he also supports Wessely's plan to publish the work *Hokhmat shelomoh*. Indeed, Wessely published his Hebrew translation of and commentary on the apocryphal Wisdom of Solomon in Berlin in 1780.

[83] Since Landau responds in this sermon for Shabat Hagadol both to Joseph II's Toleranzpatent and to Wessely's *Divrei shalom ve'emet*, it can be dated to 23 Mar. 1782.

[84] *Derushei hatselah*, sermon 39, 53*a*. This translation is largely based on that of Saperstein, *Jewish Preaching*, 365.

[85] See Wessely, *Divrei shalom ve'emet*, 4–5. Wessely bases his argument for secular studies on his non-traditional interpretation of a midrashic phrase found in *Leviticus Rabbah* 1: 15 and *Yalkut shimoni*, 'Vayikra', 429. On the basis of his alternative interpretation, Wessely asserts that a carcass is better than a scholar who knows Torah but lacks *da'at*, which he interprets as 'knowledge of etiquette and secular studies'. Traditionally, *da'at* was understood as 'common sense', not etiquette and secular knowledge.

[86] *Derushei hatselah*, sermon 39, 53*a*–*b*.

[87] Landau's first public censure of Wessely's *Divrei shalom ve'emet* occurred during his sermon for the eve of the new month of Shevat, 16 Jan. 1782. See *Kovets beit aharon veyisra'el*, 8/1 (1992), 163. On

rabbis. In the first of these, written in 1782 to a rabbi in Vienna,[88] Landau condemns *Divrei shalom ve'emet* and pronounces Wessely a 'heretic' and 'neutralist', who mocks all religion. Were it not for government restrictions, he asserts, he would issue a ban (*ḥerem*) against Wessely.[89] He then asks for assistance in garnering support against him among rabbis in nearby communities, such as Pressburg and Nicholsburg.[90]

As part of this campaign to undermine Wessely, Landau attacked him in two letters to rabbis and communal leaders in Berlin. Writing to Berlin's chief rabbi, Tsevi Hirschel Lewin, in a letter dated Sivan (May–June) 1782, he both commends Lewin's opposition to the 'cursed' Wessely and asserts that Wessely's recently published pamphlet *Rav tov leveit yisra'el* is as objectionable as his first pamphlet.[91] In a second letter from this period,[92] addressed to Berlin's Jewish communal leaders and the city's chief rabbi,[93] Landau stresses that the majority of contemporary rabbis deem Wessely a heretic. Playing on the Hebrew acronym for Wessely's first pamphlet *Divrei shalom ve'emet* (Words of Peace and Truth), he labels it and its proposed reforms *Divrei shav* (Words of Falsehood).[94] Realizing the tremendous threat that Wessely's proposed educational reforms posed to the traditional rabbinic curriculum, Landau felt compelled not only to denounce him in Prague, but to marginalize him in other important centres of European Jewry as well.[95]

the sabbath preceding Passover, 1782, he referred to this earlier homily. See *Derushei hatselaḥ*, sermon 39, 53*a*.

[88] This letter, written between Jan. and Mar. 1782, was found in the collection of Landau's writings that has now been made public (see n. 44 above). He wrote it after he had already censured Wessely in his Shevat sermon on 16 Jan. 1782. Since this letter mentions his censure of Wessely in his Shevat sermon, but not the censure in his pre-Passover homily on 23 Mar. 1782, we can assume that it was written before the latter.

[89] On Bohemian Jewry's restriction on imposing a ban, see Samuel Landau, gloss on *NB Kama*, 'YD', no. 1.

[90] *Kovets beit aharon veyisra'el*, 8/1 (1992), 162–5.

[91] *Kovets beit aharon veyisra'el*, 8/3 (1993), 123–5.

[92] This letter was probably written around Sivan/Tamuz 5542 (June 1782). It is currently in the Schwadron collection, housed in the Institute of Microfilmed Hebrew Manuscripts at the Hebrew University in Jerusalem. It is published in Assaf, *Sources for the History of Jewish Education* (Heb.), i. 239–40; Gelman, *The Noda Biyehudah and his Teaching* (Heb.), 113–15; *Kovets beit aharon veyisra'el*, 8/3 (1993), 126–7.

[93] In this letter, Landau demands that the Berlin *parnasim* secure an apology to the rabbi of Lissa from seven members of their community. Earlier in 1782 these seven had written to *parnasim* in Lissa, requesting that they criticize their chief rabbi's battle against Wessely.

[94] *Kovets beit aharon veyisra'el*, 8/3 (1993), 127.

[95] On 30 Aug. 1782, for example, David Tevele Schiff, the rabbi of the Great Synagogue of London, wrote that at first Landau 'preached against it [Wessely's pamphlet] at Prague, now, however, he is obliged to remain quiet in public and is working quietly to arouse rabbis of other famous congregations'. For this letter and its English translation, see Duschinsky, *Rabbinate of the Great Synagogue London*, 176–8, 246–50.

Interestingly, Samuel Landau promotes many of the educational goals advanced by Wessely that his father had vociferously denounced. Samuel recommends that when a child reaches the age of 6 or 7, he should be introduced to German and secular subjects. He implores parents to 'ensure that their children succeed in both Torah and *derekh erets*', secular learning, a rallying cry for later neo-Orthodox German Jews.[96] Even more surprising, Samuel suggests, like Wessely, that only gifted pupils aged at least 12 should pursue talmudic studies. Even these students may focus solely on secular subjects. Samuel's advocacy of teaching young children secular disciplines alongside Torah as well as limiting those who should study Talmud is a far cry from the limited permission granted by his father to secular instruction, once again pointing to the rapid acculturation of Prague Jewry and its leadership.

In short, although Landau appreciated certain aspects of secular knowledge, as shown by his responsa and several of his approbations, he was an unrelenting critic of the contemporary Haskalah. The assertions of scholars such as Samet that Landau was open to the Haskalah are inconsistent with the wide array of sources in which he strongly censures Mendelssohn, the 'Jewish philosophers of his day', various maskilic projects, and any emphasis on secular studies.

His polemic against the maskilim, or *me'asefim* (a term derived from the maskilic journal *Hame'asef*), even made its way into his talmudic commentary, where he defends the aggadah and the importance of pure faith from their rationalist views. Landau's recently discovered correspondence concerning Wessely indicates that his hesitancy over banning Wessely and Mendelssohn stemmed largely from governmental restrictions imposed on the Jews' autonomy. To be sure, Landau was harsher and more systematic in his denunciation of Wessely, whose proposed overhaul of the entire traditional curriculum posed a greater threat to rabbinic culture.

The radical maskilim sensed his antagonism and uncompromising stance towards them and made him into a symbol of intransigent rabbinic opposition to cultural reform. From the late 1780s until after his death, many of these maskilim, such as David Friedländer, Isaac Euchel, and Marcus Herz, vilified Landau and his Prague students in the pages of *Hame'asef*.[97] Samet asserts that the

[96] Samuel Landau, *Ahavat tsiyon*, sermon 12, 19*a*. On both the use of the phrase *torah im derekh erets* and the promotion of this ideal by later Orthodox rabbis, see Hirsch, *Die Religion im Bunde mit dem Fortschritt*; Liberles, *Religious Conflict in Social Context*, esp. 154; Ellenson, *Rabbi Esriel Hildesheimer*, esp. 11, 116–35; Eliav, *Jüdische Erziehung in Deutschland*, 201, 207, 291–5, 302, 307.

[97] See e.g. Marcus Herz's censure of Landau's defence of the Jewish practice of early burial, published in a German appendix to *Hame'asef* in 1787; see Isaac Euchel, *Hame'asef* (1787), 133; Friedländer, 'Sendschreiben an die deutschen Juden', published in an appendix of *Hame'asef* in 1788. In this article Friedländer condemns the traditional Pentateuch translation endorsed by the 'Prague rabbis', i.e. Landau and Fleckeles. See also Wolfsohn, 'Siḥah be'erets haḥayim'. Several scholars

radical maskilim's adoption of Landau as an 'anti-Haskalah' icon has biased scholarly views of his response to Mendelssohn and the Jewish Enlightenment.[98] The sources suggest, however, that the maskilic portrayal of Landau, though exaggerated, was no accident.

Landau's harsh view of Mendelssohn and the Haskalah is revealed, in an ironic manner, through an unusual eulogy written for him by the maskil Joseph Ha'efrati of Tropplowitz, who lived in Prague during the 1790s.[99] The title page of this work, *Alon bakhut*, bears a picture of Landau and Mendelssohn embracing in the Garden of Eden. The eulogy, which largely consists of a lengthy description of the imaginary reconciliation between these two figures in the hereafter, seems to indicate this maskil's recognition that Mendelssohn never secured Landau's approval during the latter's lifetime. Still, Landau's appreciation of secular studies caused certain moderate maskilim to claim him as their own.

The Inversion in the Traditional Hierarchy of Study

The maskilim's educational reforms contributed to a larger threat that was already facing rabbinic culture during the latter half of the eighteenth century. Prague was witnessing a decline in the status of talmudic and halakhic studies, previously almost the exclusive focus of education. This decline was engendered by the influence of Enlightenment ideals, state-mandated secular education, and the increasing acculturation of Prague Jewry. In about 1775, six years before the issuance of the Toleranzpatent and the publication of Wessely's *Divrei shalom ve'emet*, Landau bewails that now 'Satan dances amongst Prague Jews, who are abandoning the divinely revealed Torah to study outside [secular] books that have recently emerged."[100]

Landau comments with a sense of irony that 'all the greatness in our time is not derived from the wisdom of Torah. Rather people excel in etiquette, nature, and in the knowledge of secular books. Some excel in dance and some in song. No one toils at all in the study of Torah'.[101] Echoing these ideas, he asserts in a 1785 approbation for Fleckeles' sermon collection, *Olat ḥodesh*, that the heads of households should read this work instead of 'secular books, written in unintelligible language and in a foreign tongue, which because of our great sins are a

conjecture that the anonymous rabbi mocked in this piece is Landau. See e.g. Lowenstein, *Berlin Jewish Community*, 232 n. 33. On occasion, however, *Hame'asef* endorsed Landau's actions. It both applauded and printed his German address to the first Jewish recruits to the Austrian army (*Hame'asef* (1789), 252–5) and praised and published a section of his sermon on the occasion of Austria's siege of Belgrade, *Hame'asef* (1790), 62–4.

98 See Samet, 'Mendelssohn, Wessely, and the Rabbis of their Time' (Heb.), 240.

99 This eulogy was published in Vienna in 1793.

100 *Derushei hatselaḥ*, sermon for Shabat Hagadol, 55*b*.

101 *NB Tinyana*, 'YD', no. 119.

pernicious plague' in this generation.[102] While some of these criticisms are undoubtedly overstated, his condemnation of the shifting focus of study in a variety of his writings reflects his belief that this development affected a wide cross-section of Jewish society.[103]

At times, Landau specifically directs his criticism of the educational priorities of the community at parents, who divert their children from Torah studies. Instead of raising their sons for a life of Torah, the heretics of his day regularly teach them secular books.[104] He explains that since in our days an increasing number of Jews deny the authority of the rabbinic sages' teachings, they 'deliberately prevent the boys from studying the Oral Torah'.[105] In several homilies, he censures Prague parents more generally for their lax attitude towards providing a Torah education for their sons.[106] His laments resonate with extant evidence from this period.

Tensions arising from the transformation of Prague's educational priorities and the increasing focus on secular activities had repercussions for members of the Landau family. Disapproving of the acculturation of Prague Jews, Israel Landau's wife demanded that they return with their two sons to Poland, where their children could be brought up properly and receive an acceptable traditional education. When Israel refused, she demanded a divorce. The two sons, Eleazar and Joshua, later became rabbis in Poland.[107] The moderate maskil Israel later remarried a more 'modern' Dutch woman, and the product of this union was the progressive leader of the next generation of Prague Jews, Moses Landau.

A contemporary of Israel Landau, Fleckeles, in numerous Prague sermons and eulogies delivered during the 1780s and 1790s, also railed, like his teacher Ezekiel Landau, against Prague Jewry's preference for secular books and its dismissal of Torah studies. In his eulogy for Landau, he criticizes his generation, whose youth does not engage in dialectical study of the Talmud and the legal code *Shulḥan arukh*. He ascribes the shift to the changing values of the older generation, who no longer want their children to excel in Torah. Instead they primarily encourage them to hone their skills in grammar, writing, and mathematics.[108] Fleckeles'

[102] Landau's approbation for Fleckeles' *Olat ḥodesh*, dated 23 Sivan 5545 (1 June 1785).

[103] See e.g. *Tselaḥ, Ber.* 28*b* (p. 110).

[104] *Derushei hatselaḥ*, sermon 14, 24*a*–*b*.

[105] Ibid., sermon 39, 54*a*.

[106] See *Ahavat tsiyon*, sermon 3, 5*b*, and sermon 5 for the first day of *Seliḥot* prayers (1774), 8*b*, where he criticizes parents for taking their young children to the market in order to conduct business, instead of teaching them Torah.

[107] The oldest son, Eleazar (1778–1831), became a prominent rabbi in Brody and the second son, Joshua, became a rabbi in Olkusz.

[108] Fleckeles, *Olat ḥodesh hashelishi*, sermon 17 (Fleckeles' second eulogy for Ezekiel Landau, dated 26 Iyar 5553; 8 May 1793), 76*a*.

Prague sermon collections *Olat ḥodesh hasheni* and *Olat ḥodesh hashelishi* are replete with similar complaints that secular disciplines are replacing Torah study. He mourns that men and women devote their time to 'foreign' books and elevate the status of illusory secular studies, while the glorious Torah 'lies in the corner'.[109]

Both Fleckeles and Landau, then, championing rabbinic Judaism's age-old emphasis on talmudic study, attempted to curb the shift in Prague Jewry's intellectual priorities that resulted from acculturation, philosophical trends, and educational reforms.

Sabbatianism

Even more ominous in the eyes of the Prague rabbinate than the threats posed to traditional Judaism by contemporary philosophical trends[110] were the Sabbatians and the Frankists.[111] During the latter half of the eighteenth century, Prague was a hotbed of Sabbatianism and its later, more radical manifestation, Frankism.[112] Both the majority of Sabbatians, who believed in the Jewish pseudo-messiah, Sabbatai Zevi (1626–76), and the Frankists, who maintained that Zevi was reincarnated in their Polish leader, the apostate Jacob Frank (1726–91), espoused anti-rabbinic doctrines. Although by the eighteenth century numerous Sabbatians rejected certain aspects of overt messianism, the majority harboured messianic notions that conflicted with traditional Judaism.

[109] See Fleckeles, *Olat ḥodesh hasheni*, sermon 1, 13*b*; id., *Olat ḥodesh hashelishi*, 38*a*.

[110] On the debate as to whether there was a connection between the Sabbatians and the Haskalah in Prague, see Scholem, 'Redemption through Sin' (Heb.), in his *Studies and Texts Concerning the History of Sabbatianism and its Metamorphoses* (Heb.), 66–7; J. Katz, 'On the Question of the Connection between Sabbatianism, Enlightenment, and Reform' (Heb.), in his *Halakhah in Straits* (Heb.), 261–78; Werses, *Haskalah and Sabbatianism* (Heb.), 94.

[111] For a general discussion of Sabbatianism and Frankism, see Scholem, *Sabbatai Sevi*; id., *Messianic Idea*, 9–67; id., *Major Trends in Jewish Mysticism*, 287–324; id., *Researches in Sabbatianism* (Heb.); id., *Kabbalah*, 244–309; Balaban, *History of the Frankist Movement* (Heb.); Werses, *Haskalah and Sabbatianism* (Heb.); Liebes, 'Sabbatian Messianism' (Heb.); Carlebach, *Pursuit of Heresy*, esp. 90–104, 161–94; Doktór, 'Conversions within Shabateanism'; id., 'Jacob Frank und sein messianisches Reich'; id., 'Jakub Frank, a Jewish Heresiarch and his Messianic Doctrine'; Hundert, *Jews in Poland–Lithuania*, esp. 121–5, 153–9; Wacholder, 'Jacob Frank and the Frankists'; Duker, 'Frankism as a Movement of Polish–Jewish Synthesis'.

[112] On Sabbatianism and Frankism in Prague during the 18th c. and the first decades of the 19th c., see the anonymous polemical work against the Sabbatians and Frankists, *Dialogue between the Year 1800 and the Year 1801* (Heb.), and Fleckeles' anti-Sabbatian and anti-Frankist tract, *Ahavat david*. See also Scholem, 'Frankist Document from Prague'. For secondary writings on the subject, see Kestenberg-Gladstein, *Neuere Geschichte*, 173–91; Žáček, 'Zwei Beiträge zur Geschichte des Frankismus in den böhmischen Ländern'; Klein, 'Zuschrift an Herrn Moses Mendelson in Hamburg', 526; Werses, *Haskalah and Sabbatianism* (Heb.), 63–98; Scholem, *Kabbalah*, 306–7; Mahler, *History of Modern Jewry*, 266–8; Tishby, *Wisdom of the Zohar*, i. 39; Carlebach, *Pursuit of Heresy*, 173; J. Katz, *Halakhah in Straits* (Heb.), 261–78.

They largely based these doctrines on their interpretation of zoharic and Lurianic kabbalah.[113]

Prague served as a Sabbatian centre from the beginning of the eighteenth century. Jacob Emden describes the spread of Sabbatianism among Prague's rabbinic scholars, asserting that the Prague *kloiz* (elite private house of study and prayer) established by Abraham Broda was filled with scholars who espoused Sabbatianism.[114] While this depiction by Emden, a relentless antagonist of the Sabbatians, is probably exaggerated, there was clearly a Sabbatian element at this *kloiz*. The most famous rabbi to study with the disciples of Broda was Jonathan Eybeschütz,[115] who later headed his own yeshiva in Prague. Emden spent a large portion of his career accusing Eybeschütz of harbouring Sabbatian beliefs. Interestingly, numerous modern scholars concur with Emden's allegations.[116] Emden also reports that during the 1725–6 anti-Sabbatian campaign in central and eastern Europe, the head of Prague's rabbinical court saw to it that students leaving Prague for their homes in Vienna and Pressburg were searched for copies of the Sabbatian manuscript *Va'avo hayom el ha'ayin* ('I came this day to the well', from Gen. 24: 42), attributed to their teacher, Eybeschütz.[117] Prague's rabbinate promulgated a ban against the Sabbatians, pronounced in all the city's synagogues on Yom Kippur eve, 1725, ironically signed by Eybeschütz.[118]

Various eighteenth- and nineteenth-century sources portray the nature of the Sabbatian and Frankist presence in Prague during Landau's tenure as chief rabbi.[119] During these years, the Frankist sect emerged in eastern and central Europe, and developed into a more radical antinomian form of Sabbatianism. Unlike many of the Frankists in other countries, Bohemia's Frankists did not convert to Christianity but remained outwardly observant Jews.[120] Prague's

113 The nature of Sabbatianism in the 18th c. is complex and remains somewhat elusive. It is the subject of much current research. On 18th-c. Sabbatianism, see Carlebach, *Pursuit of Heresy*. The Sabbatian focus on kabbalah and the challenge it posed to the traditional curriculum is discussed in Chapter 6.

114 Emden, *Sefer hitabekut*, 1. On this passage, see Carlebach, *Pursuit of Heresy*, 173–4.

115 R. Abraham Broda left Prague in 1709.

116 See Perlmuter, *Rabbi Jonathan Eybeschutz and his Relationship with Sabbatianism* (Heb.); Scholem, *Kabbalah*, 407–8; D. Kahana, *History of the Kabbalists, Sabbatians, and Hasidim* (Heb.).

117 See Emden, *Sefer hitabekut*, 1–2. Although the Sabbatian manuscript *Va'avo hayom el ha'ayin* appeared as an anonymous work, both Sabbatians and their opponents attributed it to Eybeschütz. Perlmuter, a 20th-c. scholar of kabbalah, also identified Eybeschütz as the author of this treatise. See Perlmuter, *Rabbi Jonathan Eybeschütz and his Relationship with Sabbatianism* (Heb.); Carlebach, *Pursuit of Heresy*, 9, 176–7, 188.

118 See Klemperer, 'Rabbis of Prague' (1950), 150; Carlebach, *Pursuit of Heresy*, 181.

119 See *Dialogue between the Year* 1800 *and the Year* 1801 (Heb.), 27–9; Klein, 'Zuschrift an Herrn Moses Mendelson in Hamburg', 526. Dr Klein reports claims by some of Landau's contemporaries that the majority of Prague Jews were Sabbatians during this period.

120 See Kestenberg-Gladstein, *Neuere Geschichte*, 28–9, 174; Scholem, *Kabbalah*, 289–90, 299–300, 308; Tishby, *Wisdom of the Zohar*, i. 39.

Frankist leaders, Joshua Bondi, Jonas Wehle (1752–1823) and his son-in-law Löw Hönig von Hönigsberg (1770–1811), were members of influential Jewish families. Other Prague Frankists, including those from the Porges, Mauthner and Zerkowitz families, belonged to Prague's economic elite.[121] An article written in 1848, by a Dr Klein who attended the Landau yeshiva from 1829 to 1832, relates that during the late eighteenth century, the Prague Sabbatians had their own synagogue and study house, where the primary focus of study was the Bible and the Zohar.[122]

The tension between Landau and the Sabbatians and Frankists is manifest in his many denunciations, which appear in almost all genres of his work as well as in other sources from the period.[123] In one homily, he declares that the Sabbatian teachings are even more despicable than the abhorrent doctrines of the deists.[124] At the beginning of his Prague career, in October 1758, he issued a ban against the Sabbatians by means of a traditional excommunication ceremony accompanied by the 'blowing of the *shofar* and the extinguishing of candles'.[125] It stated that the paths of penitence are open to all sinners except for these sectarians. This ban was renewed annually by a proclamation made in Prague synagogues on Yom Kippur eve.[126] In a 1780 responsum sent to Fleckeles, Landau expresses his harsh assumption that all those suspected of Sabbatianism were indeed somewhat guilty of adhering to this heresy.[127] Fleckeles further reports, in his anti-Frankist tract *Ahavat david*, and in his

[121] On these Prague Frankists, see Scholem, *Kabbalah*, 306–7; id., 'Frankist Document from Prague', 787–9; Klein, 'Zuschrift an Herrn Moses Mendelson in Hamburg', 526; Werses, *Haskalah and Sabbatianism* (Heb.), 81–94; McCagg, *History of Habsburg Jews*, 69, 76; Kestenberg-Gladstein, *Neuere Geschichte*, 111–12, 175–7, 182–3.

[122] Klein, 'Zuschrift an Herrn Moses Mendelson in Hamburg', 540.

[123] See e.g. *NB Kama*, 'ḤM', no. 16, in which Landau disapproves of the practice of appending Psalm 21 (which the Sabbateans manipulated to yield hidden meanings) to the Shaharit morning service. See also ibid., 'YD', no. 6; *Derushei hatselaḥ*, sermon 39, 53*b*, and sermon for Passover, 59*a*; Landau's approbation for Zahlin's *Hadarat eliyahu*. In these denunciations Landau does not distinguish between the Sabbatians and Frankists, and often refers to both as Sabbatians. This practice was standard among most Jews.

[124] See *Derushei hatselaḥ*, sermon 25, 40*a*, where he asserts that the Sabbatians, unlike the philosophers, deny even the unity of God. This alludes to the fact that Sabbatians deified Sabbatai Zevi by proclaiming that he had become part of the Godhead, or more specifically part of the sixth *sefirah*, Tiferet. This deification is clearly antithetical to traditional rabbinic monotheistic teachings.

[125] See for example Fleckeles, *Ahavat david*, 23*b*; id., *Teshuvah me'ahavah*, i., no. 8. There he reports that Landau issued this ban against the Sabbatians and Frankists on the eve of Hoshanah Rabah during the Hebrew year 5519.

[126] In 1848 Dr Klein writes that he saw this ban, which stipulated that it should be renewed annually on Yom Kippur eve. See Klein, 'Zuschrift an Herrn Moses Mendelson in Hamburg', 527. On the ban, see also Kamelhar, *Mofet hador*, 61; Wind, *Rabbi Ezekiel Landau* (Heb.), 19, 20; id., 'Ezekiel Landau', 83.

[127] Ezekiel Landau's responsum, dated 1 Adar I, 5540 (7 Feb. 1780), in Fleckeles, *Teshuvah me'ahavah*, i, no. 112; see also ibid., no. 8.

collection of responsa, *Teshuvah me'ahavah*, that Landau had recounted numerous vilifying tales about these sectarians.[128]

The anonymous author of the anti-Frankist tract *A Dialogue between the Year 1800 and the Year 1801*, published in Prague in 1800, observes that since the Prague Sabbatians were intimidated by Landau's authority and his anti-Sabbatian stance, they did not discuss their heretical doctrines publicly during his lifetime.[129] Only in 1792, a year before Landau's death, did the identity and beliefs of a few Prague Frankists become more widely known. At that time, he confronted these Frankists, and denounced their beliefs.[130]

Nevertheless, Sabbatians and Frankists remained a subversive influence in Prague throughout Landau's career. The already powerful and wealthy Frankist families in the city were further strengthened by their numerous familial and social ties to nihilistic and influential Frankists, residing in Poland, Prussia, and Moravia, who sent both emissaries and literature to Prague.[131] These contacts with the more radical elements of the sect probably induced Prague Frankists to adopt certain antinomian practices. In addition, both their covert promulgation of anti-rabbinic teachings and their diminished focus on talmudic study threatened Prague's norms and practices.[132] Throughout his Prague tenure, Landau attempted to arrest the growth of these sects and to protect traditional Judaism from their innovations and teachings.

He was not entirely successful. After his death, the assault by Prague's Sabbatians and Frankists became more public and intense.[133] In 1800, partly inspired by the apocalyptic 'Red Epistles' written by the Frankists at Offenbach, the Frankists in Prague and elsewhere became particularly aggressive. In response, the Prague court issued a ban against the Frankists. Echoing earlier rabbinic reactions, on the eve of Yom Kippur 1800, Prague's anti-Sabbatian ban along with a new clause against the Frankists was read in all the city's synagogues

[128] See Fleckeles, *Ahavat david*, introd. See also Fleckeles, *Teshuvah me'ahavah*, i, no. 8, where Fleckeles recalls Landau's comments that the principle that one should not suspect the innocent does not apply to the Sabbatians and Frankists, for all those who are suspected of Sabbatianism or Frankism are somewhat guilty. Fleckeles cites Landau on this point in order to buttress the legal opinion that he records in this responsum, forbidding Jews from marrying anyone suspected of Sabbatianism.

[129] *Dialogue between the Year* 1800 *and the Year* 1801 (Heb.), 29.

[130] Since *Dialogue between the Year* 1800 *and the Year* 1801 was published in 1800 and its author recalls that this confrontation between Landau and the Frankists occurred eight years previously, we can date it to 1792. For a detailed discussion of this confrontation, see Part II below.

[131] On the social, intellectual, and familial ties between Frankists in Prague and in other European cities, see Scholem, *Kabbalah*, 302, 304–6. On Prague Frankists visiting the Frankist court at Offenbach, for example, see Scholem, 'Frankist Document from Prague', 788; id., *Major Trends*, 304.

[132] Some Frankists even referred to themselves as the 'anti-talmudists'.

[133] See *Dialogue between the Year* 1800 *and the Year* 1801 (Heb.), 27, 30. On the clashes between Prague's rabbis and Frankists after Landau's death, see Fleckeles, *Teshuvah me'ahavah*, introd. See also Kestenberg-Gladstein, *Neuere Geschichte*, 180–2.

and posted on their doors. The same year saw the publication of Fleckeles' collection of anti-Sabbatian sermons, *Ahavat david*.

Hasidism

The increasing popularity of the 'new hasidim', or pietists, during the last decades of the eighteenth century also threatened traditional rabbinic authority and culture. Hasidism, or rather, the new hasidic movement, emerged in Podolia, a region in southeast Poland. It then spread northward to Volhynia and later to Belorussia, Lithuania, and Galicia.[134] The founder of hasidism, Rabbi Israel ben Eliezer Ba'al Shem Tov, commonly referred to as the Besht, did have followers from the 1740s until his death in 1760, but studies of the last few decades, such as those of Immanuel Etkes and Ada Rapoport-Albert, show that only a small group of mystics joined the Besht's circle at this stage.[135] According to this recent scholarship, hasidism first developed into a movement between 1766 and 1772, under the guidance of one of the Besht's leading disciples, Rabbi Dov Baer, the *magid* of Mezhirech (d. 1772). By the 1770s, the missionary activities of Rabbi Dov Baer and his disciples had transformed hasidism from a diffuse set of practices and beliefs characteristic of a few scholarly circles into a mass movement.[136] While there were no hasidim in Prague, hasidism had made inroads in nearby east European Ashkenazi communities, and thereby posed a threat to Prague's rabbinic culture.

In almost all of Landau's references to this movement, he labels its followers as the 'new hasidim'. Several scholarly studies have shown that the seventeenth- and eighteenth-century Ashkenazi communities of Poland and Galicia had adopted the term *ḥasid* (pietist), which had largely fallen into disuse by that time, to designate the adepts of elite mystical cadres that existed in the region. During the eighteenth century, an increasing number of people were drawn to the mystical-pietistic circles of these 'old-style' hasidim. These groups generally

[134] For a general discussion of early hasidism, see Dubnow, *History of Hasidism* (Heb.); Dinur, 'Origins of Hasidism' (Heb.), in id., *At the Turning of the Generations*; Etkes, 'Hasidism as a Movement'; id., *Beginning of the Hasidic Movement* (Heb.); id., *Ba'al Hashem the Besht* (Heb.); Rosman, *Founder of Hasidism*; Piekarz, *Beginning of Hasidism* (Heb.); Hundert (ed.), *Essential Papers on Hasidism*; Rapoport-Albert (ed.), *Hasidism Reappraised*; Idel, *Hasidism*; Heschel, *Circle of the Baal Shem Tov*; Hundert, *Jews in Poland–Lithuania*, esp. 160–210; Wodzinski, *Haskalah and Hasidism in the Kingdom of Poland*; Jacobs, *Hasidic Prayer*; Katz, *Rabbinate, Hasidism, Haskalah* (Heb.); Krassen, *Uniter of Heaven and Earth*; Gries, *The Book in Early Hasidism* (Heb.); id., 'Between Literature and History' (Heb.); Schatz-Uffenheimer, *Quietistic Elements in Eighteenth-Century Hasidic Thought* (Heb.); Joseph Weiss, *Studies in East European Jewish Mysticism and Hasidism*.

[135] See Etkes, *Beginning of the Hasidic Movement* (Heb.); id., 'Hasidism as a Movement', 1–26; Rapoport-Albert, 'God and the Zaddik'.

[136] See Krassen, 'Devequt and Faith in Zaddiqim', 411. See also Jacobs, *Hasidic Prayer*, 10–11.

adhered to a regimented way of life, emphasized kabbalistic study, had a thorough foundation in rabbinic texts, and stressed the importance of asceticism and devotional prayer. Although the new-style hasidim differed from the old-style pietists in a number of ways, the most pronounced of which was the rejection by some of asceticism, the two groups had much in common.[137] One of the most famous of these pre-Beshtian pietistic groups was located at the *kloiz* of Brody, situated in the Lvov district of Poland.[138] Landau belonged to this *kloiz* from 1732 to 1745.

Several of Landau's associates from his forty years in Poland and Galicia, and particularly from the Brody *kloiz*, later became prominent figures in the new hasidic movement. Among these were Rabbi Abraham Gershon of Kutow (d. *c.*1760),[139] the brother-in-law and eventual follower of the Besht. While residing in Brody and Yampol,[140] Landau worked with Abraham Gershon, whom he met at the Brody *kloiz*, on both legal and charitable activities. Various responsa, letters, and communal records show that Landau and Abraham Gershon continued to correspond for many years after Landau left Brody.[141] In one responsum attesting to this correspondence, Landau praises Abraham Gershon's excellence in 'Torah and *ḥasidut*' as well as his knowledge of 'secrets'.[142] In Poland, Landau also interacted with Rabbi Nahman of Kosov (d. 1746), another early hasidic leader, who was in contact with the Besht. Nahman is known for his innovative teachings on *devekut* (cleaving to God or mystical union).[143] Although the details of the relationship between Nahman and Landau remain obscure, a number of passages in Emden's writings indicate

[137] See Rosman, *Founder of Hasidism*, 27–41; Piekarz, *Beginning of Hasidism* (Heb.), 79; Jacobs, *Hasidic Prayer*, 8. In contrast to portrayals in much of the scholarship on hasidism, some new-style hasidim also espoused ascetic practices.

[138] On the Brody *kloiz* and Landau's involvement with this institution, see Gelber, 'History of the Jews of Brody' (Heb.), 62–73; Reiner, 'Wealth, Social Position and the Study of Torah' (Heb.), 310–3; Heschel, *Circle of the Baal Shem Tov*, 50–2; Scholem, *Kabbalah*, 83–4; id., *Major Trends*, 328; Hundert, *Jews in a Polish Private Town*, 124. The Brody *kloiz* is discussed in greater detail in Part II.

[139] On R. Abraham Gershon, see Heschel, *Circle of the Baal Shem Tov*, 44–112; Joseph Weiss, 'Circle of Pneumatics in Pre-Hasidism', 211–12; Scholem, *Kabbalah*, 83; Jacobs, *Hasidic Prayer*, 10.

[140] After leaving Brody in *c.*1745, Landau served as chief rabbi of the Polish city of Yampol, in the district of Volhynia, for nearly ten years.

[141] It seems that both Abraham Gershon and Landau had to leave Brody after accusing the wife of a prominent member of Brody's community of adultery.

[142] *NB Kama*, 'EH', no. 73. One of the expressions employed by Landau to describe Abraham Gershon **וחסידות, לו עשר ידות** is also used by him to praise another Brody *kloiz* member, Moses Ostrer. On Landau's praise of Abraham Gershon as a hasid and sage, see also *NB Kama*, 'EH', no. 74.

[143] On Nahman of Kosov, see Piekarz, *Beginning of Hasidism* (Heb.), 23–30; Dinur, 'Origins of Hasidism', 160; Heschel, *Circle of the Baal Shem Tov*, 113–51; Joseph Weiss, 'Circle of Pneumatics in Pre-Hasidism', 199–210; Dubnow, *History of Hasidism* (Heb.), i. 102; Hundert, *Jews in a Polish Private Town*, 83, 127.

that it was Landau's letter of introduction that made Nahman a welcome visitor in the early 1740s in Opatów, Landau's birthplace.[144] Since Landau spent the first half of his life in and around the cradles of hasidism, his circle of hasidic acquaintances was probably more extensive.

At the Brody *kloiz*, Landau also formed close relationships with some of the most distinguished old-style pietists, many of whom had familial and social ties to the new hasidim. The Besht and other new-style hasidim were admirers of Landau's primary teacher at the *kloiz*, the renowned kabbalist Rabbi Hayim ben Menahem Zanzer (d. 1783).[145] The extent of this affection is shown by the fact that a child of Rabbi Jacob Joseph of Polonnoye (d. 1782), one of the Besht's leading disciples, married a child of Zanzer.[146] According to the *pinkas* (record book) of the *kloiz*, the Besht was close to another leading Brody *kloiz* kabbalist, Rabbi Moses ben Hillel Ostrer (d. 1785).[147] Ostrer, who was both an in-law of Abraham Gershon and had personal ties to other new hasidim, also befriended Landau.[148] In addition to Landau's contact with hasidim, both old-style and new-style, he endorsed several works containing kabbalistic ideas remarkably similar to those espoused by new hasidim.

Although the old-style and new-style hasidim were products of the same geographical area and cultural milieu and often interacted with one another, the old hasidim were largely at odds with the new hasidic offshoot. For instance, the *pinkas* of the Brody *kloiz* records Zanzer's opposition to the Besht during the nascent stage of hasidism.[149] Nevertheless, initially the distinctions between the old and new hasidim were somewhat fluid, and the old hasidim's resistance was rather muted. By the 1770s, however, when hasidism had developed into a mass movement, the differences became more obvious and the old-style hasidim's antagonism more pronounced. Despite their espousal of many similar kabbalistic

[144] Emden, *Sefer hitabekut*, 147*b*; id., *Petaḥ einayim*, 14*b*; id., *Shevirat luḥot ha'even*, 50*a*. See also Dinur, 'Origins of Hasidism' (Heb.), in id., *At the Turning of the Generations*, 160–1.

[145] This admiration, however, does not seem to have been reciprocal. See n. 149 below. On Hayim Zanzer, see Gelber, 'History of the Jews of Brody' (Heb.), 63; Piekarz, *Beginning of Hasidism* (Heb.), 60–1; Nahum Zwi Fish, *Mital hashamayim* ('From the Dew of Heaven'), introd. to Hayim Zanzer, *Ne'edar bakodesh*, 1–32.

[146] Scholem, 'Two Letters from Palestine' (Heb.), 436 n. 16. Jacob Joseph of Polonnoye was the chief transmitter of Israel Ba'al Shem Tov's teachings.

[147] Moses Ostrer was the second most important kabbalist of the Brody *kloiz*. On Moses Ostrer, see Gelber, 'History of the Jews of Brody' (Heb.), 71–2, 334; Piekarz, *Beginning of Hasidism* (Heb.), 79–81, 213; Ostrer, *Commentary on the Psalms* (Heb.); Reiner, 'Wealth, Social Position and the Study of Torah' (Heb.), 312–13.

[148] Scholem, 'Two Letters from Palestine' (Heb.), 436 n. 16. On Landau's acquaintance with Ostrer, see the approbation he gave for Ostrer's *Arugat habosem*.

[149] See Gelber, 'History of the Jews of Brody' (Heb.), 334; Piekarz, *Beginning of Hasidism* (Heb.), 61, 81, 235. The *pinkas* describes Zanzer as the *ba'al pelugta* (opponent) of the Besht.

teachings, the old-style hasidim repudiated the new hasidim's dissemination of kabbalistic lore to the uninitiated masses.[150]

During Landau's Prague career, he remained in contact with former colleagues from eastern Europe and was able to follow hasidism's development in the provinces where he had been educated and held his first rabbinic posts. Although Landau may not have opposed the new hasidim in person, since there were none in Prague, his criticism of their practices and followers, which appears in all his Prague works—responsa, talmudic commentary, sermons, and letters—had a wide impact. A telling example appears in a recently discovered letter from 1773, revealing that he even sent an epistle of rebuke to the eminent chief rabbi of Frankfurt, Pinhas Horowitz (1730–1805), a disciple of the early hasidic leader Dov Baer, reproaching him for belonging to the hasidic sect.[151] More commonly, however, in his Prague writings, Landau, like several *kloiz* kabbalists, denounces the members of this new 'sect', who are uneducated in traditional texts, but nevertheless 'label themselves as hasidim' and claim to know kabbalistic secrets.[152]

Landau's fierce condemnation of the new hasidim was due in part to the threat they posed to the traditional rabbinic hierarchy of values.[153] The hasidim rejected the primacy of intellectual talmudic studies,[154] and particularly repudiated *pilpul*, the casuistic method of talmudic study that was popular in seventeenth- and eighteenth-century Ashkenazi rabbinic culture, a method that Landau deftly and frequently uses in his talmudic commentaries.[155] During the

150 See Piekarz, *Beginning of Hasidism* (Heb.), 377–92; Reiner, 'Wealth, Social Position and the Study of Torah' (Heb.), 323–4; Rosman, *Founder of Hasidism*, 39. Since the initial ideas of the new hasidim were largely similar to those espoused by the old hasidim, the opposition to hasidism was primarily due to its social innovations.

151 This letter, sent on 28 Feb. 1773 by the rabbi of Fuerth, Joseph Steinhardt, to Landau, speaks of an earlier letter Landau had sent to Horowitz in which he chastised him for his affiliation with the hasidic sect. Since Horowitz was appointed chief rabbi of Frankfurt in 1771, Landau must have written this letter between 1771 and 1773. It is housed in the archival collection of the Karlin-Stolin hasidim. See *Kovets beit aharon veyisra'el*, 9/3 (51) (1994), 129–39.

152 See e.g. *Tselaḥ*, *Ber.*, preface.

153 On the general controversies between the early hasidim and their opponents, see Wilensky, *Hasidim and Mitnagedim* (Heb.); id., 'The Hostile Phase', 89–113; Dubnow, *History of Hasidism* (Heb.); Weinryb, *Jews of Poland*, 282–301; Fishman, *Russia's First Modern Jews*, 7–21.

154 See J. Katz, *Tradition and Crisis*, 202–4. Although the new hasidim at first accorded a lower status to intellectual Torah study, various hasidic groups later changed their attitude towards it. See Wilensky, 'Hostile Phase', 109.

155 Dimitrovsky argues that Landau was one of the last great masters of the *pilpul* method. See Dimitrovsky, 'On the *Pilpul* Style' (Heb.), 176–81. While Dimitrovsky contends that the writings of Landau and his sons were the last links in the Ashkenazi chain of *pilpul*, Ta-Shma wishes to date this turning point to the writings of R. Jacob Joshua Falk (1680–1756), the Penei Yehoshua. (It should be noted that despite the strength of Ta-Shma's article, he misrepresents Dimitrovsky's incisive analysis of Landau's attitude towards *pilpul*.) However, even Ta-Shma concedes that Landau's *Tselaḥ* is replete with the *pilpul* method. See Ta-Shma, 'On the Book "Pnei Yehoshua"' (Heb.), 281.

1770s, the hasidim implored the masses to reduce their emphasis on intellectualism and instead focus on their spiritual and ethical development. This new religious revivalist movement viewed the ideal of Judaism as the attainment of *devekut*, cleaving to or achieving a mystical union with God.[156] In this spirit, the new hasidim elevated prayer above all other commandments, including the intellectual study of Torah,[157] which was traditionally regarded as the most important Jewish value. These developments were disturbing to Prague's rabbis.

The new hasidim presented other challenges to the traditional view of the privileged status of intellectual Torah study. Where conventional rabbinic Judaism viewed Torah study as a goal per se, the new hasidim often regarded Torah study as a means of achieving *devekut*.[158] The mitnagedim, or opponents of hasidism, were also threatened by the hasidim's reversal of the traditional hierarchy of knowledge, through their emphasis on kabbalah for the masses who were inadequately schooled in Talmud and the legal codes. Their characterization of the hasidim is illustrated by the 1772 anti-hasidic ban issued in Brody, which asserts that the hasidim 'despise the entire Oral Law and state that they study only kabbalah'.[159] In addition, the mitnagedim accused the hasidim of precipitating the neglect of Torah study by promoting the goal of joy and consequently spending their days merrymaking instead of studying Torah.[160] In a 1782 Prague sermon, Landau, like the mitnagedim, attacks the hasidim through his criticism of an unnamed contemporary sect who, instead of studying Torah, 'make all their days into holidays and constantly fill their bellies' with delicacies.[161]

[156] On the importance of the mystical goal of *devekut* in hasidism, see Scholem, *Messianic Idea in Judaism*, 203–27; Idel, *Hasidism*; Jacobs, *Hasidic Prayer*; Nigal, 'Sources of *Devekut* in Early Hasidic Literature' (Heb.).

[157] The new hasidim particularly stressed the importance of prayer since they viewed it as one of the best means to attain *devekut*. See Jacobs, *Hasidic Prayer*, 17–21; Krassen, 'Devequt and Faith in Zaddiqim', 404–5; Wilensky, 'Hostile Phase', 96.

[158] Their different views of Torah study led to distinctions in their approach to learning. Whereas the mitnagedim promoted Torah study even if it was driven by flawed motives, the new hasidim emphasized that such study needed the *kavanah* (intention) of achieving *devekut*. See Wilensky, 'Hostile Phase', 105. For a discussion of hasidic views of Torah study as a vehicle to achieving *devekut*, see Idel, *Hasidism*, 171–85; Krassen, 'Devequt and Faith in Zaddiqim', 271–4, 404–5; Piekarz, *Beginning of Hasidism* (Heb.), 305, 346–50. On the mitnagedic claim that the hasidim neglected Torah study, see Wilensky, 'Hostile Phase', 105–9.

[159] This ban against the hasidim is published in Wilensky, *Hasidim and Mitnagedim* (Heb.), i. 44–9.

[160] Wilensky, 'Hostile Phase', 106.

[161] *Derushei hatselah*, sermon 39, 53*b*. Landau's criticism here, which is often used in polemical works against the hasidim (see Piekarz, *Beginning of Hasidism* (Heb.), 337; Wilensky, 'Hostile Phase', 105–8), seems to be directed against the new hasidim. In this barb, Landau is playing with a talmudic phrase in BT *Shab.* 151*b*, which criticizes those who abandon the study and observance of the Torah's laws and spend their days celebrating invented holidays, two accusations that were often levelled against the new hasidim.

Apart from undermining the conventional hierarchy of rabbinic values, hasidism also challenged the traditional rabbinate's authority. In contrast to the communal rabbi, largely chosen on the basis of his knowledge of talmudic law, the hasidic rabbi or *tsadik* (lit. righteous individual), was 'revealed'.[162] Since the new hasidim viewed the spiritual ability to achieve *devekut* as a prerequisite for this revelation, hasidic leaders were often adepts in kabbalah and not necessarily halakhic scholars. The new social-organizational structure introduced by hasidism during the 1770s and 1780s also threatened the conventional rabbinate. In this new pattern of organization, the hasidic *tsadik* often held sway over a geographically widespread group of followers, weakening the formerly exclusive authority of the local rabbis. These leaders were usually unaffiliated with local communal institutions, such as the rabbinic court and the yeshiva. This new organizational pattern undermined the traditional structure of the *kehilah* in numerous Ashkenazi communities.[163] Although these developments never made their way to Prague, Landau and other central European rabbis condemned these hasidic innovations in nearby Poland and Galicia, which challenged the hegemony of traditional Ashkenazi rabbinic leadership and institutions.

The historian Moshe Rosman argues that the opposition to hasidism primarily stemmed from the old-style pietists and not necessarily from 'the rabbis', who were a diverse group.[164] Landau's affiliation with Brody's *kloiz* has received scant attention, but is consistent with Rosman's thesis. However, Landau and other rabbinic figures who opposed the new hasidim were as much members of the normative rabbinate as they were old-style pietists; the normative seventeenth- and eighteenth-century Ashkenazi rabbinic elite was often closely intermingled with old-style hasidism. This point is well illustrated by the Landau family. Several members of the family were both active in various kabbalistic *kloizn* and held distinguished rabbinic leadership positions in eastern and central Europe. Scholarship's categorization of the legalistic rabbis on the one hand and the kabbalists and pietists on the other obscures the extent of the intersection between these categories. Many rabbis were both involved in Jewish legal and communal matters and deeply committed to kabbalistic study and a pietistic lifestyle. The recurrent convergence of these categories, as best demonstrated by the rabbinic giants Landau and Elijah, the Gaon of Vilna, has often been overlooked. Much of the opposition to the new hasidim came neither from 'the rabbis' nor from 'the pietists', but rather from a group of normative rabbinic

[162] On the *tsadik* in hasidic writings, see Piekarz, *Hasidic Leadership* (Heb.).

[163] See J. Katz, *Tradition and Crisis*, 203–5, 209–11; Piekarz, *Beginning of Hasidism* (Heb.), 392.

[164] See Rosman, *Founder of Hasidism*, 35, 38, 224 n. 32.

authorities, such as Landau, Emden, and Elijah of Vilna,[165] who were both rabbis and pietists. These rabbis wished to defend normative rabbinic Judaism from the incursions made by the new hasidim.

Much of the extensive folklore surrounding Landau relates both to his interaction with and attitude towards the new hasidim. Many of these tales point to the common kabbalistic and halakhic orientation of the hasidim and Landau, despite their different views on mystical authority.[166] Several stories depicting Landau's opposition to the Besht's 'revealed' teachings, particularly pertaining to halakhic matters, reflect the traditional rabbinate's fear of the hasidic leadership. In contrast, many hasidic folk-tales demonstrate the hasidim's tremendous respect for Landau's halakhic authority and religious stature. In this vein, stories relate that the hasidic *tsadik*, Rabbi Shneur Zalman of Lyady (1740–1813), the founder of Habad hasidism, asserted that Landau never made a mistake in halakhic decisions, and that Rabbi Baruch of Miedzybóz (1757–1810), the Besht's grandson, stated that the heavenly court declared that Jewish law is always in accordance with Landau's rulings.[167] Regarding Landau's spiritual qualities, a legend recounts that the Besht pronounced Landau endowed with a rare 'new soul', which, according to Lurianic kabbalah, did not partake in Adam's sin and therefore had special redemptive capabilities.[168] Other stories, probably composed by hasidim or their supporters, even portray Landau's eventual acceptance of hasidism. While they are inaccurate, these tales express the hasidim's desire for his approval.[169]

During Landau's tenure, hasidism grew from a handful of elite circles into a mass movement, with numerous charismatic 'revealed' leaders who threatened the hegemony of conventional rabbinic authority. Although Landau was educated in a pietistic *kloiz*, he strenuously opposed the innovations of the new hasidim. His writings and various folk-tales about him suggest that his censure

[165] Although Elijah of Vilna did not hold an official communal position, I maintain that he was not only one of the 'normative rabbis' but also an influential figure within this group. On the Gaon of Vilna, see Etkes, *Unique in his Generation* (Heb.). On the influence of kabbalah on the Gaon of Vilna, see Werblowsky, 'Mystic Life of the Gaon Elijah of Vilna' in his *Joseph Karo: Lawyer and Mystic*, 311–16; Avivi, *Kabalat hagerah*; Brill, 'Mystical Path of the Vilna Gaon'; Wolfson, 'From Sealed Book to Open Text'; Shohat, 'The Vilna Gaon's Commentary on *Mishnat hasidim*' (Heb.).

[166] For some of the folk-tales on Landau and his interactions with various hasidim, see Kamelhar, *Mofet hador*, 58–9; Gelman, *The Noda Biyehudah and his Teaching* (Heb.), 69–71, 77–8; anon., *Noda Biyehudah* (Heb.), 84–145.

[167] Another tale relates that the hasidic rabbi Hayim of Zanz (1793–1876) remarked that Landau was one of the three pillars upon which the world stands. See Weingarten, *The Noda Biyehudah*, 132.

[168] On the Lurianic notion of a 'new soul', see Scholem, *Kabbalah*, 163.

[169] See e.g. Kamelhar, *Mofet hador*, appendix; Gelman, *The Noda Biyehudah and his Teaching* (Heb.), 71. See anon., *Divrei no'am*, which depicts a dialogue between Landau and the hasidic rabbi Jacob Samson of Shepetovka (d. 1801).

of the hasidim was not a reaction to their general mystical-religious orientation or even their espousal of specific esoteric kabbalistic teachings, but was primarily in response to their challenge to the prevailing hierarchy of Jewish values and traditional rabbinic authority, both already threatened by other trends.

Landau was the first Prague rabbi forced to contend with the new trends of this era and the incipient stages of modernization. During his career, he responded to the major political, social, and ideological challenges of his day: the increasing centralization of the Habsburg state, its curtailment of the official authority of Prague's rabbinate, government-imposed secular education, acculturation, the Haskalah, Sabbatianism, the emergence of new-style hasidism, and the reordering of the traditional Ashkenazi curriculum. Despite steady advances made by these modernizing and mystical trends, Prague's rabbinic culture continued to thrive.

PART II

THE CENTRALITY OF KABBALAH IN LANDAU'S THOUGHT AND WRITINGS

INTRODUCTION

PARADOXICALLY, while various modernizing and mystical movements threatened to undermine Prague's traditional values at the end of the eighteenth century, kabbalah remained an integral aspect of the city's thriving traditional rabbinic culture. Kabbalah influenced the thought, and, at times, the practices of Prague Jews, whose distinguished institutions, including their academies and court system, were administered according to the principles of halakhah and largely devoted to halakhic study. Notably, many of the illustrious scholars who headed these legal and educational institutions, such as Landau, Eybeschütz, and Fleckeles, were deeply immersed both in the intricacies of halakhah and the esoteric lore of kabbalah.

While the enormous contribution of Landau, the most influential of these eighteenth-century Prague rabbis, to Jewish legal development has long been established, the centrality of kabbalah for this eminent halakhic authority has been overlooked. This section explores Landau's extensive use of kabbalah and his belief that halakhah and kabbalah enhance and reinforce one another. Strikingly, kabbalah plays a pivotal role in Landau's education, worldview, and, on occasion, even his halakhic reasoning. In addition, unlike many other rabbinic authorities who engage in kabbalah, Landau does not entirely reserve his esoteric knowledge for the initiated elite. Close analysis reveals the repeated use of kabbalistic notions in all his works: the talmudic commentaries written for his students, responsa addressed to rabbinic scholars, and most of his homilies intended for Prague Jewry at large.

FOUR

Historiography, Personal History, and Folk Tales

THE MAJOR SCHOLARLY WORKS on both kabbalah and central and east European Jewry do not address the importance of kabbalah in Landau's thought and writings.[1] As mentioned earlier, historical studies of Habsburg Jewry during his period, such as the works of Kestenberg-Gladstein and McCagg, focus on the modernization of a small group of late eighteenth-century Jews.[2] Since these studies do not examine the contributions of leading rabbinic figures, they consequently do not deal with the significance of kabbalah in their thought and works. Even the few scholars who have treated eighteenth-century rabbinic culture and leaders have often been biased. Much of the research on the rabbinate produced by these nineteenth-century scholars, promoting the Wissenschaft des Judentums (the scientific or critical-historical study of Judaism), either ignores or mockingly dismisses the influence of kabbalah. Many of these scholars viewed this lore as a foreign element grafted onto Judaism's core and antithetical to the rationalism which they prized.[3]

The scholar most responsible for redressing the Wissenschaft historians' neglect of kabbalah was Gershom Scholem,[4] the pioneer of the academic study of kabbalah during the twentieth century. His portrayal of the rabbinate, however, retains some of the Wissenschaft biases. In Scholem's dialectical schematization of Jewish history, kabbalah is the creative force which opposes the rigidity of normative rabbinic Judaism. He accordingly depicts the rabbis as an unyielding group who stifle mysticism and creativity.[5] Not surprisingly, Scholem frequently

1 The major academic works on kabbalah, such as those by Scholem, Tishby, Wolfson, Idel, and Liebes, make no mention of the centrality of kabbalah for Landau. Even the rather long entry on Landau in the *Encyclopaedia Judaica* fails to note his mystical leanings. See Samet, 'Ezekiel ben Judah Landau'.

2 See McCagg, *History of Habsburg Jews* and Kestenberg-Gladstein, *Neuere Geschichte*. Although Kestenberg-Gladstein occasionally depicts Landau's political influence, she neglects most of his rabbinic writings.

3 See e.g. H. Graetz, *History of the Jews*, ed. Löwy, vol. v.

4 For Scholem's critique of the Wissenschaft scholars' treatment of kabbalah see e.g. his *Major Trends*, 251.

5 Several scholars, such as Eliezer Schweid and Elisheva Carlebach, have noted this weakness in Scholem's work. See Schweid, *Judaism and Mysticism According to Gershom Scholem*. Schweid calls on

neglects the incorporation of kabbalah in the writings of many rabbinic leaders during the second half of the eighteenth century. Instead, he categorically claims that during this period 'the *rabbis* were withdrawing further and further from any manifestation of a mystical tendency or a leaning toward the kabbalah' (emphasis added).[6]

Both the hagiographic studies of Landau and the thematic works on him and his thought also de-emphasize or misconstrue the significance of kabbalah in his writings. While some books, such as Jekuthiel Kamelhar's *Mofet hador* and Aryeh Leib Gelman's *The Noda Biyehudah and his Teaching*, do acknowledge that Landau possessed knowledge of kabbalah from his youth, they allot only a few lines to this. The scholars of these informative, albeit hagiographic, studies accept at face value Landau's oft-repeated claim that he does not delve into esoteric matters.[7] In this vein, Kamelhar writes that 'a kabbalistic teaching was never heard from his [Landau's] mouth . . . for he always presented himself as one who did not know such things'.[8] Similarly, in Israel Hess's unpublished MA thesis, 'Rabbi Ezekiel Landau and his Position in the History of the Halakhah', he contends that even though Landau was familiar with kabbalah, he opposed its dissemination.[9] Solomon Wind alleges, in his *Rabbi Ezekiel Landau*, that although Landau mastered kabbalah, this knowledge was merely an 'ornament to his wisdom' and he 'did not ascribe much worth to it'.[10] Remarkably, in a recent anthology by leading scholars of Jewish thought, *On Faith: Studies in the Concept of Faith and its History in the Jewish Tradition*, Benny Brown argues that Landau did not engage in esoteric matters.[11] Given the importance of kabbalah in eighteenth-century central European Jewish culture in general,[12] and in the

future scholars to portray the kabbalistic elements found in numerous 18th-c. rabbinic works. Carlebach similarly points to the need for critical rabbinic biographies in order to correct scholarship's distorted depictions of many rabbinic figures. See Carlebach, *Pursuit of Heresy*, 16–17.

[6] Scholem, 'Kabbalah', 85. The citation is a classic example of Scholem's monolithic treatment of 'the rabbis'.

[7] See e.g. Gelman, *The Noda Biyehudah and his Teaching* (Heb.), 41.

[8] Kamelhar, *Mofet hador*, 6–7. Nevertheless, Kamelhar points out that, despite Landau's concerted efforts, his kabbalistic views do 'shine through' in several places.

[9] See Hess, 'Rabbi Ezekiel Landau' (Heb.), 272. Somewhat similarly, Piekarz's *Beginning of Hasidism* (Heb.), which briefly discusses Landau, also overlooks the prevalence of kabbalah in his writings. Piekarz asserts that, notwithstanding Landau's kabbalistic tendencies, he denounced public kabbalistic discourse. He even analyses several places where Landau repudiates public discussion of kabbalah. See ibid., 335–7.

[10] Wind, *Rabbi Ezekiel Landau* (Heb.), 11. This comment seems to be a reversal of Wind's previous position, as seen in the short article 'Ezekiel Landau', 95, where he asserts that Landau espoused kabbalistic doctrines.

[11] Halbertal, Kurzweil, and Sagi (eds.), *On Faith* (Heb.), 406–10. Brown writes that Landau makes almost no use of kabbalistic sources and terms in his writings.

[12] On the popularization of kabbalah in Ashkenazi society during the late 17th and 18th cc., see Hundert, *Jews in Poland–Lithuania*, 119–53; Idel, 'Perceptions of Kabbalah'; Rosman, 'Innovative

Prague Jewish community in particular, scholarship's neglect of the prominence of kabbalah in Landau's work is glaring.

Although the conflict between his stated attitude towards kabbalah and his immersion therein is not addressed by these scholars, this tension is the subject of various folk tales. Several of these oral traditions, most of which have no historical grounding, portray Landau's clandestine kabbalistic knowledge. There is, however, one historically noteworthy anecdote. According to this story, Landau possessed a secret box where he kept his kabbalistic sources. After his death, when his descendants opened the box, they found his copies of the Zohar, Lurianic writings, and his new insights on kabbalistic matters.[13] This oral tale has been lent some credence by the recent discovery of Lurianic manuscripts that were owned by Landau.[14]

Landau's manuscripts of the *Derekh ets ḥayim* and *Peri ets ḥayim* by Hayim Vital, the principal formulator of Luria's teachings, reveal that he commented on these classic kabbalistic works: his extensive notes and annotations appear throughout the margins of both manuscripts. Some of his complex glosses show that he was both well-versed in these texts and a master of the profound intricacies of Lurianic kabbalah. There can also be little doubt that Landau viewed these works as sacred, since he penned the following inscription on the cover of his copy of *Derekh ets ḥayim*: 'Blessed is God who gave us this holy book, and may He give me merit to understand all that is written herein.'[15]

Other folk tales depict both his observance of kabbalistic customs and his concealed knowledge of kabbalah. A well-known anecdote describes how he cried nightly for the exiled Shekhinah, until he would drink a cup filled with his tears of sorrow.[16] Another legend recounts the visit of Rabbi Isaac Halevi Horowitz (1715–67), a relative of Landau and his friend from the Brody *kloiz*, to

Tradition', 528–9, 547–51, 560; Gries, *Conduct Literature* (Heb.); Scholem, *Sabbatai Sevi*, 77–87; Piekarz, *Beginning of Hasidism* (Heb.); Huss, '*Sefer ha-Zohar* as a Canonical, Sacred, and Holy Text'; Hubka, 'The "Zohar" and the Polish Synagogue'. Many of the pre-eminent 18th-c. rabbis, including the Gaon of Vilna, Jacob Emden, and Jonathan Eybeschütz, were also acclaimed kabbalists.

[13] See Kamelhar, *Mofet hador*, 6 n. 13. According to this tale, Samuel Landau is said to have originally transmitted this story.

[14] Landau's copies of Vital's *Derekh ets ḥayim* and *Peri ets ḥayim* were discovered by R. Hayyim Schneebalg of New York City. They are currently owned by a private collector.

[15] We can date this inscription from Landau's use of the phrase *hareni kaparat mishkavo* ('I am the atonement for where he rests'), which is traditionally uttered by children during the first year of mourning for a parent's death (see BT *Ked.* 31*b*). Accordingly, he wrote this inscription within the first year of the death of his father, Judah Landau, who passed away at the end of the year 1737. This inscription therefore dates from 1737–8, when Landau was about 25 years old.

[16] See anon., *The Noda Biyehudah* (Heb.), 53. On the mystical practice of weeping, see Wolfson, 'Weeping, Death, and Spiritual Ascent'; Idel, *Kabbalah*, 75–88.

Prague.[17] During the visit, the two adjourned to a special room to discuss kabbalistic teachings. Afterwards, Horowitz is reported to have remarked that Landau's proficiency in kabbalah equalled his expertise in legal matters.[18] These popular tales suggest that although Landau hid his kabbalistic knowledge in locked boxes and behind closed doors, this lore formed an integral part of his intellectual and spiritual world.

Landau's Biography: Ties to Kabbalah

There are numerous indications of the prominence of mysticism in Landau's education in Poland. He probably received his first exposure to kabbalah at an early age from his family in Opatów, in the region known as Malpolska (Little Poland), where he was born in 1713. A child prodigy, Landau was first educated by his father Judah and later by Rabbi Isaac of Vladimir. Around 1728, various members of the prominent and wealthy Landau family, many of whom were versed in kabbalah, established a *kloiz* in Opatów. This *kloiz*, housed in the home of Landau's uncle, Rabbi Isaac, who served as its rabbi, was probably a centre of kabbalistic study. Landau's father was also actively involved in the *kloiz*. Besides this participation, both Judah and Isaac Landau belonged to a larger network of east European mystics. There is also evidence that some Opatów rabbis, probably including Judah and Isaac, had connections with the eminent Padua kabbalist, Rabbi Moses Hayim Luzzatto (1706–46), commonly referred to as Ramhal.[19] Most significantly, the scholars of kabbalah in Opatów had close ties to the renowned cadre of mystics and old-style hasidim in Brody. Growing up in this environment, in which kabbalah played a central role, must have influenced the young Landau.

Many members of the Landau family, especially those in the generation after Isaac and Judah, were involved with and assumed leadership positions at the distinguished kabbalistic Brody *kloiz*. Like the Opatów study house, it was founded at the beginning of the eighteenth century, and was the most important centre of kabbalah in Poland from the time of its establishment until the beginning of the

[17] Isaac Halevi Horowitz is also known as Isaac Hamburger. On the relationship between Landau and Horowitz, see *NB Kama*, 'YD', nos. 43 and 46, where Landau refers to Isaac Horowitz as 'my in-law and relative'. On Isaac Horowitz, see Gelber, 'History of the Jews of Brody' (Heb.), 57–8; Kamelhar, *Dor de'ah*, 44–7; Reiner, 'Wealth, Social Position and the Study of Torah' (Heb.), 311–12; Raphael, introd. to his edition of Isaac Halevi Horowitz, *Mishnat halevi*, 9–51; id., 'The Relationship between R. Ezekiel Halevi Landau and R. Isaac Halevi Horowitz' (Heb.).

[18] See Kamelhar, *Mofet hador*, 6 n. 13. See also anon., *The Nodah Biyehudah* (Heb.), 50.

[19] It is difficult, however, to determine the exact nature of Judah's and Isaac's involvement with kabbalah, since neither produced written works. See Hundert, *Jews in a Polish Private Town*, 82–3, 123–4; Ginzburg, *Rabbi Moses Hayim Luzzatto and his Contemporaries* (Heb.), 264; Benayahu, *Kabbalistic Writings of Hayim Luzzatto* (Heb.), 218.

nineteenth century.[20] Several of Landau's relatives were related to the *kloiz*'s founder, Rabbi Jacob Ba'abad.[21] Landau's cousin, Rabbi Hayim ben Abraham Landau, who was Ba'abad's son-in-law, enjoyed a long tenure as the head of the *kloiz*.[22] Similarly, another relative, Rabbi Isaac Halevi Horowitz, also a son-in-law of Ba'abad, seems to have served as the *kloiz's* head for a brief period. Landau's cousins Rabbi Wolf Halevi and Rabbi Joseph were involved with the *kloiz* as well.

Undoubtedly, Landau's years at the Brody *kloiz* constituted his most intense period of kabbalistic study. Entering the *kloiz* at the age of about 18 a few months after his marriage in 1732,[23] he probably spent six years there before attaining full membership. During this time, at the early age of 20, he became the first judge of one of Brody's four Jewish courts.[24] However, since the title *morenu* ('our teacher') was one of the prerequisites for becoming a full member of the *kloiz*, he probably only received full membership after obtaining this title in *c.*1738, at the age of 24.[25] After seven years of full membership, he left the *kloiz* in 1745.[26] Landau thus spent the formative years of his late teens and twenties immersed in the kabbalistic and scholarly milieu of the Brody *kloiz*.

The members of the *kloiz* comprised an elite group of old-style hasidim devoted to kabbalistic study and practice in a traditional framework. Their immersion in kabbalah commenced only after attaining proficiency in Talmud and codes,[27] which they continued to study alongside kabbalah. Since members

[20] See Gelber, 'History of the Jews of Brody' (Heb.), 62; Scholem, *Kabbalah*, 83. In the introduction to the *Noda biyehudah, Kama*, Landau writes that shortly after getting married (in 1732), he and others established the *kloiz*.

[21] On the prominent status of Jacob Ba'abad's family at the Brody *kloiz*, see *NB Kama*, 'YD', no. 43, where Landau asks two of Ba'abad's sons-in-law, R. Isaac Halevi Horowitz and R. Hirtz, as well as other Brody *kloiz* members, for their consent for one of his rulings. On Isaac Halevi Horowitz, see n. 17 above.

[22] Hayim Landau was also a significant patron of the Brody *kloiz*. See Reiner, 'Wealth, Social Position and the Study of Torah' (Heb.), 310–11; Hundert, *Jews in a Polish Private Town*, 124.

[23] Landau also studied in Brody from 1727 to 1732 before going to Dubno for a few months to get married. Shortly thereafter he returned and entered the Brody *kloiz*. In his eulogy for his wife Liba (*Ahavat tsiyon*, sermon 7), delivered on 28 Tevet 5550 (14 Jan. 1790), Landau states that they had been married for fifty-eight years.

[24] See Jacob Landau, *Divrei yedidot*.

[25] See *NB Kama*, introd., where Landau records that he began to answer halakhic queries at the age of 24, which is probably when he received the title *morenu*, which conferred the authority to render halakhic decisions. See Reiner, 'Wealth, Social Position and the Study of Torah' (Heb.), 289, 319; J. Katz, *Tradition and Crisis*, 142, 167–8.

[26] In *c.*1744–5 Landau seems to have been forced to leave Brody after accusing the wife of a prominent community member of adultery. See also Kamelhar, *Mofet hador*, 8, 9. On 16 Nov. 1744 Landau signed the approbation for Moses ben Jekuthiel's *Magid mishnah* as a member of the Brody *kloiz*, even though the heading of the approbation states that he had been appointed as the chief rabbi of Yampol.

[27] See Reiner, 'Wealth, Social Position and the Study of Torah' (Heb.), 288 n. 2 and Gelber, 'History of the Jews of Brody' (Heb.), 62.

of the *kloiz* were regarded as authorities on esoteric matters, many kabbalistic books published in eighteenth-century Poland were first sent to the *kloiz* for approval.[28] As a member of the *kloiz*, Landau gave approbations for several kabbalistic works during his residence in Brody.

Numerous extant sources demonstrate the *kloiz* members' immersion in kabbalah and adherence to kabbalistic customs. For instance, the 1772 anti-hasidic ban promulgated in Brody explicitly notes the *kloiz* members' use of the Lurianic prayer rite.[29] This ban prohibits several kabbalistic practices observed by the hasidim, such as the use of the Lurianic prayer book. The assembly, however, exempts the Brody *kloiz* from this ban, stating,

> with the exception of the remnant to whom God calls, who pray in the first *shtibl* at the side of our community's *kloiz*. For it is clear that these men . . . are full of revealed learning, the Talmud and the codes, and they have a great reputation in the secrets of kabbalah. *They have already used the prayer book of the Ari for many years.*[30] (emphasis added)

The exemption afforded to the *kloiz* demonstrates both the traditional rabbinate's respect for the institution and the adherence of the *kloiz* kabbalists to the Lurianic rite, with its attendant *kavanot* (extra-liturgical mystical intentions), for many years. In 1781, nine years after the issuing of this ban, the Brody *kloiz* even published its own edition of the *Sidur ha'ari* (Lurianic prayer book), which is replete with *kavanot*.[31] Considering Landau's extended tenure at the *kloiz*, it is likely that he too used the Lurianic siddur, at least while living at the *kloiz*.

The Brody scholars resided at the *kloiz* six days a week, returning to their spouses only on the sabbath. Although individuals often left their hometowns to study, the practice of an entire group separating from their spouses during the week is much rarer.[32] This custom could very possibly be rooted in the kabbalistic convictions of members of the *kloiz*. In particular, it may have been inspired by kabbalistic teachings found in the Zohar and in the later ethical-mystical *musar* literature, such as Elijah de Vidas's *Reshit ḥokhmah*.[33]

[28] Scholem, *Kabbalah*, 83–4.

[29] This ban, written in Yiddish, was promulgated by the rabbinic assembly that convened in Brody. See Wilensky, *Hasidim and Mitnagedim* (Heb.), i. 44–9.

[30] This excerpt from the ban is found in Wilensky, *Hasidim and Mitnagedim* (Heb.), i. 47; Reiner, 'Wealth, Social Position and the Study of Torah' (Heb.), 287. For an English translation of part of this ban, see Jacobs, *Hasidic Prayer*, 40–1. My translation is based on that of Jacobs.

[31] This *Sidur ha'ari* was published in Zolkiew.

[32] Still, the custom of residing at a *kloiz* was central to this institution in general. See Reiner, 'Wealth, Social Position and the Study of Torah' (Heb.), 315. On the talmudic discussion of the practice of individual students separating from their wives to study Torah, see BT *Ket.* 62*b*.

[33] While the notion that scholars perform their marital duties only once a week (on Friday nights) is mentioned in BT *Ket.* 62*b*, this custom was not widely promoted in rabbinic (non-kabbalistic) circles. Many kabbalists, however, did advocate such practices. See e.g. Zohar, ii. 89*a–b*, which states that the companions who study Torah 'abstain from sexual intercourse during the six weekdays while

Landau mentions his observance of this custom while living in Brody, in two sources written over thirteen years apart. In 1790, in his eulogy for his beloved wife Liba, he recollects that, 'in her youth she would remain alone, and I would stay enclosed all six days of the week in my house of study'.[34] Similarly, in his introduction to the *Noda biyehudah*, published in 1776, he reminisces that shortly after his marriage, Liba would stay alone during the week while he was at the Brody study house.[35]

The kabbalistic character of the *kloiz* is further exemplified by two of its pre-eminent teachers, Hayim Zanzer and Moses Ostrer, who were among the most fervent eighteenth-century mystics. Teaching at the *kloiz* shortly after its foundation, these charismatic kabbalists both shaped its orientation and gave the *kloiz* its reputation as one of the most important institutions of kabbalistic study in Poland.[36] As a result, they attracted other mystics either to reside in or to visit this kabbalistic centre.

At the Brody *kloiz*, Landau attained a mastery of kabbalah and met many of the leading mystics of the era.[37] He was particularly close to the most renowned *kloiz* kabbalist, Hayim Zanzer, his teacher in both law and kabbalah. As Jacob Landau relates in his biography of his father, *Divrei yedidot*,

> he, our father . . . filled himself with the knowledge of Talmud and the early codes. And all mysteries of the 'secrets of the Lord' (Ps. 25: 14) were not hidden from him. As I heard in faith from the holy . . . saintly kabbalist, Hayim Zanzer. For, as we know, he [Zanzer] was a good friend of his [Landau] in their studies of divine esoteric matters.[38] He [Zanzer] used to say that all the holy writings of the Ari and the rest of the kabbalistic books found

they labour at the Torah' (unless otherwise noted, citations are from Reuven Margaliot's edition of the Zohar; here the translation is by David Goldstein in Tishby, *Wisdom of the Zohar*, iii. 1391). On this notion in the *musar* literature, see e.g. de Vidas, *Reshit ḥokhmah*, 'Sha'ar ha'ahavah', ch. 3, 390; 'Sha'ar hakedushah', ch. 7, 152.

[34] Landau, *Ahavat tsiyon*, sermon 7, 11*a*.

[35] This is rather surprising since, in general, Jewish law strongly discourages conjugal separation during the first year of marriage. For an extensive discussion of this topic, see Frankel, *Simḥah temimah*.

[36] Reiner, 'Wealth, Social Position and the Study of Torah' (Heb.), 312–13.

[37] In his introduction to *NB Kama*, however, Landau denies his involvement with kabbalah at the *kloiz*.

[38] Elhanan Reiner offers a different reading of the above-mentioned praise: see his 'Wealth, Social Position and the Study of Torah' (Heb.), 313. According to Reiner's reading, this praise was conferred upon Hayim Zanzer, Landau's principal teacher at the Brody *kloiz*; according to my reading, this praise refers to Landau, not Zanzer. Although the pronouns in this citation are ambiguous, Reiner's reading does not work for two reasons. First, Jacob Landau wrote this piece to describe his father. All the sentences preceding this citation describe Landau, not Zanzer. Second, it is clear that the end of the sentence, which refers to the *kloiz* elders' admiration for Landau, plays on the name Ezekiel, and undoubtedly refers to him. It would be strange to argue that the first and second halves of this sentence refer to different people. Reiner's reading is problematic in view of both the content and style of this citation. Nonetheless, even this reading admits Zanzer's profound influence on Landau.

in this land, in addition to the *Guide of the Perplexed*,[39] [are] combined and hidden in him. Similarly, the rest of the sages at the *kloiz* here, the elders of that generation, would also exclaim that they had seen the visions of Ezekiel in those days.[40]

Typically, at the Brody *kloiz*, the education of exceptional students who had a particular interest in kabbalah was overseen by a *kloiz* member.[41] Jacob Landau's words reveal that Landau had this special teacher-disciple relationship with Zanzer, with whom he studied both general kabbalistic works and Lurianic kabbalah. Jacob Landau further attests that Zanzer praised his student for mastering and integrating the thought of various kabbalistic schools. The *kloiz* scholars' exclamations about having seen 'visions of Ezekiel' playfully allude both to the prophet Ezekiel's mystical vision of the chariot and to Landau's first name, Ezekiel, and bear witness to their appreciation of his kabbalistic expertise. In several writings from his Prague years, Landau likewise exhibits tremendous respect for his Brody peers and especially for Zanzer. In his responsa, he employs various rabbinic epithets of great distinction, such as 'the light of the exile' and 'the *ḥasid*', to refer to Zanzer.[42]

Moses Ostrer, the old-style hasid and second most important Brody *kloiz* kabbalist, also had ties to Landau. It seems that the two studied law and kabbalah together, as alluded to in Landau's approbation for Ostrer's book, *Arugat habosem*.[43] Landau writes that Ostrer, who 'sat with us in our study house . . . is superb in both revealed and esoteric matters . . . He has enormous strength in the wisdom of kabbalah and has descended to the chambers of the divine Chariot.[44] He has also mastered all the Ari's holy writings.' Punning on the meaning of the name Ari, 'lion', and alluding to Samson's riddle in the book of Judges,[45] Landau goes on to assert that Ostrer took honey, namely kabbalistic knowledge, from the 'corpse of the lion', namely the Ari. As attested in this approbation, he greatly valued Ostrer's kabbalistic expertise.

Landau met other prominent kabbalists in Brody. He befriended Rabbi Perez ben Moses,[46] an ardent kabbalist of the *kloiz*, and wrote an approbation for

[39] Moses Maimonides wrote the classical Jewish philosophical work, the *Guide of the Perplexed*, between the years 1185 and 1190.

[40] Jacob Landau, *Divrei yedidot*, 32.

[41] Reiner, 'Wealth, Social Position and the Study of Torah' (Heb.), 317–18.

[42] See e.g. *NB Kama*, 'YD', nos. 45 and 46.

[43] Landau's approbation for Ostrer's *Arugat habosem*, dated 9 Adar I 5505 (11 Feb. 1745). I assume that Landau wrote the text of this approbation since he was the first of the two people who endorsed this approbation to sign it. Jacob Emden denounced Ostrer's *Arugat habosem* as a Sabbatian work; see his *Torat hakenaot*.

[44] The phrase 'the divine Chariot' alludes to the mystical vision of Ezekiel. Here, as is often the case, this phrase denotes kabbalah in general.

[45] See Judg. 14: 14, 18.

[46] On R. Perez b. Moses, see Gelber, 'History of the Jews of Brody' (Heb.), 60–1, 63; Piekarz, *Beginning of Hasidism* (Heb.), 86–8.

Perez's collected sermons, *Beit perets*.[47] He also met Rabbi Moses ben Jekuthiel Zalman, and in 1744 composed an approbation for the latter's Lurianic commentary, *Magid mishnah*.[48] He recounts that Moses visited the *kloiz* and studied 'both revealed and esoteric matters . . . In esoteric matters the sages also watched over him and the members of the *kloiz* declared his words righteous.' These approbations reveal that the Brody kabbalists not only respected Landau, but even sought his approval for their kabbalistic writings.

Among the other Brody kabbalists with whom Landau had a close connection were Rabbi Nathan ben Levi[49] and Rabbi Mordecai Margoliot.[50] Rabbi Nathan made such an impression upon him that Landau cites his words in the introduction to the *Tselaḥ* on *Berakhot*, published in 1791, almost fifty years after he had left Brody. There, he employs Nathan's teachings in order to explain the importance of kabbalistic study. In several of his works Landau also refers to the kabbalistic and talmudic insights of Rabbi Mordecai of Brody.[51] These interpretations often reflect Mordecai's knowledge of kabbalistic sources and tenets. As alluded to in the folk tale discussed earlier, there is also a possibility that Landau studied kabbalah with his relative and friend at the *kloiz*, Isaac Halevi Horowitz. In short, during his thirteen-year stay at the Brody *kloiz*, he both studied and interacted with many of the most illustrious eighteenth-century kabbalists and talmudists, who either resided there permanently or passed through this kabbalistic centre.[52]

Several months after leaving Brody,[53] Landau assumed the positions of chief rabbi and head of the yeshiva in the nearby Polish city of Yampol, in the district

[47] Landau's approbation for *Beit perets* is dated 5513. Since an exact date is not given, one cannot determine whether it was written in 1752 or 1753. Landau is the only person who signed this approbation and is therefore clearly its author. Perez's affiliation with the *kloiz* is mentioned on the title page of *Beit perets*.

[48] Landau's approbation for the *Magid mishnah*, a commentary on *Mafte'aḥ ha'olamot* ('Key of the Worlds'), the first volume of Raphael Emmanuel Hai Ricchi's Lurianic *Mishnat ḥasidim*, is dated 11 Kislev 5505 (16 Nov. 1744). I assume that Landau wrote the text of this approbation since he is the first of the two signatories; the other is Hayim Zanzer.

[49] On R. Nathan b. Levi, see Gelber, 'History of the Jews of Brody', 63, 67–8. On his father, Levi b. Solomon, who was involved with practical kabbalah, see ibid. 71.

[50] On R. Mordecai Margoliot, also known as R. Mordecai Hahasid, see ibid. 64, 71, 80 n. 137, 334, 339; Piekarz, *Beginning of Hasidism* (Heb.), 87 n. 66. Moses Ostrer was R. Mordecai Hahasid's instructor in kabbalah. The inscription on R. Mordecai's tombstone reads 'a hasid, a modest person, and a master of revealed and esoteric matters'.

[51] See e.g. *Tselaḥ*, *Ber.* 33*b* (p. 126). See also *Derushei hatselaḥ*, sermon 3, 6*b*.

[52] On Landau's acquaintance with other rabbis who spent time at the *kloiz*, see e.g. his 1753 approbation for Abraham Aryeh Leib of Minsk's unpublished *Mishnah berurah vehalakhah berurah al masekhet berakhot* ('Clarifications and Elaborations on the Mishnah and Halakhah of Tractate *Berakhot*'), where he writes that he met Aryeh Leib at the Brody *kloiz*. This approbation is housed in the Schwadron collection at the Hebrew University in Jerusalem.

[53] During these months between his residence in Brody and Yampol Landau returned with his wife and father-in-law to Dubno, in the Ukrainian province of Volhynia. See Kamelhar, *Mofet hador*, 8, 9.

of Volhynia.[54] He remained in these posts for almost ten years (1745–54) until he was appointed chief rabbi of Prague.[55] In Yampol he taught many students and enacted various ordinances.[56] In particular, he gained a reputation for his responsa and for his intricate and casuistic homilies, later published in *Doresh le-tsiyon*.[57] In 1750, he was also given the title 'prince of the land of Israel'.[58] In this capacity he administered charitable funds collected in Poland and the surrounding areas for the poor in the land of Israel.

While the hagiographic studies on Landau assert that his writings from Yampol relate only to legalistic matters,[59] his mystical orientation also manifests itself occasionally in his works from this period. For example, in *Igeret orḥot olam*, published by his son Israel in 1793, Israel cites a mystical interpretation of the nature of prophecy offered by his father in a Yampol homily. Israel's account is extremely valuable since it is taken from a manuscript in his possession more than thirty years before his father's Yampol sermons, *Doresh letsiyon*, were first published. In this homily, Landau states that all those who attained prophecy first and foremost had faith and cleaved to God. He explains that because they 'cleaved to the Creator, the Creator in His grace and mercy opened the channels of influence to their intellects and they perceived what is beyond the human intellect. [In this way] they saw visions of God.'[60] Landau's description of cleaving to God as the essential criterion for achieving prophecy draws upon both Maimonidean and kabbalistic imagery.[61] His employment of such mystical concepts in a Yampol homily exhibits that his kabbalistic education already influenced his writings in Yampol.

[54] Landau seems to have been appointed chief rabbi of Yampol in 1744. See n. 26 above and Jacob Landau, *Divrei yedidot*, 33. In any case, by 11 Feb. 1745 he had already signed his approbation for Ostrer's *Arugat habosem* as a resident of Yampol.

[55] As in Brody, Landau antagonized a prominent family in Yampol by pronouncing one of its members an adulteress who could no longer live with her husband. See *NB Kama*, 'EH', no. 72. Some scholars, such as Dr Klein and Kamelhar, assert that he had to leave Yampol because of this incident. See Klein, 'Zuschrift an Herrn Moses Mendelson in Hamburg', 526; Kamelhar, *Mofet hador*, 16–17. Others, such as Gelman, disagree. See Gelman, *The Noda Biyehudah and his Teaching* (Heb.), 13.

[56] For some of the ordinances Landau enacted for the Yampol Hevrah Kadishah, see Gelman, *The Noda Biyehudah and his Teaching* (Heb.), appendix A. Other ordinances that he enacted in Yampol are mentioned in his responsa. See e.g. *NB Kama*, 'OḤ', no. 33.

[57] The title *Doresh letsiyon* can be read in two ways: 'seeking Zion' and a 'preacher for Zion'. Landau is clearly playing with both these ideas. In Yampol, he delivered two sermons a year, like most rabbis, on the sabbaths before Yom Kippur and Passover.

[58] Gelber, 'History of the Jews of Brody' (Heb.), 45–6.

[59] See e.g. Gelman, *The Noda Biyehudah and his Teaching* (Heb.), 5. Gelman writes that while living in Yampol, Landau 'only focused on new interpretations of Torah and Jewish law'.

[60] Israel Landau citing the words of his father in *Igeret orḥot olam* (in the section commenting on *Igeret teiman*), 60–1 n. 1.

[61] For a discussion of both Maimonides' references to *devekut* and the ideal of *devekut* in prophetic and Cordoverian kabbalah as well as in Landau's writings, see Part III.

His veneration of kabbalah is once again evident in his famous compromise letter, *Igeret hashalom* (Epistle of Peace), written in Yampol in 1752, in an attempt to halt the Emden–Eybeschütz controversy.[62] This dispute, which divided much of European Jewry,[63] revolved around Jacob Emden's accusations that Jonathan Eybeschütz, a leading eighteenth-century rabbi, espoused heretical messianic doctrines and had issued Sabbatian amulets.[64] Although Landau's compromise letter, sent to rabbis throughout Europe, suggests that the amulets be removed and given to the courts, he does not demand their destruction. Instead, he recommends that the courts either bury them in the same manner as old holy books or return them to Eybeschütz. He likens Eybeschütz's mystical amulets, which are an obstacle to the people, to the biblical book of Ezekiel, which the sages had wished to conceal because of its mystical content.[65] Landau seems to express here that, despite the problematic nature of Eybeschütz's amulets, they should be treated as sacred texts like the book of Ezekiel.

Largely because of the great acclaim Landau received among European Jewry for his compromise letter, *Igeret hashalom*, in 1753 he was appointed chief rabbi of Prague, one of Europe's most distinguished rabbinic posts.[66] Beginning his tenure in 1754,[67] Landau became Prague Jewry's most venerated leader for nearly forty years.

Landau's years in Poland, particularly his studies and interactions with the Brody *kloiz* kabbalists, left a lasting impression upon him. In his later Prague works he refers both to his memories from Poland and to various kabbalistic ideas that he absorbed there. His responsa also include correspondence with several kabbalists whom he met at the Brody *kloiz*. Although neglected or dismissed by scholars and hagiographic studies, his kabbalistic education and experiences in eastern Europe influenced his personal theology and writings throughout his career.

62 *Igeret hashalom* is published in full in Emden's *Petaḥ einayim*, where Emden also accuses Landau of belonging to the Sabbatian sect. See *Petaḥ einayim*, 13*a* and Emden, *Sefer hitabekut*, 147*b*–148*b*. A section of *Igeret hashalom* appears in Eybeschütz's *Luḥot edut*, 41*b*–43*a*, and in the recent anonymous work *The Wisdom of the Noda Biyehudah*, 11–13.

63 For a discussion of this controversy's effect on 18th-c. Jewry, see Abramsky, 'Crisis of Authority', 15–17.

64 On the question of Eybeschütz's Sabbatianism, see Perlmuter, *Rabbi Jonathan Eybeschütz and his Relationship with Sabbatianism* (Heb.); Liebes, 'New Writings in Sabbatian Kabbalah from the Circle of Rabbi Jonathan Eybeschütz' (Heb.); Leiman, 'When a Rabbi Is Accused of Heresy'.

65 See *Yalqut Shimoni, Ezekiel, Remez* 346, BT *Shab.* 13*b*, *Ḥag.* 11*b*, 13*a*, and *Men.* 45*a*. These rabbinic sources state that at one time the talmudic sages considered eliminating the book of Ezekiel from the canon, so that its problematic laws and mystical account of the Chariot would not circulate.

66 His letter of appointment to the Prague rabbinate is dated 20 Kislev 5514 (16 Dec. 1753).

67 See Jacob Landau, *Divrei yedidot*. It appears, however, that Landau first came to Prague alone. He then returned to Yampol in order to bring his family to Prague in the summer of 1755. See *NB Kama*, 'EH', no. 36. In this responsum, dated 6 Av 5515 (14 July 1755), Landau writes that he plans to move from Yampol in a few days.

FIVE

Promotion of Kabbalistic Study, Books, and Customs

A RANGE OF kabbalistic customs, books, and teachings were promoted by Landau as a result of his kabbalistic orientation. In several approbations and other writings, he endorses kabbalistic works and the dissemination of kabbalistic ideas. Due to Landau's view that kabbalah is the key to understanding the inner truth of the aggadah, he both espouses the pedagogic importance of knowing kabbalistic concepts and offers kabbalistic readings of enigmatic *agadot*. His kabbalistic worldview also extends beyond the theoretical, affecting his opinions and recommendations in the realm of praxis. In addition to personally observing numerous kabbalistic and ascetic customs throughout his life, he encourages Prague Jews to perform these rituals as well. On occasion, his belief in kabbalah even informs his legal analysis and defence of halakhic positions.

While residing in Poland and then Prague, Landau issued approbations for several mystical works. He began giving approbations for kabbalistic treatises at the Brody *kloiz*, and continued to do so after leaving Brody. Of the sixty-eight approbations he wrote during his lifetime, five were for kabbalistic books. The first of these five was for Moses ben Jekuthiel Zalman's *Magid mishnah*, a commentary on the first volume of the Lurianic *Mishnat ḥasidim*.[1] In this approbation, composed in 1744, he describes the currently confused state of Lurianic writings and the tremendous contribution of Moses ben Jekuthiel towards alleviating the problem. He writes:

> [Moses] increased understanding of the *Mishnat ḥasidim*, which until now has been like the writings of sealed books, since it is written in an extremely abbreviated manner . . . Also, hitherto no one has looked at the *Ets ḥayim*, whose ways are hidden. This is because there are many editions of the *Ets ḥayim*, some of which contradict one another. They are also not placed in [correct] order, from beginning to end . . . Now both problems are corrected. For he [Moses] has shown the order of the *Ets ḥayim* in accordance with the *Mishnat ḥasidim* . . . Our request is that one should strengthen him. When his book . . . is published, those who are fearful of the word of God should jump to buy this book.[2]

[1] *Mishnat ḥasidim* consists of a work on Lurianic *kavanot* (extra-liturgical mystical intentions) and an abridgement of part of Vital's *Ets ḥayim*. See Ch. 4 n. 48.

[2] Landau's approbation for Moses b. Yekutiel Zalman's *Magid mishnah*.

Landau praises the author for adding some order to the chaotic state of Lurianic publications, extant in numerous and often contradictory editions. Notably, instead of condemning the *Magid mishnah* for promoting these esoteric teachings, he insists that the God-fearing 'should jump to buy this book'. His endorsement of this work calls for a re-evaluation of his alleged opposition both to the use of *kavanot* and to the wider spread of kabbalah.[3]

Several months after endorsing the *Magid mishnah*, Landau supported another kabbalistic work that also popularizes kabbalistic ideas: the eminent Brody *kloiz* mystic Moses Ostrer's *Arugat habosem*. This treatise includes Ostrer's commentary on the Song of Songs, based on the Zohar and Lurianic kabbalah; material culled from a commentary on the Song of Songs by the biblical exegete and mystic Rabbi Moses Alshekh (d. after 1593); and Ostrer's kabbalistic remarks on the Friday evening liturgy, particularly the poem *Lekhah dodi*. At the beginning, Ostrer presents several aids to understanding his book, such as an elaborate explication of Luria's kabbalistic principles and a sefirotic diagram. These aids probably opened this work to an audience less schooled in kabbalah. On the title page, which Landau may have seen, Ostrer explicitly states that he hopes that the writing, and presumably the reading, of these kabbalistic teachings will hasten the advent of the messianic age. In Landau's approbation for this treatise, written in Yampol in 1745, he strongly recommends its publication, thereby supporting the diffusion of kabbalistic themes to the public at large.

During his tenure as chief rabbi of Yampol, in *c.*1753, Landau composed another approbation for a Brody *kloiz* kabbalist's work replete with mystical teachings and written for a broad audience: Perez ben Moses' *Beit perets*. Unlike some of Landau's other approbations, in this endorsement, he asserts that he 'saw the composed book', so he must have known of its kabbalistic content.[4] In the treatise's introduction, Perez explains that this collection of homilies addresses both revealed and esoteric matters, and adds a kabbalistically influenced prayer asking for his soul to be spared from transmigration.[5] Undoubtedly aware of the mystical character of both the treatise and its author, Landau nonetheless endorsed the printing of *Beit perets*, which he claimed would benefit the masses.

In both Yampol and Prague, Landau also wrote approbations for the biblical commentaries of the sixteenth-century Safed rabbi and mystic Moses Alshekh.[6]

[3] Landau's complex attitude towards the *kavanot* is addressed in Part IV.

[4] In this approbation Landau only praises Perez's treatment of aggadah and *musar*. However, I maintain that he also knew and approved of its kabbalistic contents.

[5] This work is largely based on Perez's weekly sabbath and holiday sermons, which he delivered at the Brody *kloiz*.

[6] On Alshekh, see Shalem, *Rabbi Moses Alshekh* (Heb.); Pachter, 'Concept of Devekut'.

Although Alshekh employs kabbalah in a less explicit manner than the previously discussed books, his works incorporate kabbalistic ideas and reveal his mystical outlook. In Landau's first approbation for an Alshekh commentary, given in Yampol, he encourages the general public to read Alshekh's commentary on the Later Prophets.[7] Over ten years later,[8] in Prague in 1765, he wrote two approbations for a German translation of Alshekh's Genesis commentary.[9] In the first of these, he supports the use of this source by preachers, calling it a 'faithful foundation' upon which they can lean. Thus in several approbations Landau promotes the publication and wider dissemination of works which popularize zoharic and Lurianic ideas as well as other doctrines of Safed kabbalah.

Landau endorses the dissemination of kabbalistic teachings in his own writings as well, both implicitly and explicitly. Particularly during his Prague years, he emphasizes the significance of kabbalistic tenets by frequently including them in glosses and sermons, addressed respectively to his students and the larger community. His publication of some of these works further attests to his desire to popularize these kabbalistic notions.

Especially noteworthy is his introduction to the *Tselaḥ* on *Berakhot*, where he explains the pedagogic import of kabbalistic study and emphasizes the necessity of achieving fluency in kabbalistic terminology in order to attain insight into the truths of biblical and aggadic texts. By placing this discussion at the beginning of the *Tselaḥ* on *Berakhot*, which was published by his son in Prague during his lifetime,[10] he displays his desire to convey this understanding to a wide readership. Notably, these remarks on the need to study kabbalistic concepts are not directed at established scholars, but rather at his students, who, at least at this stage, did not belong to the learned elite.[11] In a revealing passage in this introduction, he recounts:

I heard in my youth . . . from Rabbi Nathan ben Levi of Brody concerning the ten *sefirot beli mah*,[12] and the thirty-two paths of wisdom . . . and the three aspects in the ten *sefirot*: right, left, and centre, and in them the three aspects: Grace, Judgement, and Mercy. It is beyond the reach of our human reason to comprehend the manner in which such concepts are applied on high, where such terms do not exist . . . But all these terms are a

[7] Landau signs his approbation for Alshekh's *Marot hatsove'ot* as 'Ezekiel Landau, a resident of Yampol'.

[8] Landau left Yampol in 1754–5. He consequently gave this approbation at least ten years later.

[9] His approbations for *The Book of Genesis with Translation in Judendeutsch* (Heb.) are dated 16 Aug. and 13 Sept. 1765.

[10] Israel Landau published this commentary with its introduction in 1791, during his father's lifetime and therefore clearly with his approval.

[11] In various places, Landau writes that he composed his *Tselaḥ* commentary for his students, e.g. *Tselaḥ*, *Ber.* 52*a* (p. 210) and *Pes.*, introd.

[12] On this term, which first appears in the mystical treatise *Sefer yetsirah*, see Part III.

distant introduction for us, and serve a purpose similar to teaching a child the alphabet. However, if we have but a slight knowledge of these notions, then we will merit that, in the future, when the material will be removed from our form, we will be enlightened . . . Then we will understand in truth the foundation of the Torah.[13]

Two important conclusions can be drawn from this reflection on the lessons of Landau's youth in Brody. First, it demonstrates that he not only concurs with Rabbi Nathan's statement, but adopts it as a goal in his talmudic commentary. He wants to familiarize his readers with kabbalistic concepts that he contends are a prerequisite for understanding the future revelation of profound mysteries. This passage also shows the tremendous impact of his studies at Brody, which he had left almost fifty years earlier.[14]

In accentuating the centrality of kabbalah in an introduction to his talmudic commentary, Landau deviates somewhat from the traditional hierarchy of study. Traditionally, kabbalah was only taught to individuals who had already attained proficiency in talmudic studies. In addition to this restriction, some halakhic authorities also maintain that kabbalah should only be taught to men over the age of 40.[15] Other eminent halakhists, such as the influential Rabbi Ya'ir Hayim Bacharach (1639–1702, known as the Havat Yair), frequently cited by Landau, even allege that one should distance oneself entirely from kabbalistic study since its subject matter is too lofty.[16] Clearly Landau, who promoted kabbalistic study in his talmudic commentary, intended especially for his students, did not follow these opinions. Nowhere in his introduction does he indicate that one should study kabbalah only after mastering a requisite amount of Talmud or achieving a specific age. His repeated use of kabbalistic terms in both his sermons and commentaries reveals that he disseminated kabbalistic concepts to the broader public who, at least by traditional standards, were not necessarily sufficiently prepared to study them.

A related motif, established by Landau in this introduction, is the connection between aggadah and kabbalah, and the need to study aggadah in order to understand the future revelation of esoteric matters. To demonstrate this point, he presents a parable in which a terrible storm leaves a group of sages and a pregnant woman shipwrecked on a deserted island. On this island, the woman

[13] *Tselaḥ*, *Ber.*, introd.

[14] As described above, Landau engaged in both rabbinic and kabbalistic study at the Brody *kloiz*. Members of the *kloiz* seem to have advanced simultaneously on the rabbinic and kabbalistic fronts. In this introduction he also stresses the importance of studying aggadah, which integrates both these disciplines, a notion that was probably also emphasized in Brody.

[15] See e.g. Shabetai b. Meir Hakohen (1621–62, known as the Shakh), *Siftei kohen*, gloss no. 6 on the *Shulḥan arukh*, 'YD', no. 246. This practice, however, was not universally accepted. For a discussion of this custom, see Idel, 'History of the Interdiction on the Study of Kabbalah before the Age of 40' (Heb.).

[16] Bacharach, *Ḥavat ya'ir*, no. 210.

gives birth to a son, whom the wise men educate. As the boy grows older, one of the men attempts to teach him the sounds of the letters of the alphabet,[17] but the boy, already having attained much knowledge, deems this study infantile. Only later, when 'God opens their eyes' and sends them a ship which returns them to civilization,[18] does the boy comprehend that without this rudimentary knowledge he cannot read books and obtain their great wisdom.

Using this parable, Landau emphasizes the importance of studying aggadah, which might seem abstruse and meaningless and which, during this period, was particularly denigrated by maskilim, who stressed the virtues of human reason and logic.[19] But aside from serving as part of his larger defence of rabbinic Judaism, his discussion of the significance of aggadah is largely a result of his mystical understanding of these texts.[20] He explains that the words of the aggadah

> are all only in parable, and in them a great light is hidden. But since a material cloud covers our human reason, we cannot gaze at this light. Nonetheless, without a superficial introduction to these aggadic teachings, we will not be able, even in the future, to comprehend or look at this hidden light.[21]

The introduction to *Berakhot*, containing this parable as well as the citation of Rabbi Nathan quoted earlier, evinces both Landau's belief in a mystical truth embedded in the aggadah and his conviction that everyone should study aggadah and kabbalah.

In both the *Tselaḥ* and his responsa Landau presents the aggadah as the outer form of kabbalistic truth and the foundations of religion. In one responsum he pronounces that all the *agadot* are rooted in secrets from above.[22] Echoing this sentiment in another responsum, he asserts that all the words of the talmudic sages, including the aggadah, 'were given from one Shepherd'.[23] If we find them

17 Here Landau likens the study of aggadah to teaching a child the alphabet. Interestingly, in this introduction he makes the same analogy with the study of kabbalah.

18 *Tselaḥ*, *Ber.*, introduction. Landau employs the same phrase here—'God opens their eyes'—as that used in Gen. 3: 5, 7, where it is used to depict the comprehension of good and evil acquired by Adam and Eve after eating from the Tree of Knowledge. Perhaps, through this play on words, he intended to compare that first revelation of knowledge with the future revelation of kabbalistic secrets.

19 On Landau's defence of the aggadah against the derision of the maskilim, see Part I.

20 Maimonides preceded Landau in claiming that the aggadah contains deeper layers of meaning. See his *Guide of the Perplexed*, introd. and i. 71; id., *Commentary on the Mishnah*, introd.; id., *Perek ḥelek*, introd.; id., *Letter on Astrology*, and elsewhere. Landau's view of the aggadah, however, is markedly different. Whereas for Maimonides the aggadah alludes to metaphysical truths, for Landau it points to kabbalistic doctrines. Landau's conception of the aggadah as housing esoteric truths is quite similar to some of the teachings of the 16th-c. Judah Loew of Prague (Maharal). For a discussion of various medieval and early modern rabbinic, philosophical, and kabbalistic approaches to the aggadah, see Elbaum, 'Rabbi Judah Loew of Prague and his Attitude to the Aggadah'; Saperstein, *Decoding the Rabbis*, 1–20.

21 *Tselaḥ*, *Ber.*, introd.

22 *NB Kama*, 'OḤ', no. 24.

23 This phrase is from Eccles. 12: 11. His response here is based on a talmudic passage in BT *Ḥag.* 3*b*, which also cites this biblical phrase in order to refer to the divine origin of the plurality of

senseless, it is due to our inability to perceive what the sages hinted at in the *agadot* 'which deal with the principal matters of faith'.[24]

Nevertheless, one should note that although a few of Landau's responsa point to his tremendous veneration for the aggadah and the secrets hidden therein, he usually refrains from discussing *agadot* in his responsa. On the few occasions where he does, he addresses these matters rather briefly, stating that, since he is primarily involved with halakhah, he does not have time to dwell on aggadah.[25] His attitude expresses his determined attempt to focus exclusively on halakhic matters in his responsa as well as his acute ambivalence about disseminating esoteric teachings.

In the body of the *Tselaḥ*, however, addressed to his Prague students and a wider Ashkenazi audience, Landau promotes the importance of studying aggadah and even discusses some of its esoteric secrets in a more open manner. He repeatedly emphasizes the necessity of gaining familiarity with aggadah, stressing that it needs to be comprehensible at the literal as well as at other levels.[26] He sometimes attempts to reveal kabbalistic concepts and deeper mystical layers required for a more profound understanding of this literature. Nonetheless, even here, in a gloss on an enigmatic *agadah*, he warns that although the 'enlightened'—a term for those who know kabbalah—can grasp some of the hidden nuances hinted at in the aggadah, these truths will remain veiled to most people. He even resigns himself to the reality that, at present, the deepest stratum of the aggadah eludes all mankind. In one gloss, in which he laments that aggadic texts remain largely obscure, he prays for a second revelation like that at Sinai, in which God will disclose their full meaning.[27] Characteristically, immediately after this prayer, he presents a kabbalistic interpretation of the recondite *agadah* at hand.

Landau's occasional interchanging of the terms Torah and aggadah underscores his view that both are divine teachings containing esoteric dimensions. Echoing his remarks on the aggadah, he asserts that the esoteric meaning of the Torah and its commandments will be disclosed in the future.[28] Likewise, in the preface to the *Tselaḥ* on *Berakhot*, he remarks that, in the future God will

halakhic opinions. Landau's extension of the passage to affirm the divine origin of the aggadah is a subtle but noteworthy innovation.

[24] *NB Tinyana*, 'YD', no. 161. In this responsum he scorns those who mock the aggadah.

[25] On Landau's repeated claim that he does not deal with the aggadah in his responsa, see my discussion below and n. 87.

[26] See *Tselaḥ*, *Ber.* 18*b* (p. 74), where he writes that even though all the *agadot* contain hidden esoteric teachings, their literal interpretation needs to be comprehensible in a manner that does not contradict natural law. See also ibid., *Ber.* 54*b* (p. 213).

[27] Ibid., *Ber.* 34*b* (pp. 129, 130).

[28] See e.g. ibid., where he writes that the 'secrets of the Torah which are concealed and reserved will be revealed in the future'.

'reveal the secret reasons of the Torah and other hidden mysteries'. For Landau, then, knowledge of basic kabbalistic tenets is necessary in order to partake in the forthcoming revelation of the mysteries of the aggadah and Torah.

Kabbalistic Customs

Besides promoting the pedagogic importance of studying kabbalah and aggadah, Landau's kabbalistic convictions compelled him to observe and advocate various kabbalistic customs.[29] Although in his responsa he professes that one should only follow customs prescribed by the Talmud or the early talmudic commentators,[30] he does not always keep to this principle. What is more, despite claims by scholars such as Wind and Hess that Landau contends that customs based on kabbalistic teachings should be abolished,[31] he actually exhorts Prague Jews to follow certain kabbalistic rituals.

Several sources from Landau's years in Prague indicate his kabbalistic proclivity and practices. In the two eulogies Fleckeles composed for his teacher,[32] he vividly portrays Landau's consistent observance of kabbalistic customs as well as his mystical knowledge. In the second eulogy, Fleckeles attests that Landau was a light in both matters of Talmud and 'the divine Chariot', namely the kabbalah.[33] Since Fleckeles remained in close contact with him from when he entered Landau's academy in 1768 until Landau's death in 1793,[34] he probably observed his teacher's facility with kabbalistic texts as well as his practice of kabbalistic rituals for many years. In the first eulogy, Fleckeles relates that 'never did a midnight pass upon him, until close to his death, in which he did not mourn

29 On the relationship between kabbalah and various Jewish customs, see Hallamish, *Kabbalah in Liturgy, Halakhah, and Customs* (Heb.); J. Katz, *Halakhah and Kabbalah* (Heb.).

30 See e.g. *NB Tinyana*, 'OḤ', no. 15, where he asserts that there is no room for legal discussions concerning matters that are rooted neither in the Talmud nor in the early codes. In a similar vein, see also *NB Kama*, 'EH', no. 9, where, despite a contravening custom, he permits a man to marry a *katlanit* (lit. killer), a halakhic term denoting a woman who has been widowed three times, since this custom is not talmudic.

31 See Wind, *Rabbi Ezekiel Landau* (Heb.), 89; Hess, 'Rabbi Ezekiel Landau' (Heb.), 270.

32 The first eulogy was delivered at Landau's funeral on 30 Apr. 1793 (Lag Ba'omer), and the second on 8 May 1793 at the Klaus synagogue in Prague. See Fleckeles, *Olat ḥodesh hashelishi*, sermon 17, 71*a*–78*a*.

33 Fleckeles, *Olat ḥodesh hashelishi*, 73*a*. Appropriating a talmudic phrase that describes R. Yohanan's erudition (BT *Suk.* 28*a* and *BB* 134*a*), Fleckeles states that 'Landau mastered both the small and the great matters, the small matters meaning the dialectics of Abaye and Rava [i.e. the Talmud], the great matters meaning the divine Chariot.' The medieval rabbinic commentators debated what the Talmud means by 'great matters'. Notably, Fleckeles sides with the group of interpreters who view the 'great matters' as referring to mysticism.

34 Spitz, *Zikhron elazar*, 3. Fleckeles came to Landau's academy at the age of 14. They remained in close contact even while Fleckeles served as the rabbi of Kojetin in Moravia from 1779 to 1783.

the destruction of the Temple and the exile of the Shekhinah, as it were.'[35] This description refers to Landau's nightly performance of the kabbalistic *tikun ḥatsot* vigil,[36] a ritual not found in any talmudic source.[37] While apparently originating in thirteenth-century kabbalistic writings from Gerona, this ritual first developed into a full rite of lamentation in the sixteenth-century mystical community of Safed.[38] Fleckeles' description of Landau's observance of *tikun ḥatsot* echoes accounts of this ritual found in numerous sixteenth-century Safed kabbalistic writings.[39]

Fleckeles further recounts Landau's nightly ritual of 'joining day and night with Torah and prayer',[40] a custom which is also rooted in kabbalistic sources, such as the Zohar and the writings of Safed kabbalism.[41] By studying Torah until daybreak, Landau seems to have deliberately integrated his nightly and daily learning in order to attain the kabbalistic ideal of connecting 'the quality of night and day', or the attributes of justice and mercy.

Aside from the evidence that Landau observed kabbalistic customs, there is even an account of his personal mystical experience. In a eulogy delivered in 1769, he describes a prophetic dream vision he had received.[42] The eulogy, which is included in neither *Ahavat tsiyon* nor *Derushei hatselaḥ*, was first printed only in the twentieth century, in a collection of Eybeschütz's writings.[43] It was

[35] Fleckeles, *Olat ḥodesh hashelishi*, sermon 17, 72*a*.

[36] For a discussion of *tikun ḥatsot*, see Scholem, *Kabbalah and its Symbolism*, 146–50; Fine, *Safed Spirituality*, 13, 17–18; Robinson, 'Messianic Prayer Vigils'; Horowitz, 'Coffee, Coffeehouses, and the Nocturnal Rituals of Early Modern Jewry'; Magid, 'Conjugal Union, Mourning and *Talmud Torah*'; Idel, *Messianic Mystics*, 308–20.

[37] Although BT *Ber.* 3*a* states that God roars like a lion during the three watches of the night, the Talmud does not encourage conducting vigils at these times.

[38] While the Zohar and other 13th-c. kabbalistic sources stress the importance of rising at midnight, the custom of lamenting the exiled Shekhinah at midnight did not develop into a full rite until the 16th c. On 16th-c. Safed kabbalists' emphasis on the necessity of praying and studying at midnight on behalf of the exiled Shekhinah, see e.g. de Vidas, *Reshit ḥokhmah*, 'Sha'ar hakedushah', esp. ch. 7, 143–88. However, although the Safed kabbalist Joseph Karo includes *tikun ḥatsot* in his legal codex *Shulḥan arukh* ('OḤ', 1: 2), he does not, in this work, promote wailing for the exiled Shekhinah at this hour, as do other kabbalists, including Landau.

[39] See e.g. de Vidas, *Reshit ḥokhmah*, 'Sha'ar hakedushah', ch. 7, 185, where de Vidas states that at midnight one should mourn and pray for the downtrodden Shekhinah and the destroyed Temple, engaging in Torah study afterwards.

[40] Fleckeles' first eulogy for Landau, *Olat ḥodesh hashelishi*, sermon 17, 72*a*.

[41] The Zohar states that a person must engage in Torah study until daybreak in order to join the attributes of the night to the attributes of the day (Zohar, ii. 46*a*, 130*b*). Safed kabbalists reiterate this zoharic idea in various writings. See e.g. de Vidas, *Reshit ḥokhmah*, 'Sha'ar ha'ahavah', ch. 3, 390, and 'Sha'ar hakedushah', ch. 7, 143, 161–4.

[42] The connection between dreams and prophecy is discussed in several places in rabbinic literature. A passage in BT *Ber.* 57*b* states that a dream is one-sixtieth part of prophecy. Elsewhere, however, the Talmud notes that prophetic dreams bear no significance. See e.g. BT *Hor.* 13*b*.

[43] 'Ezekiel Landau's Eulogy for Meir Fischels Bumsla' (Heb.), 18 Kislev 5530 (17 Dec. 1769).

composed for Meir Fischels (Bumsla), who (as described in Chapter 2) presided over the Jewish High Court and a large yeshiva during his forty-year Prague career, and includes Landau's assertion that he was ordered to deliver this funeral speech 'from the heavens'.[44] He explains that two weeks earlier,[45] he received a vision in his sleep, in which he was told a biblical verse. In this visionary state, he proceeded to ask 'those who spoke to him' for the meaning of the vision. The voices told him of Meir Fischels's immanent death, and instructed him to use the verse in his eulogy for Fischels.

Exhibiting his typical ambivalence about discussing mystical matters, Landau declines to reveal the rest of the dream after disclosing this part of it. He does, however, advise his audience to pay close attention to all the ideas that he will convey, stating that the 'enlightened' (*hamaskil*)—a standard code word for kabbalistic initiates—will understand the teachings that he cannot fully disclose.[46] He also reports that because of the distressing information revealed in this vision, received on a Friday night, he fasted on the following Saturday and Sunday.[47] His fasting on the sabbath, a day on which one is halakhically obligated to feast and ordinarily prohibited from fasting,[48] demonstrates the gravity of this vision in his eyes. Notably, Landau includes both a description of this vision and an allusion to its deeper meaning in a eulogy delivered at this prominent official's funeral, which was undoubtedly widely attended. Despite his professed reluctance to discuss the vision's details, he wanted Prague Jewry to know of his 'prophetic' dream from 'the heavens' and the significance he ascribed to it.

Landau also advocates that members of Prague Jewry observe several kabbalistic rituals. He particularly urges them to conduct the midnight vigil for the

[44] Ibid. 52*b*.

[45] Although the printed copy states that this vision occurred on the seventh day of Kislev, I maintain that it transpired on 2 Kislev because Landau states that it had occurred on a Friday fifteen days previously. 7 Kislev, however, was a Wednesday and only twelve days earlier.

[46] 'Ezekiel Landau's Eulogy for Meir Fischels Bumsla' (Heb.), 53*a*. Interestingly, the Hebrew words used by Landau to describe his dream vision (*mareh*, *ḥalom*) are the same words found in the Bible's description of prophetic visions. See Num. 12: 6.

[47] Rabbinic works discuss the notion of a *ta'anit ḥalom*, a fast held after a bad dream. Various rabbinic sources maintain that if one has a nightmare on a Friday night one should even fast on the sabbath, a day on which fasting is usually prohibited (see n. 48 below). See BT *Shab.* 11*a*, *Ta'an.* 12*b*; *Tur*, 'OḤ', 288; Karo, *Beit yosef*, 'OḤ', 220, 288. However, some rabbinic texts state that those who fast on the sabbath need to fast once more on a weekday in order to atone for dishonouring the sabbath. See BT *Ber.* 31*b*; *Tur*, 'OḤ', 288; *Shulḥan arukh*, 'OḤ', 288: 4. Landau's fasts on this occasion seem to follow these rabbinic teachings.

[48] On the halakhic imperative to feast on the sabbath, see Karo, *Beit yosef*, 'OḤ', 288. In Jewish law, the notion that one must feast on the sabbath is said to be *divrei kabalah* (lit. words of tradition), and is based on the biblical phrase 'call the sabbath delight' (Isa. 58: 13). In halakhah, *divrei kabalah* are commonly accorded a status in between a biblical and a rabbinic commandment. On the prohibition against fasting on the sabbath, see *Tur*, 'OḤ', 288; *Shulḥan arukh*, 'OḤ', 288: 1, 5, 8; 578: 1.

exiled Shekhinah. Three years after arriving in Prague, he delivered a sermon on the sabbath before Yom Kippur,[49] in which he laments Prague Jewry's neglect of this custom. He exclaims:

both the learned and the unaccomplished, first and foremost, should organize to conduct the *tikun ḥatsot* regularly in order to shed tears for the exiled Shekhinah . . . especially in our time . . . We should wage a war of intrigue against the *kelipot* [shells; evil forces] and weaken their strength through the *tikun ḥatsot*.[50]

Like the Safed kabbalists,[51] Landau insists that everyone, not just the learned elite, be diligent in their observance of this nightly ritual and that they shed tears for the forlorn Shekhinah. In accordance with zoharic teachings,[52] he points to the urgency of observing this custom after so many years of exile. He explains that the *tikun ḥatsot* helps to subdue the demonic *kelipot*, whose existence prolongs the exile of both the Shekhinah and the Jewish people.

The kabbalistic *tikun ḥatsot* is promoted in some of his other writings. For example, in one homily he laments that while one should rise at midnight, when God visits His ruined Temple, 'in our great iniquities, the heads of households are not present at their watches' during this hour.[53] Echoing these ideas, he stresses in another Prague sermon that

it is a mitsvah to rise during the middle of the night. Moreover, a great thing was instituted here to conduct vigils. Yet in our many sins, this has ceased for some people because they are too slothful to attend . . . One should make the utmost effort to uphold this ritual.[54]

The note of urgency in his plea here is probably a reaction to the dwindling of Prague's *tikun ḥatsot* confraternity, which he hoped to revive. He may also be decrying the spreading influence of the Sabbatian sect in Prague. Some Sabbatians annulled the *tikun ḥatsot* vigil because they believed that since they were already

[49] See *Derushei hatselaḥ*, sermon 4. This homily is from *c.*1757. At the beginning of the sermon, Landau states that this is his third annual Shabat Teshuvah homily in Prague. Since he moved to Prague with his family in the summer of 1755, he probably delivered his first Shabat Teshuvah sermon there in that year.

[50] Ibid. 9*b*. Landau explains that it is particularly urgent that all individuals observe the *tikun ḥatsot* vigil in his generation, since the evildoers are strengthening the *kelipot*, thus contributing to the lengthy exile.

[51] See e.g. de Vidas, *Reshit ḥokhmah*, 'Sha'ar hakedushah', ch. 7, 154, where the author emphasizes that both the sages and the masses should participate in studying Torah at midnight in order to honour the Shekhinah.

[52] See Zohar, i. 242*b*. The Zohar claims that those who observe *tikun ḥatsot* subjugate the *kelipot*. This idea is also cited in de Vidas, *Reshit ḥokhmah*, 'Sha'ar hakedushah', ch. 7, 143.

[53] See *Derushei hatselaḥ*, sermon 9 (5 Oct. 1769), 18*b*. Although the idea that God laments the destroyed Temple at midnight has talmudic origins (BT *Ber.* 3*a*), the notion that an organized vigil should be conducted at midnight for the exiled Shekhinah is uniquely kabbalistic. Landau also refers to these teachings in the source cited below.

[54] *Derushei hatselaḥ*, sermon 25, 39*a*.

living in messianic times *tikun ḥatsot* was obsolete.[55] One of Landau's responsa similarly exhibits his belief in the importance of mourning at midnight.[56] Instead of simply insisting that a particular penitent confess his sins, Landau, in line with numerous kabbalists, advises him to weep heavily over the Exile every midnight.[57]

Corresponding to Landau's promotion of *tikun ḥatsot* in his own writings are several recently found Prague *tikun ḥatsot* prayer books (discussed in Chapter 1). These reveal that such liturgical works were published in Prague on at least three occasions during Landau's tenure, and indicate their use by Prague Jews.[58] These publications were almost certainly produced with his knowledge, if not his outright endorsement.

Landau also observed numerous ascetic customs, as did many medieval Jewish mystics and later kabbalists,[59] and was especially influenced by ascetic practices espoused by sixteenth-century Safed kabbalists.[60] In Fleckeles' eulogies for his teacher, he records a wide range of ascetic practices observed by Landau. Among the most dramatic of these are that he habitually slept fully dressed in a chair, regularly donned sackcloth, frequently fasted, and always went to the *mikveh* after nocturnal seminal emissions, even in the cold of winter.[61] Even if Fleckeles' portrayal is exaggerated, it is clear that Landau regularly observed an array of ascetic rituals.

[55] See Scholem, *Sabbatai Sevi*, 501. Other Sabbatians did recite the *tikun ḥatsot*, but not in the regular manner. See Scholem, *Kabbalah and its Symbolism*, 150. Kamelhar suggests that Landau's criticism here is directed at the 'new hasidim' who annulled the *tikun ḥatsot*. See Kamelhar, *Mofet hador*, 59.

[56] *NB Kama*, 'OḤ', no. 35 (1769 or 1770). This responsum is addressed to a scholar who had an adulterous relationship with a married woman who later—oddly enough—became his mother-in-law.

[57] Ibid. Interestingly, Landau promotes the observance of this kabbalistic custom immediately after telling the penitent that he should only study passages in Isaiah Horowitz's kabbalistic *musar* work *Shenei luḥot haberit*, which are not influenced by kabbalah.

[58] *Tikun ḥatsot* prayer books were published in Prague in 1767, 1782, and 1787. See Ch. 1.

[59] On asceticism in rabbinic culture and kabbalistic writings before the 16th c., see Urbach, 'Askesis and Suffering in Talmudic and Midrashic Sources' (Heb.); Fraade, 'Ascetical Aspects of Ancient Judaism'; Wolfson, 'Eunuchs who Keep the Sabbath'.

[60] On asceticism in the writings and practices of the 16th-c. Safed kabbalists, see Werblowsky, *Joseph Karo*, esp. 38–83, 133–9, 161–5; Pachter, 'Concept of Devekut', 200–10; Schechter, 'Safed in the Sixteenth Century', esp. 244–6, 283; Fine, 'Purifying the Body in the Name of the Soul'; id., *Safed Spirituality*, 11–16. Even the Safed kabbalists Cordovero and de Vidas, who are often noted for promoting the importance of joy in worship, stress the value of asceticism. See e.g. de Vidas, *Reshit ḥokhmah*, 'Sha'ar ha'ahavah', ch. 11, 635.

[61] See Fleckeles' two eulogies for Landau, *Olat ḥodesh hashelishi*, sermon 17, 72*a* and 77*a*. As mentioned, Fleckeles lists other forms of self-mortification practised by Landau into his old age. Almost all ascetic practices listed are rooted in medieval mystical and pietistic sources and later kabbalistic works, particularly Cordoverian and Lurianic writings. On the practice of going to the *mikveh* after nocturnal seminal emissions, see e.g. BT *Ber.* 22*a*, though the Talmud states there that this practice is no longer required. In contrast, many 16th-c. kabbalistic sources do promote the ascetic rituals observed by Landau. See e.g. de Vidas, *Reshit ḥokhmah*, 'Sha'ar hakedushah', ch. 7, 185; Cordovero, 'Rules of Piety', in Fine, *Safed Spirituality*, 34–8, and esp. 51.

Like the sixteenth-century Safed kabbalists and authors of later *musar* treatises, Landau often promotes ascetic practices. He particularly entreats Prague Jews to adhere to ascetic customs as part of their repentance process, albeit occasionally warning them that these practices are senseless without the appropriate accompanying remorse. Moreover, in consonance with medieval and early modern Ashkenazi pietistic, Lurianic and *musar* writings, he specifically implores his community to perform *teshuvat hamishkal* (commensurate repentance) by fasting and weeping in proportion to the sins they have committed.[62] Employing mythical and kabbalistic notions, he repeatedly claims that both *teshuvat hamishkal* and other acts of self-mortification effectively destroy the *kelipot* and other demonic powers.[63] Although most of Landau's endorsements of ascetic ideals appear in his homilies, in one responsum he painstakingly lists and prescribes numerous ascetic penances, including a life-long regimen of scheduled fasts, for a particular penitent.[64]

In a 1765 eulogy, Landau also advocates the kabbalistic custom of praying at the graves of *tsadikim* (righteous individuals).[65] While some halakhic authorities,

[62] See e.g. *Ahavat tsiyon*, sermon 2, 4*b*; *Derushei hatselah*, sermon 1, 3*b*, 4*b*; sermon 2 for the Ten Days of Repentance, 6*a*; sermon 5 for the first day of *Selihot* prayers, 10*b*; sermon 19, 29*a*; sermon 20 for the Ten Days of Repentance, 31*a*; sermon 30, 46*a*. At times, Landau explicitly asserts that these ideas are found in the *musar* literature. See ibid., sermon 1, 4*b*; *NB Kama*, 'OH', no. 35. *Teshuvat hamishkal* is particularly stressed in the works of the medieval Hasidei Ashkenaz, especially *Sefer haroke'ah*, written by R. Eleazar b. Judah of Worms (*c.*1165–*c.*1230). On *teshuvat hamishkal* and other acts of self-mortification in Ashkenazi rabbinic culture, see Elbaum, *Repentance and Self-Flagellation* (Heb.).

[63] See e.g. *Derushei hatselah*, sermon 2, 6*a* , and sermon 19, 29*a*. Unlike the concept of *teshuvat hamishkal*, which appears in both mystical and non-mystical ethical and halakhic works, the notion of the demonic *kelipot* is found only in kabbalistic writings.

[64] See his dramatic response in *NB Kama*, 'OH', no. 35: 'Even though I am lenient regarding fasting, mortification, and *teshuvat hamishkal* for this individual, we cannot dismiss him without imposing anything . . . For the remainder of the summertime, he is to fast one day each week, except for the month of Elul, during which he is to fast two or three times, according to his ability; during the Ten Days of Repentance he is to fast day after day; and during the wintertime . . . he is to fast three days each week, of which one should be a complete night and day. He is to act in this manner for three consecutive years. [. . .] Other mortifications were already mentioned by his excellency, that he does not sleep on a bed at all, and this is sufficient. He is to avoid mirth, and not laugh during these three years [. . .] All the days of the week he is not to drink wine, whisky, or any drink . . . all his life he is to fast one day each week, and in the summer, on the eve of the new moon . . . during the [Ten] Days of Repentence, he is to fast every day.' Further, although Landau professes to dismiss the importance of the penitential requirements insisted upon by various pietists and mystics, he nonetheless stresses here a kabbalistic view of the theurgical effects of sin upon the supernal realm and that acts of penitence are required in accordance with the frequency and severity of a sin. In fact, like the pietistic work *Sefer haroke'ah*, he prescribes an extremely rigorous penitential regimen for the sinner as a result of these mystical notions.

[65] Landau, *Ahavat tsiyon*, sermon 6 ('Eulogy for Samuel Heilman and Asher Anshel Oizers, 10 Feb. 1765)'. Various hasidic leaders also endorsed this practice. See e.g. the Besht's request in a letter to Abraham Gershon of Kutow that the latter mention his name during his pilgrimages to gravesites. See Vilnai, *Holy Tombstones in the Land of Israel* (Heb.), 17.

such as Maimonides, did not support this practice,[66] Landau, like other rabbis and kabbalists,[67] especially those of sixteenth-century Safed,[68] asserts that this custom could secure the intercession of the deceased in times of need.[69] However, his contention that the power of the deceased *tsadik* is restricted to the area of his grave is not rooted in any specific rabbinic or kabbalistic source, but seems to be his own idea.[70] In the aforementioned eulogy, he elaborates that although a *tsadik* serves as the generation's intercessor without any stimulus from others during his lifetime, after his death his power extends only to those who arouse him directly at his grave. During times of disaster, people should therefore rejoice to find a grave of a *tsadik*, where they can pray for his intercession.[71] This notion of localizing the power of deceased *tsadikim* may have prompted Landau's congregants to visit and pray at gravesites of distinguished individuals in Prague and its environs.[72] Interestingly, he includes these kabbalistic ideas in a eulogy for two prominent rabbis, which he probably delivered to a large audience.

[66] Maimonides even objects to marking the burial places of the righteous (*Mishneh torah*, 'Laws of Mourning', 4: 4). He concludes this ruling by stating that people should refrain from going to cemeteries. On the one occasion that he does describe the practice of visiting a cemetery, the purpose of the visit is to serve as a sober reminder of man's mortality (see *Mishneh torah*, 'Laws of Fasts', 4: 18). This comment seems to be based on one opinion cited in BT *Ta'an.* 16*a*, and appears to reject the alternative opinion cited there, namely that the purpose of the visit is to ask for the intercession of the righteous. The Tosafot seem to embrace this alternative opinion. See Tosafot, BT *Sot.* 34*a*.

[67] The notion of praying at the graves of pious individuals appears only in a few talmudic passages. See BT *Ta'an.* 16*a*, 23*b*, *Sot.* 34*b*, *BM* 85*b*. For a later rabbinic source that mentions the custom of praying at the graves of the righteous in order to obtain their intercession, see Joseph b. Meir Teomim (*c.*1727–92), *Peri megadim* on *Shulḥan arukh*, 'OḤ', 581. Several rabbinic authorities nevertheless claim that one should not use deceased *tsadikim* as intercessors. They emphasize that if one prays at a *tsadik*'s grave because it is holy ground, one should always pray directly to God, and not to the *tsadik*. See e.g. the opinion of the Maharil (Jacob b. Moses Moellin, *c.* 1360–1427) quoted in Judah Ashkenazi's commentary *Be'er hetev* on *Shulḥan arukh*, 'OḤ', 581: 17 and the remarks of Israel Meir Hakohen (Hafets Hayim), *Mishnah berurah* on 'OḤ', 581: 4. In contrast, the Zohar asserts that in times of crisis people should go to the graves of righteous individuals in order to ask for intercession (see Zohar, iii. 70*b*–71*a*). On praying at gravesites in classical kabbalah, see Giller, 'Recovering the Sanctity of the Galilee'. On cemetery prayer in early modern Jewish society, see E. Horowitz, 'Speaking to the Dead'.

[68] On Cordovero's and Luria's practice of praying at the gravesites of righteous individuals, see Liebes, 'New Directions in the Study of the Kabbalah' (Heb.), 165. On this custom in Lurianic and Cordoverian kabbalah, see Meroz, 'Redemption in Lurianic Teaching' (Heb.), 287–91.

[69] On the powers of the *tsadik* in kabbalistic and hasidic literature, see Piekarz, *Hasidic Leadership* (Heb.).

[70] The closest source to this idea is *Hazharot nosafot letsava'at yehudah heḥasid* ('Additional Prohibitions of Judah Hehasid's Will'), no. 5, published in Judah Hehasid, *Sefer ḥasidim*, 32. In this will, Judah Hehasid (13th c.) instructs those who have a graveyard in their city to refrain from praying to the dead in another city for this will cause the deceased of their own town to harm them. However, he does not mention the idea of localizing the power of the *tsadik*, as found in Landau's writings.

[71] Landau, *Ahavat tsiyon*, sermon 6, 10*a*–*b*.

[72] Since many illustrious rabbis are buried in the Old Jewish Cemetery of Prague, Landau's congregants may have prayed there. Prague Jews may also have made pilgrimages to the gravesites in the vicinity: such pilgrimages were a prevalent practice in numerous hasidic communities.

Another kabbalistic ritual which Landau appears to sanction is the monthly fast day, Yom Kippur Katan (Minor Day of Atonement).[73] This fast, first mentioned in the *Reshit ḥokhmah*,[74] originated in sixteenth-century Safed, where it was observed by both men and women. Held on the day before each new moon, the fast has its own liturgy, which, like that of the *tikun ḥatsot*, focuses on the exile and the anticipated redemption of both the Shekhinah and Israel.[75] That this kabbalistic fast day along with its liturgical service was observed in Prague during Landau's career is evident from the inclusion of its liturgy in most Prague prayer books published during the latter half of the eighteenth century, specifically in 1757, 1782, 1785 and 1798.[76] In fact, these prayer books refer to minor variations in the Yom Kippur Katan liturgy adopted by the Prague Jewish community.[77] Notably, in Landau's talmudic commentary on *Pesaḥim*, he 'finds merit' for a divergent liturgical variation in this service adopted in other communities. He even takes exception to other authorities' vituperative condemnation of these communities' particular style of reciting these prayers.[78] Both his defence of a disputed variation of this liturgy and his tolerance, if not outright support, of the publication of this kabbalistic service in several Prague prayer books indicate his general approval of this kabbalistic rite.

Landau also seems to have adopted various kabbalistic liturgical practices.[79] In a responsum in *Teshuvah me'ahavah*, Fleckeles notes that Landau employed numerous Sephardi prayer formulations and customs in private.[80] Landau's

[73] On Yom Kippur Katan, see Scholem, *Kabbalah and its Symbolism*, 151–3; Fine, *Safed Spirituality*, 12.

[74] De Vidas, *Reshit ḥokhmah*, 'Sha'ar hateshuvah', ch. 4, 762–4.

[75] The Yom Kippur Katan liturgy emphasizes that just as the moon, through its monthly cycles of waxing and waning, never remains incomplete, likewise Israel and the Shekhinah should be unified with God and not remain incomplete.

[76] See *Maḥzor*, published by Yehudah Lipmann and his brothers (Prague, 1756 or 1757), ii. 55*a*–57*a*; *Maḥzor*, published by Bezalel b. Samuel Fleckeles and Samuel b. Leizer Bahur (Prague, 1782), ii. 55*a*–57*a*; *Maḥzor*, Elfenwangerfehen publishers (Prague, 1785), ii. 77*b*–82*a*. For the inclusion of the Yom Kippur Katan liturgy in an earlier Prague work, see *Seder shomerim laboker* (1692), 49*a*–69*b*.

[77] These prayer books state that it was the custom in Prague not to recite the phrase *barukh shem kevod malkhuto* ['Blessed be the Name of His glorious Kingdom'] after reciting the Shema Yisra'el during the Yom Kippur Katan liturgy. Interestingly, in Landau's commentary (see below, n. 78), he not only defends the practice of reciting this phrase, but also that of reciting it out loud, rather than in the customary whisper. Perhaps this had been his custom in Poland.

[78] *Tselaḥ*, *Pes.* 56*a* (p. 219).

[79] For a discussion of Landau's defence of several liturgical formulations on the basis of kabbalistic notions, see p. 126 below.

[80] Fleckeles, *Teshuvah me'ahavah*, i, no. 90, 54*b*. However, Fleckeles states that Landau did not institute the use of these customs among Prague Jews. In a gloss in his talmudic commentary, Landau even criticizes Ashkenazi Jews who adopt a certain Sephardi liturgical formulation, claiming that individuals should not deviate from their family customs. See *Tselaḥ*, *Ber.* 11*b* (pp. 43–4). This passage, however, seems to be primarily directed against the 'new hasidim' who appropriated Sephardi, or Lurianic, liturgical customs.

appropriation of these Sephardi liturgical practices probably stems from his kabbalistic orientation, since *nusaḥ sefardi* (Sephardic rite) commonly refers to the Lurianic prayer rite.[81]

One of the most powerful indications of both Landau's endorsement of kabbalistic liturgical texts and the Prague community's use of them is the publication of the Prague prayer book *Tikun nefesh* in 1786.[82] Landau not only contributed to this work, largely devoted to prayers for gravely ill people, but was also probably active in its compilation. In fact, some studies attribute this prayer book to him.[83] The first section of *Tikun nefesh* is made up of psalms that he suggests individuals should recite on behalf of the sick. The three other sections contain numerous prayers and confessions, replete with kabbalistic terms and motifs. Many of these concepts, such as the *sefirot*, *kelipot*, *tikun* (restoration), the four emanated worlds, and *gilgul* (transmigration) are also found in Landau's sermons and commentaries. The confession text in *Tikun nefesh* likewise dwells on a kabbalistic motif discussed in his writing: the demonic sons, created through the spilling of seed in vain, which disturb the corpse at the time of death, and the required penances for this transgression.[84] Landau undoubtedly supported the publication of this liturgical work since his name appears on its title page, it contains prayers he recommended as well as ideas he incorporated in his sermons, and it was published in Prague at the height of his career as chief rabbi. His endorsement of this prayer book is a striking example of his advocacy of the use of kabbalistic prayers and confessions for Prague Jewry at large.

Tikun nefesh seems to have been employed by Prague Jews for many years: it was reprinted in 1796 in nearby Vienna only ten years after its first appearance. Continual demand for this prayer book probably occasioned this second printing. On the title page of the third edition, published in Prague in 1821, the

[81] On *nusaḥ sefardi* signifying the Lurianic prayer rite, see Wilensky, 'Hostile Phase', 92.

[82] *Tikun nefesh* was published by members of the Hevrah Kadishah Gomlei Nefesh, the association for the terminally ill.

[83] See e.g. Jerold Weiss, *Zion Hamtzuyenes*, 38. In *Derushei hatselaḥ*, sermon 30, 45*a*, Landau employs the term *tikun nefesh* to describe the ideal state that a person should attain before death, explaining that on Rosh Hashanah individuals fear that they might die before achieving the necessary *tikun nefesh*. It is therefore possible that he appropriated this phrase as the title of a prayer book for the terminally ill. It should be noted that the third of the Lurianic *tikunim* is also called *tikun hanefesh*. (The first, which focuses on the Shekhinah's exile, is called *tikun raḥel*, and the second, which focuses on redemption, is called *tikun le'ah*.) By using this title, Landau may have wished to evoke this mystical layer of meaning and goal.

[84] See *Derushei hatselaḥ*, sermon 23, 35*b*, and see *Tikun nefesh*, 27*b*–28*a*. These ideas are also found in Hayim Vital, *Sha'ar hakavanot*, pt. 1, 'Inyan derushei halailah', 362–5 and the anonymous Sabbatian work *Ḥemdat yamim*, ii. 98*b*. For further discussion of this motif, see Scholem, *Kabbalah and its Symbolism*, 155–6; id., *Kabbalah*, 322.

publishers explicitly state that they decided to reprint *Tikun nefesh* because of dwindling supplies. Evidently, this liturgical treatise, with its numerous kabbalistic motifs and prayers, was widely used both in Prague and elsewhere in the Habsburg empire for at least thirty-five years.

Aggadah and Halakhah

Mirroring his critique of customs based on extra-legal sources, Landau voices opposition to the use of non-halakhic materials, such as the aggadah, in legal discussions. On several occasions he states that he does not wish to address aggadic matters in his responsa since one does not derive legal rulings from aggadah.[85] However, when he either has a high regard for a particular correspondent[86] or when aggadah has some bearing upon halakhah,[87] he does analyse aggadic texts in his responsa.

He expresses an even greater reluctance to use kabbalistic ideas and sources in legal rulings.[88] For example, in one responsum where he alludes to a kabbalistic interpretation, he immediately pronounces that 'in any event, one does not derive halakhah from the Zohar'.[89] However, despite his protestations, his belief in kabbalah occasionally does inform both his legal analysis and his justification of liturgical innovations.

In one striking instance, he allows the kabbalistic doctrine of *gilgul neshamot*, the transmigration of souls, to influence his reasoning in a halakhic ruling.[90] This responsum concerns an infant who died before his eighth day of life and was buried uncircumcised.[91] After the burial, a rabbi asked Landau whether they should open the grave in order to circumcise the corpse. The linchpin of this case is the talmudic concept of *ḥaredat hadin*, 'the fear of the judgement', a

[85] See *NB Tinyana*, 'ḤM', no. 14 and 'YD', no. 161.

[86] This is the case with his responses to the queries of R. Isaiah b. Judah Berlin (also known as Isaiah Pick, the name of his father-in-law) of Breslau. See e.g. *NB Tinyana*, 'OḤ', no. 87.

[87] See ibid., 'YD', no. 161, where he states that he only discusses aggadic matters when they touch on halakhic issues.

[88] On the relationship between halakhah and kabbalah, see J. Katz, *Halakhah and Kabbalah* (Heb.); id., 'Post-Zoharic Relations between Halakhah and Kabbalah'; id., 'Kabbalah in the Legal Decisions of R. Joseph Karo' (Heb.); id., 'Luria's Status as a Halakhic Authority' (Heb.); Hallamish, *Kabbalah in Liturgy, Halakhah and Customs* (Heb.); Bonfil, 'Halakha, Kabbala, and Society'. For an example of an esoteric notion that was included in mainstream halakhic writings, see Wolfson, 'Circumcision and the Divine Name'.

[89] See *NB Kama*, 'YD', no. 74. See also his reluctance to discuss the kabbalistic idea of the exile of the Shekhinah in *NB Tinyana*, 'OḤ', no. 107, dated 24 Mar. 1780. Nevertheless it should be noted that while he at first berates the questioner for asking him about this kabbalistic motif, he does then proceed to offer an interpretation which has strong parallels with zoharic descriptions. See Zohar, iii. 45*b*, and i. 84*b*–85*a*.

[90] On Landau's use of the kabbalistic concept of *gilgul neshamot* in his sermons and commentaries, see Part IV.

[91] *NB Tinyana*, 'YD', no. 164.

notion that prohibits opening graves because such a disturbance scares corpses into thinking that the Day of Judgement has arrived. The rabbi enquires whether this concept applies to an infant, who, according to the traditional understanding of Jewish law, is not responsible for its actions and hence not subject to the Day of Judgement.

Landau replies that the infant may indeed be subject to the Day of Judgement, since the soul may have transmigrated. In this event, it would be liable for its actions in previous transmigrations. Still, he reasons, even if the soul has undergone *gilgul*, the corpse should be circumcised in order to avoid shaming it during the future resurrection. He therefore rules that the grave be opened and the corpse circumcised, which will benefit the infant whether his soul has transmigrated or not. His ruling not only confirms his acceptance of the notion of *gilgul*, but also shows his willingness to allow kabbalistic considerations to influence his legal decisions. Further, he exhibits his kabbalistic proclivity here by initiating this unsolicited mystical discussion, which could have been avoided.[92]

Another illustration of kabbalistic influence on Landau's halakhic reasoning appears in his remarks on fasting during the Ten Days of Repentance, between Rosh Hashanah and Yom Kippur.[93] On this issue, Landau supports a minority halakhic position on the basis of a kabbalistic tradition. This position is that of the ninth-century *gaon* Natronai ben Hilai, who claims that with the exception of the first day of Rosh Hashanah one may fast on all the remaining Ten Days of Repentance including the sabbath because of their unique nature. The author of the authoritative legal codex *Arba'ah turim*, Rabbi Jacob ben Asher (*c.*1270–1340), records the opposition of his father (Rabbi Asher ben Yehiel, *c.*1250–1327, the Rosh), to Rabbi Natronai's teaching. Both Rabbi Asher and Rabbi Jacob maintain that Rabbi Natronai's position is inconsistent, since if one cannot fast on the first day of Rosh Hashanah because it is sanctified by biblical law, the same prohibition should apply to the sabbath, a day also sanctified by biblical law. In a responsum dealing with this matter, Fleckeles recounts Landau's defence of Rabbi Natronai's minority position, claiming that its underpinning is a kabbalistic teaching espoused by the Ari.[94] According to this Lurianic tradition, also cited in a homily by Landau,[95] on each of the Ten Days of Repentance one can atone for the sins committed on that day of the week during the previous year. Landau uses this Lurianic idea to justify fasting on the

92 The original question that prompted this responsum mentioned neither the kabbalistic doctrine of *gilgul neshamot* nor the legal complexities that would result from it.

93 There is a tradition that pious individuals fast during the Days of Repentance. See *Shulḥan arukh*, 'OḤ', 581: 2.

94 Fleckeles, *Teshuvah me'ahavah*, ii, no. 273 (notes on *Shulḥan arukh*, 597).

95 *Derushei hatselaḥ*, sermon 19, 29*a*.

sabbath during these penitential days,[96] despite the halakhic principle that one must feast on the sabbath.[97]

In his responsa and talmudic commentaries, Landau also selects and justifies several liturgical formulations on the basis of kabbalistic and aggadic principles.[98] An example appears in a responsum sent by him to the distinguished rabbi of Breslau,[99] Rabbi Isaiah ben Judah Loeb Berlin (Pick) (1725–99).[100] Rabbi Isaiah had asked Landau why a certain prayer recited every Saturday night, according to the Polish prayer rite, reads 'everywhere you find His *gedulah* [greatness]',[101] while the phrase in the Talmud and in the Yom Kippur liturgy reads 'everywhere you find His *gevurah* [strength]'.[102] Landau's response hinges on the kabbalistic notion that *gevurah* is associated with judgement. He explains that whereas the Polish rite uses the more common biblical term, *gedulah*, the special version recited on the last of the days of judgement, Yom Kippur, deliberately stresses the term *gevurah*.[103] He similarly invokes this kabbalistic association in numerous sermons and commentaries.[104]

In light of Landau's generally conservative attitude towards liturgical innovation, his use of kabbalah in discussions concerning prayer is noteworthy. Both in his responsa and talmudic commentary, he repeatedly denounces suggested changes to prayer formulations.[105] His opposition, however, is primarily directed against the 'new sects' of his day,[106] and has little, if anything, to do with

[96] See Fleckeles, *Teshuvah me'ahavah*, ii, no. 273. Fleckeles relates here that, according to Landau, one can fast on the sabbath during these ten penitential days in order to attain atonement, even though fasting is usually prohibited on the sabbath. The reason Landau pemitted this is that it would serve as an atonement for all the sins transgressed on the sabbaths of the past year, some of which might otherwise incur the death penalty; and, according to rabbinic law, one may transgress the sabbath in order to save one's life. Following this Lurianic teaching, Landau asserts that there is still no need to fast on the first day of Rosh Hashanah, which is the first of the Ten Days of Repentance, because the day of the week on which Rosh Hashanah falls occurs twice during the Days of Repentance. Remarkably, it appears that, were this not the case, he would probably have suggested that the aforementioned Lurianic principle also outweighs the halakhic notion that one should feast on the first day of Rosh Hashanah.

[97] On the halakhic obligation to feast on the sabbath, see n. 48 above.

[98] See e.g. his use of aggadic and kabbalistic notions to defend the wording of a particular prayer formulation in the following gloss in *Tselah, Ber.* 60*b* (pp. 218–9), s.v. *atah yatsarta bi*.

[99] *NB Tinyana*, 'OḤ', no. 20.

[100] On this author of several important rabbinic works, who also contributed to *Masoret hashas* (a reference guide published in the margins of every tractate of the Vilna Talmud), see Kamelhar, *Dor de'ah*, 87–9. Although Landau admired R. Isaiah of Breslau, he had a complex relationship with him.

[101] This phrase appears in the prayer *Vayiten lekha*.

[102] BT *Meg.* 31*a*.

[103] On the kabbalistic association of judgement and *gevurah*, see e.g. Zohar, iii. 254*b* (*Ra'aya mehemna*), and iii. 303*a* (*Tosefta*).

[104] See e.g. *Derushei hatselah*, sermon for Rosh Hashanah, 6*a*; *Tselah, Ber.* 58*a* (p. 215). For a more extensive discussion of this topic, see Part III.

[105] See e.g. *NB Tinyana*, 'OḤ', no. 127, dated 13 Aug. 1781.

[106] See e.g. *NB Kama*, 'OḤ', nos. 17 and 35.

his attitude towards kabbalah. He reiterates that these new sects—probably referring to the hasidim and Sabbatians—instituted various liturgical changes.[107]

Strikingly, as well as personally espousing kabbalistic tenets and practices, Landau advocates their importance for Prague Jewry and supports the publication of an array of kabbalistic works. This is probably the result of his belief that one must first study aggadah and be fluent in the terminology of kabbalah in order to comprehend the future revelation of esoteric truth. His discussion of the kabbalistic layers of various aggadic texts reinforces the significance he ascribes to knowing kabbalistic teachings. But Landau's mystical excursion is not limited to intellectual pursuits. He regularly conducts and repeatedly recommends the observance of the nightly *tikun ḥatsot* vigil as well as the practice of numerous ascetic customs espoused by Safed kabbalism. These, he asserts, hasten the processes of both repentance and redemption. In the realm of praxis, he also endorses the Prague liturgical work *Tikun nefesh*, which disseminates prayers replete with kabbalistic concepts to members of his community. In addition, while he officially renounces the use of kabbalah in halakhic deliberations in both his responsa and talmudic commentary, he defends variant prayer formulations and minority rabbinic opinions on the basis of kabbalistic notions. However, despite his frequent promotion of kabbalistic ideas and customs, various factors (discussed in the next chapter) cause his discomfort with the public discussion of kabbalah.

[107] See e.g. *Tselaḥ, Ber.* 11*b* (pp. 43–4). On the hasidic use of the Lurianic rite, see e.g. Wilensky, *Hasidim and Mitnagedim* (Heb.), i. 45–6. The 1772 Brody ban against the new hasidim explicitly criticizes them for introducing changes in the Ashkenazi prayer rite. For a hasidic explanation of the reason for using different prayer formulations, see Dov Baer of Mezhirech, *Magid devarav leya'akov*, 16*a*–*b*. On Landau's critique of liturgical innovations introduced by the Sabbatians, see e.g. *NB Kama*, 'ḤM', no. 16, where he criticizes the Sabbatian practice of reciting Psalm 21 at the end of the prayer service. The Sabbatians adopted this practice, as he explains, because the numerical value (*gematriyah*) of one of the psalm's words referring to salvation, *uviyeshuatekha*, equals that of the name Sabbatai Zevi. On the Sabbatian practice of reciting this psalm, see Scholem, *Sabbatai Sevi*, 424; Hundert, *Jews in Poland–Lithuania*, 130 n. 32.

SIX

Tension

Although Landau employs kabbalah extensively in his work and even allows mystical notions to influence his views on some legal practices, his writings convey a tension, discernible in many kabbalistic sources, between the conception of kabbalah as restricted lore that needs to be safeguarded for the educated elite, on the one hand, and the desire to disseminate kabbalistic truth, on the other.[1] This reluctance to disseminate kabbalistic doctrines is heightened by his opposition to the trends of Sabbatianism, Frankism, and hasidism, which based their tenets on kabbalah. His resistance to discussing kabbalistic concepts in public is also a response to the rearrangement of educational priorities in the eighteenth-century Prague Jewish community, and he and other Prague rabbis repeatedly lament Prague Jewry's replacement of the core disciplines of Talmud and halakhah with the non-essential study of kabbalah and secular disciplines.

Landau's ambivalence regarding the disclosure of kabbalistic ideas is frequently manifested by the concealed manner in which he reveals these notions. The stratified texture of some of his writings combines exoteric and esoteric layers.[2] These different levels of meaning are made apparent by his use of tropes which only a kabbalistic initiate could comprehend. He generally signals to his reader those passages which are pregnant with kabbalistic motifs, remarking that 'these matters are deep' or the 'enlightened will understand.' By alluding to the kabbalistic dimensions of numerous biblical and rabbinic texts, he invites careful readers to explore further the esoteric ideas at which he only hints in his writings.[3]

[1] On the intrinsic tension between revealing and concealing secrets in medieval Jewish esoteric writings, including 12th- and 13th-century kabbalistic works, see Halbertal, *Concealment and Revelation*. Elliot Wolfson specifically discusses the general paradox of kabbalistic works, which often only reveal esoteric matters by concealing them. See Wolfson, 'From Sealed Book to Open Text', 145–78; id., *Through a Speculum That Shines*; id., 'Occultation of the Feminine'.

[2] This stratified manner of writing bears out Leo Strauss's claim in *Persecution and the Art of Writing*, 22–37, that one frequently needs to read 'between the lines' in order to decipher an author's esoteric teachings.

[3] He particularly wishes to familiarize his students, to whom he dedicated his talmudic commentary, with these esoteric teachings. This complements Strauss's suggestion that the esoteric ideas found in exoteric works are often addressed to young potential philosophers. See Strauss, *Persecution and the Art of Writing*, 36. Somewhat similarly, Landau's esoteric teachings are probably addressed to young students who may develop into kabbalistic initiates.

It is primarily internal considerations, such as fidelity to the dictates of tradition, that drive Landau to conceal mystical tenets in public discussions,[4] but his obscure style is also a defensive response to social and political stimuli.[5] In fact, his suppression of kabbalistic teachings is evident in the political arena as well. Wary of the threat posed to rabbinic Judaism by the spread of the mystical sects of Sabbatianism and Frankism in Prague, he probably instigated Joseph II's 1785 ban against the importation of kabbalistic books into the Habsburg empire.[6]

Political considerations may also have spurred Landau to give two out of his three approbations repudiating public kabbalistic discourse to books published in Prague during that same year.[7] Ironically the third work, *Pa'amonei zahav* (Golden Bells), for which he gives an approbation commending its author for refraining from addressing esoteric matters, is replete with kabbalistic notions.[8] Since Landau writes that he examined *Pa'amonei zahav*, unlike some of the other books for which he gives an approbation,[9] he must have known of its kabbalistic content. This approbation captures his ambivalence towards popularizing kabbalistic teachings. His desire to disseminate kabbalistic ideas, however, overrides his concerns about their esoteric and potentially subversive nature. This leads to his numerous, if somewhat restrained, discussions of kabbalistic concepts.

Nonetheless, his reservations repeatedly drove him to deny his involvement with kabbalah. Appropriating a phrase from the apocryphal work Ben Sira, cited in the Talmud,[10] Landau professes in all genres of his writings that he 'does not engage in esoteric matters'.[11] Occasionally he explains that his focus on the

[4] Several rabbinic texts assert that the study of esoteric ideas should be restricted, and should certainly not be discussed in public. See Mishnah *Ḥag.*, 2: 1; BT *Ḥag.* 11*b*.

[5] Strauss claims that the esoteric truths embedded in many texts are often suppressed by their authors because of political persecution. On dissimulation and the use of hidden meanings in early modern Europe as a result of religious persecution, see also Zagorin, *Ways of Lying*.

[6] It stands to reason that, as Prague's chief rabbi, Landau informed the Habsburg authorities of the pernicious influence of kabbalah on the Sabbatians and Frankists. The first ban on importing kabbalistic works was issued on 2 Nov. 1785, the second was issued by emperor Francis II on 7 June 1794. On both these bans, see Fleckeles, *Teshuvah me'ahavah*, i, no. 26, 15*a–b*

[7] In spite of several approbations in which he supports the dissemination of kabbalistic works, in three approbations Landau expresses his opposition to exoteric kabbalistic discussions. See his approbations for Elijah Zahlin's *Hadarat eliyahu*, dated 13 Dec. 1785, Issachar Bloch's *Binat yisakhar*, dated 20 July 1785, and David b. Joseph Katz's *Pa'amonei zahav*, dated 16 Aug. 1768. In the second of these, Landau writes that unlike other contemporary preachers, Issachar has not arrogantly revealed the secrets that God has concealed.

[8] A superficial glance at this commentary on Psalms reveals its use of numerous kabbalistic works, including the Zohar, Vital, *Ets ḥayim*, and de Vidas, *Reshit ḥokhmah*.

[9] By contrast, see Landau's other approbations for Zahlin, *Hadrat Eliyahu* and Bloch, *Binat Yissakhar* (see above, n. 7), which indicate that, at best, he was only able to carry out a cursory examination of these works.

[10] Landau often uses this phrase from Ben Sira, which is cited in BT *Ḥag.* 13*a*.

[11] See e.g. *NB Kama*, 'YD', no. 74; *Tselaḥ*, *Ber.* 33*b* (p. 126); *Derushei hatselaḥ*, sermon 12, for the first day of *Seliḥot* prayers, 20*a–b*.

Talmud and codes leaves him with no time to deliberate upon meta-halakhic disciplines, such as aggadah and kabbalah.[12]

Particularly remarkable are the instances where, on the heels of such disclaimers, he immediately proceeds to introduce kabbalistic notions. In conjunction with this tactic, he sometimes also appropriates authoritative rabbinic sources in order to veil his kabbalistic teachings and justify his mystical excursions. An excellent example of this is found in his talmudic commentary on *Pesaḥim*. Expounding upon the biblical depiction of the patriarch Jacob's attempt to reveal to his sons what will transpire at the *kets hayamim* ('end of days', Gen. 49: 1),[13] he writes that Jacob

> investigated if they had not blemished the right or the left, for at times man . . . blemishes the right, which is the attribute of grace . . . and some struggle against the punishments . . . which are meted out by the attribute of judgement, and this blemishes the left. But *we do not engage in esoteric matters*, only this is what we found in Rashi's commentary on the biblical verse, the 'right of the Lord' (Exod. 15: 6).[14] (emphasis added)

Landau seeks to minimize the novelty of his kabbalistic interpretation by implying that it was the medieval commentator Rashi, and not he, who introduced this kabbalistic reading. However, neither Rashi's commentary on this biblical narrative concerning Jacob,[15] nor other glosses of Rashi's on the biblical phrase the 'right of the Lord',[16] equate the right side with divine grace or the left side with divine judgement, as does Landau.[17] By asserting that Rashi introduced these kabbalistic readings centuries earlier, he attempts, albeit unconvincingly, to buttress his claim that he does not engage in kabbalistic exegesis. He employs the same tactic in other talmudic glosses and sermons,[18] repeatedly citing Rashi as the source of his kabbalistic portrayal of the right side as mercy and the left side as judgement.

A related gloss in the *Tselaḥ* on *Pesaḥim* again betrays the tension between Landau's wish to popularize kabbalistic ideas and his discomfort with this enter-

[12] See *NB Tinyana*, 'OḤ', no. 109 and 'YD', no. 201; Landau's approbation for Zahlin, *Hadarat eliyahu*.

[13] The Talmud's rendition of this phrase is *kets hayamin* (ending with the letter *nun* rather than *mem*), which in Aramaic means 'the end of days'. On the use of this phrase in Aramaic, see Dan. 12: 13. Following Rashi's gloss on BT *Pes.* 56*a*, Landau picks up on the unusual rendition of this phrase in the context of Jacob's blessing. Like Rashi, he interprets *hayamin* in this talmudic passage according to its Hebrew meaning: 'the right side'.

[14] *Tselaḥ*, *Pes.* 56*a* (p. 218).

[15] Rashi on Gen. 49: 1 s.v. *ve'agidah lakhem*; Rashi at BT *Pes.* 56*a* s.v. *kets hayamin.*

[16] Rashi on Exod. 15: 6 s.v. *yeminekha*.

[17] By contrast, the correspondence between the right side and divine grace and the left side and divine judgement is found in numerous kabbalistic sources. For a discussion of the Zohar's portrayal of these aspects of the *sefirot*, see Wolfson, 'Left Contained in the Right'.

[18] See e.g. *Tselaḥ*, *Ber.* 30*b* (p. 117), 58*a* (p. 215); *Derushei hatselaḥ*, sermon for Rosh Hashanah, 6*a*; sermon 5, 11*a*; sermon 28, 44*a*.

prise. Here he uses kabbalistic concepts to explain the talmudic description of the patriarch Jacob's recitation of an insertion to the Shema prayer that Moses did not recite.[19] He then claims that these kabbalistic notions also provide the key to understanding the abstruse 'parable of the princess' cited in the Talmud in this context.[20] However, after laying the foundation for his kabbalistic reading of this parable, he writes that

> since the rabbis spoke in riddles and hints, I will not act as a talebearer and reveal secrets. What I have written is already enough, and if God forbid this was a mistake, may the good Lord atone for me.[21]

The mistake referred to here is the disclosure of kabbalistic secrets.[22] These comments exhibit Landau's conflicting views about the importance of concealing and revealing kabbalah. Interestingly, however, his ambivalence does not hinder him from publishing these kabbalistic insights. Numerous other examples from his talmudic commentary similarly illustrate his desire to share kabbalistic teachings, contravening his assertion that they should remain esoteric.[23]

In several sermons permeated by kabbalistic tenets, Landau likewise expresses his uneasiness with conveying kabbalistic notions.[24] For example, in one homily where he refers to kabbalistic ideas in Vital's *Ets ḥayim*, he introduces these motifs with the disclaimer that such matters are 'deep secrets hidden from us'. Nonetheless, he proclaims, 'I will explain [them] to you according to revealed teachings.'[25] The ensuing discussion is replete with kabbalistic concepts, including the divine 'male and female waters', theurgy, and the existence of numerous

[19] See *Tselaḥ*, *Pes.* 56*a* (pp. 218–19): *amri rabanan heikhi ne'evid*. This passage deals with a description of the patriarch Jacob's recitation of the phrase *barukh shem kevod malkhuto le'olam va'ed*, inserted into the Shema prayer. Landau interprets this passage by explaining that, unlike Moses, Jacob was accompanied by the angel who represented the joining of divine judgment and divine mercy and therefore recited this phrase, which, according to kabbalists, also represents the unification of divine judgement and divine mercy.

[20] BT *Pes.* 56*a*. On the parable, see Chapter 11.

[21] *Tselaḥ*, *Pes.* 56*a* (p. 219).

[22] Baruch Brandeis, one of Landau's students, records that Landau orally decoded the talmudic 'parable of the princess' by relating it to the kabbalistic liturgical formulation of the 'wisdom of unification', *yiḥud*, which facilitates the joining of divine judgement and mercy. See Brandeis, *Leshon ḥakhamim*, pt. 1, 'Hilkhot tefilah', 21. Landau's complex attitude towards kabbalistic 'unifications' is discussed in Chapter 11.

[23] See e.g. *Tselaḥ*, *Ber.* 6*a* (p. 21), s.v. *Minayin shehakadosh barukh hu meniaḥ tefilin*. Although Landau claims here that 'we do not engage in esoteric matters', his analysis is replete with kabbalistic concepts, the scope of which goes beyond the simple clarification of the text. At times, however, he is slightly more restrained and just hints at the esoteric meaning of a passage. See e.g. ibid., *Ber.* 31*b* (p. 122), s.v. *ḥanah hetiḥah devarim*; ibid. *Pes.* 54*a* (p. 216), s.v. *shivah devarim nivre'u kodem nivra ha'olam*.

[24] See e.g. *Ahavat tsiyon*, sermon 2, 3*a*–4*b*. Following a disavowal at the beginning of this homily of any discussion of esoteric material, he proceeds to deliver what is probably his most mystical sermon.

[25] *Derushei hatselaḥ*, sermon 25, 40*a*.

emanated worlds. In this manner, he makes recondite kabbalistic doctrines more accessible to his audience.

Occasionally, however, his reluctance to address the 'secrets' publicly does lead him to offer only abbreviated kabbalistic remarks. In one sermon, where he hints at the kabbalistic idea that identifies the creation of the evil inclination and the minimization of the moon as one event, he immediately states that 'these are deep matters which should not be elaborated upon.'[26] Such truncated comments reflect moments when his instinct to conceal kabbalistic truths suppresses his impulse to reveal them.

In his talmudic commentary, Landau alludes to the reason for his hesitancy to discuss kabbalah. Commenting on a famous talmudic narrative,[27] he explains

> there are several paths and they *are paths of life*, but these paths have various obstacles along the way. And whoever does not know to be careful falls . . . Likewise in earlier generations, the sages of the Mishnah attained a great understanding of the supernal worlds in the heavens above and gazed upon the mysteries of the divine Chariot. And although this is a path of life, it is extremely dangerous.[28] (emphasis added)

In order to emphasize the perils of the mystical enterprise, Landau relates that mysticism led even some of the greatest Jewish authorities astray, and consequently suggests that one should avoid this authentic but dangerous religious path.[29] In several sermons he similarly conveys his simultaneous belief in the truth of kabbalah and his conviction that its study should be limited due to its potential hazards.[30]

[26] See ibid., sermon 12, 21*a*. For his limited discussion of other kabbalistic matters, see also ibid. 20*a*–*b*. In various kabbalistic sources, the creation of the evil inclination, which is rooted in the demonic realm, is associated with the minimization of the moon. For example, this notion is found in zoharic texts as well as in the writings of Todros Abulafia and Moses de Leon.

[27] BT *Ber.* 28*b*. In this talmudic narrative, the disciples of R. Eleazar ask him which of the many paths of life they should follow in order to merit the next world.

[28] *Tselaḥ*, *Ber.* 28*b* (p. 109). He continues to explain that even many of the great sages of the Mishnah therefore refrained from studying mystical matters.

[29] This gloss is replete with his denunciations of the 'new hasidim's' arrogant use of kabbalah.

[30] See e.g. *Derushei hatselaḥ*, sermon 39, 53*a*–54*a*, where Landau states (53*b*) that 'we will merit to gaze upon the beauty of the Lord (Ps. 27: 4) *even* if we do not study any esoteric matters.' His use of the word 'even' in this context denotes his belief in the truth of esoteric teachings. It also shows his contention that those who engage in both revealed and esoteric studies follow a righteous and possibly superior path to those involved solely in revealed matters. His guarded attitude towards studying kabbalah, in this sermon, is not simply a reflection of a general concern about the dangers of mystical study, but also a response to contemporary trends. In this homily, he denounces the Sabbatians, Jewish 'philosophers', acculturating Jews, and a new hedonistic sect, probably a reference to the 'new hasidim'.

Reasons for the Discrepancy

Landau's reluctance to disclose kabbalistic ideas in public was partly fuelled by the numerous trends threatening the hegemony of traditional rabbinic culture at the end of the eighteenth century.[31] Several of these trends or movements were steeped in kabbalistic teachings. Of these, he most vehemently opposed the Sabbatians and Frankists, who rooted much of their anti-rabbinic theosophy in zoharic and Lurianic texts.[32]

The anonymous maskilic author of the anti-Sabbatian and anti-Frankist tract *A Dialogue between the Year 1800 and the Year 1801* portrays the centrality of kabbalah for Prague's Sabbatians, describing how they

> study the book of the Zohar and engage in the writings of the Ari. Their entire preoccupation, both the men and the women, is with kabbalistic books . . . They study esoteric matters for one or two hours every day. And the mundane discussion of these women is not like the mundane discussion of other women, for they are filled with the spirit of the Zohar and kabbalah.[33]

Later in the treatise, the author similarly criticizes the Prague Sabbatians for teaching their youngest pupils midrash, the *agadot* in the *Ein ya'akov*, the Zohar, and the rest of the kabbalistic canon.[34] Echoing these sentiments, Fleckeles, in his anti-Frankist treatise *Ahavat david*, also published in Prague in 1800, writes that 'both young and old, children and women come to hear the deceptive kabbalah of Jacob [Frank] and to study together defiled mysteries of the Chariot . . . and the writings of the Ari'.[35] Furthermore, both Landau and Fleckeles lament

[31] He seldom explicitly identifies his motives for hesitating to discuss kabbalah publicly. Nevertheless, they can be discerned from various social factors that he mentions in passages written specifically for the purpose of discouraging Prague Jews from engaging in kabbalah. See e.g. *Tselah*, *Ber.* 28*b*, and *Derushei hatselah*, sermon 39, 53*a*–54*a*, where (53*b*), after denouncing several contemporary sects, he states that 'we do not care if these sects mock us. We will continue to tread the path taken by the Rif [Isaac Alfasi], Rambam [Maimonides], Rosh [Asher b. Jehiel], and Tosafot . . . They did not engage in esoteric matters, yet they attained eternal life.'

[32] For a discussion of the centrality of zoharic and Lurianic kabbalah in Sabbatian and Frankist circles, see Scholem, *Sabbatai Sevi*, 297–300, 465–6; Tishby, *Wisdom of the Zohar*, i. 28, 38–40; Idel, 'Perceptions of Kabbalah', 56–7; Werses, *Haskalah and Sabbatianism* (Heb.), 76–9; Huss, '*Sefer ha-Zohar*', 284–7.

[33] *A Dialogue between the Year* 1800 *and the Year* 1801 (Heb.), 11–12. He goes on to state that the conversation of these women is replete with kabbalistic concepts, including those pertaining to the *sefirot*, male and female aspects of the Divine, the demonic realm, etc. For a discussion of this treatise, see Chapter 3.

[34] Ibid. 14. *Ein ya'akov* is a collection of many of the *agadot* found in the Babylonian and Palestinian Talmuds. This 16th-c. work was widely studied in subsequent centuries.

[35] Fleckeles, *Ahavat david*, 25*b*.

these sectarians' advocacy of antinomian practices, particularly those having to do with food and sexuality, which they based on kabbalistic doctrines.[36]

At times, Landau's rejection of the Sabbatians and Frankists leads directly to his public denunciation of kabbalistic study.[37] He expresses this explicitly in one responsum, where he states that 'in our generation, the Sabbatian heretics have increased. We therefore ought to limit the study of the Zohar and kabbalistic books.'[38]

He also rails against the mystical enthusiasm found in Prague, presumably among these sectarians. The phenomenon of enthusiasm, the claim of direct divine inspiration without ecclesiastical mediation, was well known in early modern Europe. Numerous seventeenth- and eighteenth-century Protestant and Jewish religious leaders denounced enthusiasm since it undermined the role of traditional religious authority as the sole channel to divine truth.[39] Cases of enthusiasm were widespread among the Sabbatians:[40] both erudite and ignorant believers in Sabbatai Zevi attested to receiving revelations of the mysteries.[41] The *Dialogue between the Year 1800 and the Year 1801* particularly criticizes the Sabbatian and Frankist women who 'prophesy . . . and reveal deep kabbalistic secrets'.[42] In his sermons Landau specifically condemns enthusiastic claims of prophecy made by lay individuals. He writes that, despite the enthusiasts' ignorance of the revealed Torah, they arrogantly declare that they have merited the gift of the Holy Spirit and knowledge of esoteric matters.[43] The threat posed to rabbinic leadership by the enthusiasts' claim of a direct divine connection and

[36] See *Derushei hatselah*, sermon 25, 40*a*, where Landau asserts that they consider 'all the prohibitions to be *mitsvot*'. He states that they eat forbidden foods and engage in prohibited sexual practices. See also ibid., sermon 39, 53*b*. On Sabbatian antinomianism and the Frankist notion of the holiness of sin, see Scholem, *Messianic Idea*, 78–141. See also Fleckeles, *Ahavat david*, 12*b*; id., *Teshuvah me'ahavah*, i., preface.

[37] Jacob Katz maintains that Landau's, Fleckeles' and other rabbis' criticism of the study of kabbalah, which had been a core component of rabbinic culture for centuries, was largely motivated by its importance for the Sabbatians. See J. Katz, 'On the Question of the Connection between Sabbatianism, Enlightenment, and Reform' (Heb.), 272–3.

[38] *NB Kama*, 'YD', no. 74, in which he addresses a query about a zoharic teaching.

[39] On enthusiasm and responses to this phenomenon, see Heyd, 'The Reaction to Enthusiasm in the Seventeenth Century'; id., 'Protestantism, Enthusiasm and Secularization in the Early Modern Period'; Scholem, *Sabbatai Sevi*, 418; Goldish, 'Rabbi Jacob Sasportas', 116–36. Various eminent 18th-c. rabbis, such as Emden and Landau, repudiated the enthusiastic claims of prophecy that were prevalent in their day.

[40] Scholem writes that the 'gift of prophecy was infectious' among this sect. See Scholem, *Sabbatai Sevi*, 383,

[41] 17th- and 18th-c. writings, as well as later historical works, record cases of lay enthusiasm among the Sabbatians. See e.g. Sasportas, *Tsitsat novel tsevi*, 96, 148, 162–3, 182, 298, 315; Scholem, *Sabbatai Sevi*, 254, 382–3, 418–23; Goldish, 'Rabbi Jacob Sasportas', 122, 128.

[42] *A Dialogue between the Year* 1800 *and the Year* 1801 (Heb.), 24; see also 27.

[43] *Derushei hatselah*, sermon 32 for the sabbath of Hanukah, 47*a*.

attainment of mystical knowledge probably contributed to Landau's inclination to limit his kabbalistic discussions.

The emergence of the 'new hasidim' during the last decades of the eighteenth century also played a role in Landau's discomfort with exoteric kabbalistic discourse. As mentioned earlier, the nascent hasidic movement was heavily steeped in kabbalistic teachings and often led by charismatic mystical leaders.[44] This posed a potential challenge to traditional rabbinic authority, which was largely based on its halakhic expertise.

All genres of Landau's writings from the 1770s and 1780s contain denunciations of the 'new hasidim's' popularization of esoteric concepts and observance of certain kabbalistic customs.[45] In the preface to his commentary on *Berakhot*, for example, he ridicules those of his generation who refer to themselves as hasidim and arrogantly 'disseminate secrets publicly'. Despite these activities, he mocks, they fail to reveal the Torah's secrets, because of their ignorance.[46] Elsewhere in this commentary, he derides the hasidim, 'who claim to be masters of kabbalah', and who conceitedly spread nonsense about the kabbalah in order to aggrandize themselves in the eyes of the masses.[47] In a Prague sermon he further attacks the hedonistic ways of an unnamed group involved in kabbalah.[48] Here he is probably referring to the embrace of worldly pleasures by many hasidim as a means of worshipping the Divine, an innovative hasidic concept based on earlier kabbalistic notions.[49] His repudiation of the 'new hasidim's' mystical practices heightened his opposition both to certain kabbalistic customs which gained popularity during his day[50] and to the dissemination of kabbalistic teachings.

Landau's apprehensions about the misuse of kabbalah were exacerbated by Prague Jewry's reordering of its traditional curriculum of study, a phenomenon challenging Ashkenazi culture more generally during this period. In traditional Ashkenazi culture, kabbalah was regarded as a discipline to be studied only by

[44] There are numerous studies on the centrality of kabbalah in hasidism. For some of the best scholarly works on this topic, see Scholem, *Messianic Idea*, 203–27; id., *Major Trends*, 325–50; Rapoport-Albert (ed.), *Hasidism Reappraised*, pts. I and IV; Idel, *Hasidism*; Piekarz, *Beginning of Hasidism* (Heb.); Jacobs, *Hasidic Prayer*; Joseph Weiss, *Studies in East European Jewish Mysticism and Hasidism*; Lamm, *Religious Thought of Hasidism*.

[45] See, for example, Landau's repudiation of the hasidic appropriation of kabbalistic prayer formulations in *NB Kama*, 'YD', no. 93, dated 9 June 1776.

[46] *Tselaḥ*, *Ber.*, preface.

[47] Ibid., *Ber.* 28*b* (p. 109).

[48] *Derushei hatselaḥ*, sermon 39, 53*b*. Landau's juxtaposition of contemporaries with kabbalistic interests and this hedonistic sect echoes the criticism of other opponents of the new hasidim.

[49] Although this idea was largely an innovation of the hasidim, many claimed to base it on kabbalistic doctrines. For Landau, who was both an ascetic and a mystic, this hasidic blend of mysticism must have been particularly problematic. On the hasidic conception of worship through corporeality, see Lamm, *Religious Thought of Hasidism*, 323–36.

[50] These included the use of *kavanot* and the Lurianic prayer rite.

individuals whose 'bellies were already filled' with knowledge of the Talmud and codes.[51] Several seventeenth- and eighteenth-century kabbalistic and halakhic sources reiterate this traditional view, indicating that this restriction was not always followed.[52] On various occasions, Landau ridicules those who engage in kabbalah without a proper foundation in the revealed law. In two approbations for works published in Prague, he specifically criticizes contemporary preachers who arrogantly profess to reveal secrets.[53] They do this, he writes, even though some 'have not learned a single [talmudic] tractate properly. [Consequently] they appropriate teachings which are unworthy and give advice in matters over which they have no mastery.' He recommends that one should distance oneself from such preachers and their words.[54]

Many of Landau's comments decrying the reversal in the order of study, particularly the focus on kabbalah, are directed against the Sabbatians.[55] The anti-Sabbatian *Dialogue* explains that Prague Frankists lead their pupils astray at an early age, stating 'why spend your time studying the Talmud . . . Above all, carefully study the book of the Zohar and the rest of the kabbalistic works.'[56] Landau similarly often censures the Sabbatian focus on kabbalah at the expense of talmudic study. In one responsum denouncing the Sabbatians he explicitly addresses this issue: 'How infuriated I am against those who study the Zohar and kabbalistic books publicly! They cast aside the yoke of the revealed Torah from their necks, and talk and chirp about the Zohar, and are able to master neither. In this manner, the Torah is forgotten in Israel.'[57] Although he does not usually single out the Sabbatians, as he does here, in his comments critiquing contem-

[51] This tradition is based on a teaching found in the classical Ashkenazi work of R. Moses Isserles, where he claims that one should only study esoteric matters, or *pardes*, after one is proficient—or 'filled'—in Jewish law. See his gloss on *Shulḥan arukh*, 'YD', 246: 4. His formulation is based on Maimonides' teaching in *Mishneh torah*, 'Laws of the Foundations of the Torah', 4: 13, where Maimonides also suggests that the study of *pardes* be restricted to individuals who are proficient in Jewish law. For Maimonides, however, the term *pardes* denotes metaphysics, not kabbalah.

[52] Even kabbalists, such as Moses Ostrer of the Brody *kloiz*, warn that one needs to be proficient in Jewish law before studying kabbalah. See Ostrer, *Arugat habosem*, 67*a*. The halakhist Shabetai b. Me'ir Hakohen also states that the kabbalists' accepted order of study was that one should first attain fluency in Torah and Talmud and only thereafter engage in kabbalistic study: see his *Siftei kohen*, gloss no. 6 on *Shulḥan arukh*, 'YD', no. 246. The 'new hasidim' were often accused of ignoring this order of study; see e.g. the 1772 anti-hasidic ban promulgated in Brody.

[53] See Landau's approbation for *Hadarat eliyahu* (see above, n. 7). Landau's criticism of preachers who reveal what is concealed by God, the Ancient of Days (*atik yomin*), is a play on a passage in BT *Pes.* 119*a*, in which an individual who conceals what the *atik yomin* concealed is praised.

[54] Landau's approbation for Bloch, *Binat yisakhar*, July 1785.

[55] In fact he denounces the Sabbatian influence on some of the preachers he condemns in his approbation for *Hadarat eliyahu*, discussed above.

[56] *A Dialogue between the Year* 1800 *and the Year* 1801 (Heb.), 15–16.

[57] *NB Kama*, 'YD', no. 74. On this text, see also Tishby, *Wisdom of the Zohar*, i. 39.

porary curricular priorities these remarks are often made with the Sabbatians in mind.

A passage in the *Dialogue*, overlooked by most scholars, explicitly demonstrates Landau's condemnation of the reordering of the traditional curriculum by the Sabbatians. The author recalls that when the existence of a Prague group of Sabbatians came to Landau's attention in 1792, he met them and excoriated them as follows:

> Why do you gaze upon the heavens? Is it not enough to know your course on earth? . . . Why do you engage in kabbalah? 'It is exceedingly deep; who can find it out' (Eccles. 7: 24)? 'The righteous walk in them [i.e. its ways], but the sinners shall stumble in them' (Hos. 14: 10). Busy yourselves with Talmud, medieval and later codifiers, Bible and aggadah. These alone will serve for you as a guide.[58]

As in most of Landau's statements regarding kabbalah, here he denies neither its truth nor that the righteous 'walk in its ways'. He only warns of its potential danger, especially for those lacking the requisite foundation.

Fleckeles, like his teacher, also frequently criticizes the inverted order of study adopted by some Prague Jews, especially the Sabbatians.[59] In the preface to *Teshuvah me'ahavah*, he bemoans that because of 'our many sins . . . people who are not experts in the Talmud and codes gather in groups and study the Zohar and the writings of the Ari'.[60] He repeatedly echoes this lament in his anti-Sabbatian tract *Ahavat david*, stating that the distinguishing characteristic of the Sabbatians is that the members of this group, including children and women, study aggadah and the book of the Zohar without having mastered the Talmud and codes. 'This is for you the sign of the impure *tsav* according to its kind' (Lev. 11: 29), he remarks, playfully alluding to a biblical verse and the name Sabbatai Zevi.[61] Although Fleckeles' campaign against the Sabbatians reached its peak around 1800,[62] his criticism of the Sabbatians' focus on kabbalah without requisite talmudic knowledge is probably grounded in his

58 *A Dialogue between the Year* 1800 *and the Year* 1801 (Heb.), 28–9. His remarks here echo other comments of his in which he claims that one cannot study the ways of heaven before knowing the fundamental teachings on earth. See Brandeis, *Leshon ḥakhamim*, pt. 1, 'Hilkhot tefilah', 21.

59 This theme appears repeatedly in Fleckeles' *Ahavat david*. See e.g. *Ahavat david*, 4*b*, 5*a*, 11*b*, 17*b*, 18*a*.

60 Fleckeles, *Teshuvah me'ahavah*, i, preface.

61 The word *tsav* means 'lizard' in biblical Hebrew and is one of the animals listed as impure in the Bible. In a word-play, Fleckeles uses this biblical verse to refer to the impure followers of Sabbatai Zevi. Fleckeles, *Ahavat david*, 6*b*; see also ibid. 27*a*.

62 The Prague authorities imprisoned Fleckeles and Samuel Landau from 11 to 15 Nov. 1800 on the basis of Frankist accusations against them. On Fleckeles' campaign against the Sabbatians and Frankists, see his introductions to *Ahavat david* and *Teshuvah me'ahavah*. See also S. Lieben, 'Rabbi Eleasar Fleckeles', 18–21; Werses, *Haskalah and Sabbatianism* (Heb.), 63–74; Žáček, 'Zwei Beiträge zur Geschichte des Frankismus', 370–410.

impressions as a youth in Prague and as a member of Prague's Jewish court during Landau's lifetime.[63]

Besides the threat of sectarians, enthusiasts, and the changing order of study, other factors contributed to the Prague rabbinate's simultaneous dismissal of kabbalah and staunch defence of Talmud. Like most Ashkenazi rabbis, Landau believed in the primacy of talmudic and halakhic subjects, maintaining that these alone were critical for perpetuating Judaism. Accordingly, he advised students to limit the time they spent on extra-talmudic disciplines. His 1789 approbation for a Hebrew grammar book attests to his promotion of this ideal. He typically qualifies his endorsement by insisting that young men spend all day studying the Talmud and codes, the main components of Torah, and only about half an hour or an hour studying the Bible and Hebrew grammar.[64] His advocacy of concentrating almost exclusively on Talmud and halakhah left hardly any room for studying extra-talmudic subjects, such as kabbalah. In fact, he had already voiced concern about kabbalah detracting from Torah studies in an approbation written over twenty years earlier. There he lamented that emphasis on kabbalah causes people 'to forget the enjoyable study of the Talmud and codes which have been transmitted with certainty by us from one generation to the next, from the time the law was revealed to Moses at Sinai'.[65]

During the last decades of the eighteenth century, Landau felt compelled to reinforce the Ashkenazi rabbinic ideal of the centrality of talmudic study in response to both governmental policies and social forces promoting secular studies. These included Joseph II's decree of mandatory secular education and the focus on secular disciplines by the maskilim and acculturating Jews. Even the limited secular studies available at Prague's Jewish Normalschule took away time traditionally devoted to learning Torah. Indeed, as mentioned, Landau and Fleckeles frequently bewail Prague Jewry's increasing emphasis on secular subjects and the concomitant decline in rabbinic studies. The precarious state of Torah education in Prague spurred Landau to intensify his efforts to promote talmudic study.

In short, many of Landau's writings exhibit his ambivalence towards exoteric kabbalistic discourse. His reluctance stemmed both from his mystical perspec-

[63] See S. Lieben, 'Rabbi Eleasar Fleckeles', 18. As discussed in Chapter 2, Fleckeles served on Prague's Jewish high court from 1783.

[64] Landau's approbation for Elijah b. Asher Halevi Ashkenazi's *Sefer habaḥur*, dated 15 Av 5549 (7 Aug. 1789). Landau warns his students not to be too drawn to this discipline (i.e. grammar and Bible), explaining that they should not substitute the 'vegetables for the meat, which is the study of Talmud and codes. For the study of Talmud and codes is our life and the main staple of Torah.' (The phrase 'substituting vegetables for meat' is based on a talmudic idiom in BT *Shab.* 140*b*.) Notably, even though Landau recommended only limited use of this grammar book, he was the first of the *Prenumeranten* (pre-subscribers) for this work.

[65] Landau's approbation for D. Katz, *Pa'amonei zahav*, dated 16 Aug. 1768.

tive that kabbalistic study should remain limited, and from his repudiation of contemporary trends, including Sabbatianism and hasidism, which rooted their teachings in kabbalah. He also wanted to uphold the Ashkenazi rabbinic paradigm of the primacy of talmudic studies, leaving little room for extra-talmudic disciplines, such as secular and kabbalistic subjects. Joseph II's educational reforms and maskilic ideology, which challenged the traditional rabbinic curriculum, gave this Ashkenazi rabbinic ideal particular urgency during this era. As a result of these factors, Landau often prefaces his kabbalistic remarks with the ironic claim that he does not engage in esoteric matters. Notwithstanding these protestations, his belief in kabbalah and desire to share some of its teachings prompted him to produce works replete with kabbalistic doctrines and ideals central to several kabbalistic schools.

PART III

KABBALISTIC SCHOOLS IN LANDAU'S WORKS

INTRODUCTION

KABBALISTIC IDEAS from divergent schools, sources, and trends permeate all genres of Landau's writing. A thorough study of his works reveals that these kabbalistic sources formed an integral part of his spiritual and mystical universe, and that, to a certain extent, he felt compelled to disseminate their teachings.

Modern scholarship has identified two primary models, or trends, of kabbalah: the theosophical-theurgical and the ecstatic.[1] Nevertheless, it should be stressed that both types often appear in a single kabbalistic work. The theosophical-theurgical model is predominantly concerned with the configuration of the ten potencies of the Godhead known as *sefirot*, and the influence of ritual upon them. The ecstatic, or prophetic, trend of kabbalah, founded by the Spanish mystic Abraham Abulafia (1240–91),[2] focuses mainly on the mystic's attempt to attain the prophetic experience of *devekut*.[3] The zoharic and Lurianic schools largely conform to the theosophical-theurgical model, though they also contain ecstatic elements, while the Cordoverian school integrates the ideals of the ecstatic model into its theosophical worldview. Landau's works, like those of Cordovero and other kabbalistic writings, include both trends of kabbalah.

Many of the theosophical-theurgical and ecstatic goals that Landau emphasizes in his sermons and commentaries, such as *tikun*, *berur hanitsotsot* (selection of the supernal sparks), and *devekut*, are based on central zoharic, Cordoverian, and Lurianic teachings. Although Landau does not usually disclose the original sources of the kabbalistic ideas he uses, they are frequently rooted in these kabbalistic texts. On occasion, rather than presenting original kabbalistic interpretations directly, he weaves them into his discussions of tenets originating in zoharic, Cordoverian, and Lurianic works. These innovative kabbalistic remarks are most prominent in his comments on *devekut* and the nature of sin. This section shows that Landau employs a variety of kabbalistic concepts specific to the

[1] These trends were first designated in Scholem, *Major Trends*, 124. For a discussion of them, see Idel, *Kabbalah*, esp. pp. xi, 250. Although the categorization of kabbalistic ideas as either theosophic or ecstatic cannot be rigidly applied, it is a good heuristic tool.

[2] On Abraham Abulafia and ecstatic kabbalah, see Scholem, *Major Trends*, 119–55; Idel, *Mystical Experience in Abraham Abulafia*; id., *Studies in Ecstatic Kabbalah*; id., *Language, Torah, and Hermeneutics in Abraham Abulafia*; Wolfson, *Abraham Abulafia*.

[3] The use of the term *devekut* in kabbalistic literature is varied, referring to states ranging from moderate to complete union with the Divine. While Scholem asserts that *unio mystica* is not found in Jewish mystical texts, Idel argues that unitive descriptions appear in kabbalistic sources as often as they occur in non-Jewish mystical works. See Scholem, *Messianic Idea*, 203–4, 227; id., *Major Trends*, 122–3; Idel, *Kabbalah*, 60, 62; id., *Hasidism*, 55; id., 'Universalization and Integration'.

major schools and trends of kabbalah in numerous writings disseminated among Prague Jewry.

This investigation of the importance of zoharic, Cordoverian, and Lurianic kabbalah in Landau's writings serves as a corrective to much of the scholarship on eighteenth-century kabbalah as well as to the hagiographic studies of Landau. Until recently, the dominant view of scholarship, most pronounced in the works of Scholem, was that the kabbalah studied and cultivated in eighteenth-century Europe was almost exclusively Lurianic.[4] In addition, as emphasized earlier, both the scholarship on kabbalah and the hagiographic books on Landau overlook not only the significance of ecstatic and Cordoverian notions in his writings, but also the prominence of zoharic and Lurianic concepts in his work.[5] This section identifies the various kabbalistic schools that form the foundation of many of the kabbalistic ideals promoted by Landau. It should be remembered, however, that he often uses these sources in an eclectic and syncretistic fashion.[6]

Landau was probably introduced to a range of kabbalistic schools and trends as a young man in Brody. As mentioned previously, there was a great emphasis on Lurianic kabbalah at the Brody *kloiz*. Several of its kabbalists, such as Zanzer and Ostrer, seem to have been instrumental in the first printings of Lurianic treatises in the nearby city of Korets in 1784.[7] A close examination of the writings of Brody mystics, however, shows that, in contrast to portrayals in modern scholarship, the kabbalah studied and venerated at the *kloiz* was not limited solely to Lurianic texts.

Works like *Beit perets*, by the Brody kabbalist Perez ben Moses, which stresses the mystical goal of *devekut* and cites Cordoverian *musar* writings, demonstrate that the ideals of ecstatic and Cordoverian kabbalah were important to several *kloiz* members with whom Landau had contact. Besides Perez's own advocacy of *devekut*,[8] he records the remarks of another Brody kabbalist, Nathan ben Levi, concerning this mystical ideal. These include Nathan's striking assertion that the 'main objective [of Torah] is to cleave to God',[9] a sentiment echoed in

4 See Scholem, *Major Trends*, 284–7, 327; id., *Kabbalah*, esp. 87. More recent studies, however, such as those of Idel, Sack, and Tishby, have done much to dispel this view. See my discussion of this topic in the Introduction.

5 Since the hagiographical studies maintain that Landau concealed his familiarity with zoharic and Lurianic kabbalah, they neglect the wealth of zoharic and Lurianic motifs in his writings. His promotion of the ecstatic conception of cleaving to God remains completely unnoted in these works as well as in academic studies.

6 This is analysed in Part IV below.

7 Scholem, *Kabbalah*, 83, 425; id., *Major Trends*, 328; Reiner, 'Wealth, Social Position and the Study of Torah' (Heb.), 313.

8 Perez b. Moses, *Beit perets*, 28*b*.

9 Ibid. For a discussion of *devekut* and Torah study, see Piekarz, *Beginning of Hasidism* (Heb.), 346–56; Idel, *Hasidism*, 171–88.

numerous hasidic writings. Landau, who quoted Nathan ben Levi many years after leaving Brody, seems to have been particularly influenced by him.[10] Thus in addition to Lurianic kabbalah, Landau probably also became acquainted with other mystical schools and ideas in Brody.

There are various indications that his encounters with Brody kabbalists, who promoted both ecstatic and Lurianic ideals, had an impact upon him that lasted throughout his career. In about 1753, almost eight years after leaving Brody, Landau gave an approbation for the aforementioned *Beit perets*, a book replete with both ecstatic and Lurianic concepts. In several Prague works, he also recounts specific *musar* teachings that he had heard years earlier, as well as certain kabbalistic customs that he had observed acquaintances perform during his youth.[11] These comments probably refer to kabbalistic notions and practices that he had encountered at the Brody *kloiz*. Exposure to different kabbalistic trends as a young man undoubtedly influenced his later thought.

In his Prague writings, Landau sporadically cites a wide range of mystical texts and teachings. These include *Sefer yetsirah*, biblical glosses of Nahmanides (Rabbi Moses ben Nahman, 1194–1270), the Zohar, oral teachings of Luria, and Vital's *Ets ḥayim*. He also quotes several *musar* and homiletic treatises as a source for some of the kabbalistic concepts that he appropriates and expands upon. Among these are Bahya ibn Pakudah's *Ḥovot halevavot* (eleventh century), Cordovero's disciple de Vidas's *Reshit ḥokhmah*, the homiletic writings of Alshekh (both from the sixteenth century), and the seventeenth-century Prague rabbi Isaiah Horowitz's kabbalistic *musar* treatise, *Shenei luḥot haberit*. On a few occasions, Landau also refers to kabbalistic texts in a generic fashion, stating that a specific idea is discussed in the 'works of the kabbalists' or in the '*musar* writings'. Most frequently, however, he employs kabbalistic doctrines without alluding either to their general kabbalistic provenance or to their specific kabbalistic source.

One should bear in mind that some of the kabbalistic texts cited by Landau may have been known to a wider Prague audience through their publication in Prague. Examples of such works are *Sefer yetsirah* and Cordovero's popular *musar* treatise *Tomer devorah*, which were published there in 1621 and 1624. Other kabbalistic books aimed at popularizing recondite kabbalistic texts and tenets, especially those of the Zohar and Cordoverian kabbalah, were also published in Prague during the seventeenth century. These include various introductory works to the Zohar by Issachar Ber Petahiah, as well as several introductory kabbalistic treatises influenced by Cordoverian concepts by the Prague kabbalist Shabetai Sheftel Horowitz.

[10] See Landau, *Tselaḥ*, *Ber.*, introd.

[11] See e.g. the end of *NB Kama*, 'YD', no. 93.

This section charts and analyses Landau's use of doctrines which, although not usually presented as such, are rooted in early mystical texts, zoharic, Cordoverian, or Lurianic writings. It also demonstrates his presumption that his audience was familiar with many of these kabbalistic teachings.

SEVEN

Zohar and Early Mystical Sources

CONCEPTS ORIGINATING IN *SEFER YETSIRAH* (Book of Creation) are found in several of Landau's writings, and zoharic motifs repeatedly appear in his Prague works. At times he even refers to these mystical texts by name. In a few sermons and commentaries, he describes the supernal realm in terms of the ten *sefirot beli mah*,[1] a term from *Sefer yetsirah*.[2] Countless other writings by Landau appropriate theosophical-theurgical notions emphasized in the Zohar, such as the depiction of the sefirotic realm's three major aspects (the right, left, and centre), and Israel's ability to influence them through their deeds.

Sefer yetsirah and Other Possible Mystical Works

Sefer yetsirah was the first systematic Hebrew mystical treatise,[3] composed between the third and sixth centuries,[4] and is the oldest mystical text used by Landau. It begins with the pronouncement that God created the world through 'thirty-two secret paths of wisdom', defined as the 'ten *sefirot beli mah*' and the 'twenty-two basic letters' of the Hebrew alphabet.[5] In his introduction to the *Tselaḥ* on *Berakhot*, Landau cites concepts from *Sefer yetsirah*, including the ten *sefirot beli mah* and the thirty-two paths of wisdom, about which he had heard in

[1] Scholars disagree about the meaning of this phrase. Some claim that its derivation is from a verse in Job 26: 7 and is similar in meaning to the verse's parallel term *tohu* (chaos). Others claim that it is derived from the word *balum* (locked, closed), found in a phrase in *Sefer yetsirah*, 1: 8 (p. 142): *balum pikha miledaber* ('close your mouth [and refrain] from speaking'), where it denotes that one should not speak about such esoteric matters. After the phrase *sefirot beli mah* was introduced in *Sefer yetsirah*, it became an accepted trope in kabbalistic literature.

[2] The term *sefirot* first appears in *Sefer yetsirah*, though it primarily denotes numbers there. See Scholem, *Kabbalah*, 23–8; Idel, *Kabbalah*, 112.

[3] Although *Sefer yetsirah* dates from a period preceding the emergence of the first historical stages of the kabbalah, which, according to modern scholarship, occurred in late 12th-c. Provence, I include it in my discussion of the kabbalistic sources that influenced Landau, since the kabbalists read *Sefer yetsirah* as a kabbalistic work. Despite the indeterminate nature of the phrase *sefirot beli mah* in *Sefer yetsirah*, the kabbalists, and probably Landau, interpreted it through the prism of their theosophical understanding of the term *sefirot*.

[4] There are three extant versions of this text that date from the 10th c., although the work was written before the 6th c. See Gruenwald, 'Preliminary Critical Edition of *Sefer Yezira*'; references are to this edition.

[5] Gruenwald, 'Preliminary Critical Edition of *Sefer Yezira*', 1: 1 and 2 (p. 140).

his youth. He also refers to *Sefer yetsirah* and its doctrines when expounding on the significance of the Hebrew letters or specific numbers in other Prague commentaries and sermons.[6] For instance, in a 1761 homily, he asserts that the mishnaic statement that the world was created with ten utterances 'alludes to the ten *sefirot beli mah* discussed at the beginning of *Sefer yetsirah*'.[7]

Besides using the general term *sefirot*,[8] Landau, unlike *Sefer yetsirah*, also mentions individual *sefirot* by name. In his sermons he frequently refers to the final *sefirah*, Malkhut (Kingdom) and, albeit less often, the first *sefirah*, Keter (Crown).[9] Elsewhere he alludes to other *sefirot* and their respective attributes and mates, particularly the two supernal pairs, Hokhmah (Wisdom) and Binah (Understanding) and Hesed (Grace or Love) and Gevurah (Strength, Rigour) or Din (Judgement).[10] Since many of these sefirotic names and symbols appear in texts written after *Sefer yetsirah* but before the Zohar, such as *Sefer habahir* (Book of Bright Light) and other early kabbalistic treatises,[11] these works could have served as the source for his remarks on individual *sefirot*. However, these comments may be based on the Zohar, a text he frequently employs.

[6] See e.g. *Tselaḥ*, *Ber.*, preface, where he discusses the connection between the 22 letters of the Hebrew alphabet and the ten *sefirot beli mah* mentioned in *Sefer yetsirah*. See also ibid, *Ber.* 30*b* (p. 117), where Landau states that, according to its esoteric meaning, the talmudic recommendation that 'one should direct one's heart to God' during prayer alludes to the fact that one should focus on the 32 paths of Hokhmah (Wisdom) discussed in *Sefer yetsirah*. Landau is playing here with the notion that the numerology of the Hebrew letters for the word *lev*, 'heart', equals 32.

[7] *Ahavat tsiyon*, sermon 2, 3*b*.

[8] See e.g. *Derushei hatselaḥ*, sermon 25, 40*a*. Like many kabbalists, he also uses the general term *midot* to refer to the *sefirot*. See e.g. *Tselaḥ*, *Pes.*, 54*a* (p. 216).

[9] See *Derushei hatselaḥ*, sermon 9, 17*b*; *Ahavat tsiyon*, sermon 2, 3*a*. On Landau's use of numerous symbols associated with the *sefirah* Malkhut, see Part IV.

[10] See e.g. *Tselaḥ*, *Ber.* 30*b* (p. 117), s.v. *ein omdin*. Landau's linking of the *sefirah* Hokhmah with the *sefirah* Hesed in this gloss hinges on the kabbalistic notion that Hokhmah, which is on the right side in the sefirotic realm, is directly above Hesed, and is therefore designated as upper-Hesed. Binah is similarly designated as upper-Gevurah, since it is directly above Gevurah on the left side in the sefirotic realm. In this gloss, his explanation is based on the kabbalistic conception of these two parallel sefirotic pairs, Hokhmah and Binah, and Hesed and Gevurah. He also plays with the idea of Hokhmah and Binah as sefirotic mates in the introduction to the *Tselaḥ* on *Berakhot*, where, immediately after mentioning the 32 paths of Hokhmah, he refers to the talmudic notion of the 50 gates of Binah (BT *RH* 21*b*; *Ned.* 38*a*). On Landau's description of these *sefirot*, see also *Tselaḥ*, *Ber.* 34*b* (pp. 129–30).

[11] *Sefer habahir* is one of the first works to describe the *sefirot* as divine attributes and in a symbolic manner. Scholem describes it as the first treatise to discuss the sefirotic realm and therefore the first kabbalistic work. The earliest extant manuscript of *Sefer habahir* was copied in 1298, and it was first printed in its entirety in 1651, in Amsterdam. On this work, see Scholem, *Origins of the Kabbalah*, 49–198; id., *Kabbalah*, 313–16; *The Book Bahir*, ed. Abrams (Heb.).

The Zohar

Landau's Prague writings are replete with citations from the Zohar, one of the central works of Jewish mysticism,[12] composed largely during the last decades of the thirteenth century.[13] By the eighteenth century the Zohar was regarded as a sacred text in many Jewish circles.[14] Scholars argue, however, over the extent to which its contents were known to the Jewish public in eastern and central Europe. The recent research of the art historian Thomas Hubka has shown that major zoharic motifs were incorporated into the architectural design and interior decorations of numerous seventeenth- and eighteenth-century Polish synagogues. These widely-used visual motifs probably familiarized a large audience in eastern Europe, including those who were not literate—or at least could not read Hebrew or Aramaic—with zoharic symbols. Whether zoharic motifs were used at all in Prague as part of the visual vernacular is difficult to ascertain, as scant evidence remains.[15] Still, Landau's Prague writings, particularly his sermons, with their frequent use of zoharic concepts, indicate his congregants' basic familiarity with them. Nonetheless, in one responsum he states that in his generation it would be appropriate 'to restrict the study of the Zohar'.[16] In this case, however, the remark was primarily meant to denounce the Sabbatians'

[12] On the Zohar's authoritative status as well as its themes and structure, see Scholem, *Major Trends*, 156–243; id., *Kabbalah*, 213–43; id., *Kabbalah and its Symbolism*, 89; Tishby, *Wisdom of the Zohar*; Liebes, *Studies in the Zohar*; id., 'Zohar and Eros' (Heb.); Huss, '*Sefer ha-Zohar*', 257–307. On the Zohar's influence on Ashkenazi Jewish culture in the late 16th and 17th cc., see Elbaum, *Opening and Withdrawal* (Heb.), esp. 183–222, 184 n. 3; J. Katz, 'Post-Zoharic Relations between Halakhah and Kabbalah'; id., *Halakhah and Kabbalah* (Heb.).

[13] Most contemporary academic scholars maintain that the Zohar was largely composed in Castile by a group of kabbalists and that the most famous member of this group was Moses de Leon. For a discussion of how the Zohar was composed, see Liebes, *Studies in the Zohar*, 85–134. In his *Halakhic Residue in the Zohar* (Heb.), 51–2, Ta-Shma places the Zohar's author in the school of Nahmanides in Gerona during the 1260s or 1270s. For a critique of this thesis, see Liebes, 'The Zohar as a Halakhic Book' (Heb.).

[14] On the Zohar's prominence in the 18th c., see Scholem, *Major Trends*, 156–67; Tishby, *Wisdom of the Zohar*, i. 29–30; Gries, 'Between Literature and History' (Heb.); id., 'The Copying and Printing of Kabbalistic Books' (Heb.); Huss, '*Sefer ha-Zohar*'. Contrary to Tishby and Scholem, Gries asserts that the Zohar was not widely disseminated until the 18th c., and that even then it never became a canonical text. In a similar vein, Huss suggests that the wider dissemination of the Zohar during the 18th c. only reflects its use as a holy book, not necessarily its canonical status. See Huss, '*Sefer ha-Zohar*', 297. More recently, Hubka has pointed to the importance of visual modes as a means of diffusing zoharic ideas during the 17th and 18th cc. See Hubka, 'The "Zohar" and the Polish Synagogue', 182–6.

[15] Although some of the synagogues and other communal buildings that existed in 18th-cent. Prague still stand, most of their interiors have been entirely remodelled.

[16] *NB Kama*, 'YD', no. 74. Immediately preceding this quote, Landau repudiates the ideas of the Sabbatians.

specific focus on the Zohar.[17] A detailed examination of Landau's works shows that both he and Prague's Jews incorporated the Zohar's essential doctrines into their larger world-view and regarded it as a sacred and authoritative text.

Many of Landau's explicit references to the Zohar appear in his Prague homilies and eulogies. An example appears in his 1762 eulogy for the Prague High Court judge Isaac Wolf Austerlitz. At the beginning of the eulogy, recorded in a manuscript by one of Landau's students,[18] he asserts that Austerlitz, who passed away on a sabbath afternoon, died at a time of *ratson* (grace). Citing the Zohar and appropriating its language,[19] he explains that while the forces of judgement prevail during weekday afternoons, on sabbath afternoon the powers of grace are dominant.[20] This idea provides the foundation for much of the eulogy. Landau similarly cites zoharic notions in numerous Prague writings, demonstrating both his extensive knowledge of this classic kabbalistic work and his conviction that zoharic concepts had already become an integral aspect of the popular culture and 'grammar' of his congregants.[21]

The Zohar is often used by Landau as a tool to bolster his rebuke of Prague Jews for their religious laxity. In a homily of about 1757, he admonishes worshippers who talk during the synagogue service, exclaiming that 'they have no share in the God of Israel, as explained in the holy Zohar.'[22] In another sermon, in which he again harshly censures this group, calling them apostates, he subsequently remarks that 'heaven forbid that these words are my own, rather they are solely the words of the Zohar.'[23] He also invokes the Zohar's authority as a means to rebuke Prague Jewry for their careless observance of several laws pertaining to *tefilin* (phylacteries).[24] Zoharic views are similarly cited in order to encourage certain paths of penitence.[25] Clearly, Landau, a traditional rabbinic

[17] Because of their emphasis on the Zohar (see Part II) the Frankists even referred to themselves as 'Zoharites'. See Emden, *Sefer mitpaḥat sefarim*, 20. See also Scholem, *Messianic Idea*, 173, 358 n. 19; Werses, *Haskalah and Sabbatianism* (Heb.), 147.

[18] This eulogy, delivered by Landau on 28 Mar. 1762, was first printed in *Kerem shelomoh*, 7 (1991), 6–8. He mentions its delivery in *NB Kama*, 'EH', no. 10.

[19] See Zohar, ii. 88*b*. On sabbath afternoon as a time of grace, see Ginsburg, *Sabbath in the Classical Kabbalah*, 201–2.

[20] Landau, 'Eulogy for Isaac Wolf Austerlitz' (Heb.), 6.

[21] See e.g. *Derushei hatselaḥ*, sermon 24, 37*b*, where he asserts that Prague Jews should perform certain commandments for the sake of the *neshamah* (soul) and supports this plea by citing a zoharic teaching. See also ibid., sermon 23, 36*a*, where he quotes the Zohar's portrayal of King David's confession to the prophet Nathan.

[22] Ibid., sermon 4, 9*b*. This exact phrase and idea appears in the Zohar (ii. 131*b*). For a discussion of this theme in kabbalistic sources, see Hallamish, *Kabbalah in Liturgy, Halakhah, and Customs* (Heb.), 401–33.

[23] *Derushei hatselaḥ*, sermon 24, 38*a*.

[24] Ibid., sermon 4, 9*a*. He cites the zoharic idea that when God asks for a Temple this refers to the *tefilin*. See Zohar, i. 129*a–b* (*Midrash hane'elam*). He asserts that one should therefore observe the laws of *tefilin* meticulously.

[25] See *Ahavat tsiyon*, sermon 2, 4*a*, where he discusses penitence based on an elevated fear as described in the Zohar. See Zohar, i. 11*b* and see below, Chapter 8, for a discussion of the concept of 'elevated fear'.

authority, and as such primarily concerned with praxis, would not have used the Zohar in this manner unless he was confident that it would effect changes in his community's normative conduct.[26]

His responsa and commentaries also contain explicit references to the Zohar and zoharic concepts. In a 1789 responsum sent to the Jewish court of the Moravian city of Trest he addresses a mysterious zoharic notion. The city had just experienced a severe drought, and certain members of Trest's Jewish court wanted permission, should such a drought recur, to take a Torah scroll to the cemetery in order to pray with it. Quoting the Zohar, they contend in a query sent to Landau that these actions would arouse the dead to plead for mercy on their behalf. In response, Landau writes:

> what you claim as obvious, namely, that according to the Zohar this practice is permissible, is incorrect. The truth is that I do not engage in the secret mysteries . . . But since you already saw the Zohar, is it not explained there that if, God forbid, this Torah scroll is missing even one letter, this practice will cause great harm . . . Therefore Heaven forbid that we should observe this custom.[27]

Despite Landau's protestations that he does not engage in kabbalah, this responsum reveals that he is well versed in the Zohar.[28] Interestingly, he does not dismiss the validity of the zoharic custom suggested by the Trest judges. Instead, he appears to take this practice seriously, and discusses the necessary conditions for invoking the compassion of the dead. He warns that since there are hardly any perfect Torah scrolls extant, performing this custom could cause great damage, as depicted in the Zohar. In several talmudic glosses he likewise displays his veneration for the Zohar, both by referring to zoharic biblical exegesis and by insinuating that early halakhic *posekim* did not deliberately dismiss this text.[29]

[26] Landau's use of the Zohar in this fashion reflects his belief that it had authoritative status for Prague Jews. However, in one remark in *Derushei hatselaḥ*, sermon 4, 9*a*, he seems to express somewhat different sentiments, indicating that although his community respects the Zohar, they regard its teachings as beyond the norms required by halakhah.

[27] *NB Tinyana*, 'OḤ', no. 109. This responsum is dated 16 Sivan 5549 (10 June 1789). Landau continues to stress his point by asking where the community could even find a Torah scroll that had been certified as not having extra or missing letters. On Trest, see Fiedler, *Jewish Sights of Bohemia and Moravia*, 186–7.

[28] See Zohar, iii. 71*a–b*, the passage to which Landau refers in this responsum. The Zohar relates there that although certain individuals took a Torah scroll to the cemetery, they were unable to influence the souls of the Patriarchs to pray on behalf of the world because the scroll had an extra letter *vav* in the word *perasot* (hooves), a word found in Lev. 11: 3.

[29] See e.g. *Tselaḥ*, *Pes.* 53*b* (p. 216), and *Ber.* 3*a* (p. 9), where Landau comments, in the context of a discussion on midnight as a time of grace, that the earlier *posekim* did not engage with the Zohar on this topic because this book was not available during their era. This remark implies that he views the Zohar as an important and authoritative source, and does not even entertain the notion that earlier authorities might have dismissed this kabbalistic text.

Aside from citing the Zohar explicitly, Landau often draws on zoharic tropes without mentioning their provenance. Many of his remarks on the soul, resurrection, eschatology, and the demonic realm are heavily influenced by this classic text, as are many of his teachings on the holidays, and other kabbalistic images found in his writings.[30] One of the zoharic concepts he uses most is the notion that the *sefirot* are divided into three aspects: Hesed (grace or love) on the right side,[31] Gevurah (strength, rigour) or Din (judgement) on the left side, and Rahamim (mercy) in the centre.[32]

In his talmudic commentary, he employs the motif of the right side of grace and the left side of judgement in order to explain various complex concepts and passages.[33] For instance, in the course of interpreting a cryptic aggadic dictum in *Berakhot*, he asserts that from the time of the six days of creation 'the right, the left, and the median which are grace, judgement, and mercy, are contained in one another.'[34] He goes on to invoke a related esoteric zoharic motif, namely that the legs of the Heavenly Throne are comprised of the three Patriarchs, who symbolize Hesed (right, Abraham), Gevurah (left, Isaac), Rahamim (centre, Jacob).[35] Expanding on these ideas, Landau, like the Zohar, often portrays divine providence in terms of these sefirotic aspects,[36] and particularly applies these terms to the relationship between the Land of Israel and other lands.[37]

[30] See e.g. *Derushei hatselah*, sermon 24, 38*a*; sermon 22, 34*a*, where he mentions the zoharic notion of the *ushpizin* (guests), who arrive on Sukkot.

[31] Like other kabbalists, Landau is not always systematic in his use of the names Hesed and Rahamim and occasionally interchanges them.

[32] These three aspects are mentioned in *Sefer habahir* and certain descriptions of the left, right, and centre are even found in *Sefer yetsirah*, particularly in its discussion of the significance of the elements of fire, water, and air. See *Sefer yetsirah*, 2: 1 (p. 151); 3: 2 (p. 151). However, Landau's use of the notion of the three aspects of the sefirotic realm seems to be influenced primarily by zoharic teachings. On the Zohar's portrayal of these three divine aspects, see Wolfson, 'Left Contained in the Right'.

[33] Landau's introduction to the *Tselah* on *Berakhot* states that there are 'three aspects in the ten *sefirot*, right, left, and centre, and in them are the three aspects grace, judgement, and mercy'. See also *Tselah*, *Ber.* 4*b* (p. 16).

[34] Ibid. *Ber.* 34*b* (p. 130). In the remainder of this gloss, he appropriates various other zoharic tropes, such as the *shabat elyon* (supernal sabbath). On the Zohar's discussion of the supernal sabbath, see e.g. Zohar, i. 5*b*.

[35] *Tselah*, *Ber.* 34*b* (p. 130). The idea that the Heavenly Throne consists of the three patriarchs appears in various zoharic passages. See Zohar, i. 99*a*, 154*b*, 229*a*. Elsewhere in the *Tselah*, Landau also refers to Abraham and Isaac as representing Hesed and Gevurah. See e.g. *Tselah*, *Pes.* 56*a* (p. 218).

[36] e.g. his explanation of the talmudic statement that those who recite the Ashrei prayer three times a day will merit the world to come. After citing Rashi's interpretation of this statement, Landau offers his own, more mystical, explanation. See *Tselah*, *Ber.* 4*b* (p. 16), where he states that reciting the Ashrei prayer three times a day alludes to man's need to thank God for His particular interaction with him through His distinctive combination of one, two, or three of the primary divine aspects, Hesed, Gevurah, and Rahamim. See also *Tselah*, *Pes.* 56a and *Ber.* 16*b* (p. 67).

[37] Ibid., *Ber.* 62*b* (p. 221), where he writes that the right side, Hesed, alludes to the Land of Israel, and the left side, Din (Gevurah), refers to lands outside Israel.

On occasion, Landau even suggests that the Zohar's conception of Hesed, Din, and Rahamim form the underlying foundation of various talmudic arguments and biblical narratives. An example appears in a lengthy comment in the *Tselaḥ*, where he uses these notions to explain each sage's position in a four-way talmudic dispute.[38] In this argument, each of the four sages presents an image which he claims persuaded God to halt the plague visited upon King David, as described in 1 Chronicles 21: 15. Drawing on several zoharic concepts,[39] Landau maintains that each of these four images represents the kabbalistic ideal of joining divine mercy and divine judgement.[40]

The zoharic trope of the divine left of judgement and the divine right of grace also serves as a *leitmotif* in many of Landau's sermons, especially in discussions concerning penitence.[41] He asserts that the various names of the Divine represent, 'justice and mercy, which are the left and the right, *as it is known* . . . That is, one may return either to the right or to the left side' (emphasis added).[42] Later in the same homily, however, he states that since people are removed from God because of their sins, penitents initially can only approach the left side (judgement), for the 'right side of mercy' is closed off to them.[43] His repeated use of this imagery in diverse genres of his work in order to portray the Divine and the atonement process shows that he not only espoused these notions but thought in terms of these kabbalistic categories. These writings also indicate his assumption that these kabbalistic concepts were 'known' to Prague Jews.[44]

Two related zoharic ideals also appear frequently in Landau's writings: the transformation of the divine left of judgement into the divine right of grace and

[38] Ibid., *Ber.* 62*b*, s.v. *mai ra'ah*.

[39] He claims that each concept functions like the sacrificial incense used in the Temple (see Exod. 30: 7–8), which had the extraordinary power to terminate plagues by joining divine mercy and divine judgement. On the Zohar's portrayal of incense as unifying the *sefirot* and thereby linking divine justice and mercy, see Zohar, ii. 218*b*–219*b*, 230*a*. The Zohar explains that since the incense removes fury in this fashion, the high priest Aaron used it to stay the plague depicted in Num. 17: 11–13. In addition to appropriating these ideas, Landau also echoes the zoharic notion that incense is particularly important during the afternoon, when the principle of judgement holds sway. See Zohar, ii. 230*a*. In this gloss he also interprets other biblical verses in accordance with the zoharic conception of the three principal aspects within the divine realm.

[40] Landau suggests, however, that the last image in this talmudic passage alludes to the related zoharic ideal of containing divine judgement within divine mercy.

[41] See e.g. *Derushei hatselaḥ*, sermon 17 for Rosh Hashanah, 27*b*; sermon 5, 10*b*.

[42] Ibid., sermon 5, 11*a*. As noted above, Landau, like other kabbalists, occasionally interchanges the terms Rahamim (Mercy) and Hesed (Grace).

[43] Ibid. 11*b*. He therefore explains that on Rosh Hashanah, also called Yom Hadin (the Day of Judgement), a person first awakens the left side and only later attempts to rouse mercy, on the right side. For a similar portrayal of Yom Hadin, see *Derushei hatselaḥ*, sermon 12, 20*a*.

[44] See *Derushei hatselaḥ*, sermon for Rosh Hashanah, 6*a*; sermon 35 (for Hanukah), 49*a*, where he introduces several comments on the divine right and left with the assertion that the motif 'is known'.

the containment of the divine left within the divine right.[45] In numerous passages where he uses these motifs,[46] he ascribes them to Rashi's commentary on the biblical phrase the 'right hand of the Lord' (Exod. 15: 6).[47] Curiously, Rashi's remarks are devoid of any mention of either the divine attributes of grace and judgement or the containment of the divine left within the divine right.[48] Landau's comments on changing divine judgement into divine grace or containing judgement within grace originate not in Rashi, but in the Zohar.

Landau also uses the zoharic tropes of the divine left turning into, or being contained by, the divine right in his biblical exegesis; an example is his portrayal of the biblical miracle of the splitting of the Red Sea. Mirroring zoharic teachings, he asserts that, at the height of Israel's redemption—the splitting of the Red Sea—divine judgement turned into grace. Drawing further on zoharic ideas, he writes that although the punishment meted out to the Egyptians seemed like the product of *gevurah*, it turned into *gedulah* (greatness),[49] terms which, in the Zohar, respectively denote the divine left of judgement and the divine right of grace.[50] He appropriates both this motif and the concept of containing the divine left within the divine right in his exegesis of other biblical narratives and verses.[51]

In a similar vein, he emphasizes that Israel's deeds can cause the divine left to be contained by the divine right or even turn the divine left into the divine right. In his Prague sermons and commentaries, he repeatedly notes that 'when Israel performs the divine will . . . the left is transformed into the right'.[52] In con-

[45] In the Zohar, these motifs represent grace turning into judgement, and the harmony of grace and judgement in the sefirotic realm, respectively. On the Zohar's discussion of the transformation of the divine left into the divine right, or vice versa, see e.g. Zohar, ii. 36*a*, 63*a*, 152*b*, iii. 15*b*, 30*b*, 65*a*, 207*b*. On the zoharic trope of containing the divine left within the divine right, see Zohar, i. 16*b*, ii. 84*a*, 84*b*, 98*b*, 162*b*, iii. 178*a*. For analysis of this trope, see Wolfson, 'Left Contained in the Right'.

[46] See e.g. *Derushei hatselaḥ*, sermon 28, 44*a*, and sermon for Rosh Hashanah, 6*a*; *Tselaḥ*, *Ber.* 30*b* (p. 117), *Pes.* 56*a*, and *Ber.* 58*a* (p. 215).

[47] Rashi on Exod. 15: 6. See the discussion of this in Chapter 6.

[48] Although Rashi's glosses do mention the 'left' and the 'right', they do not refer to the kabbalistic notions of changing divine judgement into divine grace, or containing divine judgement within divine grace.

[49] *Tselaḥ*, *Ber.* 58*a* (p. 215). Echoing the Zohar, he exegetically connects the phrase 'the *right* [hand] of the Lord' (Exod. 15: 6) from the Song of the Sea with the verse 'and Israel saw the *great* hand which the Lord wrought against the Egyptians' (Exod. 14: 31). See Zohar, ii. 52*b*. He claims that these two descriptions refer to God's *ḥesed*, grace, which in the Zohar is represented both by the right side and by the term *gedulah*, 'greatness'.

[50] On the Zohar's use of the term *gedulah* to refer to the fourth *sefirah*, Hesed, see e.g. Zohar, ii. 59*b*. In kabbalistic literature, the term *gevurah* often designates the fifth *sefirah*, also known as Din (divine judgement).

[51] See e.g. his exegesis of Israel's victory over the Amorites in *Tselaḥ*, *Ber.* 58*a* (p. 215). See also his discussions of these concepts in *Ber.* 4*b* (pp. 15–16) and 62*b* (p. 221).

[52] See *Derushei hatselaḥ*, sermon 14, 24*b*; sermon 17, 27*b*; sermon 28, 44*a*; sermon for Rosh Hashanah, 6*a*; *Tselaḥ*, Pes. 56*a*, and *Ber.* 6*a* (p. 21).

sonance with the Zohar, he specifically stresses that the *shofar* blasts sounded on Rosh Hashanah turn the divine judgement of the left side into the divine compassion of the right side.[53] Prayer, he similarly contends, has the power to alter the sefirotic balance. Using the hermeneutical method of *gematriyah* (numerology), he alleges that the talmudic dictum that people should direct their hearts to God during prayer intimates that individuals should direct their prayers to Gevurah and Hesed. This, he explains, will help contain the divine left within the divine right.[54] Clearly, his conception of Israel's theurgical powers is integrally linked to his understanding of the zoharic tropes of the divine left and right.

Many of Landau's Prague writings both quote the Zohar and *Sefer yetsirah* explicitly, and adopt their tenets without citing the provenance of these ideas. Besides using the Zohar directly, he may have also appropriated zoharic concepts found in later kabbalistic works, such as Cordoverian and Lurianic texts, and especially the *musar* writings of Cordovero's disciples, which are heavily indebted to the Zohar.[55] Since he respected and was familiar with a wide range of these later kabbalistic texts, his zoharic teachings were, at times, also interpreted through this later kabbalistic lens.

[53] On the Zohar's depiction of the effect of the *shofar* blasts on the sefirotic realm, see Zohar, i. 114*a*–*b*, iii. 99*a*–100*b*, 149*b*. On Landau's use of this motif, see *Derushei hatselaḥ*, sermon for Rosh Hashanah, 6*a*. Although in this homily Landau mentions a midrash from *Leviticus Rabbah* 29: 4 which states that the *shofar* blast causes God to move from the throne of judgement to the throne of compassion, this text does not refer to the kabbalistic trope of the divine right and left. See also Landau's remarks on the shofar in *Derushei hatselaḥ*, sermon 12, 20*a*–*b*.

[54] *Tselaḥ, Ber.* 30*b* (p. 117).

[55] Citations from the Zohar are frequently found in Cordoverian, Lurianic, and *musar* writings. For instance, the zoharic ideal of containing divine judgement within divine grace is also stressed in the work of Cordovero's disciple, Elijah de Vidas. See e.g. de Vidas, *Reshit ḥokhmah*, 'Sha'ar ha'-ahavah', 1, 22 (p. 358), and 3, 25 (p. 395).

EIGHT

The Path to Devekut: *Ecstatic and Cordoverian Teachings*

ASIDE FROM availing himself of zoharic teachings in all his works, Landau also appropriates Cordoverian expressions, motifs, and ideals.[1] The central mystical goal of *devekut*, promoted in both ecstatic and Cordoverian writings, is so significant to him that he claims that nothing less than the structure of the universe, the purpose of human activity, reward and punishment, and the nature of the next world all relate to this state.[2] In line with various ecstatic and Cordoverian kabbalists, such as Abulafia and de Vidas, he also frequently advocates the ideal of *devekut* and related mystical concepts in terms borrowed from Maimonides' philosophical and legal works.[3] However, despite his use of Maimonidean terminology, Landau presents this mystical material in a highly ecstatic and impassioned manner.

Using ideas that bear a striking similarity to elements of ecstatic and Cordoverian kabbalah, he both promotes the ideal of *devekut* and advances a range of techniques for achieving this mystical state. The presence of the goal of *devekut* and the techniques leading to it are characteristic features of the ecstatic trend of kabbalah, and are regularly incorporated into Cordoverian works. Landau's advocacy of techniques to attain *devekut* indicates that his discussions of this ideal are not merely exegetical, but are influenced by ecstatic and Cordoverian tenets. As in many Cordoverian writings, he stresses the value of both nomian and anomian, or

[1] On Moses Cordovero, see Ben-Shlomo, *Mystical Theology of Moses Cordovero* (Heb.); id., 'Moses Cordovero'; Sack, *Kabbalah of Rabbi Moses Cordovero* (Heb.).

[2] On the mystical goal of *devekut*, see Idel, *Kabbalah*, pp. xi, 62; id., *Hasidism*, 52, 55–6, 86; Scholem, *Messianic Idea*, 203–27. The ideal of *devekut* appears in the book of Deuteronomy (10: 20; 11: 22; 13: 5; 30: 20). However, both the techniques used to attain *devekut* and its meaning were first discussed by medieval Jewish philosophers and particularly by the ecstatic kabbalists.

[3] On Abulafia's use of Maimonidean terms, which are largely based on Aristotelian terminology, see Idel, *Studies in Ecstatic Kabbalah*, 2–3, 16–17. On the use of Maimonidean terms in de Vidas' writings on *devekut*, see e.g. *Reshit ḥokhmah*, 'Sha'ar ha'ahavah', 8, 4 (p. 533). For a general discussion of various kabbalists' use of Aristotelian terminology in their portrayal of *devekut*, and the commonality between some philosophical terms and goals and those of ecstatic kabbalah, see Idel, *Kabbalah*, 39–40; id., *Studies in Ecstatic Kabbalah*, 103–69. On Maimonides' writings and mysticism, see Blumenthal, 'Maimonides'; Shmidman, 'Maimonides' "Conversion" to Kabbalah'.

a-halakhic, avenues to *devekut*, often claiming that the proper observance of the commandments leads to an individual's cleaving to God. Like ecstatic and Cordoverian kabbalists,[4] he also suggests that intensified forms of emotional states prescribed by normative law, such as heightened love and fear of God, foster different levels of *devekut*—ideas echoed in numerous hasidic writings. In this vein, he advocates focusing all one's thoughts on the Divine in order to achieve and maintain these emotions and the mystical state of *devekut*.[5] Again drawing on ecstatic and Cordoverian traditions,[6] Landau also endorses several anomian vehicles as a means to attain *devekut*, including *hitbodedut* (solitary contemplation), enthusiasm, and desire. Strikingly, he offers an innovative mystical portrayal of what he calls the ultimate form of devotion, the fear of losing one's *devekut*.

Sources, Terms, and Motifs

Landau's teachings on the mystical and ecstatic ideal of *devekut* and its associated techniques are probably derived from the works of Cordovero and his disciples. The ecstatic kabbalists' notions were probably available to him through Cordovero's anthologies of earlier kabbalistic writings, which contain extensive passages from Abulafia.[7] Conceptions of *devekut* are also emphasized in the *musar* literature of Cordovero's students.[8] During the seventeenth and eighteenth centuries the dissemination of these ethical-mystical treatises steadily increased until they became widespread among central and east European Jews.[9] Cordoverian

[4] There is a running debate in kabbalistic writings as to whether the love of God or the fear of God is the higher preparatory state for *devekut*.

[5] The ecstatic and Cordoverian kabbalists probably inherited the tradition of the importance of focusing exclusively on the Divine from Maimonides. See *Mishneh torah*, 'Laws of Repentance', 10: 2–6; *Guide of the Perplexed*, iii. 51–4.

[6] For a discussion of anomian techniques promoted in ecstatic and Cordoverian kabbalah as a means of attaining *devekut*, see Idel, *Kabbalah*, 74–111; id., '*Hitbodedut* qua "Concentration" in Ecstatic Kabbalah' (Heb.). It should be noted that Landau does not mention the full range of ecstatic anomian techniques, omitting such practices as permutations of letters and visualization of colours.

[7] See Idel, *Hasidism*, esp. 58–60; id., *Studies in Ecstatic Kabbalah*, esp. 126–8.

[8] On the centrality of *devekut* in *musar* writings and in other works of Cordovero's disciples in Safed, see Pachter, 'Concept of Devekut'. See also id., 'Homiletic and Ethical Literature' (Heb.); Werblowsky, *Joseph Karo*, 38–83.

[9] On the transmission of Cordoverian and *musar* literature to eastern Europe, see Pachter, 'The Book *Reshit ḥokhmah*' (Heb.); Elbaum, 'Trends and Courses in Jewish Speculative and Moralistic Literature' (Heb.); id., 'Aspects of Hebrew Ethical Literature'; id., *Opening and Withdrawal* (Heb.); Piekarz, *Beginning of Hasidism* (Heb.); Idel, *Hasidism*, esp. 11; Krassen, 'Devequt and Faith in Zaddiqim'; Gries, *Conduct Literature* (Heb.); id., *The Book in Early Hasidism* (Heb.); id., 'Between Literature and History' (Heb.), 157–9. Gries asserts that *musar* literature was not widely available until the 18th c. On the dissemination of kabbalah through the *musar* literature, see also Scholem, *Major Trends*, 251.

teachings were also disseminated in seventeenth-century kabbalistic works, such as *Shefa tal* and *Nishmat shabetai halevi* by Shabetai Horowitz, which popularized Cordoverian concepts. (As mentioned earlier, both *Nishmat shabetai halevi* and Cordovero's influential *musar* tract *Tomer devorah* were published in Prague during the seventeenth century.) By the mid-eighteenth century, Cordovero's theoretical writings became increasingly well known in central and eastern Europe as well.[10] Such books, widely circulated in Poland and Prague, probably popularized the ecstatic ideals and Cordoverian doctrines mentioned and promoted by Landau.

Several Cordoverian sources are clearly employed in his writings. Although he never mentions these works by name, he appropriates idioms and motifs originally found in Cordovero's seminal book, *Pardes rimonim*, and his zoharic commentary, *Or yakar*.[11] On a few occasions, however, Landau does cite two prominent *musar* treatises replete with Cordoverian teachings: *Reshit ḥokhmah*[12] and *Shenei luḥot haberit*.[13] He particularly emphasizes ideas found in *Reshit ḥokhmah*[14] and repeatedly refers to the work of Alshekh,[15] who similarly integrates Cordoverian notions into his writings. Since he also often cites *musar* works in a generic manner, in remarks such as 'it is explained thus in the *musar* treatises',[16] or 'this is already known in all the *musar* books',[17] it is likely that he used other treatises of this genre, including *Sefer ḥaredim* by Eleazar Azikri

[10] Idel, 'Perceptions of Kabbalah', 77; id., *Hasidism*, 42. Several of Cordovero's books were in print for over a century and therefore easily accessible. Idel also lists other reasons for the increased popularity of Cordoverian kabbalah during the 18th c. He asserts that, in contrast to Lurianic sources, the study and printing of Cordoverian works was not restricted during this period. In addition, Cordoverian kabbalah was viewed as a necessary prerequisite for the study of Lurianic texts. Moreover, many preferred the scholastic language of Cordoverian kabbalah to the highly anthropomorphic language of Lurianic kabbalah.

[11] On the importance of *Pardes rimonim* in Ashkenazi culture during the 16th and 17th cc., see Elbaum, *Opening and Withdrawal* (Heb.), esp. 198. On the *Or yakar*, see Sack, *Kabbalah of Rabbi Moses Cordovero* (Heb.), 25–7.

[12] See *Derushei hatselaḥ*, sermon 23, 34*b*. During the 18th c., de Vidas' *Reshit ḥokhmah* was one of the most influential *musar* treatises. See Pachter, 'The Book *Reshit ḥokhmah*' (Heb.).

[13] See *Derushei hatselaḥ*, sermon 16 for Shabat Teshuvah (1768), 26*b*, and sermon 19, 29*b*. For a discussion of the strong influence of Cordoverian kabbalah on Horowitz's *Shenei luḥot haberit*, see Sack, 'Influence of Cordovero', 366–70.

[14] For example, in *Derushei hatselaḥ*, sermon 23, Landau explicitly cites teachings on repentance from *Reshit ḥokhmah*. In numerous other homilies, however, he employs concepts from this work without citing it.

[15] For Landau's citations of Alshekh, see *Tselaḥ*, *Ber.* 17*a* (p. 67); *Derushei hatselaḥ*, sermon 7 for the Fast of Gedaliah, 14*a*; sermon 9, 17*b*; sermon 15, 25*a*; sermon 18 for the second day of Rosh Hashanah, 28*a*; *Ahavat tsiyon*, sermon 1, 2*b*. On the ideal of *devekut* in Alshekh's writings, see Pachter, 'Concept of Devekut', 186–8.

[16] *Ahavat tsiyon*, sermon 5 (1774), 8*a*.

[17] *Derushei hatselaḥ*, sermon 25, 39*b*. For other examples of Landau's generic citation of the *musar* literature, see *Tselaḥ*, *Ber.* 15*b* (p. 65); *Derushei hatselaḥ*, sermon 1, 4*b*; sermon 3, 7*b*; sermon 15, 25*a*; *Ahavat tsiyon*, sermon 8, 12*b*.

(1533–1600) and *Ḥesed le'avraham* by Abraham Azulai (*c.*1570–1643).[18] Many Cordoverian tenets espoused by Landau appear in these works. He may have also been influenced by the *musar* treatise *Mesilat yesharim* written by his contemporary, the kabbalist Moses Hayim Luzzatto, with whom his father and uncle probably had some connection.[19] *Mesilat yesharim* likewise emphasizes the mystical ideal of *devekut*.

In addition to his frequent use of *musar* writings in his sermons and commentaries, Landau also exhibits his esteem for this genre. Notwithstanding the fact that in his responsa he occasionally hesitates to discuss kabbalistic concepts and practices found in *musar* treatises, even here his high regard for this literature is revealed.[20] One indication of this is a recommendation, appearing in both his sermons and a responsum, for individuals to include these texts in their personal curriculum of Torah study.[21] Given his respect for and use of *musar* writings, it is likely that this genre is the source of some of the Cordoverian notions found in his works without attribution.

Landau uses several phrases and concepts that first appear in Cordoverian works without citing their original source. A striking illustration of this is his appropriation of two Cordoverian tropes: the *or yashar* (direct light) and the *or ḥozer* (reflected light), elaborated upon in *Pardes rimonim*.[22] These terms convey Cordovero's conception that the entire sefirotic world is created by the coupled process of the direct light, an expression of God's mercy, emanating downward, and the returning light, the source of divine judgement, reflecting this process upward. The weakened returning light, or attribute of judgement, was necessary

[18] Azikri was among Cordovero's most famous students. On *devekut* and other Cordoverian ideals in his *Sefer ḥaredim*, see Werblowsky, *Joseph Karo*, 57–65; Pachter, 'Concept of Devekut', 202–9; Idel, *Studies in Ecstatic Kabbalah*, 132–4. On the use of Cordoverian kabbalah in Azulai's *Ḥesed le'avraham*, see Sack, 'Influence of Cordovero', 372–9.

[19] See Chapter 4.

[20] See e.g. *NB Tinyana*, 'OḤ', no. 107, where he expresses annoyance with a questioner for asking him about the esoteric practice of mourning for the Shekhinah that is discussed in the *musar* literature. Nonetheless, even on this occasion, he proffers an abbreviated response rather than dismissing the *musar* works as unimportant. On his ambivalence about using *musar* writings in his responsa, see also *NB Kama*, 'OḤ', no. 35, where he mocks the basis of many of the ascetic practices promoted in the *musar* literature while conceding that these materials and practices cannot be ignored altogether.

[21] See e.g. *Derushei hatselaḥ*, sermon 6, 13*a* and *NB Kama*, 'OḤ', no. 35, where he advises a penitent that he should include *musar* works, such as Bahyah ibn Pakuda's *Ḥovot halevavot* and Horowitz's *Shenei luḥot haberit*, in his Torah study. Even here, however, his ambivalence towards kabbalistic study is apparent, for although he promotes the study of Horowitz's largely kabbalistic *musar* work he warns the penitent not to focus on its kabbalistic sections.

[22] The trope of the *or yashar* and *or ḥozer* appears in many places in *Pardes rimonim* (such as Sha'ar 15: 'From Below to Above'). For a discussion of Cordovero's use of the term *or ḥozer* and its connection to judgement, see Ben-Shlomo, *Mystical Theology of Moses Cordovero* (Heb.), 270–4; id., 'Moses Cordovero', 402–4.

for completing the creation of the world.[23] Cordovero and other kabbalists maintain that during Rosh Hashanah, which commemorates the world's creation, the supernal state which existed during creation is replicated. Consequently, during Tishrei, the month in which Rosh Hashanah falls, the direct light retracts and the reflected light is dominant.[24]

The month of Tishrei is likewise associated with the *or ḥozer* in Landau's writings. In several homilies, he points out that the Hebrew letters of the word Tishrei— ת.ש.ר.י —are in reverse alphabetical order, thereby alluding to the *or ḥozer*, the attribute of judgement. Like these letters, he alleges, the *or yashar*, representing God's mercy, retracts at this time, making the *or ḥozer* dominant. Similarly, in both his talmudic commentary and sermons, Landau employs this trope to explain the reason for the diminishing numerical value of the letters used to signify the different *shofar* blasts sounded on Rosh Hashanah ת.ש.ר.ק.[25] This order of the letters, he claims, 'hints at the attribute of judgement, the *or ḥozer*'.[26]

Cordoverian parables and motifs also appear in Landau's works. In *Or yakar*, Cordovero writes that during the previous exiles the role of the Shekhinah was to guard the Jews, but in this last and harshest of exiles, the downtrodden Shekhinah needs assistance as well. Comparing the Shekhinah to an exiled princess, Cordovero notes that, in this final exile, 'if a servant brings the princess even a moist blade of grass, it is of greater value to her than all the delicacies she had in the king's palace'.[27] Analogously, in this exile, the Shekhinah appreciates all deeds that Israel performs on her behalf, no matter how small. An almost identical parable appears in one of Landau's Prague sermons. There he states

[23] On this idea, see Ben-Shlomo, *Mystical Theology of Moses Cordovero* (Heb.), 272, 274. Ben-Shlomo discusses the similarities between Cordovero's conception of the *or ḥozer* and Luria's notion of *tsimtsum*. Both these concepts necessitate a retraction of the Divine in order to allow for creation.

[24] Tishrei is therefore a period of divine judgement which inspires the awe and fear of God. On the association between Rosh Hashanah and divine judgement in various kabbalistic sources, see Krassen, 'Devequt and Faith in Zaddiqim', 303–8, 304 n. 199.

[25] In *gematriyah*, Hebrew numerology, *taf*, which represents the *shofar* sound *tekiyah*, is 400; *shin*, which represents the sound *shevarim*, is 300; *resh*, which represents the sound *teruah*, is 200; and *kuf*, which represents *tekiyah*, is 100.

[26] By contrast, Landau writes that the first Hebrew letters of the word Nisan, the month in which the Jews were redeemed from Egypt, are in ascending order. This alludes to the *or yashar*, or divine mercy, which prevails during this period. See *Tselaḥ, Ber.* 4*b*; *Derushei hatselaḥ*, sermon for Rosh Hashanah, 6*a*, and sermon 3, 6*b*. In this last source, Landau presents Nisan in terms of both the *or yashar* and the *or ḥozer* since, according to various kabbalistic works, Israel's redemption from Egypt involved divine judgement and divine mercy. These sources explain that although God redeemed Israel in his mercy, the redemption was carried out by the attribute of judgement. See e.g. Zohar, ii. 52*b*.

[27] Cordovero, *Or yakar*, vol. v, 'Vayetse', 219. On Cordovero's use of this parable, see Sack, 'The Exile of Israel' (Heb.); repr. in id., *Kabbalah of Rabbi Moses Cordovero* (Heb.), 249–66; id., 'Influence of Cordovero', 374–5.

that although originally the princess, or Shekhinah, had everything, in her exile no one does even the slightest thing for her. Therefore, if she finds someone who will assist her in the most minute way, she will value this more highly than anything done for her while she lived in the palace.[28] In another homily, he offers a slightly different variation on the same parable.[29] The similarity between these tales and the parable in Cordovero's commentary is striking. Landau may have encountered the original parable in *Or yakar*, in Azulai's rendition of it in *Ḥesed le'avraham*,[30] or in a variation found in *Reshit ḥokhmah*.[31]

The Ideal of *Devekut*

Besides appropriating Cordoverian expressions and parables, Landau often stresses the importance of *devekut*, as did the ecstatic and Cordoverian kabbalists. Although the ultimate aim of *devekut* is *unio mystica*, a total union with the Divine, both Cordoverian kabbalists and Landau use the term *devekut* to describe a range of stages of communion with God. As in the *musar* literature, which popularized the esoteric notion of *devekut*, Landau promotes this mystical ideal as a religious goal in various sermons and commentaries.

The centrality of *devekut* in his works is manifest both in the significance he assigns to it and the frequency of its appearance in his writings. In one homily he asserts that the 'purpose of everything is to achieve *devekut* with God'.[32] In another Prague sermon, in which he mentions the goal of cleaving to God over thirty times, he goes so far as to claim that the structure of the entire universe is related to this goal. In order to enable *devekut*, he explains,

> Ein Sof, blessed be He, emanated, created, formed, and made all of the worlds from the outer circumference of the Supernal Anthropos until the innermost realm of Malkhut within [the *sefirah* of] Malkhut in the World of Making. In this structure, all the worlds were included.[33]

[28] *Derushei hatselaḥ*, sermon 4, 8*a*.

[29] See ibid., sermon 6, 12*b*, where, in a lengthy narrative, Landau likens the Shekhinah to a king in a distant land where no one recognizes him. He explains that in this exile the king derives more pleasure from the small space that he is allotted than he had had from his entire kingdom at the height of his glory.

[30] Azulai reproduces Cordovero's parable in his *Ḥesed le'avraham*, 6*b*.

[31] See de Vidas, *Reshit ḥokhmah*, 'Sha'ar ha'ahavah', 8, 10 (p. 536): de Vidas recounts a parable that he attributes to his teacher, Cordovero, in which an exiled king appreciates a piece of bread and a glass of water that he receives in exile as much as he had appreciated the finest foods in his kingdom.

[32] *Derushei hatselaḥ*, sermon 39, 53*a*.

[33] *Ahavat tsiyon*, sermon 2, 3*a*–4*b*. The quotation is from 3*a*. Landau offers some of his most powerful remarks on *devekut* in this homily. According to many kabbalists, each of the ten *sefirot* have another, more attenuated, version of the ten *sefirot* within them, i.e. within Malkhut are elements of the *sefirot* of Keter, Hokhmah, Binah, etc. Thus Malkhut within Malkhut signifies the lowest divine element, Malkhut, within the lowest *sefirah*, Malkhut.

Since Landau, like all kabbalists, believes that the transcendent aspect of God, the Ein Sof (lit. infinite), is beyond all human experience,[34] he maintains that it is only through the sefirotic emanations, often portrayed by kabbalists in the shape of the Supernal Anthropos,[35] and through the many supernal worlds that humans have an opportunity to cleave to the Divine. The four verbs he uses in this passage to describe Ein Sof's formation of these worlds: 'emanated', 'created', 'formed', and 'made', allude to the kabbalistic doctrine of the four worlds of emanation: *olam ha'atsilut* (World of Emanation), *olam haberiyah* (World of Creation), *olam hayetsirah* (World of Formation), and *olam ha'asiyah* (World of Making), in which the *sefirot* are active to varying degrees.[36] This doctrine of the four worlds was fully developed in sixteenth-century Safed, particularly in the works of Cordovero and Luria.[37] Landau's comments on these worlds, the *sefirot*, and their connection to *devekut* are probably the product of sixteenth-century Safed writings. In any event, what is clear is that his explanation of these kabbalistic doctrines in terms of *devekut* points to the pivotal place of this mystical ideal in his understanding of the universe and religious world-view.

He bases other teachings on the ideal of *devekut* (particularly as to how it relates to the commandments) on mystical ideas, especially from Cordoverian kabbalah. Like Cordoverian kabbalists,[38] he subscribes to the belief that the path of *devekut* consists of numerous stages in which the highest aspect of the soul, the *neshamah*, progressively returns to its divine root in accordance with an individual's virtues and piety.[39] In line with many Cordoverian writings,[40] he also frequently alleges

[34] For a discussion of the term Ein Sof, see Scholem, *Kabbalah*, 88–91; Tishby, *Wisdom of the Zohar*, i. 229–68; Hallamish, *Introduction to the Kabbalah*, 121–5.

[35] The Hebrew term used in this passage is *adam kadmon*, the highest manifestation of God, configured in the shape of a man.

[36] According to many kabbalists, each of these worlds represents a different realm: *olam ha'atsilut*, the sefirotic realm; *olam haberiyah*, the realm of the Throne and Chariot; *olam hayetsirah*, the domain of the angels; and *olam ha'asiyah*, the terrestrial world. The names of these worlds are based on verbs used in Isa. 43: 7 and 45: 18. For a discussion of the different worlds in kabbalah, see Scholem, 'Evolution of the Doctrine of the Worlds' (Heb.); id., *Kabbalah*, 118–19; Tishby, *Wisdom of the Zohar*, ii. 555.

[37] The doctrine also appears in some sections of the Zohar, albeit usually without this specific terminology.

[38] On the notion, in both the *musar* treatises and the homiletical writings of Cordovero's disciples, that *devekut* is achieved through the *neshamah* see de Vidas, *Reshit ḥokhmah*, 'Sha'ar ha'ahavah', 1, 36 (p. 366) and 'Sha'ar hakedushah', 6, 14 (p. 88). See also Pachter, 'Concept of Devekut', 193, 221–2; Scholem, *Kabbalah*, 174.

[39] See *Ahavat tsiyon*, sermon 2, 3*a*–*b*. Echoing de Vidas and other Cordoverian kabbalists, Landau also asserts here (p. 3*b*) that a wicked person can never attain *devekut* since his 'sins are a screen of separation' between him and the Divine. Although this idea appears in the Zohar, Landau's connection of this trope to the ideal of *devekut* seems to stem from the influence of Cordoverian sources. See e.g. *Reshit ḥokhmah*, 'Sha'ar ha'ahavah', 3, 31 (p. 399).

[40] See e.g. *Reshit ḥokhmah*, 'Sha'ar ha'ahavah', 4, 24 (pp. 421–2).

that prayer, good deeds, and observance of the commandments all lead to *devekut* with God, and the Shekhinah in particular,[41] and that 'when a righteous person performs the commandments his intention is to achieve *devekut* with the supernal roots'.[42] In one of his most striking comments on this theme, found in both a Prague address and a talmudic gloss, he even pronounces that *devekut* 'is the main element in the fulfilment of a commandment'.[43] In the future, he suggests in another gloss, one will merit to see retroactively the *devekut* one achieved through the fulfilment of each commandment.[44]

The attainment of *devekut*, he further claims, is the ultimate reward that can be achieved both in this world and the next. Without the possibility of attaining *devekut*, he states in a sermon, one could not receive reward or punishment for performing or violating the commandments.[45] This is due to the fact that the principal 'enjoyment in this world is *devekut* with the Shekhinah, which one achieves by ascending from level to level and from world to world . . . All ten [*sefirot*] were created in order to bestow a good reward.'[46] While the pious temporarily attain the ultimate reward of *devekut* in this world, in the World to Come they will continuously be in this state of '*devekut* with the Shekhinah',[47] a concept he probably bases on Maimonides' use of this talmudic expression. Like one case in Maimonides' writings but unlike the Talmud,[48] Landau employs this phrase to depict a state that an individual *can* attain.

However, in accordance with the ecstatic kabbalists (especially Abulafia), in his discussions of *devekut* he often adapts Maimonidean ideas and terms to his own mystical perspective. For example, instead of associating the goal of achieving '*devekut* with the Shekhinah' with the union of the righteous with the Active

[41] e.g. *Derushei hatselaḥ*, sermon 1, 3*b*; sermon 6, 13*b*; sermon 24, 37*a*; sermon 28, 43*a*; sermon for Passover, 57*b*; *Ahavat tsiyon*, sermon 2, 3*b*.

[42] *Ahavat tsiyon*, sermon 2, 3*b*.

[43] Ibid., sermon 3 to the Hevrat Gemilut Hasadim (Charitable Works Society; 1761 or 1762), 5*a*. See also *Tselaḥ*, *Ber.* 28*b* (p. 109). Despite the absence of the ideal of *devekut* in the talmudic account of R. Eliezer's advice to his students when he fell ill (depicted in BT *Ber.* 28*b*), Landau employs the term *devekut* over ten times in his gloss on this narrative. Further, although he strongly warns against the dangers of mysticism in this gloss, he repeatedly stresses the significance of the mystical ideal of *devekut*. Similarly, in his responsa he promotes the ideal of *devekut* in connection to the performance of specific commandments, albeit in a more limited fashion. See e.g. *NB Kama*, 'OḤ', no. 35.

[44] *Tselaḥ*, *Ber.* 33*b* (p. 126).

[45] *Ahavat tsiyon*, sermon 2, 3*b*. See also *Tselaḥ*, *Ber.* 28*b* (p. 109).

[46] *Ahavat tsiyon*, 3*b*.

[47] In his talmudic commentary Landau describes the World to Come in a similar manner. See *Tselaḥ*, *Ber.* 16*b* (p. 66).

[48] See BT *Ket.* 111*b*. Despite the Talmud's assertion that man *cannot* attain direct *devekut* with the Shekhinah (see also BT *Sot.* 14*a*), Maimonides in one instance uses the talmudic phrase *dibek bashekhinah* (lit.: cleaving to the Shekhinah) to describe the state of a person who has repented. See *Mishneh torah*, 'Laws of Repentance', 7: 7. Interestingly, elsewhere Maimonides reiterates the talmudic teaching that man cannot attain direct *devekut* with the Shekhinah: see *Mishneh torah*, 'Laws of Character Traits', 6: 2; id., *Sefer hamitsvot*, 6.

Intellect, as does Maimonides,[49] Landau employs Cordoverian and ecstatic notions of *devekut* to interpret this ideal. He explains the reward of '*devekut* with the Shekhinah' in terms of the ten *sefirot*, the soul's ascent, and other mystical tropes foreign to Maimonidean rationalism. In other comments on *devekut* he also adopts Maimonidean concepts, particularly in his comments on the states leading to the supreme love of God, a prerequisite for cleaving to Him.[50] Landau's frequent incorporation of Maimonidean and kabbalistic notions in his remarks on *devekut* points to the influence of ecstatic kabbalah, in which Maimonidean terminology is prominent, on his understanding of this ideal.

Methods Leading to *Devekut*

In consonance with ecstatic and Cordoverian kabbalah, Landau not only promotes *devekut* and the role of the commandments in attaining this goal, but also advocates heightened nomian emotional states as well as anomian practices (such as *hitbodedut*) as ways of achieving this ideal. Accordingly, he repeatedly recommends intensified forms of the nomian emotional states of love and fear of God as paths to *devekut*, and appropriates numerous teachings on these devotional modes from the *musar* literature.[51] Although medieval kabbalistic sources, such as the Zohar, had already suggested that love or fear of God leads to *devekut*,[52] the merits of each of these modes and their respective relationship to *devekut* are particularly stressed in Cordoverian works as a result of their general emphasis on this mystical goal.[53] Drawing on these views, Landau frequently asserts that both the fear and love of God can lead to certain degrees of *devekut*.

[49] On the Active Intellect in Maimonides' writings, see e.g. *Guide of the Perplexed*, ii. 18; iii. 51, 52.

[50] For example, like Maimonides (*Guide of the Perplexed*, iii. 51; *Mishneh torah*, 'Laws of Repentance', 10: 3, 6), Landau promotes the ideal of focusing exclusively on God in order to induce the ultimate love of Him.

[51] Although the ideals of love and fear of God are biblical commandments (see Deut. 6: 5, 10: 20; Maimonides, *Sefer hamitsvot*, 3 and 4), the connection between love, fear, and *devekut* receives greatest emphasis in kabbalistic sources.

[52] On the connection between love and cleaving to the Divine see Zohar, iii. 68*a*. For a discussion of love and fear as preparatory states leading towards *devekut*, see Scholem, *Kabbalah*, 175. The ideal love of God is also discussed in non-kabbalistic medieval sources. See e.g. *Mishneh torah*, 'Laws of Repentance', 10: 2–6, where Maimonides emphasizes that love of God emanates from knowledge of God. See also his *Guide of the Perplexed*, iii. 51–4. For a general discussion of the love of God in medieval Jewish thought, see Vajda, *L'Amour de Dieu*, 73–297.

[53] See e.g. Azikri's mystical diary, most of which appears in JTS MS 3541 (formerly known as Adler 74) and has not been published. Azikri depicts *devekut* as a spectrum of ecstatic states which include intense love and fear of God; see e.g. JTS MS 3541, 202*a*. De Vidas, in *Reshit ḥokhmah*, similarly presents the fear of God as a necessary condition for cleaving to the Divine, and the sublime love of God and *devekut* as interdependent. On both Azikri's mystical diary and the significance of love in *Reshit ḥokhmah*, see Pachter, *Milei deshemaya*; id., 'Concept of Devekut', 203, 210, 224.

In both his sermons and glosses, he accentuates that love of God engenders a state of cleaving to the Divine and that love and *devekut* are completely intertwined.[54] In a homily, he states, like de Vidas,[55] that 'since the love of God brings about *devekut*, the Torah paired the notions of love and *devekut* in several places'.[56] He similarly explains in a talmudic gloss that a taste of the ultimate *devekut* can be attained in this world by those who cleave to God out of love. One should particularly recite the first section of the Shema prayer, especially the words 'and you shall love' (Deut. 6: 5) with the intention of losing oneself in a state of *devekut*, since 'love is *devekut*'.[57]

Echoing the *Reshit ḥokhmah*, *Sefer ḥaredim*, *Shenei luḥot haberit*,[58] and other *musar* treatises, he contends that the aim of both the love of God and *devekut* is a state in which all of one's thoughts focus solely on the Divine. Elaborating upon these ideas, he observes in a sermon that 'this is the aim of the love [of God. A person should love until], due to the great cleaving of his love, he thinks no other thoughts, not even those concerning pleasure or benefit for himself. For he thinks only of his love for the Creator'.[59] In this vein, he concludes another homily with the entreaty that God should grant him and the Prague Jewish community the strength to love and fear God constantly 'in all our thoughts and to cleave to Him'.[60] Strikingly, like the *Reshit ḥokhmah*, *Sefer ḥaredim*, and *Shenei luḥot haberit*, he promotes the mystical states of love, fear, and total concentration on the Divine as worthy goals for the entire community.

Aside from encouraging these mystical states and discussing their connection to *devekut*, the contrast between worshipping out of love and out of fear is a leitmotif in Landau's sermons. This debate, found in many kabbalistic sources,[61] is particularly emphasized in Cordoverian texts.[62] Expanding on this tradition, Landau distinguishes between several forms of worship out of fear, although not

[54] See e.g. *Derushei hatselaḥ*, sermon 30, 44*b*; sermon 39, 53*a*; sermon 23, 34*b*; *Ahavat tsiyon*, sermon 2, 3*b*.

[55] *Reshit ḥokhmah*, 'Sha'ar ha'ahavah', 1: 36 (p. 366).

[56] *Derushei hatselaḥ*, sermon 7, 15*a*.

[57] *Tselaḥ*, *Ber.* 16*b* (p. 66).

[58] De Vidas writes that all 'alien' thoughts must be removed before a complete love of God and *devekut* can be achieved. See *Reshit ḥokhmah*, 'Sha'ar ha'ahavah', 11, 23 (p. 611) and 4, 8 (p. 412). Azikri likewise recommends a state in which one only thinks of one's love for God. See *Sefer ḥaredim hashalem*, 51. Isaiah Horowitz stresses that one should cleave to God in all one's thoughts. Even when one is involved in mundane matters, one should not depart from this *devekut* for a moment. See *Shenei luḥot haberit*, 'Sha'ar ha'otiyot', 104*a*.

[59] *Derushei hatselaḥ*, sermon 7, 15*a*. See also sermon 13, 23*b*.

[60] Ibid., sermon 30, 46*a*.

[61] On the comparison between fear and love of the Divine, see e.g. Zohar, i. 11*b*–12*a*. On this theme, see also Scholem, *Kabbalah*, 175. The comparison is also found in Maimonides' writings. See *Mishneh torah*, 'Laws of Repentance', ch. 10, 'Laws of the Foundations of the Torah', 2: 2; id., *Guide of the Perplexed*, iii. 51–4.

[62] See e.g. *Reshit ḥokhmah*, 'Sha'ar ha'ahavah', preface 2 (pp. 345–6) and 1, 3 (p. 346). De Vidas repeatedly states that the love of God, which is integrally connected to *devekut*, is superior to the fear of God.

always in a systematic or consistent manner,[63] and describes their respective relationships to love and *devekut*. Like the *Reshit ḥokhmah* and other *musar* treatises,[64] he maintains that the lowest form of fear, the fear of punishment, is inferior to worship motivated by love.[65] Nonetheless, he presents two other types of fear that are preferable to love. In conformity with kabbalistic teachings, he claims that one of these is an elevated fear of God's awesome powers.[66] There is an even higher fear, however: that of losing the ability to cleave to God. This state, which he deems the ultimate form of worship, is original to his thought.[67]

Landau portrays this supreme fear in several writings. In one of his most mystical depictions of the various levels of love and fear, he asserts that the highest state of religious worship consists of the dread experienced by a person cleaving to God. Such an individual fears that his '*devekut* with the *adam elyon* [Supernal Anthropos, a configuration of the ten *sefirot*], will cease'.[68] Elaborating upon the steps leading to this elevated state, Landau exclaims:

When a person accustoms himself to holiness his soul is kindled, and the fire of the love of God begins to become inflamed in his heart . . . Indeed, a person who worships out of love . . . when he merits this kind of *devekut*, he does not separate from his contemplation of God at all . . . He then merits the most exalted of all lofty states, the supreme fear . . . He now fears that through sin his connection of cleaving to God will cease, and he will therefore become distanced from the essence of holiness. This is the fear of His majesty. This is the fear of God and not the fear of punishment.[69]

The stages Landau describes here as precursors to *devekut* resemble those found in Cordoverian texts. Like de Vidas, he contends that one must first attain *kedushah* (holiness) in order to proceed along the mystical path which culminates in the supreme fear of God.[70] Echoing zoharic and Cordoverian writings, he alleges that one must transcend the stage of worshipping the Divine out of the fear of punishment before achieving *devekut*. After passing these milestones, one

[63] Landau's remarks on the fear and love of God are sometimes inconsistent. For example, in *Derushei hatselaḥ*, sermon 30, 44*b*, he claims that worship out of sublime fear is a higher form of devotion than worship out of love because the former is not concerned with the reward of *devekut*. Elsewhere, however, he claims that the highest form of devotion is a fear that one's state of *devekut* should cease.

[64] Various *musar* works identify two distinct forms of fear of God. See e.g. the last chapter in Ibn Pakuda's *Ḥovot halevavot*, 'Gate of Love'.

[65] See e.g. *Derushei hatselaḥ*, sermon 19, 29*b*.

[66] The Zohar and other kabbalistic and ethical works give this type of fear paramount status. See e.g. Zohar, i. 11*b*. This teaching is cited in both Azikri, *Sefer ḥaredim*, 50 and de Vidas, *Reshit ḥokhmah*, 'Sha'ar hayirah', 1, 2 (p. 30) and 'Sha'ar hakedushah', 7, 107 (p. 195). Landau explicitly writes in *Ahavat tsiyon*, sermon 2, 4*a*, that 'this fear of the Zohar is more important than love.' Again appropriating both zoharic language and this zoharic idea, he asserts in *Derushei hatselaḥ*, sermon 30, 44*b*, that the elevated fear of God's sublime powers is a higher form of worship than divine love.

[67] Despite some variation, Landau presents the same hierarchy in many passages, namely the fear of punishment, followed by the love of God, followed by the awe of God's greatness, and finally the fear of losing one's *devekut*.

[68] *Derushei hatselaḥ*, sermon 13, 24*a*.

[69] Ibid. 23*b*.

[70] See e.g. *Reshit ḥokhmah*, 'Sha'ar ha'ahavah', 11, 67 (p. 634) and 'Sha'ar hakedushah', preface (p. 5).

who worships God with a passionate love can merit the mystical state of *devekut*, in which all one's thoughts cleave to God. Only at this stage can one reach the highest level, the awe of God's greatness and the sublime fear of losing one's *devekut*.[71] Notably, he does not hesitate to describe techniques leading to this elevated *devekut* in this and other sermons that he probably delivered to the public at large. He apparently wanted Prague Jewry to know and perhaps practise these mystical forms of worship in order to enjoy the various levels of *devekut* that they fostered.

Elsewhere, Landau expands on this theme of the sublime fear of God.[72] In a Prague homily in which he describes three types of fear, he explains that the most exalted of these is trepidation that

> if one sins one will be cut off from one's root; this is the fear of *devekut*. In this state, one wishes to cleave to the Divine and fears that [through sin] one will fall downward, and one's *devekut* will cease. This fear does not cease for one moment and one cannot forget it. This is the fear that contains desire and excessive love. This fear includes love . . . for one loves to be in a state of *devekut* and have roots in such a supernal place.[73]

Addressing the debate as to whether the love or fear of God is the more effective way to acquire *devekut*, Landau suggests that in the highest mode of devotion, in which *devekut* is attained, the love of God is contained within the fear of Him. Although he does distinguish between various levels of fear and love, he maintains that, ideally, these modes are inextricably intertwined, and both are necessary for achieving *devekut*. While some of these notions appear in the Zohar, *Reshit ḥokhmah*, and *Shenei luḥot haberit*,[74] Landau's portrayal of the supreme state of worship as incorporating both the elevated fear of losing one's *devekut* and the love of this mystical state cannot be traced to any particular kabbalistic source.

In line with many kabbalistic works, especially those of de Vidas and early hasidic writings,[75] he also contends that the process of repentance is inextricably

[71] In his talmudic commentary Landau also portrays, albeit less dramatically, the sublime fear of losing one's *devekut*. See *Tselaḥ*, *Ber.* 28*b* (p. 109), where he plays with the Hebrew root *ḥbr* and explains that R. Eliezer's advice to be careful about the honour of one's *ḥaver* (friend) is an allusion to the *ḥibur* (connection) of *devekut*. (The words *ḥaver* and *ḥibur* have the same Hebrew root.) In this gloss, he emphasizes that the ultimate fear is that one's connection of *devekut* will be severed as a result of sin.

[72] See e.g. *Derushei hatselaḥ*, sermon 23, 34*b*.

[73] *Ahavat tsiyon*, sermon 2, 4*a*.

[74] See e.g. Zohar, i. 11*b*; de Vidas, *Reshit ḥokhmah*, 'Sha'ar hayirah', 1, 2 (p. 30) and 'Sha'ar hakedushah', 7, 107 (p. 195); Horowitz, *Shenei luḥot haberit*, 'Sha'ar ha'otiyot', 104*a*. In fact Landau cites the Zohar at the beginning of the passage quoted here.

[75] Like Landau's homiletic writings, many hasidic works are replete with mystical ideas on repentance drawn from diverse kabbalistic sources in general and *musar* writings in particular, principal among them *Reshit ḥokhmah*. On the role of this work in hasidic writings, see Sack, 'Influence of *Reshit ḥokhmah* on the Teachings of the Maggid of Mezhirech'; Pachter, 'Traces of the Influence of R. Elijah de Vidas' *Reshit ḥokhmah*' (Heb.); Idel, *Kabbalah*, 50–1; Nigal, 'Sources of *Devekut*' (Heb.), 345–6.

connected with certain levels of fear, love, and *devekut*.[76] Corresponding to his view of the different stages of *devekut*, Landau distinguishes between three forms of penitence. In a homily delivered *c.*1770 he explains that the two lower forms are motivated by fear. In order to reach the highest type of repentance, 'it is fitting that one be in a state of enthusiasm all day in order to cleave to God. Also, at night when one is lying in bed, one's soul should cleave in love to the Creator.'[77] The supreme form of penitence thus consists of continuously cleaving, or at least attempting to cleave, to God in an ecstatic, perhaps erotic, fashion. In a responsum he similarly stresses the connection between repentance, love, the sefirotic realm, and *devekut*.[78] These and other passages demonstrate that his understanding of repentance is largely shaped by mystical ideas concerning fear, love, and *devekut*,[79] and that, like many kabbalists, he believes that, in its ideal form, repentance is another vehicle leading to and intertwined with *devekut*.[80]

Paralleling ecstatic and Cordoverian kabbalists, he also identifies anomian avenues to *devekut*, including serving God with intense enthusiasm, desire, and longing. Many of his remarks on these forms of devotion and their connection to *devekut* are laced with ideas stressed in the *Reshit ḥokhmah*.[81] Echoing the exact language of de Vidas and other Cordoverian kabbalists,[82] Landau proclaims that

[76] See e.g. *Reshit ḥokhmah*, 'Sha'ar hateshuvah', preface 1 (p. 665), and 'Sha'ar hayirah', preface 5 (p. 28).

[77] *Derushei hatselaḥ*, sermon 1, 4*a*.

[78] See *NB Kama*, 'OḤ', no. 35.

[79] See e.g. *Tselaḥ*, *Ber.* 4*b* (p. 16) s.v. *a[mar] r. ele'azar bar avina*, where he alleges that 'the one who repents from love: when he hears that the Holy One, blessed be He, desires his punishment, he repents. But his intent is not out of fear of the punishment. Rather . . . he senses by himself that he is certainly distant from the Holy One, blessed be He, since He distances him with His left. Therefore, he [the penitent] draws closer with his right, and repents in order to cleave to his Creator. . . . The Maharsha [R. Samuel Eliezer ben Judah Edels] wrote in *Ḥidushei agadot* that Michael is from the side of grace, and Gabriel is from the side of judgment. And I say that their names teach of their attributes: Michael, who[se name] alludes to *mi khe'el* [who is like God], proclaims the greatness of the Creator and therefore the sinner should recognize from whom he is distancing himself. And due to this awareness of the greatness of the Creator, he will repent; this is repentance from love. Gabriel's name teaches [of fear] of the *gevurah* of the Creator, in whose hand is [the power] to punish the sinner . . . this is repentance from fear.' In this gloss, replete with kabbalistic language, Landau intertwines several kabbalistic concepts concerning penitence, love, fear, *devekut*, and the angels Michael and Gabriel, who, according to Landau and kabbalistic sources, represent the divine right, grace, and the divine left, judgement, respectively.

[80] See also e.g. *Derushei hatselaḥ*, sermon 30, 46*a*. Azikri, de Vidas, and other kabbalists of the Cordoverian school also understand repentance in terms of love, fear, and *devekut*. On the connection between repentance and *devekut* in the writings of Azikri and Karo, see Pachter, 'Concept of Devekut', 202–3.

[81] See *Reshit ḥokhmah*, 'Sha'ar ha'ahavah', 3, 42–4 (pp. 405–6), where de Vidas maintains that there are three successive stages leading towards the ultimate *devekut*: *devikah* (cleaving to the Divine), *ḥashikah* (desiring the Divine), and *ḥafitsah* (lust for the Divine). On de Vidas' teaching that one can achieve these stages through performing the commandments and studying Torah with enthusiasm and desire, see e.g. ibid., ch. 4, 18 (p. 417).

[82] See e.g. *Reshit ḥokhmah*, 'Sha'ar ha'ahavah', 4, 32 (p. 426).

one who serves God out of love always desires 'to acquire *devekut* with the Holy One Blessed Be He . . . and desires the love of the Torah';[83] accordingly, he admonishes his community in several sermons for failing to invest their worship with the requisite enthusiasm and desire.[84] He dramatically explains the benefits of such desire in a 1782 homily: 'when the heart is inflamed with the desire of enthusiasm then we will be filled with exultation.'[85] Notably, he advocates this goal of desire to achieve *devekut* in sermons addressed to the wider Prague Jewish community.[86]

Another preparatory state for *devekut* promoted by Landau is *simḥah* (joy).[87] Since this conception appears almost exclusively in ecstatic and Cordoverian writings, these works were almost certainly the source of his views on the subject. His specific comments on the necessity of joy for achieving *devekut* also closely resemble those found in Cordoverian texts. For example, in a 1761 sermon, Landau, like de Vidas, interprets the talmudic dictum that 'the Shekhinah does not dwell in a place of sadness'[88] in terms of the ideal of *devekut*, stating that only those who 'awaken the happiness of their soul' can cleave to God.[89]

The mystical technique of *hitbodedut* (solitary contemplation) is also portrayed by Landau as a vehicle for achieving *devekut*. While this idea appears in ecstatic and Cordoverian works,[90] such as those of Abulafia, Azikri, and de

[83] *Derushei hatselaḥ*, sermon 19, 29*b*. Here Landau, like the kabbalists, seems to equate God and the Torah by drawing a parallel between desire to cleave to God and desire to love the Torah. His remarks on desire for the Torah probably also imply desire to cleave to God. For a discussion of the kabbalists' identification of the essence of the Torah with God and their conception that one can therefore cleave to God through the Torah, see Pachter, 'Concept of Devekut', 187; Krassen, 'Devequt and Faith in Zaddiqim', 274, 278–82. Again, like the ecstatic kabbalists, Landau appropriates Maimonidean language in his discussion of desire and *devekut*. See e.g. *Mishneh torah*, 'Laws of Marriage', 15: 3.

[84] See *Derushei hatselaḥ*, sermon 5, 12*a* , and sermon 39, 53*a*. Like de Vidas and other Cordoverian kabbalists, Landau underscores that performing *mitsvot* with intense desire fosters *devekut*. See *Tselaḥ*, *Ber.* 28*b* (p. 108).

[85] *Derushei hatselaḥ*, sermon 39, 54*a*. In this sermon Landau also explains that the theurgical efficacy of the commandments hinges upon performing them with joy and desire.

[86] This is made clear by the fact that he admonishes his community in many of these sermons.

[87] The importance of joy and its connection to *devekut* is advanced in many Cordoverian writings. For example, de Vidas devotes the entire tenth chapter of *Reshit ḥokhmah*'s 'Sha'ar ha'ahavah' to the significance of joy in religious worship, the ultimate expression of which is found in *devekut*. Some medieval Jewish thinkers similarly recommend observing the commandments in a state of joy. See e.g. Maimonides, *Mishneh torah*, 'Laws of Sukkah and Lulav', 8: 15. For Maimonides, however, joy is not specifically connected with the ideal of *devekut*.

[88] See BT *Shab.* 30*b*, *Pes.* 117*a*; de Vidas, *Reshit ḥokhmah*, 'Sha'ar ha'ahavah', 2, 22 (p. 378).

[89] *Ahavat tsiyon*, sermon 2, 3*b*. In the same passage Landau also pronounces that great joy accompanies *devekut*, the highest level of which is attained by the completely righteous.

[90] For a discussion of the importance of *hitbodedut* in ecstatic and Cordoverian kabbalah, see Idel, *Studies in Ecstatic Kabbalah*, ch. 7, 103–69. As Idel shows, the works of Cordovero and his disciples disseminated the ecstatic kabbalah's teachings on *hitbodedut* as a preparatory step for *devekut*.

Vidas,[91] the technique of *hitbodedut* is almost entirely absent, with a few notable exceptions, from zoharic and Lurianic kabbalah.[92] In remarks on *hitbodedut*, de Vidas explains that solitary contemplation of the Divine Name engenders joy,[93] a necessary prelude to *devekut*. Echoes of many of these notions are found in a Prague sermon containing some of Landau's most vivid depictions of the stages leading to *devekut*. He states: 'The pious can merit a hint of the World to Come already in this world if they cleave with joy, good heartedness, *hitbodedut*, song and praise, and total desire [of God], particularly at night.'[94] In this manner, he continues, the soul of a pious individual will cleave to God. Like ecstatic and Cordoverian kabbalists, he explains that through solitude, joy, and intense desire the pious can achieve *devekut* in this world. Remarkably, in this passage and others, he feels compelled to share both the mystical ideal of *devekut* and classic preparatory techniques for attaining it with his community.

Hierarchical Stages to the Holy Spirit

Aside from love, fear, joy, and *hitbodedut*, Landau, like most ecstatic and Cordoverian kabbalists, also describes other means to achieve a mystical experience. He cites the *baraita* (tannaitic material not included in the Mishnah) of Rabbi Pinhas ben Yair, a second-century sage, in a Prague sermon.[95] This *baraita* presents an ascending hierarchy of moral and ascetic virtues, which progressively enable an individual to receive the gift of the Holy Spirit.[96] As Landau reiterates, these stages include purity, abstinence, holiness, modesty, and piety. Pinhas ben Yair's *baraita* was extremely popular among Cordoverian kabbalists

[91] On the significance of *hitbodedut* in Azikri's mystical diary, see e.g. JTS MS 3541, 23*a*, 202*a*; in *Sefer ḥaredim*, see 226–9, 234. For a discussion of *hitbodedut* in Azikri's work in general, see Pachter, 'Concept of Devekut', 205–9; Idel, *Studies in Ecstatic Kabbalah*, 132–3. On de Vidas' portrayal of the connection between *hitbodedut* and *devekut*, see e.g. *Reshit ḥokhmah*, 'Sha'ar ha'ahavah', 4: 31 (p. 426) and 10: 31 (p. 587), 'Sha'ar hakedushah', 6, 16 (p. 89). In *Mesilat yesharim*, 334, Moses Hayim Luzzatto also claims that *hitbodedut* fosters *devekut*. Luzzatto's writings on this ideal may have influenced Landau.

[92] For a discussion of the marginal role of *hitbodedut* in Lurianic kabbalah, see Idel, *Hasidism*, 10–11. The ideal of *hitbodedut* is promoted, however, in Vital's *Sha'arei kedushah*, particularly in its final section, 'Ma'amar hitbodedut', on which see Scholem, *Kabbalah*, 181; Idel, *Studies in Ecstatic Kabbalah*, 132.

[93] *Reshit ḥokhmah*, 'Sha'ar ha'ahavah', 10: 28 (p. 585).

[94] *Ahavat tsiyon*, sermon 2, 3*b*. Some of these ideas are similar to teachings in *Reshit ḥokhmah*, 'Sha'ar ha'ahavah', 10, 32 (p. 587). In consonance with prophetic kabbalah, the preparatory states that Landau lists here as leading to *devekut* correspond to Maimonides' description of the necessary states for attaining prophecy. See Maimonides, *Mishneh torah*, 'Laws of the Foundations of the Torah', 7: 4.

[95] *Derushei hatselaḥ*, sermon 5, 11*a*.

[96] This *baraita* appears in several places in the Talmud. See BT *AZ* 20*b* and parallels. For a discussion of 12th- and 13th-c. kabbalists' experiences of divine revelation, or the gift of the Holy Spirit, see Heschel, 'Inspiration in the Middle Ages' (Heb.).

and authors of *musar* treatises, such as Luzzatto and de Vidas,[97] since fulfilment of its stages provided a path to attain the immediate presence of God, or *devekut*, through the 'gift of the Holy Spirit'.[98]

Although Landau asserts that during our time of 'darkness' we no longer have a direct path to attain the gift of the Holy Spirit,[99] he nonetheless lists many of the virtues promoted by Pinhas ben Yair as prerequisites for meriting this gift.[100] Like the *musar* treatises, he seems indirectly to encourage his community to acquire these traits, which several mystics claim foster *devekut*. His engagement in such discourse attests to his high regard for the gift of the Holy Spirit and *devekut* and the path leading to these mystical states.

Landau's repeated promotion of these mystical goals and the techniques necessary to attain them, as well as his appropriation of Cordoverian expressions and motifs, reflects the tremendous influence exerted upon him by both ecstatic ideals and other teachings advanced by Cordovero and his disciples.

[97] Luzzatto even employed these stages as the basis for his *Mesilat yesharim*, and states this explicitly; see *Mesilat yesharim*, 12, 14, 336. De Vidas similarly organized the *Reshit ḥokhmah* according to the order of the virtues mentioned in this *baraita*. See e.g. *Reshit ḥokhmah*, 'Sha'ar hakedushah', preface 3 (p. 6). On de Vidas' use of this *baraita*, see also ibid., 'Sha'ar ha'ahavah', 11, 59–74 (pp. 629–40).

[98] *Reshit ḥokhmah*, 'Sha'ar ha'ahavah', 11, 3 (p. 600).

[99] Landau explains that the gifts of the Holy Spirit and prophecy ceased with the Second Temple prophets Haggai, Zechariah, and Malachi. This notion appears in BT *San.* 11*a*, *Yoma* 9*b*, *Sot.* 48*b*.

[100] *Derushei hatselaḥ*, sermon 5, 11*a*. Landau continues here that, in order to ensure that people will come closer to God and not sink into the morass of sins without the Holy Spirit, He sends His left (i.e. punishment), which is usually associated (by kabbalists) with judgement and harshness, but which in this case is an act of God's mercy.

NINE

Lurianic Kabbalah: Berur, *Final Sparks, and the Mission of Exile*

ZOHARIC AND CORDOVERIAN sources are by no means the only kabbalistic texts Landau uses. Despite the tremendous influence of Cordoverian doctrines in central and eastern Europe during the eighteenth century, Lurianic kabbalah was still the dominant kabbalistic school and it had a prominent place in Landau's writings.[1] Named after its founder, Rabbi Isaac Luria, who briefly studied in Safed with Moses Cordovero,[2] this branch of kabbalah primarily deals with complex systems of theosophical and theurgical doctrines, at the expense of ecstatic traditions.[3] The ideal of *devekut* and the modes of worship promoted in ecstatic kabbalah, such as enthusiasm and *hitbodedut*, play a subsidiary role in most Lurianic works.[4]

Both Landau's education in Brody and his glosses on Vital's *Derekh ets ḥayim* and *Peri ets ḥayim*, two central theosophical–theurgical Lurianic texts, reflect his intense involvement with Lurianic kabbalah during his youth in Poland. He draws on this knowledge and employs Lurianic tenets in many Prague sermons and talmudic commentaries, often explaining biblical and rabbinic narratives, rites, and prohibitions in terms of Lurianic concepts and ideals. In these discussions, he frequently uses the precise linguistic phrases, terms, and ideas found in Lurianic writings on the same themes, revealing his deep immersion in these sources. Nevertheless, in his Prague writings he only mentions a single Lurianic text by name—Vital's *Ets ḥayim*—and only on one occasion at that.

Although many of Landau's kabbalistic teachings appear to stem from Vital's rendition of Lurianic kabbalah, it is usually difficult to determine the exact source

[1] On the prominence of Lurianic kabbalah during this period, see Idel, *Hasidism*, 31, 33.

[2] Luria studied with Cordovero in 1570. See Fine, *Safed Spirituality*, 61; Scholem, *Kabbalah*, 74. On the similarities between various doctrines found in Lurianic and Cordoverian kabbalah, see Sack, *Kabbalah of Rabbi Moses Cordovero*; id., 'Moses Cordovero and Isaac Luria' (Heb.); Liebes, 'New Directions in the Study of the Kabbalah' (Heb.), 162, 165.

[3] On Luria and Lurianic kabbalah, see Scholem, *Major Trends*, 244–86; id., *Kabbalah*, 74–9, 128–44, 162–3, 167–8; id., *Kabbalah and its Symbolism*, 109–17, 127–9; Fine, *Physician of the Soul*; Meroz, 'Redemption in Lurianic Teaching' (Heb.); id., 'Faithful Transmission versus Innovation', 257–74; Tishby, *Doctrine of Evil* (Heb.); Avivi, *Binyan ari'el*; Idel, *Kabbalah*, 256–67; Liebes, 'Myth vs. Symbol' (Heb.).

[4] Idel, *Hasidism*, 10, 31, 90; id., *Kabbalah*, pp. xv, 57. See also Chapter 8, n. 92.

or sources which served as the basis for his Lurianic remarks.[5] This is mainly because of the complexity of the transmission and authorship of Lurianic works, resulting from the fact that Luria transmitted his teachings in diverse formulations and almost exclusively orally. Consequently, it was Luria's chief disciple, Hayim Vital, who wrote one of the first and most comprehensive books of Lurianic theosophy, the *Ets ḥayim*, also called *Shemonah she'arim* (Eight Gates) because of its division into eight sections,[6] including the volumes *Sha'ar hapesukim* (Gate of Biblical Verses), *Sha'ar hakavanot* (Gate of Mystical Intentions), and *Sha'ar hagilgulim* (Gate of Transmigration). Contributing to this complex transmission process, other recensions of Vital's literary output were published by students of Lurianic kabbalah, such as the Ashkenazi kabbalist Meir Poppers (d. 1662), who was born in Prague and lived for many years in Jerusalem. Poppers divided his edition of Vital's writings into three parts: *Derekh ets ḥayim*, *Peri ets ḥayim*, and *Nof ets ḥayim*.[7] Popper's rendition of Lurianic kabbalah was the most popular in Poland and Germany during the late seventeenth and eighteenth centuries. We know that, at the very least, Landau owned the first two of Popper's volumes, *Derekh ets ḥayim* and *Peri ets ḥayim*, though it should be emphasized that the Lurianic notions that he promotes are found in many of the aforementioned treatises.[8]

Landau usually appropriates the central tropes of Lurianic kabbalah without referring to their original sources or authors. Since much of Lurianic kabbalah is grounded in the Zohar and Cordoverian kabbalah,[9] it is sometimes difficult to

[5] With the notable exceptions of Vital's *Derekh ets ḥayim* and *Peri ets ḥayim*, it is difficult to ascertain the exact Lurianic works which Landau studied and employed. Most of Vital's writings were first published at the end of the 18th c. and circulated only in manuscript until then. Although we can assume that Landau was probably introduced to many of Vital's works and teachings at the Brody *kloiz*, there is no account of the specific Lurianic sources that he studied or viewed there.

[6] Vital composed the *Ets ḥayim* shortly after Luria's death. Using this *magnum opus* as his basis, Hayim Vital's son Samuel (1598–*c.*1678) compiled his own re-edited version of *Shemonah she'arim*, which, unlike his father's original version, was eventually published. This rendition became extremely influential and many kabbalists considered it to be the most authoritative recension of Lurianic kabbalah. Many of the Lurianic texts cited in this book are from Samuel's edition of *Shemonah she'arim*. On the various recensions of the *Ets ḥayim* and other Lurianic works, see Scholem, *Kabbalah*, 423–6, 445–6; Avivi, *Binyan ari'el*; Meroz, 'Faithful Transmission versus Innovation'; Magid, 'From Theosophy to Midrash', 44 n. 22.

[7] These works encompass most of the material found in Samuel Vital's edition of *Shemonah she'arim* as well as materials from other renditions of Vital's writings. Poppers also compiled a collection of Lurianic Bible commentaries entitled *Likutei torah*. In *c.*1620 another student of Lurianic kabbalah, Benjamin Halevi, edited and compiled a compendium of Vital's writings, which included *Sefer halikutim* and *Sefer haderushim*, with which Landau may also have been familiar.

[8] Since the different recensions of Vital's works often contain variations on a Lurianic theme, I sometimes refer to several expositions of Vital on Lurianic doctrines that appear in Landau's writings. Any or all of these may have been the basis for Landau's discussions.

[9] On the centrality of zoharic and Cordoverian tenets in Lurianic kabbalah, see Liebes, 'New Directions in the Study of the Kabbalah' (Heb.), 162, 165; Tishby, *Wisdom of the Zohar*, i. 103–4, 385; Sack, 'Moses Cordovero and Isaac Luria' (Heb.).

determine the exact source of various kabbalistic concepts found in Landau's writings. Nonetheless, it is often clear that his kabbalistic discussions are based on Lurianic teachings, since they use terms and concepts unique to Lurianic kabbalah. Among these are the mythic motifs of *shevirat hakelim* (breaking of the vessels), *berur vehe'alat hanitsotsot* (selection and elevation of the supernal sparks), and the ideal of redeeming the final sparks from the heels of Adam Belial (*adam beliya'al*; Demonic Being).[10] Besides these, Landau frequently employs other notions which, albeit not exclusive to Lurianic works, are uniquely developed and especially emphasized in Lurianic texts, such as the kabbalistic goal of *tikun* (restoring the cosmos). Drawing on Lurianic views, Landau accordingly claims that the task of elevating and restoring the supernal sparks is one of the main purposes of man's deeds, Israel's exile, and even of those who convert to Judaism. Other theosophical–theurgical tenets uniquely conceptualized in Lurianic kabbalah, such as the Shekhinah's mission and the demonic forces that feed off holiness, repeatedly appear in Landau's writings. Beyond merely appropriating these Lurianic tropes, his approach to essential religious questions, such as the meaning of exile, redemption, and the messianic era, is largely shaped by these and other Lurianic doctrines.

Nevertheless, it is only in a few passages that Landau cites ideas taught by Luria and relates stories concerning him. On these occasions, however, his remarks demonstrate his veneration for Lurianic tenets. For instance, in one homily he enthusiastically points to a talmudic text that supports a Lurianic teaching he promotes.[11] His attempt to explain this Lurianic notion in accordance with talmudic concepts,[12] as he does for all legal statements made by medieval talmudic commentators, demonstrates his high regard for Lurianic materials. In a 1764 homily delivered to the Prague Hevrat Gemilut Hasadim (Charitable Works Society),[13] he even chooses a Lurianic tradition concerning God's thirteen attributes that contradicts explanations offered by the renowned medieval talmudic commentators Asher ben Yehiel (the Rosh) and the French and German exegetes known as the Tosafot.[14] Supporting his stance, he pro-

[10] Many central Lurianic doctrines, such as notions concerning theurgy and the role of exile, revolve around these original and mythic conceptions of the supernal realm. See Scholem, *Kabbalah*, 140, 142–3; Idel, *Hasidism*, 52; Meroz, 'Redemption in Lurianic Teaching' (Heb.); Liebes, 'Myth vs Symbol' (Heb.).

[11] *Derushei hatselah*, sermon 19, 29*a*. Landau must have stressed this Lurianic teaching, since Fleckeles records hearing it from Landau in his youth. See Fleckeles, *Teshuvah me'ahavah*, ii, no. 273, notes on *Shulhan arukh*, 597. Fleckeles' comment that he *heard* this idea from Landau suggests that the latter transmitted at least some mystical notions orally.

[12] The concepts he refers to are found in BT *Ḥag.* 5*b*.

[13] *Ahavat tsiyon*, sermon 4 (4 Jan. 1764, the eve of the new month of Shevat), 5*b*–7*b*.

[14] The Tosafot were a group of talmudic scholars who lived in northern France and Germany in the 12th and 13th cc.

ceeds to 'prove' that Luria's interpretation of the attributes is indeed correct.[15] His willingness to side with Luria, as opposed to these leading rabbinic authorities, again points to his enormous respect for Luria and his ideas. His backing of Luria in this instance is also noteworthy since, at least in legal matters, he generally upholds the opinion of earlier rabbinic authorities over those of later ones.[16] Here, however, he endorses the opinion of Luria, both a later authority and a kabbalist. Yet even on those rare occasions where he manifests his respect for Luria by citing teachings and tales explicitly attributed to him, he does not mention where they can be found.[17]

The one instance when Landau explicitly mentions a Lurianic text appears in a Prague sermon.[18] He refers to an esoteric section of the *Ets ḥayim* that expounds the mystical meanings of the Hebrew *ta'amim* (cantillation marks) and *nekudot* (vowels) and their relation to the 'secrets' of the eye and the ear.[19] This discussion hinges on the concept of the *mayim nukvin* (female waters), a zoharic trope reinterpreted and emphasized in Lurianic writings.[20] Like the Lurianic kabbalists, Landau explains that the arousal of the female waters is initially achieved by Israel's good deeds. These waters, in turn, stimulate the divine *mayim dukhrin* (male waters), or supernal *shefa* (abundance), to flow into the lower worlds. Since the eye is akin to the more significant male waters and the ear is akin to the female waters, 'the secret of the eye is more elevated' than that of the ear, as 'is explained in the *Ets ḥayim*'.[21] Both Landau's citation of the *Ets ḥayim* and his willingness to share these esoteric doctrines exhibit his esteem for Lurianic teachings. The use of these concepts in his sermons also indicates that Prague Jews were at least somewhat familiar with these recondite kabbalistic notions.

[15] *Ahavat tsiyon*, sermon 4, 6*b*. He states that since talmudic interpretations of the thirteen attributes are inconclusive, he can avail himself of any hint provided by talmudic sages.

[16] In legal matters Landau, like most later rabbinic authorities (*aḥaronim*), gives more weight to the opinions of medieval rabbinic authorities (*rishonim*) than to those of later *posekim*. However, it should be noted that he is one of the few *aḥaronim* who does disagree with medieval talmudic commentators, albeit on rare occasions. See the discussion on p. 53.

[17] See e.g. *Derushei hatselaḥ*, sermon 24, 38*a*. In this sermon Landau uses a story about Luria's conversation with a spirit in order to demonstrate the importance of confession. See also *Ahavat tsiyon*, sermon 1, 2a, sermon 2, 3*b*, sermon 4, 6*b*.

[18] *Derushei hatselaḥ*, sermon 25, 40*a*.

[19] Landau's citation probably refers to one of the following sections of the *Ets ḥayim*: 'Sha'ar hanekudot', 'Sha'ar ha'akudim' (spots or streaks), or 'Sha'ar tanta' (the latter is an acronym for *ta'amim*, *nekudot*, *tagin* (decorative 'crowns' on the letters) and *otiyot* (letters)). Many of the ideas Landau alludes to in this sermon are found in these sections.

[20] In Lurianic kabbalah these 'female waters' refer to the forces which form within the Shekhinah and arouse the 'coupling' of various aspects of the Godhead. On *mayim nukvin* and *mayim dukhrin* ('male waters') in Lurianic kabbalah, see e.g. Vital, *Ets ḥayim*, vol. 2, 39: 'Sha'ar mayim nukvin vemayim dukhrin', ch. 39, 65*a*–79*a*. For a discussion of this motif, see Wolfson, *Circle in the Square*, 113–15, 189 n. 174, 213 n. 96, 228 n. 168, and 230 n. 182; Scholem, *Mystical Shape of the Godhead*, 187–9; id., *Kabbalah*, 141, 143.

[21] *Derushei hatselaḥ*, sermon 25, 40*a*.

Some of Landau's other citations of Luria similarly convey his awareness of the dissemination of Lurianic tenets among Prague Jews. This is explicitly expressed in sermons delivered in 1756 and in 1764, where he states that the Lurianic teachings he discusses are 'well known'.[22]

Lurianic Terms and Motifs

As stated, Landau usually employs Lurianic motifs without citing their original sources. This section charts the primary Lurianic tenets found in his works and identifies texts that may have served as the source of these doctrines. I begin with the trope *shevirat hakelim*, an integral component of Lurianic theosophy, which originates in Lurianic writings.

Shevirat hakelim

According to this central Lurianic myth, the vessels containing the light issuing forth from the initial configuration of divine light,[23] the Adam Kadmon (primordial man),[24] were first shattered in an event known as *shevirat hakelim*, the 'breaking of the vessels'.[25] While the three vessels corresponding to the highest *sefirot* were capable of safeguarding this forceful divine light, it caused a breach in the seven lower vessels. After this cataclysmic event many of the supernal sparks (*nitsotsot*) contained in these vessels descended into the lower depths, where they were captured by the demonic *kelipot* (lit. 'shells'; demonic forces). Through good deeds, humans redeem these sparks. The ultimate goal of this process is to restore the divine realm to its idyllic state which preceded the catastrophic *shevirat hakelim*.

Landau refers to this myth in a homily, explaining that among all the nations 'there are still *shevirat kelim* (broken vessels) from the holiness, and we must . . .

[22] *Ahavat tsiyon*, sermon 1, 2*a*; sermon 4, 6*b*.

[23] In the Lurianic system, the first step in the process of creation was the *tsimtsum*, the contraction, of the infinite Ein Sof away from a single point. Adam Kadmon is the first configuration of divine light which emanated from the Ein Sof into the void produced by *tsimtsum*. On the concept of *tsimtsum* in Lurianic kabbalah, see Scholem, *Major Trends*, 260–4; id., *Kabbalah*, 129–33. On *tsimtsum* in earlier kabbalistic writings, see Idel, 'Concept of *Tsimtsum*' (Heb.).

[24] The primary aim of Lurianic kabbalah is the restoration of this highest emanated form of the Divine to its initial state. On Adam Kadmon and the ideal of restoring it in Lurianic kabbalah, see Scholem, *Major Trends*, 265, 268, 275; Idel, *Hasidism*, 52, 90. The term 'Adam Kadmon' was already in use in a work from the *Sefer ha'iyun* circle, a group of 12th-c. kabbalists in Provence and perhaps Castile. On the writings of this circle, see Scholem, *Origins of the Kabbalah*, 309–64; Verman, *Books of Contemplation*. The *Tikunei hazohar* also uses the term Adam Kadmon. On its use in zoharic writings, see Scholem, *Major Trends*, 400 n. 31.

[25] This cataclysmic event is also referred to as 'the death of the primeval kings', a phrase appropriated from the *Idrot* section of the Zohar. See Scholem, *Kabbalah*, 138–9.

gather these pieces, and liberate them from impurity into purity'.[26] The use of this trope here and in other writings of his attests to his appropriation of this distinctly Lurianic motif.[27]

Tikun

The ideal of *tikun*, restoring the unity of the cosmos that was originally disrupted by the breaking of the vessels, is central in both Lurianic and Landau's works. In almost every genre of his writings, Landau reiterates this aim, and, like Lurianic kabbalists, he even declares that the purpose of the Torah and all the commandments is to engender the restoration of the supernal worlds.[28]

The importance he attributes to the kabbalistic ideal of *tikun* is further demonstrated in his portrayal of various biblical narratives. In concordance with Lurianic kabbalah, he interprets several major biblical events, including Adam's fall,[29] the Exodus, and the sin of the golden calf, in terms of the attempt to achieve this goal. Following Vital's writings,[30] Landau asserts that Israel's experiences in Egypt almost served as the final stages in the *tikun* of Adam's sin.[31] This transgression, according to Lurianic kabbalah, repeated in the lower realm the catastrophe that the breaking of the vessels had previously produced on high.

Despite the spiritual heights that Israel reached during the Exodus, both Lurianic kabbalists and Landau repeatedly claim that just as the Jews were

[26] *Derushei hatselaḥ*, sermon 38, 52*b*.

[27] He refers to this trope elsewhere with slight variations. See e.g. *Tselaḥ*, *Ber.* 9*b* (p. 34). In this gloss he touches on the Lurianic myth of the breaking of the vessels, though he does not mention the term *shevirat hakelim*.

[28] *Ahavat tsiyon*, sermon 2, 3*b*.

[29] As in Lurianic kabbalah, Landau gives great weight to Adam's primal sin, asserting that *tikun* is, at least partly, necessary because of this transgression. For Vital's remarks on the consequences of Adam's fall, see Vital, *Sefer halikutim*, 'Bereshit', 2*a*, and 'Ekev', 56*b*; id., *Sha'ar hakavanot*, pt. 2, 'Inyan pesaḥ', sermon 1, 137; id., *Sha'ar hamitsvot*, 'Re'eh', 47*b*; id., *Peri ets ḥayim*, 'Sha'ar keriat shema', ch. 3, 164; id., *Sha'ar hagilgulim*, preface 20, 20*a*; id., *Sefer hagilgulim*, pt. 2, ch. 18, 35; id., *Sha'arei kedushah*, pt. 1, Sha'ar 1, 12. On Landau's discussion of Adam's sin in terms of Lurianic notions, see e.g. *Tselaḥ*, *Ber.* 9*b* (p. 34); ibid., *Pes.*, introd.; *Ahavat tsiyon*, sermon 2, 3*b*; *Derushei hatselaḥ*, sermon 20, 31*b*.

[30] Vital, *Peri ets ḥayim*, 'Sha'ar ḥag hamatsot', ch. 1, 490–3; id., *Sha'ar hakavanot*, pt. 2, 'Inyan pesaḥ', sermon 1, 136–49, and *Sha'ar hapesukim*, 'Shemot', 101–4. In these sources Vital reveals the secret of Israel's exile in Egypt, explaining that the Jews who were enslaved in Egypt were the product of the *nitsotsot keri* (sparks produced by diurnal and nocturnal pollutions) that Adam emitted for 430 years until the birth of his son Seth. The exile in Egypt, which also lasted 430 years, was supposed to serve as a *tikun* for this sin of Adam. According to Vital, during the Exodus from Egypt the *tikun* of these *nitsotsot* was almost completed. In Lurianic texts Adam's sin is identified as his spilling semen in vain. This understanding of his sin is exegetically connected with his sin of eating from the tree of knowledge, i.e. the biblical image is interpreted figuratively.

[31] Landau is not always consistent in his claim that during the Exodus the ideal of *tikun* and spiritual redemption were almost attained. See e.g. *Derushei hatselaḥ*, sermon 38, 52*b*, where he states that the Jews had reached the lowest depth of impurity in Egypt. If they had remained there for even a moment longer, the possibility of achieving *tikun* would have been denied to them. Such inconsistent accounts of the Jews' spiritual state during the Exodus, however, are found as early as the midrashic literature.

approaching the completion of *tikun*, they fell to one of their lowest states, as a result of the sin of the golden calf.[32] Vital writes that after the Exodus the Jews were freed from the angel of death, an aspect of the *kelipah* into whose realm they had fallen during Adam's transgression; 'however, through the sin of the calf they were once again drowned in the *kelipah*'s midst.'[33]

Landau incorporates many of these Lurianic motifs in his writings, including his introduction to the *Tselaḥ* on *Pesaḥim*, a text he published in Prague and in which he did not solely address kabbalistic initiates.[34] There he asserts:

It is known that the entire exile in Egypt served as a *tikun* for the sin of Adam who ate from the Tree of *Knowledge*. And thus, it was said to Abraham our forefather at the Covenant of the Pieces '*know*, surely that your descendants will be strangers', etc. (Gen. 15: 13). God said '*know*, surely'. In this manner, He hinted to Abraham that [the exile in Egypt] is due to Adam's transgression of eating from the Tree of *Knowledge* . . . For, when Adam sinned, his *nefesh ḥayah* [living soul] departed . . . and he became subject to death . . . Adam only had the level of *nefesh ḥayah* before his sin. Thus it is written 'the sojourning of the children of Israel, who dwelt in Egypt, was 430 years' (Exod. 12: 40). And with this number of years in Egypt they achieved *tikun* for *nefesh ḥayah*, for this is the numerical value of the word *nefesh* [soul][35] . . . And this *tikun* would have been fulfilled if they had not sinned with the calf. Then they would have been freed from the angel of death.[36] (emphasis added)

Employing hermeneutical methods prevalent in kabbalistic works, Landau interweaves various biblical narratives here, including the Covenant of the Pieces, Israel's exile in Egypt, and the sin of the golden calf, and interprets them in the light of the kabbalistic ideal of *tikun*. Following Lurianic kabbalists, he views these events as stages which either enhanced or hindered the interrelated mystical processes of restoring the cosmos and soul to their pristine states preceding Adam's fall.

Much of the imagery and terminology found in his discussion of *tikun* and the soul, in this introduction and elsewhere, is rooted in Lurianic teachings.[37] As in

[32] These ideas appear in various Lurianic sources, including Vital's *Ets ḥayim* and *Sha'ar ma'amerei rashbi*. See e.g. *Ets ḥayim*, vol. 2, '38: Sha'ar le'ah veraḥel', ch. 6, 63*a*–64*a*.

[33] Vital, *Sha'ar ma'amerei rashbi*, 'Pekudei', 169.

[34] On Landau's dedication of his talmudic commentary to his students, see Part II. This introduction to *Pesaḥim*, which appears in the first edition published in Prague, 1783, is printed alongside the introduction to *Berakhot* in the *Tselaḥ hashalem* edition of *Berakhot*, published in Jerusalem, 1995; oddly, it does not appear in the volume on *Pesaḥim*.

[35] According to *gematriyah*, the letters of the Hebrew word *nefesh* equal 430 since *shin* equals 300, *peh* equals 80, and *nun* equals 50.

[36] *Tselaḥ*, *Pes.*, introd. The last sentence in this citation plays with a phrase found in BT *AZ* 5*a*.

[37] In both his sermons and talmudic commentary he emphasizes the necessity of achieving the restoration of one's soul. The idea of *tikun neshamah*, stressed in Lurianic kabbalah, also appears in earlier kabbalistic writings, such as those of Moses de Leon. See Scholem, *Kabbalah*, 159. On Landau's use of this trope, see *Tselaḥ*, *Ber.* 58*b* (p. 216); *Derushei hatselaḥ*, sermon 30, 45*a*.

Vital's *Ets ḥayim*,[38] he describes man's soul as having been initially a *nefesh ḥayah*, a living soul, comprised of supernal dust.[39] This sublime soul, which departed when Adam sinned, was to be restored finally during the Exodus. Significantly, Landau entitles his talmudic commentary *Tsiyun lenefesh ḥayah* (*Tselaḥ*), 'A Guidepost for the Living Soul'.[40] While this title refers primarily to the memory of his mother, Hayah Landau, to whom he dedicates the commentary,[41] the many Lurianic motifs in this introduction suggest that it also alludes to Lurianic tropes regarding death and the restoration of the soul. In resonance with Vital's work, Landau also occasionally offers highly anthropomorphic descriptions of the soul and its role in *tikun*.[42]

Berur

Landau and the Lurianic kabbalists emphasize that in order to achieve the ideal of *tikun*, man must first facilitate its negative complement, *berur*—the selection and elimination of the demonic *kelipot*, a concept unique to Lurianic kabbalah.[43] *Berur*, which enables the eventual isolation and elevation of holy sparks, is necessary, according to Lurianic kabbalists, because both Adam's sin and subsequent human transgressions have caused a detrimental mixing of holy sparks with demonic forces in all spheres.[44]

Many Lurianic sources interpret Israel's exile in the context of the necessity of separating and redeeming the captive divine sparks, which have been scattered to the four corners of the earth. In *Sha'ar hapesukim*, Vital explains:

> the reason for Israel's exile among the nations is that . . . since Adam bore all the worlds and all the souls within him, when he sinned, all these souls fell from him into the realm of the *kelipot*.[45] This realm is divided among the seventy nations. Israel must disperse to

[38] See Vital, *Ets ḥayim*, vol. 2, '50: 'Sha'ar yod-ayin kitsur avsha'ar', ch. 7, 116*a*, in which he contends that through death, Adam's soul returned to the pure state of *nefesh ḥayah*.

[39] On the phrase *nefesh ḥayah* in Lurianic kabbalah, see Scholem, *Kabbalah*, 157–8. On the use of this term in the Zohar, see Tishby, *Wisdom of the Zohar*, ii. 704, 708–9; Scholem, *Kabbalah*, 156–7.

[40] See Landau's discussion in *Tselaḥ*, *Pes.*, introd.

[41] The title also alludes to the biblical phrase *nefesh ḥayah*. See e.g. Gen. 1: 24, 2: 7 (quoted by Landau), and 2: 19.

[42] Like the Lurianic kabbalists, Landau portrays the soul as containing 248 limbs and 365 sinews and maintains that all these elements are subject to injury and *tikun*, based on a man's deeds. See e.g. *Ahavat tsiyon*, sermon 2, 3*b*; Vital *Sha'ar hagilgulim*, preface 17, 17*b*, and preface 21, 20*a–b*; id., *Sha'arei kedushah*, pt. 1, Sha'ar 1, 11. Some of these ideas also appear in Zohar, iii. 222*b*. For a discussion of Landau's mystical view of the soul, see Part IV.

[43] On the importance of *berur* in the Lurianic system see e.g. Vital, *Sefer hagilgulim*, pt. 2, ch. 18, 35*a* and id., *Sefer halikutim*, 'Psalms', 89*a*.

[44] Lurianic kabbalists maintain that the breaking of the vessels on high caused the original mixture of good and evil. This mixture was exacerbated by Adam's sin below. On the significance of Adam's sin in Lurianic kabbalah, see n. 29 above.

[45] According to Lurianic kabbalah, the original soul of Adam contained all the souls, or sparks, of humanity (an idea based on *Exodus Rabbah* 40). Adam's sin caused both the scattering of these

each nation in order to gather the holy souls . . . As the Sages wrote, 'Israel went into exile among the nations in order that proselytes should join them, etc.'[46] You should understand this well.[47]

In other texts, Vital reiterates that the need for both *berur* and exile is rooted in the confused state of good and evil wrought by Adam's sin. Israel is consequently exiled to each place where holy sparks are scattered. The efficacy of Israel's mission of *berur* and elevating the sparks depends on its observance of the commandments.[48]

Landau appropriates these Lurianic motifs in several sermons and talmudic commentaries. In striking consonance with Lurianic passages on *berur* and exile, he writes in the *Tselaḥ* on *Berakhot*:

Through Adam's sin of eating from the Tree of Knowledge of Good and Evil, he caused the mixture of good and evil. In this way, holy sparks were dispersed in all the lands. And the Holy One, blessed be He, causes Israel to come to these lands in order that the holy sparks should not be banished. At times, God takes all of Israel into exile, as in the exile of Egypt. In other exiles, he takes the majority of Israel, while at other times God takes only a few individuals. All this is done in accordance with the needs of the good, which is mixed with the bad, in each place. [For, the purpose of these exiles is] to achieve *berur* of the good and to elevate it through Israel's observance of the commandments and performance of good deeds, in each place of exile. The good [in each place] thus finds its counterpart [in the holy deeds of Israel] and is elevated with Israel.[49]

Echoing Lurianic kabbalists,[50] Landau maintains that Adam's sin caused the mingling of good and evil, and the ensuing need for *berur*, and that the number of Jews dispersed in each exile is determined by the degree of purification of the sparks required in each place. Accordingly, like Vital, he stresses that in Egypt, 'the most defiled land',[51] the exile of the entire Jewish people was necessary to redeem the sparks there, while in other places, a partial exile is sufficient.

In his talmudic commentary, Landau also uses the Lurianic concepts of *berur* and elevating the sparks to explain the role of the proselytes who left Egypt along with the Israelites. In line with Vital, he comments:

individual souls among the *kelipot* and the dispersal of many of the Shekhinah's sparks. See e.g. Vital, *Sefer halikutim*, 'No'aḥ' 8*b*; id., *Sefer hagilgulim*, pt. 2, ch. 18, 35*a*. For a discussion of these ideas, see Scholem, *Kabbalah*, 163, 167. The trope of the 'exiled sparks of the Shekhinah' originates in Lurianic sources. See Scholem, *Mystical Shape of the Godhead*, 193, 244.

46 BT *Pes.* 87*b*.

47 Vital, *Sha'ar hapesukim*, 'Shemot', 101.

48 See Vital, *Peri ets ḥayim*, 'Sha'ar keriat shema', ch. 3, 164; id., *Sha'ar hamitsvot*, 'Re'eh', 47*b*; id., *Sefer halikutim*, 'Psalms' 89 *a–b*; id., *Sefer hagilgulim*, pt. 2, ch. 18, 36*a*. ; id., *Sha'ar hapesukim*, 'Bereshit', sermon 3, 13.

49 *Tselaḥ*, *Ber.* 9*b* (p. 34).

50 See Vital, *Sefer halikutim*, 'Vayishlaḥ', 22*b*.

51 Id., *Sha'ar hamitsvot*, 'Re'eh', 47*b*; id., 'Psalms' , 89*b*.

Rabbi Eleazar states that the Holy One, blessed be He, exiled Israel among the nations in order that proselytes should join them.[52]. . . The root of this, as it is known, is that through transgressions, sparks of holiness fall into the *kelipah*. Therefore Israel needs to go into exile. For in exile these sins receive *tikun* and the sparks which have fallen in that place are elevated. These are the proselytes who convert . . . and when Israel left Egypt they elevated all the sparks that were in Egypt. Therefore, numerous proselytes left Egypt with them at that time.[53]

Like Vital, Landau suggests that the proselytes who joined Israel during the Exodus housed holy sparks, and thereby assisted in the task of winnowing good from evil.

Even the biblical injunction against Israel returning to Egypt (Exod. 14: 13) is interpreted by Landau in light of the Lurianic tenet of *berur*.[54] Several Lurianic works, including *Sefer hagilgulim* and *Sefer halikutim*, disclose that the 'secret' of this biblical prohibition is that 'the *berur* of all the holy sparks was already complete at the time of the Exodus.'[55] This explanation is transmitted by Landau in both a Prague sermon and a talmudic gloss.[56] In these contexts, parallel to Lurianic teachings,[57] he interprets a number of talmudic metaphors concerning the Exodus from Egypt by relating them to the Lurianic notion that the process of *berur* is no longer necessary in Egypt.[58] Like Vital, Landau even adds that returning to Egypt can only incur harm by potentially causing the renewed admixture of good and evil there.[59] His repeated promotion of this Lurianic rationale for a biblical prohibition, despite his assertion, both in his discussion of

52 BT *Pes.* 87*b*.

53 *Tselaḥ*, *Ber.* 9*b* (p. 34).

54 Maimonides and Nahmanides list this injunction as a biblical commandment. See Maimonides, *Sefer hamitsvot*, negative commandment no. 46; id., *Mishneh torah*, 'Laws of Kings', 5: 7; Nahmanides, *Commentary on the Torah*, Exod. 14: 13.

55 Vital, *Sefer hagilgulim*, pt. 2, ch. 18, 35*b*; id., *Sefer halikutim*, 'Psalms' 89*b*.

56 *Derushei hatselaḥ*, sermon 38, 52*b*, in which he explains the injuction against returning to Egypt: 'no holy spark remained in Egypt . . . accordingly, we are never to go there'. See also *Tselaḥ*, *Ber.* 9*b* (p. 34).

57 Vital claims that the two images found in BT *Ber.* 9*b* that describe Israel's departure from Egypt, namely that they made Egypt like a snare without corn, or a pond without fish, allude to the holy sparks that Israel redeemed during the Exodus. The images allude to Exod. 12: 36, which states that during the Exodus the Jews emptied Egypt of all its valuables (see also n. 58 below). See Vital, *Sha'ar hamitsvot*, 'Re'eh', 48*a*; id., *Peri ets ḥayim*, 'Sha'ar keriat shema', ch. 3, 164. In *Sefer hagilgulim*, Vital elaborates on these metaphors and the manner in which they depict *berur* in a somewhat different manner. See *Sefer hagilgulim*, pt. 2, ch. 18, 36*a*.

58 Like Vital, Landau states that the two talmudic metaphors discussed above do not refer to the spoil taken from Egypt by the Israelites during their departure, as a non-kabbalistic interpretation would suggest, but rather to the sparks liberated by Israel. See *Tselaḥ*, *Ber.* 9*b* (p. 34). On his use of these Lurianic ideas to explain the talmudic metaphor of the pond without fish, see also *Derushei hatselaḥ*, sermon 38, 52*b*.

59 See Vital, *Sha'ar hamitsvot*, 'Re'eh', 48*a*; id., *Peri ets ḥayim*, 'Sha'ar keriat shema', ch. 3, 164–5; *Tselaḥ*, *Ber.* 9*b* (p. 34). In accordance with Lurianic tenets, Landau maintains that in places where *berur* is completed, Israel's exile is not only superfluous but forbidden.

this commandment and others, that one should not speculate about the reasons for the commandments, reflects the importance he ascribes to Lurianic kabbalah.

Notwithstanding the role that both exile and the performance of the commandments have in accelerating the process of *berur*, Landau and Lurianic kabbalists contend that the final *berur* will only occur in the era preceding the eschatological age.[60] In numerous works Vital states that during the messianic epoch the realm of holiness will be unadulterated, as it was before Adam's fall.[61] Landau advances this Lurianic conception both in *Ahavat tsiyon* and *Derushei hatselaḥ*.[62] In one sermon he relates:

> I have already preached in the name of the rabbi, the Ari, that the meaning [of the talmudic statement] that whoever will be alive in the generation [of the messiah] will be either entirely innocent or entirely guilty [see BT *Sanhedrin* 98*a*] is that there will be no mixing at that time . . . For this [commingling] was the sin of Adam, [namely] that the *nitsotsot* of holiness fell into the *kelipah*. In the generation when [the messiah] the son of David arrives, the process of *berur* will be completed.[63]

Supporting Luria's interpretation, Landau explains the enigmatic talmudic dictum that a generation that is entirely guilty will be fit for the messianic age on the basis of the Lurianic conception of *berur*. The merit of this utterly guilty generation, he asserts, is that it contains no admixture. Intriguingly, he prefers this daring Lurianic teaching to more conventional notions regarding good and evil.[64] Nevertheless, like the Lurianic kabbalists, he believes that such complete separation of good and evil will only be attained at the end of days.

Demonic Feeding on the *Nitsotsot*

Another Lurianic motif integrally bound to the concept of *berur*, the notion that the demonic forces feed on the holy sparks, repeatedly appears in Landau's writings. According to many Lurianic works, the divine sparks entrapped in the abyss of the *kelipot* during the breaking of the vessels and again during Adam's

[60] According to Lurianic kabbalah, the last stage of redemption will occur when the process of *berur* is completed. There are different views, however, concerning the role of the messiah in this process. Some works assert the messiah will only arrive after the process of *berur* is finished, while others state that he will play a special role in redeeming the final sparks. See Scholem, *Kabbalah*, 167–8.

[61] Vital, *Sha'ar ma'amerei rashbi*, 'Pekudei', 166; id., *Sha'ar hamitsvot*, 'Re'eh', 48*b*; id., *Sha'ar ha - pesukim*, 'Bereshit', sermon 3, 13; id., *Sefer halikutim*, 89*a*; id., *Sha'ar hagilgulim*, preface, 20, 19*b*; id., *Sefer hagilgulim*, pt. 2, ch. 21, 38*b*.

[62] See *Derushei hatselaḥ*, sermon 32, 47*a*, and sermon 30, 44*b*.

[63] *Ahavat tsiyon*, sermon 2, 3*b*.

[64] Elsewhere, however, he adopts the more conventional stance that the messianic age will only begin when all evil has been obliterated.

fall provided the germinal life force for the satanic realm.[65] Since the time of these cataclysmic events, mankind's continual sins perpetuate the captivity of the sparks, which in turn nourish the *kelipot*.[66] In an elaborate discussion of this theme, Vital writes:

As a result of Adam's sin, all the holy souls fell into the depth of the *kelipot* . . . These *kelipot* are by themselves called *darga demuta* [gradation of death] . . . As long as the holiness is in the midst of the *kelipot* they feed and live off it. But when the holiness is absent, the *kelipot* die, for they have no vitality and receive no divine emanation.[67]

Elsewhere Vital expounds upon the role of the wicked in this struggle between holiness and impurity, claiming that, when a wicked individual sins, 'he revives the *kelipah* and destroys the holiness'.[68]

Landau likewise discusses the demonic forces' dependence upon the holy sparks, as well as the role of wicked individuals in the clash between these two opposing forces. Appropriating concepts found in Vital's discourses on the *kelipah*, he explains in a 1769 sermon that

the *sitra aḥra* [demonic Other Side] has no vitality of its own; it is the *sitra demuta* [side of death]. It receives vitality only through the holy *nitsotsot* that fall into its realm . . . Through the few *mitsvot* which the wicked individual performs in his state of evil, the *kelipah* is granted ephemeral life until the wicked individual repents. Then he removes from the *kelipah*'s mouth that which it had swallowed.[69]

Following Vital, Landau portrays the demonic forces as feeding on the sparks, dramatically claiming that when the supernal sparks are elevated, the life force of the Other Side is 'taken from its mouth'. Using the same terminology as Vital,[70] he even designates the *kelipot* as *sitra demuta*, the side of death.

Interestingly, Landau's depiction of the struggle between holiness and evil is harsher than Vital's. Vital usually asserts that the *kelipot* are strengthened only by the nefarious acts of the wicked, while Landau claims that even good deeds performed by a wicked individual nourish the Other Side.[71] Landau's view that

[65] See Vital, *Sha'ar hagilgulim*, preface 15, 16*b*; id., *Ets ḥayim*, vol. 2, 39: 'Sha'ar mayim nukvin vemayim dukhrin', sermon 1, 65*b*; id., *Peri ets ḥayim*, 'Sha'ar keriat shema', ch. 3, 164; id., *Sha'ar hamitsvot*, 'Re'eh', 47*b*.

[66] Lurianic kabbalists therefore claim that the destruction of the evil forces will only occur at the end of days, when the final sparks are redeemed.

[67] Vital, *Sha'ar hagilgulim*, preface 15, 16*b*.

[68] Id., *Sha'ar hamitsvot*, 'Re'eh', 48*a*.

[69] *Derushei hatselaḥ*, sermon 9, 17*b*.

[70] On the terms *sitra demuta* and *darga demuta* in Vital's writings, see e.g. Vital, *Ets ḥayim*, vol. 2, 38: 'Sha'ar le'ah veraḥel', ch. 4, 62*b*; id., *Sha'ar hapesukim*, 'Vayetse', 81; id., *Sha'ar hagilgulim*, preface 15, 16*b*.

[71] The notion that demonic forces are nourished by the observance of some of the Torah's rituals, such as the offering of the goat to Azazel on Yom Kippur, appears in the Zohar. See e.g. Zohar, iii. 63*a*. While the Zohar limits its assertions about nourishing the 'Other Side' to a small number of rituals, Landau extends the scope of this idea.

good deeds can animate the demonic mirrors the paradoxical Lurianic notion that the demonic depends on holiness for its sustenance.

The Lurianic tenet that God will never forsake the sparks, which paradoxically ensures the *kelipot*'s survival, also informs Landau's discussion of the supernal sparks. In *Sha'ar hagilgulim*, Vital explains that God devises various schemes in order that not even a small spark in the midst of the *kelipot* 'should be banished'.[72] Adopting Vital's language, Landau writes that the 'Holy One, Blessed be He, causes events to occur so that the holy sparks should not be banished'.[73] Echoing the Lurianic kabbalists, he alleges that God orchestrates plans in order to safeguard and eventually liberate the sparks, which are simultaneously the prisoners and the life force of the satanic domain.

Raising Sparks from Adam Belial's Feet

Many of the kabbalistic motifs mentioned above are employed by both Landau and Lurianic kabbalists in their remarks on Adam Belial, the Demonic Being. According to Lurianic teachings, Adam Belial arose and took the place of Adam Kadmon after Adam's sin.[74] Since then Adam Belial has been nourished by the captive divine sparks, although over the course of history, these are steadily redeemed from his limbs. By the messianic epoch this purification process will be complete, and the Demonic Being will perish. Drawing on a zoharic statement,[75] various Lurianic works maintain that as the exile approaches its final stage, this process reaches the last sparks situated in Adam Belial's heels, where the forces of evil are strongest.[76] Although based on a zoharic phrase, the trope of purifying Adam Belial's heels, or feet, is unique to Lurianic kabbalah.

One of God's methods of redeeming these final and most entrenched sparks, according to both Lurianic and Landau's writings, is the exile of the Shekhinah.[77] Israel's deeds either enhance or hinder the Shekhinah in this mission, and when the Shekhinah finally succeeds in liberating the sparks from Adam Belial's heels,

72 Vital, *Sha'ar hagilgulim*, preface 15, 16*b*–17*a*.

73 *Tselaḥ*, *Ber.* 9*b* (p. 34).

74 According to Lurianic sources, Adam Belial, whose structure corresponds to the shape of Adam Kadmon, subsumed many supernal sparks into its limbs.

75 See Zohar, ii. 258*a*, where it is stated that during the eschatological age 'the feet will reach the feet'.

76 See e.g. Vital, *Sha'ar hamitsvot*, 'Re'eh', 48*b*. Variations on this Lurianic theme appear in Vital, *Ets ḥayim*, vol. 2, '39: 'Sha'ar mayim nukvin vemayim dukhrin', sermon 1, 65*b*; id., *Peri ets ḥayim*, 'Sha'ar keriat shema', ch. 3, 163–5; id., *Sha'ar hagilgulim*, preface 20, 19*b*; id., *Sha'ar ma'amerei rashbi*, 'Pekudei', 166, 169; id., *Sha'ar hapesukim*, 'Bereshit', sermon 3, 13. For a discussion of this Lurianic motif, see Wolfson, 'Walking as a Sacred Duty', 193–6; Scholem, *Kabbalah*, 167. According to other versions of this myth, the purification reaches the heels of Adam Kadmon.

77 Lurianic kabbalah reshaped the zoharic concept of the Shekhinah's exile in accordance with Lurianic mythic doctrines.

the messianic age will arrive. Divulging the 'secret' of the Shekhinah's exile, Vital states:

From the time of the destruction of the Temple . . . the Shekhinah gathers all the *nitsotsot neshamot* [sparks of souls] . . . Until the Shekhinah finishes gathering all the souls which fell among the *kelipot* of Adam Belial from his head even to those which fell into his feet, the messiah will not reveal himself and Israel will not be redeemed . . . The Shekhinah only gathers the *nitsotsot* on the basis of the deeds and prayers of the lower realms . . . If all Israel would repent fully, the Shekhinah would have the strength to liberate all the *neshamot* [souls] from Adam Belial in an instant.[78]

In various other writings Vital returns to this theme: that the exiled Shekhinah enters the demonic realm in order to elevate the holy sparks, many of which fell into the *kelipah*'s domain because of Adam's sin.[79]

In discussions of Adam Belial, several Lurianic sources, building on zoharic teachings, state that the calamitous struggle between the forces of Adam Kadmon and Adam Belial is alluded to in the verse 'There is a time when one man rules over another to his own detriment' (Eccles. 8: 9). Vital asserts that this verse refers to the '*sitra aḥra*, Adam Belial, who rules over Adam Kadmon in order to seize the oppressed souls embedded in Adam Kadmon. All this is to the detriment of Adam Belial.'[80] Elsewhere he elaborates upon the nature of this damage, stating that although the purpose of demonic rule over Adam Kadmon is to gain pleasure from holiness, 'the opposite occurs. Holy sparks which are mixed among the *kelipot*' separate from the *kelipot*'s domain.[81]

In his Prague homilies Landau disseminates many of these Lurianic tropes relating to Adam Belial, including the struggle between the Demonic Being and holiness, the redemption of the sparks from Adam Belial's heels, and the exiled Shekhinah's mission to liberate these sparks. These motifs are combined by Landau in a particularly powerful manner in a sermon for the Ten Days of Repentance suffused with Lurianic teachings. Quoting the verse 'There is a time when one man rules over another to his own detriment', he claims that the man who rules is

Samael, who is called Adam Belial, the figure of impurity. For through Adam's sin and the sin of the golden calf, some holy souls fell into this body. And the son of David [the messiah] will not come until all the souls are exhausted from this impure body.[82] We are

78 Vital, *Sha'ar hagilgulim*, preface 15, 16*b*.

79 See id., *Ets ḥayim*, vol. 2, '26: Sha'ar hatselem', ch. 1, 15*a*; id., *Sha'ar hamitsvot*, 'Re'eh', 47*b*.

80 Vital, *Sha'ar ma'amerei rashbi*, 'Pekudei', 167–8.

81 Id., *Sefer likutei torah*, 'Lekh lekha', 47*a*; id., *Sha'ar hamitsvot*, 'Re'eh', 47*b*; id., *Sefer halikutim*, 'Psalms' 89*a*.

82 Landau is playing here with an esoteric talmudic dictum: 'The son of David will not come before all the souls in the body have been exhausted' (BT *Yev.* 62*a*, *AZ* 5*a*).

obligated to gather the *nitsotsot* through our good deeds. However, because of our many sins, more *nitsotsot* have left the realm of holiness and entered the *kelipah* . . . This is the [reason for the] exile of the Shekhinah, for she must gather the *nitsotsot* from Adam Belial, from his head to the soles of his feet . . . When the exile reaches its deepest state, the Shekhinah will reach . . . the heels of this Adam Belial. Then she will gather even the *nitsotsot* in his heels.[83]

In line with many Lurianic kabbalists, Landau explains that the exiled Shekhinah's mission is to redeem the supernal sparks trapped by the Demonic Being as a result of Adam's fall and Israel's subsequent transgressions.[84] Israel can assist in this task through its good deeds. Following Lurianic sources, he also contends that the Shekhinah's release of the final *nitsotsot* from Adam Belial's heels will usher in the messianic epoch. Specifically echoing the *Ets ḥayim*, Landau interprets the cryptic talmudic dictum that the messiah 'will not arrive until all the souls in the body are exhausted' in accordance with these Lurianic tropes concerning Adam Belial.[85]

The virtues of repentance and the 'secret' of the liturgical confession are also understood by Landau in terms of redeeming the divine sparks from the Satanic Being. His comments on these themes refer once again to the Lurianic interpretation of the biblical phrase 'one man rules over another'. In this context, however, he dramatically identifies the man who is 'ruled over' as the penitent. In this vein, he states:

At first the penitent enters the depths of the *kelipot* in accordance with his sins. Yet now through his repentance he returns and elevates himself, and at this point he elevates all the holy *nitsotsot* along with him. This is the reason why Adam Belial rules over another to his own detriment, since the one whom the Demonic Being had ruled over becomes a detriment to him. For now the penitent elevates the *nitsotsot* from Adam Belial. This is the secret of confession: that one returns to the realm of the *kelipah* in order to elevate the holy *nitsotsot* . . . If we confess wholeheartedly and repent, we will then merit to save the holy city of Jerusalem, redeem the Shekhinah, and elevate all the holy *nitsotsot* from the *kelipah*.[86]

The centrality of Lurianic notions in this passage is striking. Here and in other homilies Landau appropriates Lurianic doctrines to explain the significance of confession, a principal element of the Yom Kippur liturgy, and of the practices of the *ba'al teshuvah*, the penitent.[87] By descending into the realm of sin, both the

[83] *Derushei hatselaḥ*, sermon 20, 31*b*.

[84] Landau similarly asserts elsewhere that the mission of the Shekhinah's exile is to elevate the holy sparks. See *Derushei hatselaḥ*, sermon 32, 47*a*.

[85] Vital, *Ets ḥayim*, vol. 2, 39: 'Sha'ar mayim nukvin vemayim dukhrin', sermon 1, 65*b*, and see n. 82.

[86] *Derushei hatselaḥ*, sermon 20, 31*b*.

[87] See also ibid., sermon 1, 5*a*, and sermon 26, 41*a*, in which Landau argues that the main purpose of confession is to release the divine emanation, which has descended into the *kelipah* due to our sins.

penitent and the one who recites a confession expedite the Lurianic goal of elevating the *nitsotsot*.[88] Landau's disclosure of this 'secret' is especially intriguing, since the idea that sparks can be liberated through man's descent into the demonic was a central doctrine of the Sabbatian and Frankist sects that he so reviled. The value he accords to these radical and potentially antinomian Lurianic tenets is demonstrated by his assertion that through this mode of confession and penitence, one hastens the redemption of nothing less than Jerusalem, the Shekhinah, and the divine sparks.

The Fall of the Sparks

Mirroring Lurianic writings, Landau also singles out certain transgressions that particularly engender the fall of holy sparks into the demonic sphere, such as the sin of spilling seed in vain. For Lurianic kabbalists, this transgression is one of the most egregious.[89] Besides repeating this kabbalistic notion, Landau, like Lurianic sources, stresses that his congregants should perform various penitential acts in order to atone for this sin.[90] In a sermon for the Days of Repentance he states that 'each person must repent and weep bitterly in order to elevate all the holy *nitsotsot* that we have caused to fall into the *kelipah*' due to this transgression.[91]

At times he uses halakhic analogies, such as specific laws concerning violations of the sabbath, in order to explain the kabbalistic concept of the descent of sparks into the *kelipah*. For example, in a sermon for Shabbat Teshuvah, he expounds upon the significance of the rabbinic practice of building an *eruv*, a structure which legally transforms a public domain—where one is prohibited from carrying on the sabbath—into a private domain, where such carrying is permitted. In an extremely esoteric passage, he interprets the prohibition against carrying in an open area on the sabbath in terms of the Lurianic conception of the spheres of holiness and evil, asserting that:

> This world is similar to a corridor which is open at one end[92]. . . In contrast, holiness is called a *reshut hayaḥid* [private domain], as is explained in *the books of the kabbalists*. Its width equals the four letters of the Tetragrammaton and its length equals the ten letters of the divine name of *mem heh*. However, the *kelipah* is called the *reshut harabim* [public

[88] The phrase 'elevating the *nitsotsot*', found in Landau's sermons and commentaries, originates in Lurianic kabbalah. See Scholem, *Mystical Shape of the Godhead*, 243.

[89] The rabbis base the prohibition on spilling seed in vain on Gen. 38: 10. See BT *Nid.* 13*a*. The severity of this sin is stressed in zoharic and Lurianic kabbalah. In fact, various Lurianic sources maintain that this transgression was Adam's original sin. See Vital, *Peri ets ḥayim*, 'Sha'ar ḥag hamatsot', ch. 1, 490; id., *Sha'ar hakavanot*, pt. 2, 'Inyan pesaḥ', sermon 1, 136–49; id., *Sha'ar hapesukim*, 'Shemot', 101–4. In these sources Vital asserts that for 430 years Adam transgressed by spilling his seed, thereby causing the entrapment of innumerable holy sparks in the satanic realm.

[90] See e.g. *Derushei hatselaḥ*, sermon 20, 31*b*, in which he states that chief among these penitential acts is copious weeping, 'like a stream'.

[91] Ibid. sermon 23, 35*b*.

[92] According to rabbinic law, a corridor with one opening is not considered a private domain.

domain] . . . As soon as one leaves the sphere of holiness, one falls into the realm of the *kelipah*.[93] (emphasis added)

Landau's description of the private domain here is clearly not a delineation of the dimensions of a physical space where one may carry on the sabbath, but rather a kabbalistic portrayal of the dimensions of the sefirotic world of the Godhead. In resonance with some Lurianic texts, he states that the Tetragrammaton and the *shem mem heh* represent measurements of the sefirotic realm.[94] The esoteric ideas conveyed in this passage are easier to decipher if one explores Landau's reference to 'the books of the kabbalists'. These are almost certainly the writings of Vital. In *Ets ḥayim*, Vital, like Landau, discusses the definition of private and public domains in terms of holiness and evil.[95] Adopting these and other Lurianic concepts,[96] Landau suggests that on the sabbath a sacred space, a *reshut hayaḥid*, is created, resembling the transcendent sefirotic world, often referred to by kabbalists as *olam hayiḥud* (world of unity);[97] a word play on *yaḥid* and *yiḥud* is also found in Vital's writings. Like Vital, Landau asserts that everything outside this sacred space is dominated by the *kelipah*.[98] Drawing on Vital's language and teachings as well as the rabbinic prohibition against carrying on the sabbath in a non-demarcated public domain, Landau warns his congregants that through sin one falls from the sphere of holiness into the demonic domain. The Lurianic motif of Israel's transgressions causing the descent of sparks into the demonic realm appears in many other sermons and commentaries by Landau.[99] Although he

93 *Derushei hatselaḥ*, sermon 24, 37*a*–*b*.

94 In Lurianic kabbalah, the *shem mem heh* (name of forty-five), יוד הא ואו הא, is one of the four permutations of the Tetragrammaton. It consists of ten letters and is therefore said to refer to the ten *sefirot*. It is called *mem heh* (45) because the numerology of these ten letters equals forty-five. This is also the numerological value of the name Adam. Kabbalists thus use the *shem mem heh* to show that the *sefirot* can be configured as the Adam Elyon, the Supernal Anthropos. Technically, in Lurianic texts, Adam Kadmon refers to the configuration of the divine before the emanation of the *sefirot*, while Adam Elyon refers to the human configuration of the *sefirot*, although these terms are, at times, used interchangeably. In earlier kabbalah, the two terms are almost always synonymous. For a discussion of the connection between the Tetragrammaton and the ten *sefirot*, see Scholem, *Kabbalah*, 111.

95 See Vital, *Ets ḥayim*, vol. 1, 'Sha'ar shevirat hakelim', ch. 2, 41*a*, which discusses the measurements of the public domain in terms of the seven Edomite kings, who are associated with evil in the Zohar and Lurianic kabbalah.

96 For example, Landau, like Vital, refers to the sabbath as *reshut hayaḥid*. See Vital, *Sefer halikutim*, 'Ekev', 56*b*.

97 In many kabbalistic works the world of emanation is referred to as the world of unity, while the material world is referred to as the world of separation. The Zohar speaks of the world above the heavenly throne as the world of unity and the world below it as one of separation. See e.g. Zohar, i. 155*a*–*b*. Using these ideas and playing with a halakhic term, Vital designates this world as *reshut harabim* (lit. 'the domain of the many').

98 See e.g. Vital, *Sha'ar ma'amerei rashbi*, 'Kedoshim', 179. This notion is also found in the Zohar (iii. 63*b*–64*a*). The mystical significance of violating the prohibition to carry on the sabbath is elaborated upon in *Tikunei zohar*, *tikun* no. 24, 69*a*. For a discussion of this zoharic teaching, see Tishby, *Wisdom of the Zohar*, iii. 1229.

99 See e.g. *Tselaḥ*, *Ber.* 9*b* (p. 34); *Derushei hatselaḥ*, sermon 19, 29*a*.

usually does not acknowledge the kabbalistic origin of these ideas, they are clearly rooted in specific Lurianic works.

To summarize, Landau's occasional citation of Luria's teachings and his frequent use of central Lurianic tropes, including those that stem uniquely from Lurianic sources—such as *shevirat hakelim*, *berur hanitsotsot*, and redeeming the final sparks from Adam Belial's heels—attest to his immersion in Lurianic kabbalah. His reading of numerous biblical and talmudic narratives through a Lurianic lens, his promotion of Lurianic spiritual ideals, and his depiction of various religious practices, such as confession and other rituals related to repentance, in terms of Lurianic myths convey the centrality of Lurianic doctrines in his spiritual world-view. Landau's wish to disseminate these tenets, at least to some extent, to a broader public is shown by the manifold Lurianic ideas found in his sermons and commentaries, addressed primarily to audiences of non-kabbalistic initiates. In fact, the intricacy of the Lurianic motifs in a good number of his homilies displays his assumption that Prague Jews had more than a glancing familiarity with these Lurianic concepts. Finally, his repeated use of Lurianic notions to rebuke the practices of Prague Jewry reflects his belief that members of his community not only understood, but would be swayed by these doctrines.

PART IV

KEY KABBALISTIC DOCTRINES FOR LANDAU AND PRAGUE JEWS

INTRODUCTION

BESIDES APPROPRIATING kabbalistic tenets unique to a specific kabbalistic school, Landau's Prague works often draw on doctrines that are pivotal to numerous kabbalistic systems, as well as interlacing rabbinic concepts with a range of mystical motifs. The ideas examined in this section appear in a variety of kabbalistic sources, including Nahmanidean writings, the Zohar, and Cordoverian, Lurianic, and *musar* treatises, and can neither be traced to an individual kabbalistic school nor to a particular kabbalistic work with certainty. Since Landau viewed all these texts, already inextricably interconnected, as comprising an essential core containing divine truths, he did not hesitate to use their ideas in a syncretic fashion.[1]

This section thematically portrays the central kabbalistic doctrines that Landau espoused, their relationship to rabbinic motifs, and the eclectic rabbinic, philosophical, mystical, and kabbalistic sources that shaped his views on fundamental religious issues. It also shows that his remarks frequently flow seamlessly from ecstatic ideals to theurgical notions, which for him, as for many kabbalists, are integrally linked. In a similar vein, he repeatedly incorporates concepts from different kabbalistic schools within a single passage. Accordingly, his teachings on basic tenets, such as the nature of the soul, the commandments, and the next world, are often the product of the interweaving of zoharic, Cordoverian, and Lurianic texts. Many of his writings treat kabbalistic ideas on these and other themes as axiomatic. In this manner his work indicates that his intended audience required neither an introduction to, nor a justification for, his frequent use of doctrines from diverse kabbalistic schools.

[1] Much recent scholarship has been devoted to showing the interconnectedness of zoharic, Cordoverian, Lurianic, *musar*, and numerous other kabbalistic writings. On both the centrality of zoharic kabbalah in Cordoverian works and the prominence of zoharic and Cordoverian tenets in Lurianic sources, see e.g. Sack, *Kabbalah of Rabbi Moses Cordovero* (Heb.), esp. 34–54, 57–82; id., 'Moses Cordovero and Isaac Luria' (Heb.), 311–40; Ben-Shlomo, 'Moses Cordovero', 401; Tishby, *Wisdom of the Zohar*, i. 103–5, 385; Liebes, 'New Directions in the Study of the Kabbalah' (Heb.), 162, 165; Huss, '*Sefer ha-Zohar*', 281, 294, 299.

TEN

Demons, the Soul, and the Afterlife

ALL LANDAU'S PRAGUE works incorporate kabbalistic teachings related to the soul, including *gilgul neshamot* (transmigration), *ibur* (impregnation; entry of another soul into a living being), *ḥokhmat hapartsuf* (metoposcopy), and the mythical conception of the soul's limbs and garments. His Prague homilies and commentaries are also replete with kabbalistic concepts concerning demonic spirits and the afterlife. These writings, other Prague sources, and recent research on popular Jewish and non-Jewish culture in pre-modern Europe, reveal that the Jews of Prague were obsessed with notions concerning the satanic realm, the soul, and the idea that invisible demons inhabit and cause suffering everywhere. As in numerous eighteenth-century eastern and central European communities,[1] these themes played a prominent role in the spiritual life and outlook of Prague Jews during this era. In addition, many of Landau's mythic and daring remarks concerning the soul and the demonic are predicated on his mystical understanding of these entities. In order to comprehend the kabbalistic tenets that Landau takes as a given for himself and Prague Jews and to discover some of his original kabbalistic insights, we must investigate aspects of the fundamental teachings on these mystical topics.

The Soul

Following most kabbalistic sources,[2] Landau describes three levels of the soul: the *nefesh* (vital soul), *ruaḥ* (spirit), and the divine *neshamah* (superior soul).[3] Like

[1] See Rosman, 'Innovative Tradition', 528–9; id., 'Prolegomenon to the Study of Jewish Cultural History', 117; Hundert, *Jews in Poland-Lithuania*, 143–7.

[2] On the three levels of the soul mentioned in the Zohar, see e.g. Zohar, i. 205*b*–206*a*, ii. 142*a*–*b*, 163*a*, 182*a*, iii. 25*a*–*b*, 71*b*, 83*a*–83*b*; ibid., i. 81*a* (*Sitrei torah*); ibid., iii. 29*a*–*b* (*Ra'aya mehemna*). For a discussion of the tripartite division of the soul in the Zohar and other kabbalistic sources, see Tishby, *Wisdom of the Zohar*, ii. 684–98; Scholem, *Kabbalah*, 154–7, 161. On the doctrine of the soul in kabbalah, see also Hallamish, *Introduction to the Kabbalah*, 247–79.

[3] *Derushei hatselaḥ*, sermon 1, 3*b*; sermon 20, 31*a*; *Tselaḥ*, *Ber.* 60*b* (p. 218); *Derushei hatselaḥ*, sermon 13, 22*b*. In the last source, Landau implies that only Jews are endowed with a tripartite soul. In contrast to Jewish philosophers, many kabbalists distinguish between the nature of Jewish and non-Jewish souls. This distinction first appears in 13th-c. kabbalistic writings. See e.g. in Moses de Leon, *Sefer harimon*, ed. Wolfson, 211: 8–212: 13, 308: 12–14; Zohar, i. 131*a*, 220*a*. On this topic, see Wolfson, 'Mystical Rationalization of the Commandments in *Sefer ha-Rimmon*', 242.

his sources, he draws on the tripartite divisions of the soul found in Platonic and Aristotelian philosophy, and adapts them to his mystical views.[4] In accordance with zoharic and later kabbalistic texts,[5] he stresses that these aspects of the soul, particularly the *neshamah*, are acquired through Torah study and the performance of other commandments.[6]

The majority of Landau's comments on the soul are devoted to its highest aspect, the *neshamah*. Like all kabbalists, he uses biblical, rabbinic, and kabbalistic tropes to depict the *neshamah*'s supernal origins,[7] repeatedly describing it as a 'part of the Divine above',[8] a phrase found in many kabbalistic portrayals.[9] He also frequently invokes the mystical image of the *neshamah* as hewn from God's Throne of Glory, which again appears in numerous kabbalistic works.[10] Drawing on kabbalistic teachings, he preaches that the soul yearns to return to its sacred origin.[11] However, unlike rabbinic portrayals in the aggadah,[12] he, like the kabbalists, views the divine *neshamah* as providing a continual connection between man and God. Critically, his kabbalistic conception of man's ability to affect the Divine is largely rooted in his understanding of this link.

[4] Like many kabbalists, Landau does not always employ the terms *nefesh*, *ruaḥ*, and *neshamah* consistently. Occasionally he uses the terms *nefesh* or *neshamah* to denote all three parts of the soul.

[5] See e.g. Zohar, iii. 25*b*; *Tikunei zohar*, *tikun* no. 21, 49*a*; de Vidas, *Reshit ḥokhmah*, 'Sha'ar hakedushah', 4, 27 (p. 57), and 30 (p. 59).

[6] *Derushei hatselaḥ*, sermon 20, 31*a*, and sermon 24, 37*b*. On the kabbalistic view that one needs knowledge of the Torah and its mysteries in order to possess the three levels of the soul, see Scholem, *Mystical Shape of the Godhead*, 218.

[7] For a discussion of kabbalistic portrayals of the divine origin of the *neshamah*, see Scholem, *Kabbalah*, 155–7; Ginsburg, *Sabbath in the Classical Kabbalah*, 192. Ginsburg points out that the kabbalistic belief in the divine nature of the soul contradicts the talmudic view that the soul is created, and therefore not divine.

[8] This is a play on the biblical expression *ḥelek elo'ah mima'al* found in Job 31: 2, where it refers to the portion, *ḥelek*, that one hopes to receive from the Divine. Landau and other kabbalists, however, play with this phrase, using another meaning of the word *ḥelek*, namely 'a part', to portray the *neshamah* as a part of the Divine. On Landau's use of this phrase to describe the *neshamah*, see *Ahavat tsiyon*, sermon 5, 9*a*; *Derushei hatselaḥ*, sermon 26, 41*a*, and sermon 25, 38*a–b*.

[9] See e.g. de Vidas, *Reshit ḥokhmah*, 'Sha'ar hayirah', 14, 9 (p. 281), 'Sha'ar ha'ahavah', 2, 22 (p. 378), 'Sha'ar hakedushah', 6, 47 (p. 103). See also de Leon, *Sefer hamishkal*.

[10] The Talmud describes the souls of the righteous as *hidden* under the Throne of Glory (BT *Shab.* 152*b*). Some kabbalistic sources, expanding on this notion, claim that the souls of the righteous are *hewn* from God's Throne of Glory, replacing the word *genuzot*, hidden, with the word *ḥatsuvot*, hewn. See Vital, *Sha'ar hapesukim*, 'Bereshit', sermon 3, 11; de Vidas, *Reshit ḥokhmah*, 'Sha'ar hakedushah', 6, 25 (p. 93). In line with these kabbalistic sources, Landau employs the term 'hewn', *ḥatsuvah*, in his description of the soul's relationship to the Throne of Glory. See e.g. *Tselaḥ*, *Pes.*, introd.; *Derushei hatselaḥ*, sermon 26, 41*a*, and sermon 25, 38*a*; *Ahavat tsiyon*, sermon 5, 9*a*.

[11] *Derushei hatselaḥ*, sermon 26, 41*a*.

[12] See Tishby, *Wisdom of the Zohar*, ii. 682.

Consistent with both the kabbalists and authors of the aggadah,[13] but in contrast to prominent Jewish philosophers, such as Maimonides,[14] Landau maintains that the *neshamah* is pre-existent. Various passages in the aggadah, Nahmanides' writings, and the Zohar state that during creation all souls were placed in a supernal storehouse.[15] The Zohar describes how, when a soul is summoned into the world, it is taken from this storehouse and 'garbed in the form of the world'.[16] Echoing these ideas, Landau asserts that there is a supernal storeroom where all the *neshamot* formed during creation are housed. At the beginning of the soul's creation, it possessed no form and was only 'ready to receive form, like the hylic matter mentioned by Nahmanides in the name of the Greek sages'. Subsequently, God formed the soul so that it could clothe itself in the body.[17] Although he does not cite the Zohar in this passage, his teachings on the *neshamah*'s pre-existence point to the influence of both the Zohar and Nahmanides.

Several other kabbalistic images used to depict the *neshamah* are incorporated in Landau's writings. One of these is the rope motif, illustrating the link the *neshamah* provides between God and man, and the resultant theurgical capacity bestowed upon man.[18] On various occasions, in both his homilies and glosses, he presents the *neshamah* as possessing limbs and sinews, in the likeness of the Supernal Anthropos and, accordingly, the human form—imagery in consonance with zoharic, Cordoverian, and Lurianic works.[19] In fact, he even refers to the *neshamah*'s *shi'ur komah* (measurement of the body), a term found most prominently in Jewish mystical literature describing the Supernal Anthropos's dimensions. In this vein, he reiterates that the *neshamah* has 365 sinews and 248 limbs,[20] corresponding to the talmudic portrayal of the number of limbs in the

[13] The rabbis of the aggadah and all kabbalists contend that the soul is pre-existent at least from the time of creation. For aggadic sources discussing the pre-existence of the soul, see BT *Ḥag.* 12*b*, *Genesis Rabbah* 8: 7, Midrash *Tanḥuma*, 'Pikudei', 3. See Scholem, *Kabbalah*, 157; Tishby, *Wisdom of the Zohar*, ii. 698–9, 702–3.

[14] The medieval Jewish philosophers Sa'adiah Gaon (882–942) and Maimonides denied the soul's pre-existence. See Maimonides, *Mishneh torah*, 'Laws of the Foundations of the Torah', 4: 9.

[15] See e.g. *Zohar ḥadash*, i. 10*b*–*c* (*Midrash hane'elam*); Zohar, iii. 303*b* (*Hashmatot*).

[16] Zohar, ii. 161*b*.

[17] *Tselaḥ*, *Ber.* 60*b*, 218–19.

[18] On the kabbalistic use of the rope as a metaphor to portray the link between the *neshamah* and its divine source, see e.g. de Vidas, *Reshit ḥokhmah*, 'Sha'ar ha'ahavah', 3, 5 (p. 386), 7 (p. 387), and 8 (p. 387). On Landau's use of this imagery, see *Ahavat tsiyon*, sermon 5, 9*a*, which emphasizes the importance of this link not being severed. See also *Derushei hatselaḥ*, sermon 25, 38*a*.

[19] On the kabbalistic notion that the *neshamah* possesses limbs and sinews, see e.g. Zohar, iii. 222*b*; *Tikunei zohar*, *tikun* no. 21, 52*b*; de Vidas, *Reshit ḥokhmah*, 'Sha'ar hayirah', 7, 10 (p. 133) and 11–12 (p. 134), and 8, 4 (p. 139), 'Sha'ar hakedushah', 6, 47 (p. 103); Vital, *Sha'ar hagilgulim*, introd., 21, 20*a*–*b*.

[20] See *Ahavat tsiyon*, sermon 2, 3*b*; *Derushei hatselaḥ*, sermon 13, 24*a*; sermon 19, 30*b*; sermon 30, 46*a*; *Tselaḥ*, *Ber.* 60*b* (218–19).

human body.[21] Echoing Vital and other kabbalists, he claims that the 248 limbs of the *neshamah* match the number of positive commandments, while its 365 sinews match the number of negative precepts. Like many kabbalists, he builds on these ideas and maintains that man affects the individual limbs of his soul by observing the commandments associated specifically with them. In turn, these limbs of the soul influence the corresponding limbs of the Supernal Anthropos.[22]

The mythical notion that the *neshamah* dons ethereal garments is also frequently included in Landau's homilies. This motif appears in thirteenth- and fourteenth-century Spanish kabbalistic sources, particularly in texts originating in Nahmanides' school.[23] Zoharic writings, however, are the first to suggest that this garment is woven out of man's good deeds, and that man's transgressions stain it.[24] This zoharic conception, adopted in later *musar* treatises,[25] often recurs in Landau's sermons. He repeatedly stresses that righteous acts produce magnificent garments for the soul, while transgressions create soiled clothing for it.[26]

Kabbalistic teachings on the soul also appear in Landau's comments on the *neshamah yeterah*, the 'additional soul',[27] a concept only mentioned twice in the Talmud.[28] Most medieval Jewish works either ignore the idea that man receives an additional soul on the sabbath or treat the notion figuratively. The most elaborate and mythical portrayals of the *neshamah yeterah* as a distinct entity are

21 See BT *Mak.* 23*b*. It is stated there that the Torah contains 248 positive commandments, corresponding to the number of limbs in the human body.

22 Both Landau's and many kabbalists' understanding of theurgy and *tikun* is predicated on this structure of man's soul and its resemblance to the Godhead. See e.g. Vital, *Sha'arei kedushah*, pt. 1, Sha'ar 1, 13–14; Sha'ar 3, 19, and pt. 2, Sha'ar 3, 41–6. For a more detailed discussion of the significance of this concept in Lurianic writings, see Chapter 9.

23 See Scholem, 'The Paradisic Garb of Souls' (Heb.); id., *Kabbalah*, 134, 158.

24 On the Zohar's portrayal of the theurgical creation of clothing for the *neshamah* through Torah study and prayer, as well as the soiling of this clothing through sin, see e.g. Zohar, ii. 210*a–b*, 211*b*, 247*a*, iii. 214*a*. For a discussion of this zoharic theme, see Scholem, 'The Paradisic Garb of Souls' (Heb.), 297–300. Although the Bible uses the imagery of stained clothing to symbolize transgression (Jer. 2: 22; Zech. 3: 4), only kabbalistic works claim that sin stains the *neshamah*'s garment.

25 On the use of this zoharic motif in *musar* treatises, see e.g. de Vidas, *Reshit ḥokhmah*, 'Sha'ar hakedushah', 4, 21 (p. 53), 'Sha'ar hayirah', 8, 5 (pp. 140–1) and 14, 9 (p. 281).

26 See *Derushei hatselaḥ*, sermon 1, 5*a*: 'From every commandment a garment is made for the soul, that is, for the limb in which the commandment was observed, while a cloak for the soul, that covers its entire body, is made from the commandment of charity'. See also ibid. sermon 5, 11*b*, 12*a*; sermon 19, 30*b*; sermon 20, 31*a*; sermon 25, 39*b*.

27 For a discussion of the role of the *neshamah yeterah*, or sabbath-soul, in kabbalistic sources, see Ginsburg, *Sabbath in the Classical Kabbalah*, esp. 121–38, 260–7, 295–6; Tishby, *Wisdom of the Zohar*, iii. 1230–3, 1237. On Landau's comments on the *neshamah yeterah*, see e.g. *Derushei hatselaḥ*, sermon 38, 52*a*.

28 See BT *Beits.* 16*a*. This statement of R. Simeon b. Lakish is repeated in BT *Ta'an.* 27*b*.

found in the Zohar.[29] Landau's remarks on this theme are influenced by such zoharic teachings, which are also often incorporated in the *musar* literature.

One popular zoharic notion concerning the *neshamah yeterah* included in Landau's writings is that it needs to be regaled with original words of Torah. In a homily delivered *c.*1757, he adopts this zoharic motif to rebuke sabbath desecrators, admonishing his congregants that rather than harming the *neshamah yeterah* with their sins, they should honour it with Torah study. Appropriating a zoharic teaching,[30] he relates that every Saturday night, God asks the souls that visited Israel what new aspect of Torah they learned on earth. He adds that each soul 'reports according to its stature, one about *sitrei torah* (secrets of Torah), one about original insights on Torah', etc.[31] Notably, he not only invokes this zoharic idea, but also claims that the additional souls of the most capable people engage in the 'secrets of Torah', clearly a reference to kabbalistic mysteries. Parallel to his comments on man's primary soul,[32] on several occasions he highlights the theurgical impact of Israel's deeds on the *neshamah yeterah*, using these kabbalistic teachings in order to influence his community's behaviour, particularly to encourage them to repent.[33]

Correspondingly, his gruesome accounts of the afflictions visited upon the *neshamot* of individuals who did not repent during their lifetime are replete with kabbalistic images and ideas.[34] In various sermons and glosses, he warns that

[29] Nevertheless, Nahmanides was the first to discuss the *neshamah yeterah* explicitly as an emanated soul. For zoharic writings on the *neshamah yeterah*, see e.g. Zohar, ii. 204*b*; iii. 29*a*, 35*b*, 242*b*–243*a* (*Ra'aya mehemna*).

[30] Zohar, iii. 173*a*. This idea is repeated in ibid. iii. 173*b*–174*a*.

[31] *Derushei hatselah*, sermon 4, 8*b*.

[32] On Landau's use of zoharic teachings about the *neshamah*, see Chapter 7.

[33] See e.g. *Derushei hatselah*, sermon 2, 6*a*, in which he discusses the relationship between the *neshamah yeterah* and the *kelipah*. Landau's treatment of the *neshamah yeterah* here is rooted in zoharic teachings. On the notion that the *kelipah* rules on weekdays and that holiness and the *neshamah yeterah* reign on the sabbath, see e.g. Zohar, i. 14*b*, 20*b*, 48*a*; iii. 35*b*; iii. 255*a* (*Ra'aya mehemna*); *Tikunei zohar, tikun* no. 21, 57*a*; *Zohar hadash*, 'Tikunim', 106*c*; *Zohar hadash*, 'Yitro', 32*a*. In addition, he likens the rule of evil forces on the sabbath and the consequent banishment of the *neshamah yeterah* as a result of Israel's sins to a 'servant-girl who is heir to her mistress' (Prov. 30: 23), an image commonly used in the Zohar to portray the domination of evil over holiness. See Zohar, iii. 266*a*, 279*b*, 281*b*–282*a* (*Ra'aya mehemna*). See also ibid. i. 6*a*; *Tikunei zohar, tikun* no. 6, 21*b*, where the Zohar speaks of the subjugation of the holy Shekhinah to the 'Other Side' as a result of the desecration of the sabbath.

[34] Landau often mentions his belief in the immortality of the soul. See e.g. *Derushei hatselah*, sermon 25, 38*b*; *Ahavat tsiyon*, sermon 6, 10*b*. On his mythical portrayal of the different fates of the souls of the wicked and the pious, see e.g. *Derushei hatselah*, sermon 1, 5*a*. On this notion in midrashic literature, see *Ecclesiastes Rabbah* 3. On kabbalistic teachings concerning the different fates of the three parts of the soul and the relationship between the immortality of the soul and reward and punishment, see Scholem, *Kabbalah*, 161, 333–4. In contrast to some kabbalistic sources Landau does not systematically distinguish between the fates of the three parts of the soul. In fact, in his discussions of the punishments meted out to the soul after death, he sometimes uses the terms *nefesh* and *neshamah* interchangeably.

destructive demons, created by an unrepentant individual's sins, punish and torture his or her restive soul after the death of the body that housed it.[35] Drawing on aggadic and kabbalistic themes, he also often refers to other punishments suffered by the souls of those who do not repent fully. These include *ḥibut hakever* (beating of the dead by evil spirits), *gehinom* (hell), and general punishments of the *neshamah*.[36] Although he occasionally comforts his congregants by stating that the purpose of these afflictions is to purify souls for the future resurrection,[37] his vivid and recurrent portrayals of the horrible fates awaiting the souls of impenitent individuals reflect his belief that these mythical concepts would stir contemporary Prague Jews.

Gilgul

Other than beatings by evil spirits and *gehinom*, Landau discusses another means by which the soul is purified: transmigration of souls or metempsychosis.[38] This tenet is mentioned neither in the Talmud nor the Midrash, and medieval Jewish philosophers do not accept it.[39] However, the doctrine appears in the Zohar and other thirteenth-century kabbalistic works. By the sixteenth century, it became a popular notion in Safed kabbalah, and from there it percolated into numerous European Jewish centres,[40] including sixteenth- and seventeenth-century Prague. In 1688 an entire book devoted to the topic of transmigration, *Gilgulei*

[35] See *Derushei hatselaḥ*, sermon 1, 5*a*, and sermon 30, 46*a*; *Tselaḥ*, *Ber.* 28*b* (p. 109), where he describes the 'destructive [demonic] children' who torment the soul of the sinner after death. The phrase 'destructive [depraved] children' first appears in Isa. 1: 4. There, however, it refers to the depravity of the Israelites, not to demons.

[36] See *Derushei hatselaḥ*, sermon 1, 5*a*; sermon 13, 23*b*; sermon 28, 43*a*. On *ḥibut hakever* in kabbalistic sources, see Scholem, *Kabbalah*, 333.

[37] See e.g. *Derushei hatselaḥ*, sermon 30, 46*a*, and sermon 19, 30*b*. In several places Landau asserts that only the bodies of the righteous will be revived during the eschatological age. See e.g. *Tselaḥ*, *Ber.* 18*b* (p. 74). There are various opinions in rabbinic writings as to who will be resurrected. Some claim that only the righteous will rise again, while others contend that everyone will.

[38] Like the Zohar and other kabbalistic writings, Landau presents *gehinom* and *gilgul* as vehicles for the soul's atonement, despite the contradictory nature of these two methods of punishment and purification. For a discussion of the conflicts between these methods as well as other kabbalists' views on the subject, see Scholem, *Kabbalah*, 161, 346; id., *Mystical Shape of the Godhead*, 211.

[39] See e.g. Sa'adiah Gaon, *Emunot vede'ot*, 6: 8; Hasdai Crescas (Spain, d. *c*.1412), *Or adoshem*, 4: 7.

[40] For a comprehensive discussion of *gilgul*, see Scholem, *Mystical Shape of the Godhead*, 197–250; Hallamish, *Introduction to the Kabbalah*, 281–309. The doctrine of metempsychosis is discussed in the first known kabbalistic text, *Sefer habahir*, redacted in the 12th c. The term *gilgul*, however, first appears in kabbalistic literature in *Sefer hatemunah*, produced by a group associated with the 13th-c. Gerona kabbalists. See Scholem, *Mystical Shape of the Godhead*, 197, 209; id., *Kabbalah*, 345. For a discussion of the term *gilgul* see Scholem, 'Study of the Theory of Transmigration in Kabbalah during the Thirteenth Century' (Heb.). On both the popularity of the doctrine of *gilgul* in 16th-c. Safed and Safed kabbalists' dissemination of this tenet, see Scholem, *Major Trends*, 281–4; id., *Kabbalah*, 73, 347–8; Fine, *Physician of the Soul*, 300–58; id., *Safed Spirituality*, 24; Meroz, 'Redemption in Lurianic Teaching' (Heb.), esp. 276, 280, 291–3.

neshamot, by the eminent Italian kabbalist Menahem Azariah da Fano, was published for the first time in Prague.[41] Like many seventeenth- and eighteenth-century kabbalists, Landau believes in *gilgul*, maintaining that it enables the soul to atone for sins committed in previous incarnations.[42]

Both his discussion of *gilgul* without any preparatory remarks and the limitation of his comments on this theme to technical considerations reveal his assumption that this doctrine was widely accepted by his audience and readers.[43] This is apparent in a gloss on BT *Berakhot*, where he analyses two variant texts, one found in most editions of the Babylonian Talmud and the other in the talmudic digest of Rabbi Isaac Alfasi (1013–1103), popularly known as the Rif. Landau suggests that the discrepancies between these texts hinge on a debate concerning the workings of *gilgul*. The differences result from

> a great and deep dispute, which cannot be grasped by human reason. For *it is well known*, as has been publicized among our nation, that there is *gilgul neshamot*, and that one *neshamah* transmigrates two or three times, and that in each transmigration the *neshamah* assumes a new body.[44]

Following the teachings of several Spanish kabbalists, Landau takes for granted that the soul transmigrates approximately three times.[45] He claims that this tenet is 'well known' among eighteenth-century Jews, and asserts that the variations between the two talmudic texts are the product of different views on the question as to which body will ultimately be resurrected when several bodies have housed the same transmigrated soul. According to the passage in the Rif's digest, only the body in which the *neshamah*'s restoration was completed will be revived. In contrast, the opinion expressed in the passage in most Babylonian Talmud editions is that *all* bodies that have housed a transmigrated soul will be

[41] Menahem Azariah da Fano, a disciple of Cordovero, was one of the main disseminators of Cordoverian kabbalah in Europe. He was also influenced by Lurianic kabbalah, particularly as interpreted by Israel Sarug, its leading exponent in Italy.

[42] Although most early kabbalists viewed *gilgul* as a punishment for specific transgressions, later kabbalists regarded it as a general opportunity to heal the soul of the consequences of sins committed during previous transmigrations. On the evolution of the doctrine of *gilgul*, see Scholem, *Mystical Shape of the Godhead*, 209, 212; id., *Kabbalah*, 161, 347.

[43] In his sermons and talmudic commentaries, Landau treats the general tenets of *gilgul* as a given, and in one responsum even bases his reasoning for a legal ruling on this doctrine. See *NB Tinyana*, 'YD', no. 164. See my discussion of this responsum in Chapter 5.

[44] *Tselaḥ*, *Ber.* 58*b* (p. 216), emphasis added. For a discussion of the kabbalistic debate on the revival of the multiple bodies which have housed a single transmigrated soul, see Scholem, *Mystical Shape of the Godhead*, 216.

[45] For various kabbalistic opinions on the number of transmigrations a soul may experience, see Scholem, *Kabbalah*, 346. The most widely accepted view in Spanish kabbalah is that the soul transmigrates three times after dwelling in its first body.

resurrected.[46] Strikingly, Landau's remarks exhibit not only his belief in *gilgul* and its associated technicalities, but also his exegetical willingness to explain discrepancies between variant talmudic texts on the basis of this kabbalistic tenet.

Elsewhere in the *Tselaḥ* Landau adopts the view that he ascribes to the Rif. There, like a minority of kabbalists,[47] he alleges that even the souls of the righteous who die on account of their transgressions undergo *gilgul*. Only the last body to house the transmigrated soul of this righteous individual, he remarks, will be resurrected, for 'during the revival of the dead this *neshamah* will certainly not split into many parts'.[48]

Several sources indicate that such discussions of the practical workings of *gilgul* interested members of Prague Jewry. Even Jonas Jeitteles, referred to by the historian Kestenberg-Gladstein as 'the father of Prague's Haskalah',[49] engaged in similar technical discourses on *gilgul*. Jeitteles's son, Judah, recounts his father's defence of *gilgul* after a public theological disputation during which a priest attacked the concept, asserting that it was incompatible with the doctrine of resurrection.[50] Jonas responded that although many bodies house one *neshamah* only the first will be resurrected.[51]

Landau even warns his congregants against subversive notions that may result from misunderstanding technicalities relating to *gilgul*, again demonstrating his belief that this tenet was widely accepted. He cautions his community, 'lest you say that you will only receive punishment for your last transmigration, this is not the case. Rather, in the future you will be accountable for all deeds for which you remained unpunished [both] in the first *gilgul*'

46 *Tselaḥ, Ber.* 58*b* (p. 216). Landau also asserts here that a phrase found in the more common talmudic text (but not in the Rif's version) alludes to a further aspect of this esoteric mystery, namely that during the resurrection the single transmigrated *neshamah* that had been housed in numerous bodies will be able to sustain all of them.

47 See e.g. Zohar, iii. 216*a* (*Ra'aya mehemna*); *Tikunei zohar, tikun* no. 69, 99*b*, 102*b*. For a discussion of this theme, see Scholem, *Mystical Shape of the Godhead*, 210–11, 221. Most kabbalists, however, contend that the righteous do not undergo transmigration.

48 *Tselaḥ, Ber.* 10*a* (pp. 39, 40). Elsewhere he builds on rabbinic teachings in order to expound on the technical workings of the future resurrection. See e.g. *Derushei hatselaḥ*, sermon 32, 47*b*.

49 Kestenberg-Gladstein, *Neuere Geschichte*, 121.

50 This theological disputation was held in the Prussian city of Halle, where Jonas lived for three years. See Judah Jeitteles' biography of his father, *Benei hane'urim*, 14–20. At the end of Judah's elaborate description of his father's defence of this kabbalistic doctrine, Judah, also a *maskil*, offers various apologetic reasons for his father's teachings on transmigration (*Benei hane'urim*, 19 n. 2). One reason is that his father was young when he engaged in this debate. Judah apologetically explains that it is difficult even for the scientific researcher to discard the kabbalistic ideas he absorbed with his 'mother's milk'.

51 Jeitteles, *Benei hane'urim*, 19 n. 2. Jonas claims here, somewhat differently from Landau, that only the first body to house a soul will be revived at the end of days. Interestingly, he employs this understanding of *gilgul neshamot* to interpret the enigmatic talmudic saying that the messiah will not arrive 'until all the souls are exhausted from the body' (BT *Yev.* 62*a*, *AZ* 5*a*). See *Benei hane'urim*, 19 n. 1. On Landau's Lurianic interpretation of this talmudic dictum, see *Derushei hatselaḥ*, sermon 20, 31*b*.

and in subsequent transmigrations.[52] Recognizing that members of his community subscribe to the doctrine of *gilgul*, he attempts to hinder its misinterpretation, which he feels could have dire consequences.

Ibur

The mystical notion of *ibur*, impregnation, which also appears in Landau's writings, is intimately related to the concept of *gilgul*.[53] In the Zohar and later kabbalistic treatises, *ibur* designates the entry of a second soul into a living person, usually for the purpose of performing a specific commandment. Various kabbalistic sources, especially Lurianic works, view *ibur* as an opportunity given to righteous individuals, allowing them to fulfil outstanding obligations without having to undergo the hardships of *gilgul*. In one responsum, answering a query from Rabbi Isaiah of Breslau, Landau writes

> the words of aggadah that you mentioned and the explanation that you offered according to the secret of *ibur*, [namely] that the righteous also appear in the later generations through the secret of *ibur*. In your great stature, you know that you are completely righteous, perhaps in you it is fulfilled that the secrets of God are revealed to the God-fearers and the upright (Ps. 25: 14). But in my impoverished state, I am happy in my portion, the revealed portion of the Talmud and Codes.[54]

Since many of Landau's responsa show his tremendous respect for Rabbi Isaiah,[55] his statement that Rabbi Isaiah might have insight into secrets such as *ibur* seems to be sincere. Moreover, although Landau denies his involvement with kabbalah here, he does not dismiss the idea of *ibur*. At the end of this and other passages,[56] he prays that God should disclose the wonders of Torah to him and place him on the *derekh emet* (path of truth) followed by his teachers. While his use of the phrase *derekh emet* here seems to refer to the revealed law, it is a standard code word for kabbalah.[57] Quite possibly, Landau concluded this passage referring to *ibur* with a plea to God to guide him in the path of kabbalah,

[52] *Derushei hatselah*, sermon 25, 38*b*.

[53] For a discussion of *ibur*, see Scholem, *Kabbalah*, 348–9; id., *Mystical Shape of the Godhead*, 221–2. In kabbalistic sources composed before the end of the 13th c., the terms *gilgul* and *ibur* are not clearly differentiated.

[54] *NB Tinyana*, 'YD', no. 201. Landau refers to R. Isaiah respectfully in the third person. In order to avoid confusion, I have used the second person in my translation of this passage.

[55] Although Landau usually does not respond to questions of a non-halakhic nature, he answers all R. Isaiah's queries, including those concerning aggadah. He also expresses his high regard for R. Isaiah in some of the 27 responsa he sent him. See e.g. *NB Tinyana*, 'OḤ', no. 35, and 'YD', nos. 123, 124, 160. For a discussion of Landau's respect for R. Isaiah, see Hess, 'Rabbi Ezekiel Landau' (Heb.), 177, 294. Still, even this relationship was fraught with tensions.

[56] See e.g *Tselaḥ*, *Ber.* 10*a* (p. 39).

[57] From the 13th c. onwards the phrase *derekh emet* generally refers to kabbalah.

along with its esoteric doctrines such as *ibur*, which many of his teachers had indeed taken and mastered.

Ḥokhmat hapartsuf

Ḥokhmat hapartsuf (lit. wisdom of the face, or metoposcopy), a kabbalistic art relating to the soul, is similarly discussed in Landau's work.[58] According to this divinatory art, the lines on an individual's forehead correspond to specific facets of his or her soul, revealing its previous transmigrations and a person's moral state. In this manner, *ḥokhmat hapartsuf* facilitates both proper repentance and the process of restoring the soul. Although this concept is barely treated in rabbinic literature, several zoharic passages do refer to it.[59] The practice of metoposcopy was particularly popular in Luria's circle in Safed, and many works about it were published during the sixteenth and seventeenth centuries.[60] Strikingly, Landau uses this kabbalistic notion to explain a talmudic narrative. In a novel reading of a talmudic vignette, he asserts that the traditional blessing of *ḥakham harazim*, 'the wise who discerns secrets', mentioned in the narrative, refers not to God, as explained by classical talmudic commentators,[61] but to sages whose wisdom is discerned through *ḥokhmat hapartsuf*. Landau's introduction of metoposcopy as the key to understanding a talmudic narrative indicates his belief in this divinatory art.[62] His referral to *ḥokhmat hapartsuf* without any explanatory remarks attests to his presumption that his readers were, at the very least, acquainted with this technique of practical kabbalah, and perhaps even accepted it.

Olam haba

Landau also presents a kabbalistic view of the ultimate rewards awaiting righteous individuals in *olam haba*, the World to Come.[63] The first is gnosis. Echoing

[58] For general discussions of metoposcopy, see Thorndike, *History of Magic*, vols. vi and vii; Seligmann, *Magic, Supernaturalism, and Religion*, 256–61; Alexandrian, *Histoire de la philosophie occulte*, 201–3. On metoposcopy in kabbalistic writings, see Scholem, *Kabbalah*, 318–19.

[59] See Zohar, ii. 71*a*–78*a* (and the parallel version in *Raza derazin*); Zohar, ii. 272*a*– 276*a*; *Tikunei zohar, tikun* no. 70.

[60] The main Lurianic treatise dealing with metoposcopy is Vital, *Sha'ar ru'aḥ hakodesh*, 15–22. On Luria's practice of metoposcopy, see Fine, 'Art of Metoposcopy'; id., *Physician of the Soul*, 153–64.

[61] See Rashi at BT *Ber.* 58*a* s.v. *ḥakham harazim*; Nahmanides, *Milḥamot hashem*, 44*a* (in Alfasi, *Halakhot gedolot*, Romm edn.).

[62] See *Tselaḥ*, *Ber.* 58*b* (p. 216), *ana nami kayion deḥazetinkhu*. After Landau offers his interpretation, he states that he took pleasure in seeing that Nahmanides also uses the concept of *ḥokhmat hapartsuf* in his reading of this narrative relating to the *ḥakham harazim* blessing. Unlike Landau, however, Nahmanides claims that *ḥakham harazim* refers to God. See Nahmanides, *Milḥamot*, 44*a* (in the Rif).

[63] Although in rabbinic and philosophical literature the expression *olam haba* sometimes denotes the hereafter immediately after death, Landau, in line with the more common usage of this expression, often uses it to refer to the eschatological age.

many kabbalists, he claims that in the World to Come the secret mysteries will be revealed, especially to the righteous.[64] In his remarks on this theme, he plays with various rabbinic and kabbalistic motifs. In particular, his linking of the World to Come with the Supernal Sabbath, both represented in kabbalistic literature by the *sefirah* Binah (Insight), is an outgrowth of kabbalistic lore.[65] His association of the World to Come with the sabbath and the uncovering of secrets is primarily based on the kabbalistic notion, emphasized in the Zohar, that those who properly observe the sabbath enter the pneumatic world, attaining a glimpse of the mysteries that will be more fully disclosed in the next world.[66] Along with gnosis, Landau maintains that in the World to Come, the righteous will also merit the ecstatic state of unceasing '*devekut* with the Shekhinah'.[67] By portraying gnosis and *devekut* as the ultimate rewards the righteous will achieve in the next world, he again reveals to Prague Jews his espousal of both kabbalistic and mystical ideals.

The Demonic Realm

In contrast to Landau's limited discussion of the pleasures awaiting the righteous in the next world, his writings, particularly his sermons, are replete with vivid mythical and kabbalistic portrayals of evil and punishment. Unlike Jewish philosophers, who frequently either neglect the problem of evil or treat it in a highly abstract manner, numerous kabbalistic works focus on the problems and mechanics of evil, often offering extremely mythical depictions.[68] Landau follows this kabbalistic tradition.

---

[64] See *Tselaḥ, Ber.*, preface; *Ber.* 34*b* (p. 130). In the preface Landau uses language found in Rashi's gloss on S. of S. 1: 2, while in his comments on *Ber.* 34*b* he employs the language of BT *Pes.* 119*a*.

[65] See *Tselaḥ, Ber.* 34*b* (p. 130). In the Zohar the *sefirah* Binah is called both the 'World to Come' and the 'Supernal Sabbath'. See Ginsburg, *Sabbath in the Classical Kabbalah*, 72, 100.

[66] *Tselaḥ, Ber.*, preface, in which he compares the sabbath to the secrets to be revealed in the World to Come. The kabbalists often appropriated the rabbinic association of the sabbath with *olam haba*, or *yom shekulo shabat* (the day that is entirely sabbath). See Mishnah *Tam.* 7: 4.

[67] See *Ahavat tsiyon*, sermon 2, 3*b*; *Tselaḥ, Ber.* 16*b* (p. 66). The phrase that Landau uses in these sources, namely 'to cleave to the Shekhinah', appears in the Talmud and in Maimonides' writings. See BT *Ket.* 111*b*; *Mishneh torah*, 'Laws of Repentance', 7: 7. Landau, however, employs this talmudic expression in a mystical manner in order to describe the future communion between the souls of the righteous and the tenth *sefirah*, the Shekhinah. For a more extensive discussion of this topic, see Chapter 8. In his description of the rewards bestowed upon the righteous in the next world, he also uses the phrase *nehenim meziv hashekhinah*, 'enjoying the splendour of the Shekhinah', a phrase used in BT *Ber.* 17*a* to describe the pleasures of the righteous in the next world. He similarly applies this rabbinic phrase to his mystical view of *devekut* and the Shekhinah.

[68] See Scholem, *Mystical Shape of the Godhead*, 58–9; id., *Kabbalah and its Symbolism*, 99. On philosophical and kabbalistic approaches to evil, see Tishby, *Wisdom of the Zohar*, ii. 447–50; Hallamish, *Introduction to the Kabbalah*, 167–82.

In line with thirteenth-century and later kabbalistic texts,[69] he views the realm of evil as existing in parallel with that of holiness. Consequently, like the kabbalists, he labels it 'the Left' and the 'Other Side' (*sitra aḥra*).[70] Building on this and other notions stressed in zoharic and Lurianic works, he frequently invokes the mythical motif of the ongoing battle between the demonic forces of the Left and those of holiness. However, like many kabbalists, he is not always consistent in his depiction of the relationship between these forces, alternately describing them as integrally connected, distinctly competitive, and mutually exclusive.[71]

As in most kabbalistic sources, Landau does not clearly distinguish between evil, emanations of the Left Side, and demons.[72] In his mythological world-view, demons are a hypostatization of evil, and one does not exist without the other. In fact, like many kabbalists, he uses the popular kabbalistic term *kelipot* to represent both evil in general and demons specifically.[73] Lacing his remarks on the *kelipot* with ideas highlighted in zoharic and Lurianic kabbalah,[74] he asserts that each transgression augments the *kelipot*, creating a destructive demon on the Left,[75]

[69] For a discussion of the realm of evil or the 'Other Side' in the Zohar and other 13th-c. writings, see Tishby, *Wisdom of the Zohar*, ii. 447–528; Wolfson, 'Left Contained in the Right', 28–33; Scholem, *Kabbalah*, 321; id., *Mystical Shape of the Godhead*, 73. On the demonic realm in Lurianic kabbalah, see Tishby, *Doctrine of Evil* (Heb.).

[70] See e.g. *Derushei hatselaḥ*, sermon 9, 17*b*; sermon 22, 33*a*; sermon for Shabat Hagadol, 57*a*: 'the Left Side has no part in the prayers in the Land of Israel.' This citation is probably based on the zoharic notion that the hard shell of the 'Other Side' does not rule over the Holy Land. See Zohar, ii. 140*b*–141*a*.

[71] See e.g. *Derushei hatselaḥ*, sermon 1, 3*b*, in which Landau relates that the commission of a transgression removes the sinner from the camp of holiness to the place of the *kelipah*; and after three sins, the sinner cannot re-enter the camp of holiness by himself. See also ibid., sermon 2, 6*a*; sermon 9, 17*b*; sermon 23, 34*b*; sermon 30, 45*a*; sermon 34, 48*a*.

[72] The correspondence between demons and the lowest powers of the 'Left Side' appears in various 13th-c. Castilian kabbalistic texts, including some of the Hebrew works of Moses de Leon and zoharic writings. See Scholem, *Kabbalah*, 321. The correspondence is also elaborated upon in many later kabbalistic treatises, particularly in the *musar* literature. See de Vidas, *Reshit ḥokhmah*, 'Sha'ar hateshuvah', 3, 26 (p. 735), 'Sha'ar hayirah', 8, 8 (p. 142). For a discussion of demons in Lurianic kabbalah, see Scholem, *Kabbalah*, 325–6.

[73] On the conception of the *kelipot* in the Zohar, Lurianic kabbalah, and other kabbalistic writings, see Scholem, *Kabbalah*, 124–5, 138–9; Tishby, *Wisdom of the Zohar*, ii. 461–4; id., *Doctrine of Evil* (Heb.), esp. 61–90.

[74] In general, Landau's comments on the *kelipot* are replete with concepts found in zoharic and Lurianic texts. For instance, he asserts that they dwell in the *nukba ditehoma raba*, 'the crevice of the great deep', a phrase mentioned in the Zohar and Lurianic sources (see e.g. Zohar, i. 242*b*, ii. 163*b*, 173*b*, iii. 19*a*). However, although the notion that the *kelipot* reside in the *nukba ditehoma raba* before they are stirred up by man's sins appears in the Zohar, it is more commonly found in Lurianic works. For Landau's comments on this topic, see e.g. *Ahavat tsiyon*, sermon 1, 2*a*; *Derushei hatselaḥ*, sermon 24, 37*a*, and sermon 32, 47*a*.

[75] On the Zohar's contention that human transgressions, particularly those of Adam and his sons, generate demons, see Tishby, *Wisdom of the Zohar*, ii. 529–31. On the parallel notion that angelic advocates are created through the performance of the commandments, see *Derushei hatselaḥ*, sermon 5, 11*b*–12*a*, sermon 13, 24*a*.

and reiterates that this is taught in all the *musar* works.[76] He further warns that not only the number of sins, but also the severity of a transgression and the enthusiasm with which it is performed contribute to the potency of the evil spirits created.[77] Aside from frequently referring to general categories of demons generated and strengthened by human sin, such as *meḥabelim* (evil spirits), *mazikim* (harmful spirits), *kelipot* and *banim mashḥitim* (destructive demonic sons), he also occasionally mentions specific demonic figures, as do many thirteenth-century and later kabbalists.

In resonance with zoharic, Lurianic, and numerous other kabbalistic works, Landau presents the leader of the Other Side as Samael, or Satan,[78] and as Adam Belial.[79] Following the Lurianic custom of not pronouncing the demonic name in full, Landau usually refers to Samael by the Hebrew letters *samekh mem*.[80] In line with aggadic and kabbalistic sources,[81] he uses a wide array of images to portray Samael, including the executor of punishment, the evil inclination,[82] and the guardian of the nations ruling Israel.[83]

Although Samael appears in both rabbinic and kabbalistic sources, the notion that he has a mate, the demonic queen Lilith, is first found in thirteenth-century kabbalistic writings, such as Isaac Hakohen's *Treatise on the Left Emanation* and the Zohar.[84] Appropriating this and other kabbalistic tropes, Landau chastises his community, exclaiming that each of their sins strengthens the power of both

[76] See *Tselaḥ*, *Ber.* 5*a* (p. 18); *Ahavat tsiyon*, sermon 1, 2*a*; *Derushei hatselaḥ*, sermon 3, 7*a*; sermon 6, 12*a*; sermon 13, 23*a*; sermon 19, 30*b*; sermon 23, 36*a*; sermon 26, 41*a*; sermon 30, 46*a*; sermon 34, 48*a*.

[77] *Derushei hatselaḥ*, sermon 5, 11*b*; *Tselaḥ*, *Ber.* 28*b* (p. 109).

[78] After the Amoraic period, Satan is primarily referred to as Samael in Jewish sources. For a discussion of Samael as the leader of the 'Other Side' in kabbalistic texts, see Scholem, *Kabbalah*, 321, 323, 385, 387; Tishby, *Doctrine of Evil* (Heb.), 19, 63, 72, 93. For Landau's association of Samael and the *kelipot*, see e.g. *Ahavat tsiyon*, sermon 2, 4*a*.

[79] See *Derushei hatselaḥ*, sermon 20, 31*b*. On the use of the term Adam Belial in the Zohar, see e.g. Zohar, ii. 118*b* (*Ra'aya mehemna*). On this phrase in Lurianic writings, see e.g. Vital, *Sha'ar hagilgulim*, introd. 15, 16*b*; id., *Sha'ar ma'amerei rashbi*, 'Pekudei' 167–8.

[80] See e.g. *Derushei hatselaḥ*, sermon 23, 35*b*, and sermon 26, 41*a*.

[81] For an overview of the primary functions of Samael and the 'Other Side' in aggadic and kabbalistic sources, see Tishby, *Wisdom of the Zohar*, ii. 511–12; id., *Doctrine of Evil* (Heb.), esp. 93.

[82] See *Derushei hatselaḥ*, sermon 2, 6*a*; sermon 22, 33*a*; sermon 30, 45*a*; sermon for Passover, 59*a*. Following aggadic and zoharic teachings, he also associates Samael's evil powers with the *naḥash hakadmoni*, the 'primordial serpent'. See ibid. sermon 5, 11*b*. On the aggadic and zoharic portrayal of the connection between Samael and the primordial snake, see Tishby, *Wisdom of the Zohar*, ii. 467.

[83] See e.g. *Derushei hatselaḥ*, sermon 20, 31*b*.

[84] Lilith is mentioned in the Bible (Isa. 34: 14), works of aggadic Midrash, several talmudic passages, and numerous kabbalistic sources. See e.g. BT *Shab.* 151*b*, *Nid.* 24*b*. For a discussion of Lilith, see Scholem, *Kabbalah*, 321, 326, 356–61, 387–8; Tishby, *Wisdom of the Zohar*, ii. 531; Dan, 'Samael, Lilith, and the Concept of Evil'. On zoharic references to Samael and his consort, see Zohar, i. 148*a–b* (*Sitrei torah*), and iii. 224*b*. On the pairing of Samael and Lilith in later kabbalistic works, see e.g. de Vidas, *Reshit ḥokhmah*, 'Sha'ar hayirah', 8: 8 (p. 142).

the evil servant Lilith and of Samael.[85] Invoking a related zoharic motif,[86] in a homily in which Lilith is mentioned almost fifteen times, he laments that Israel's transgressions have allowed Lilith to 'succeed her mistress' [Prov. 30: 23], the Shekhinah.[87] Consequently, rather than being cleansed by the Shekhinah, Israel is tormented by Lilith. Such mythic portrayals of Lilith recur in several of Landau's writings.

Lilith also plays the role of a demonic temptress in both kabbalistic works and those of Landau.[88] The Zohar explains that since demons cannot procreate independently, Lilith and other female demons seduce men, using their seed to bear demonic offspring.[89] Later kabbalistic texts connect this mythical theme with man's death.[90] According to various kabbalistic sources as well as the eighteenth-century Sabbatian tract *Ḥemdat yamim*, the demons produced by man's spilling of seed during his lifetime accompany his bier at his funeral.[91] Referring to these kabbalistic ideas in a sermon for the Days of Repentance, Landau laments:

> [Because of] our great sins, through our lascivious thoughts during the day, at night Lilith comes and makes a person impure[92] . . . For through every drop [of semen] a harmful demon and *kelipah* is born. And after a person's death, at the hour when people carry his bier through the city streets, all these demonic offspring come [and] encircle his bier, causing him grief.[93]

85 *Derushei hatselaḥ*, sermon 19, 30*b*.

86 Like zoharic and later kabbalistic texts, Landau repeatedly compares the demonic servant-girl Lilith's condition with that of the holy Shekhinah. See e.g. Zohar, iii. 69*a*, which states that 'the King has dismissed the consort [the Shekhinah] from His presence and brought in a maidservant in her place, as it is said, "For three things the earth quakes . . . and for a servant-girl that is heir to her mistress" (Prov. 30: 21–3)'. Trans. in Tishby, *Wisdom of the Zohar*, i. 408. See also Zohar, i. 148*a*; de Vidas, *Reshit ḥokhmah*, 'Sha'ar hayirah', 9, 10 (p. 156).

87 *Derushei hatselaḥ*, sermon 19, 30*b*.

88 On zoharic and later kabbalistic views of Lilith as a demonic sexual power and the creation of demons through the 'pollution of seed', see Scholem, *Kabbalah and its Symbolism*, 154–7.

89 See e.g. Zohar, iii. 76*b*–77*a*. On this zoharic myth, see Tishby, *Wisdom of the Zohar*, ii. 464.

90 The idea that all the demonic children that a man has produced appear at his funeral is first found in the writings of Abraham Sabba, a 16th-c. Spanish kabbalist who emigrated to Morocco.

91 On the harm caused by such demons, see Vital, *Sha'ar hakavanot*, pt. 1, 'Inyan derushei halailah', 362–5. On the notion that they surround the bier at one's funeral see Anon., *Ḥemdat yamim*, ii. 1763, p. 98*b*: 'all those spirits that have built their bodies from a drop of his seed regard him as their father . . . On the day of his burial, he must suffer punishment; for while he is being carried to the grave, they swarm around him . . . behind his bier.' (trans. in Scholem, *Kabbalah and its Symbolism*, 155). Although *Ḥemdat yamim* is replete with Sabbatian teachings, it was extremely popular among 18th- and 19th-c. Ashkenazi Jews. On this work, see Scholem, 'Vehata'alumah be'einah omedet'.

92 Landau is playing here with the similar sounds of the Hebrew words *lailah* (night) and *lilit* (Lilith).

93 *Derushei hatselaḥ*, sermon 23, 35*b*. Interestingly, in 1717 Jakob Schudt, the director of the Frankfurt Gymnasium, wrote that Frankfurt Jews believed that the demonic sons produced by the spilling of seed accompanied a man's bier at his funeral. See Schudt, *Jüdische Merckwürdigkeiten*, iv, appendix, 43. Scholem cites this source in *Kabbalah and its Symbolism*, 156.

Endorsing kabbalistic notions, particularly concepts promoted in Lurianic kabbalah, Landau recommends, here and elsewhere, that one atone for such demons, created through nocturnal emissions, by means of weeping and other forms of penitence.[94] Notably, he uses the kabbalistic conception that illicit sexual activity strengthens Lilith's domain in order to influence his congregants' behaviour, suggesting his belief that Prague Jews subscribed to these mythical teachings.

In fact, the Prague prayer book *Tikun nefesh* indicates that these kabbalistic motifs had an impact on rituals practised by Prague Jews. Strikingly, this prayer book contains a standardized confession both for the sin of spilling seed in vain and for creating demons in this way. This confession, to be recited by an individual who is ill, bans these demonic forces, stating that after the transgressor's death they will attempt to accompany his bier 'from his home to his grave'. The sick individual vows that if he recovers he will observe the appropriate penances for this sin prescribed in Lurianic writings and other sacred works. Following the recitation of the confession, a court of three declares that the demonic forces created by the sick man's seed shall not harm him after death.[95]

Besides singling out the generation of demons through illicit sexual behaviour, Landau also emphasizes the creation of demons through various transgressions related to prayer. Touching on an issue involving both sins, he rails against Prague Jews' widespread practice of praying in private homes, exclaiming 'who knows how many *kelipot* and *mezikim*' were born in their houses, where they both pray and 'sprawl on their beds?'.[96] Even in synagogue, he cautions in one sermon, idle chatter produces demons of destruction.[97] In other comments on prayer, in both his homilies and talmudic commentary, he warns that *kelipot* created through transgressions 'fill the air', 'seizing prayers', in order to hinder them from reaching God.[98]

On occasion, he even introduces his own mystical interpretations of the demonic realm, prayer, and the soul. In one of his Prague homilies he explains that only the souls of those who pray in synagogue will ascend to heaven, stating that:

[94] See also *Derushei hatselaḥ*, sermon 20, 31*b*. On kabbalists' advocacy of various acts of penance for this transgression, see Scholem, *Kabbalah and its Symbolism*, 156–7. On the tremendous focus during the 18th c. on the sin of nocturnal seminal emissions, due to the enormous weight given to this transgression in kabbalistic sources, see Hundert, *Jews in Poland–Lithuania*, 131–7. On the Lurianic conception that this sin, in particular, engenders the fall of sparks, see Chapter 9.

[95] *Tikun nefesh*, 27*b*, 28*a–b*. This confession notes the universality of this harmful phenomenon.

[96] *Derushei hatselaḥ*, sermon 3, 7*a*. On Prague Jews' practice of praying in private minyanim, see Chapter 1.

[97] *Derushei hatselaḥ*, sermon 4, 9*a–b*.

[98] Ibid., sermon 5, 12*a*, and sermon 19, 29*a*. *Tselaḥ*, *Ber.* 30*b* (p. 117).

In my humble opinion the reason for this is that the entire Diaspora is filled with *kelipot* . . . [only] the soul which is already used to its daily ascent [to heaven], through its synagogue attendance, [knows the path to heaven] . . . Further, the slaughtering of this soul is not done by Samael. For a blemished knife [i.e. that of Samael] renders the soul unfit for sacrifice.[99]

Intriguingly, Landau reveals that the first mystical interpretation that he offers concerning the demonic *kelipot* and the heavenly ascent of the soul is 'his own opinion'.[100] In general, he does not make such admissions since, as discussed earlier, they fly in the face of his repeated claim that he does not engage in mystical matters.

Curiously, the prayer book *Tikun nefesh* employs the second kabbalistic image found in the aforementioned passage, namely that of a soul becoming ritually unfit, or possessed by Samael, because it was slaughtered with a blemished knife.[101] This idea is incorporated in a confession to be recited by a mortally ill individual, stating that Satan desires to slaughter him in this fashion in order to make him ritually forbidden.[102] In view of Landau's probable endorsement of *Tikun nefesh*, his exposition of this kabbalistic motif in a Prague homily is not surprising.

In conclusion, many of Landau's works as well as other eighteenth-century Prague sources, incorporate kabbalistic teachings on the afterlife, the soul's limbs, clothing, transmigration, and the demonic realm. His repeated use of mythic kabbalistic motifs relating to souls and demonic spirits as a tool to promote various practices, such as synagogue attendance, Torah study, and discouraging the spilling of seed in vain, reflect his assumption that Prague Jews embraced these concepts. Besides the numerous indications that these kabbalistic notions were widely known by eighteenth-century Prague Jews, the prayer book *Tikun nefesh* demonstrates that kabbalistic teachings about the demonic and the soul found in Landau's writings also influenced liturgical texts and customs.

[99] *Derushei hatselaḥ*, sermon 22, 33*a*. Here Landau draws an analogy between the souls of the dead and the sacrifices that were carried out in the Temple. A slaughtering knife with even the slightest nick rendered a sacrifice ritually unfit. On this, see BT *Ḥul.* 3*b*, 10*a–b*. On the motif of sacrificing souls, see Tosafot on BT *Men.* 110*a*, s.v. *vemikha'el sar hagadol*; Zohar, i. 80*a* (*Sitrei torah*).

[100] Landau conveys a similar idea in *Derushei hatselaḥ*, sermon 15, 25*b*.

[101] See Zohar, iii. 29*a* (*Ra'aya mehemna*).

[102] *Tikun nefesh*, 26*b*.

ELEVEN

The Banished Consort: Theurgy and the Exiled Shekhinah

THE KEY KABBALISTIC MOTIFS of the Shekhinah's exile and the theurgical role of the commandments permeate Landau's writing. His remarks on these themes reveal both their centrality for him and the diverse sources which shaped his kabbalistic views. Contrary to scholarship's portrayal of both Landau in particular and rabbinic opponents of hasidim in general, Landau's kabbalistic beliefs led him to advance various theurgical and mystical forms of devotion.[1] Accordingly, he frequently urges his congregants to pray, study Torah, and perform good deeds with the intent of redeeming the exiled Shekhinah. He also adopts elements of the ecstatic conception of *kavanah*—i.e. the intention of attaining *devekut*—particularly for prayer, stating that this mode of worship leads to this mystical ideal.[2] Notwithstanding the assertions made in most studies of Landau and in debates concerning the use of *kavanot* (lit. intentions; extra-liturgical aspects of prayer) during the eighteenth and nineteenth centuries, several primary sources attest to his respect both for general kabbalistic *kavanot* and the more esoteric Lurianic *kavanot*.

Theurgy

All genres of Landau's work take the theurgical notion that Israel's deeds, both good and bad, influence the divine upper worlds as a given.[3] Like many

[1] See e.g. Allan Nadler's assertion that the mitnagedim rejected all the endeavours of their Jewish contemporaries to partake in any type of theurgical or mystical prayer. In particular, Landau's advice to his congregants that they should have the needs of the exiled Shekhinah in mind during their prayers and not just their own temporal needs (see e.g. *Derushei hatselah*, sermon 30, 44*a*) contradicts Nadler's claim that the mitnagedim insisted that prayer should be no more than a petition for sustenance. See Nadler, *Faith of the Mithnagdim*, 69–70.

[2] These ideas are already promoted in the early kabbalistic works of Isaac the Blind and his disciples Ezra and Azriel of Gerona. For a discussion of their portrayal of *kavanah*, prayer, and *devekut*, see Scholem, *Origins of the Kabbalah*, 299–309, 414–21; Brody, 'Human Hands Dwell in Heavenly Heights'.

[3] For a discussion of the kabbalistic view that theurgy is a primary purpose of the commandments, see Matt, 'The Mystic and the *Mizvot*', 372–400; Tishby, *Wisdom of the Zohar*, iii. 1157–67; Wolfson, 'Mystical Rationalization of the Commandments in *Sefer ha-Rimmon*', 217–51; Idel, *Kabbalah*, pp. xviii, 156–99.

kabbalists, he explains in his responsa and sermons that Israel's good acts cause 'all the restorations above to occur automatically'.[4] Conversely, in the same vein as his comments on the creation of demons, he repeatedly alleges that both the gravity of a sin and its frequency determine the severity of the defect on high.[5] He consequently insists that a penitent atone for every violation of each transgression committed, as each violation causes an additional 'blemish above'.[6]

Several of his remarks on theurgy employ the ladder motif,[7] popular in both Lurianic and hasidic discussions of Israel's theurgic capabilities.[8] Using the biblical image of Jacob's ladder (Gen. 28: 12), he states that all that transpires above is the result of our deeds 'as if [we were] a ladder placed on earth, and our heads reached the heavens'.[9] Elsewhere, as in the *musar* literature,[10] he draws a connection between the angels ascending and descending Jacob's ladder and man's ability to 'ascend and cleave' or to descend in the supernal realm, depending on his deeds. In accordance with Vital and imagery that appears in hasidic works,[11] Landau stresses that through this ascent or descent man either perfects or blemishes the supernal worlds.[12]

Striking a resonant note with many kabbalistic texts, Landau maintains that the underlying rationale for the commandments (*ta'amei hamitsvot*) is their theurgical influence above. Echoing Moses de Leon and other kabbalists,[13] he explicitly states that 'the purpose of the entire Torah and the commandments' is the need of the upper world to be restored.[14] Even in places where he reiterates the rabbinic contention that one should not ponder the reasons for the *mitsvot*, but rather observe them simply because they are the decrees of the Divine King,[15] he

[4] *NB Kama*, 'YD', no. 93; *Derushei hatselaḥ*, sermon for Passover, 59*a*, and sermon for 4 Tishrei, 19*a*.

[5] *Derushei hatselaḥ*, sermon 5, 10*b*. See also sermon 11, 19*b*, where he claims that this also applies to the extent that the world of the angels is harmed or restored. See ibid., sermon for 4 Tishrei, 19*a*; *Ahavat tsiyon*, sermon 2, 3*b*; *Derushei hatselaḥ*, sermon 13, 24*a*.

[6] *NB Kama*, 'OḤ', no. 35. For a detailed discussion of this responsum, see Part II.

[7] *Derushei hatselaḥ*, sermon 25, 40*a*; *Ahavat tsiyon*, sermon 2, 3*a–b*.

[8] See e.g. Vital, *Sha'arei kedushah*, pt. 1, Sha'ar 3, 45–6.

[9] *Derushei hatselaḥ*, sermon 25, 40*a*.

[10] De Vidas also uses the motif of Jacob's ladder to describe man's ability to ascend to various spiritual levels, leading to *devekut*; see his *Reshit ḥokhmah*, 'Sha'ar hakedushah', 4: 43 (pp. 65–6).

[11] On the ladder motif in hasidic writings, see e.g. Jacob Joseph of Polonnoye, *Toledot ya'akov yosef*, 22*b*; see also Moses Hayim Ephraim of Sudylkow, *Degel maḥaneh efrayim*, 14*b*.

[12] *Ahavat tsiyon*, sermon 2, 3*a–b*.

[13] See de Leon, *Sefer harimon*, 388: 5–6, where he writes that 'the secret of the performance of the *mitsvot* [is] the perfection of all the worlds'. Cited and trans. in Wolfson, 'Mystical Rationalization of the Commandments in *Sefer harimon*', 237.

[14] *Ahavat tsiyon*, sermon 2, 3*b*. See also *Derushei hatselaḥ*, sermon 25, 40*a*, and sermon 39, 53*b*.

[15] BT *San.* 21*b* states that the reasons for the commandments should not be disclosed. While this is the predominant view in talmudic sources, it is not unanimous. See e.g. BT *Pes.* 119*a*, where a talmudic sage praises those who reveal the reasons for the commandments. Alexander Altmann mistakenly cites this latter passage as proof that the rabbis repudiated such activity. See Altmann,

nonetheless affirms their theurgical efficacy. He explains that although man does not need to investigate the reasons for the commandments, God performs above 'that which should be performed with the observance of each *mitsvah*'.[16] Intriguingly, despite his professed reluctance to reflect on reasons for the commandments, on various occasions he does offer theurgical explanations for particular rituals or commandments.[17]

In line with the kabbalists,[18] Landau contends that every detail of each commandment serves a function on high. Interestingly, he labels this approach rabbinic. Like the kabbalist Meir ibn Gabbai (1480 to after 1540) in his *Avodat hakodesh*,[19] Landau harshly criticizes what he calls the philosophical view presented by Maimonides in the *Guide for the Perplexed*.[20] There Maimonides claims that although the commandments have general reasons, their details frequently serve no significant purpose.[21] In opposition to this view, adopting a phrase found in Nahmanides' writings, ibn Gabbai's *Avodat hakodesh*, and other kabbalistic works,[22] Landau reiterates that all the attendant details of the commandments fulfil a *tsorekh gevohah*, a 'need on high'.[23] The purpose of man's creation, he argues, is to satisfy this divine need.[24] Notwithstanding Landau's tremendous

'Commandments'. On the rabbinic opinion that one should not investigate the reasons for the commandments since they are the King's decrees, see Jacob b. Asher, *Tur*, 'YD', 181, and Rashi on Lev. 19: 19. In the *Guide of the Perplexed* iii. 51, however, Maimonides advocates study of the reasons for the commandments. For a discussion of the rabbinic view that one should not investigate them, see Matt, 'The Mystic and the *Mizvot*', 367–70, 373; Tishby, *Wisdom of the Zohar*, iii. 157. On the Zohar's assertion that one is not permitted to reveal them, see *Tikunei zohar*, *tikun* no. 70, 130*b*.

16 *Derushei hatselaḥ*, sermon for Passover, 59*a* and sermon 39, 53*b*. Landau's guarded stance towards discussing the theurgical effects of the commandments in these two sermons, in which he also condemns the Sabbatians, may be motivated by concerns related to these sectarians.

17 See e.g. *Tselaḥ*, *Ber*. 9*b* (p. 34), where he asserts that the reason for the singular prohibition of returning to Egypt is because no spark of holiness remains there. See also *Derushei hatselaḥ*, sermon 20, 31*b*, where he explains the theurgic purpose of confession. Usually, however, he does not discuss the technical theurgical functions of individual commandments.

18 On the idea that every detail of the commandments serves a theurgical and mystical purpose, see ibn Gabbai, *Avodat hakodesh*, pt. 2, ch. 3, 74–7; Zohar, ii. 55*b*. This notion is also found in Cordoverian and Lurianic sources. For a discussion of this concept, see Matt, 'The Mystic and the *Mizvot*', 385; Tishby, *Wisdom of the Zohar*, iii. 1165–6.

19 See ibn Gabbai, *Avodat hakodesh*, pt. 2, ch. 3, 74–7.

20 *Ahavat tsiyon*, sermon 2, 3*a*–*b*.

21 Maimonides, *Guide of the Perplexed*, iii. 26.

22 Nahmanides on Exod. 29: 46; ibn Gabbai, *Avodat hakodesh*, pt. 2, ch. 2, 71–3. The notion that the commandments fulfil a divine need is one of the most distinctive elements of the kabbalistic conception of the *mitsvot*. See Matt, 'The Mystic and the *Mizvot*', 377, 393–4; Faierstein, 'God's Need for the Commandments'. By contrast, a well-known rabbinic and Jewish philosophical view is that the commandments are meant to test or benefit humans, not God. See *Genesis Rabbah* 44: 1; *Midrash tanḥuma*, 'Shemini', 8; Maimonides, *Guide of the Perplexed*, iii. 26, 48. There are, however, several rabbinic sources which maintain that human acts strengthen God's power.

23 See *Derushei hatselaḥ*, sermon 21, 32*a*, sermon 25, 40*a*, sermon 39, 53*b*; *Ahavat tsiyon*, sermon 2, 3*a*.

24 *Derushei hatselaḥ*, sermon 20, 31*b*.

veneration for Maimonides, he categorically rejects the latter's conception of the function of the commandments' details. In a similar vein, he also criticizes the 'overly clever' historical explanation given by Maimonides concerning the purpose of the sacrifices, namely that they served the ancient Israelites' needs.[25] Instead, Landau defends Nahmanides' view that the sacrifices, along with all their accompanying details, fulfil theurgical functions on high.

Pre-kabbalistic theurgical rabbinic notions concerning the purpose of the commandments and divine worship also surface in Landau's writings, as they do in many kabbalistic works. Citing one of the few rabbinic sources that contain theurgical concepts,[26] Landau often observes that 'when Israel performs God's will they add power to *gevurah* in the supernal realm . . . But when they anger Him, they as it were weaken the power in the supernal realm.'[27] Like other kabbalists, he views this midrashic statement through a kabbalistic lens, relating it to several kabbalistic teachings. These include the notion that Israel's good deeds add power to the *sefirah* Gevurah, which in turn causes divine *shefa* (abundance) to flow upon man.[28] Conversely, Landau also adopts the idea found in Moses de Leon's *Shekel hakodesh*, Azriel of Gerona's writings, and the Zohar,[29] that sin impedes the flow of divine *shefa*.[30]

Strikingly, some of his discussions of the commandments' theurgical role incorporate his theosophical views.[31] For instance, he writes that man's sins spur the descent of a *sefirah*, which only returns to its original level when man repents.[32] Following many kabbalistic writings, he also reiterates that the observance of various commandments assures the dominance of 'the right' side,

[25] Ibid., sermon 39, 53*b*–54*a*. On Maimonides' presentation of the rationale for the sacrifices, see *Guide of the Perplexed*, iii. 46. For Nahmanides' view, see his commentary on Gen. 4: 3.

[26] See *Lamentations Rabbah* 1: 33. This rabbinic teaching is cited in various other *midrashim*. See e.g. *Yalkut shimoni*, 'Ha'azinu', §945.

[27] *Derushei hatselaḥ*, sermon 5, 10*b*; sermon 11, 19*b*; sermon 21, 32*a*. The idea that Israel's transgressions 'weaken the heavenly household' is also found in the writings of the 16th-c. kabbalist, R. Yehudah b. Ya'akov Hunain. See MS Paris, BN 858, 98*a*, cited in Idel, *Kabbalah*, 364 n. 27.

[28] For a discussion of the kabbalistic theme that human deeds influence the flow of *shefa*, see Wolfson, 'Mystical Rationalization', 230; Matt, 'The Mystic and the *Mizvot*', 388, 395; Brody, 'Human Hands Dwell in Heavenly Heights'.

[29] See e.g. Zohar, iii. 297*a–b*, which states that sinners 'cause a defect above', thereby impeding the flow of emanation. See also de Leon, *Shekel hakodesh*, 70.

[30] *Tselaḥ, Ber.* 5*a* (p. 18), s.v. *bo ure'eh shelo kemidat hakadosh barukh hu*. In several sermons Landau similarly claims that the Jews benefit from the divine abundance awakened by their good deeds.

[31] See e.g. *Derushei hatselaḥ*, sermon 25, 40*a*. Idel points out that numerous kabbalists elaborated on the rabbinic view of theurgy by incorporating this view into their theosophical system. See *Kabbalah*, 161.

[32] See *Tselaḥ, Pes.* 54*a* (p. 216), s.v. *shivah devarim*, where he states that this descent is an expression of divine mercy, and comes instead of the destruction of the *sefirah*. For a discussion of man's sins causing a retreat of the *sefirot*, see Idel, *Kabbalah*, 182, 186.

Grace, in the sefirotic realm.[33] Nevertheless, echoing *Tikunei zohar*, *Avodat hakodesh*, and other kabbalistic sources,[34] he reminds his audience that while Israel's deeds do have an effect on the *sefirot*, they do not influence the transcendent Ein Sof.[35]

In concordance with numerous kabbalistic authors, Landau underscores the theurgical efficacy of Torah study and reading Torah out loud,[36] claiming that Torah study gives the exiled Shekhinah a place of rest.[37] Although he regularly insists that one need *not* focus on the kabbalistic functions of the commandments, he does encourage Prague Jews to bear in mind this theurgical effect. Those who study Torah with this intent, he emphasizes, increase their reward.[38] Appropriating zoharic and Cordoverian teachings on the theurgical influence of Torah study,[39] he also asserts that each utterance of Torah 'makes an impression on the world above'.[40] In support of this belief, he wrote an approbation, signed by all Prague's High Court judges, for a Pentateuch devoted to correct grammar and cantillation, in which he encourages Prague Jews to read the Torah out loud, using precise pronunciation and cantillation. These actions, he stresses, theurgically elicit the kabbalistic goal of *tikun*, while incorrect readings cause great damage above.[41]

Prayer is similarly singled out by Landau for its theurgical and mystical functions.[42] Employing ecstatic and theurgical teachings accentuated in Cordoverian kabbalah, he explains that the sounds of prayer serve as a means to connect with

[33] This is discussed in detail in Chapter 7, in the section on zoharic influences on Landau.

[34] See e.g. *Tikunei zohar*, *tikun* no. 70, 131*b*; ibn Gabbai, *Avodat hakodesh*, pt. 2, chs. 3 and 16.

[35] See e.g. *Ahavat tsiyon*, sermon 2, 3*a*.

[36] See e.g. *Derushei hatselaḥ*, sermon 25, 40*a*. For a discussion of the theurgical, mystical, and magical functions of Torah study in kabbalistic, and more specifically hasidic, texts, see Idel, *Hasidism*, 171–88. For a more general discussion of Torah study and Jewish mysticism, see Scholem, *On the Kabbalah and its Symbolism*, 32–86; Idel, *Absorbing Perfections*, esp. 164–201.

[37] *Derushei hatselaḥ*, sermon 6, 12*b*; he adds that a person is first judged regarding his Torah study (BT *Kid.* 40*b*), 'since this is most essential for the Shekhinah'. Although the general idea that the neglect of Torah study 'weakens' God appears in BT *Meg.* 11*a*, the specific notion that Torah study especially aids the downtrodden Shekhinah is kabbalistic. See e.g. Zohar, iii. 268*a*; de Vidas, *Reshit ḥokhmah*, 'Sha'ar ha'ahavah', 8: 28, 29 (pp. 546–7).

[38] *Derushei hatselaḥ*, sermon 6, 12*b*.

[39] See e.g. Zohar, iii. 105*a*. These ideas are especially accentuated in Cordoverian kabbalah. See e.g. Cordovero, *Pardes rimonim*, sha'ar 27, ch. 2: 59*b*–60*a*. De Vidas also stresses that man influences the supernal roots when he enunciates Hebrew letters during Torah reading and prayer; see *Reshit ḥokhmah*, 'Sha'ar hakedushah', 10: 19 (p. 247).

[40] *Derushei hatselaḥ*, sermon 39, 53*b*.

[41] In Landau's 1779 approbation for the revised version of Isaac Premesla's Pentateuch (Prague, 1779), he even asserts that the halakhic requirement of 'reading the Hebrew Bible text twice and the Aramaic Targum once' is best performed with a precise reading of the words. On this work and approbation, see Chapter 2, n. 26.

[42] For a discussion of theurgic, mystical, and magical views of prayer in kabbalistic and hasidic writings, see Wolfson, 'Mystical–Theurgical Dimensions of Prayer in *Sefer ha-Rimmon*'; Idel, *Hasidism*, 149–70.

and affect the sefirotic realm.[43] In a sermon suffused with mystical ideas, he describes

> the great attribute of prayer, which is performed through the five inner places of man's mouth, all of which have great roots above. And when man prays, by moving his lips below, he awakens the supernal roots . . . The supernal lights created through prayer become Keter. And all this [occurs] if a person prays with *kavanah*. And prayer is called pouring out the soul. And then one can attain *devekut* through strong and intense love.[44]

Building upon rabbinic and kabbalistic concepts, Landau alleges that supernal lights are theurgically created through prayer, which are then absorbed into the heavenly crown, Keter.[45] As in the works of Cordovero and the *musar* treatises of his disciples, de Vidas's *Reshit ḥokhmah* and Horowitz's *Shenei luḥot haberit*,[46] Landau claims that man's mouth contains five inner places, each having roots on high. By moving the lips or making sounds during prayer a connection is established between these five inner places of the mouth and their supernal roots. Echoing Cordoverian texts, he implies that this connection enables man to attain *devekut* with God. Interestingly, he contends that prayer leads both to the mystical goal of *devekut* and to theurgical efficacy, two ideals which he regards as intertwined.

The Cordoverian notion that *maḥshavah* (thought) and nonverbal *kavanah* are even more efficacious than praying aloud in terms of affecting the Divine also influenced Landau.[47] In the sermon mentioned above, he describes how the non-verbal prayers of a *tsadik* who has already attained a state of *devekut* immediately arouse supernal mercy, even before he outwardly calls upon God. Landau emphasizes that the most important elements of this elevated prayer are *kavanah* and *maḥshavah*.[48] His comments, however, suggest that only a *tsadik*, cleaving to God, can arouse Him through non-verbal *kavanah*, without the sounds of prayer

[43] On the importance of sound during contemplation and prayer in Abulafian and Cordoverian sources, see Idel, *Hasidism*, 160–2, 165.

[44] *Ahavat tsiyon*, sermon 2, 3*b*. In this passage, the phrase 'the supernal roots' refers to the *sefirot*.

[45] See *Midrash tehilim*, Ps. 88; *Pesikta rabati*, 97*a*. The notion that Israel's prayer ascends to the heavens and forms a supernal crown is found in these and other midrashic texts. See also BT *Ḥag.* 13*b*. The motif of Israel's prayers ascending to form God's crown, especially in Hekhalot texts, is discussed at length in Green, *Keter*. For a discussion of this motif, see also Idel, *Kabbalah*, 191–7. However, the idea that prayer theurgically creates supernal lights appears only in kabbalistic sources.

[46] See e.g. Cordovero, *Pardes rimonim*, Sha'ar 27. In *Reshit ḥokhmah*, 'Sha'ar hakedushah', 10: 19 (p. 247), de Vidas cites Cordovero's comments on this theme. This passage also appears in Horowitz, *Shenei luḥot haberit*, i. 112*b*.

[47] On the role of *maḥshavah* in Cordoverian kabbalah, see Cordovero, *Pardes rimonim*, Sha'ar 27, ch. 2: 59. For a discussion of the importance of non-verbal prayer in Cordoverian works, see Idel, *Hasidism*, 164–5.

[48] *Ahavat tsiyon*, sermon 2, 3*b*. Jacob Joseph of Polonnoye uses somewhat similar language in *Toledot ya'akov yosef*, 167*a*.

usually needed to 'awaken the supernal roots'. Nonetheless, it is noteworthy that in his remarks to the larger community (i.e. not only to the *tsadik*), he stresses the importance of having appropriate *kavanah* while performing the commandments, since without proper *kavanah* during worship, he warns, one cannot cleave to God.[49]

In sum, Landau's teachings on the theurgical and mystical function of prayer and other commandments, as well as his acceptance of elements of the ecstatic view of *kavanah*, belie scholarship's portrayal of him as a resolute opponent of both mystical prayer and of performing the commandments with theurgical intentions.[50]

Galut hashekhinah

Fundamental religious ideas pertaining to exile, revelation, and redemption are understood by Landau through the prism of the kabbalistic concepts of theurgy and the exile of the Shekhinah.[51] The image of redeeming the exiled Shekhinah is one of the primary lenses through which he views the role of religious activity. Israel's actions, he believes, assist in restoring the Shekhinah, thereby hastening the redemption. Attempting to incorporate these ideas into the religious life of his congregants, he frequently exhorts them to pray and repent in order to achieve these ideals.[52] His sermons are replete with kabbalistic parables and symbols relating to the exiled Shekhinah and Israel's theurgical ability to redeem her, revealing the enormous influence of kabbalah both on his own conception of the Divine and on the portrayal of God that he transmitted to his community.

[49] *Ahavat tsiyon*, sermon 2, 3*b*. While the Talmud debates the necessity of proper *kavanah* (intention, concentration) in the fulfilment of commandments (see BT *RH* 28*b*), the kabbalists deem it essential, because for them it refers to the intention to attain *devekut*. See e.g. *Tikunei zohar*, introd., 6*a*. The emphasis on the connection between *kavanah* and *devekut* is particularly prominent in the writings of ecstatic and Cordoverian kabbalists.

[50] On the depiction in previous scholarship of Landau's criticism of the use of theurgical *kavanot*, see e.g. Kamelhar, *Mofet hador*, 57–9. On my reassessment of his attitude towards kabbalistic *kavanot*, see below.

[51] Occasionally he also uses the kabbalistic motif of the divine right and left to explain God's revelation of grace and justice throughout history, in response to Israel's deeds and religious state. See e.g. *Derushei hatselaḥ*, sermon 5, 11*a*: 'When the Temple existed, His right was fully extended . . . but once the First Temple was destroyed, the prophetic *shefa* no longer remained, save for a trace at the beginning of the Second Temple . . . [But after this period] prophecy ceased once again . . . Consequently, so that we should not sink in the impurity of sin, in His mercy the Holy One, blessed be He, sends the left hand, which seemingly is the attribute of strict justice . . . but, in truth, this is mercy, to bring us back to Him . . . and it is proper . . . to repent, and then His right would draw us closer.'

[52] As shown in Chapter 5, on several occasions Landau even encourages his community to observe the kabbalistic vigil of *tikun ḥatsot* on the Shekhinah's behalf.

As in kabbalistic writings, Landau presents the Shekhinah as a female and hypostasized aspect of the Divine, using a wide array of kabbalistic symbols to portray her various functions. Although the identification of the Shekhinah with God's presence is often found in rabbinic literature, her conception as a hypostasized and feminine divine potency does not appear in pre-kabbalistic works.[53] Following kabbalistic teachings, Landau commonly depicts the Shekhinah as a passive female in need of Israel's assistance.[54] Appropriating feminine kabbalistic symbols,[55] he regularly characterizes the Shekhinah as a heavenly mother, consort, and the supernal Keneset Yisra'el (Assembly of Israel).[56] He also portrays the Shekhinah, the *sefirah* closest to the terrestrial world, as both a ruler and representative of divine providence.[57] In line with *Sefer habahir*, the Zohar, and later kabbalistic texts,[58] Landau uses both female and male regal symbols as well as the image of the 'tabernacle of David' to depict the Shekhinah in these roles.[59] Finally, in consonance with eclectic kabbalistic sources,[60] he describes the Shekhinah as a force of holiness, battling the demonic powers.[61]

In discussions of the Shekhinah, Landau often refers to the aggadic motif of the exile of the Shekhinah that became popular in many kabbalistic works, including *Sefer habahir*, the Zohar, and Cordoverian and Lurianic treatises.[62]

[53] For a discussion of the motif of the Shekhinah in kabbalistic literature, see Scholem, *Mystical Shape of the Godhead*, 140–96; Tishby, *Wisdom of the Zohar*, i. 371–87.

[54] On the kabbalistic view that the Shekhinah is dependent on Israel's deeds, see e.g. Zohar, ii. 155*b*; iii. 268*a*; de Vidas, *Reshit ḥokhmah*, 'Sha'ar hayirah', 15: 51 (p. 322), 'Sha'ar ha'ahavah', 8: 9 (p. 535), 10 (p. 536), and 28–9 (pp. 54–7). For a survey of zoharic symbols used to portray the Shekhinah as passive and feminine, see Tishby, *Wisdom of the Zohar*, i. 371–2.

[55] These symbols are found in 13th-c. and later kabbalistic writings. For a discussion of the zoharic presentation of the Shekhinah as the supernal mother and Keneset Yisra'el, see Tishby, *Wisdom of the Zohar*, i. 372, 379–81.

[56] See e.g. *Derushei hatselaḥ*, sermon 20, 31*b*; Landau, 'Eulogy for Meir Fischels Bumsla' (Heb.), 53*b*. Like the words 'wife' and 'mother', the name Keneset Yisra'el implies a feminine image because it is a feminine idiom in Hebrew.

[57] Although the Shekhinah occupies the lowest rung in the sefirotic realm, she is at the zenith of the other lower worlds. In kabbalistic literature the Shekhinah is often referred to as Malkhut, 'Kingdom', because of her dominion over the terrestrial world.

[58] For a discussion of *Sefer habahir*'s portrayal of the Shekhinah as a king and as a princess, see Scholem, *Mystical Shape of the Godhead*, 165–8. On the Zohar's presentation of the Shekhinah as both a queen and the 'fallen tabernacle of David' (Amos 9: 11), with David representing the ideal monarch, see Zohar, ii. 186*b*; Tishby, *Wisdom of the Zohar*, i. 380. On de Vidas' use of this biblical phrase to refer to the Shekhinah, see *Reshit ḥokhmah*, 'Sha'ar ha'ahavah', 8: 9 (p. 535).

[59] See e.g. *Derushei hatselaḥ*, sermon 21, 32*a* and sermon 32, 47*a*.

[60] See e.g. Zohar, ii. 219*b*. For a discussion of this zoharic motif, see Tishby, *Wisdom of the Zohar*, i. 373, 377–8.

[61] See e.g. *Derushei hatselaḥ*, sermon 6, 13*b*. As shown in Chapter 9, he sometimes employs Lurianic tropes in his portrayal of the Shekhinah's clash with the demonic, depicting her exile as a mission to elevate holy sparks from the depths of the *kelipot*.

[62] The notion of the exile of the Shekhinah originates in rabbinic aggadah. See *Mekhilta derabi yishma'el*, 'Bo', §14, p. 51; BT *Meg.* 29*a*; *Yalkut shimoni*, 'Bo', §210. On this trope in the Zohar, see

The kabbalists interpret this aggadic trope in accordance with their understanding of the Shekhinah as a divine feminine force, viewing her exile as a tearing within the godhead. According to both Landau and the kabbalists, Israel's exile parallels the exilic condition of the Shekhinah.[63]

In resonance with the Zohar and later kabbalistic sources,[64] Landau often portrays the exiled Shekhinah through inconsistent, and somewhat contradictory, motifs. In some places he depicts the Shekhinah as a supernal mother protecting Israel, while in others he describes her as a banished and downtrodden woman. He also presents her both as a compassionate ruler bestowing love and as a harsh monarch administering judgement. He is especially fond of the image, emphasized in the Zohar and later kabbalistic writings, of the Shekhinah as a merciful mother or guardian who accompanies her children in exile.[65] At times, however, he suggests that it is the supernal father's kindness, and not necessarily the mother's, which ensures that the Shekhinah carries out her lofty task. In a parable addressing this theme, he tells of a father who banishes his rebellious son but mercifully sends the mother to instruct the boy during his wanderings. Nonetheless, despite this divine mercy, Landau laments, Israel has not heeded the Shekhinah's guidance.[66] In a variation on this theme, Landau, analogously to the Zohar,[67] pronounces that the Shekhinah serves as a guarantee for Israel's redemption, presumably because the divine father will not forsake her.[68]

A range of royal personalities is also used in Landau's portrayal of the Shekhinah in order to point to her hegemony over the terrestrial world. However, as in *Sefer habahir*, the Zohar, and Cordoverian writings,[69] in several

Zohar, i. 53*b*; Tishby, *Wisdom of the Zohar*, i. 382–5. On the centrality of this theme in 16th-c. Safed, see Werblowsky, *Joseph Karo*, 58; Sack, 'The Exile of Israel' (Heb.), 157–78, repr. in Sack, *Kabbalah of Rabbi Moses Cordovero* (Heb.), 249–66; Scholem, *Kabbalah and its Symbolism*, 115–16; id., *Mystical Shape of the Godhead*, 148–9, 185; Tishby, *Doctrine of Evil* (Heb.), 91, 98.

63 On Landau's use of this motif, see e.g. *Derushei hatselaḥ*, sermon 17, 28*a*: '[Exiled] Israel elevates Keneset Yisra'el from the exile, and the first awakening is from them'. See also ibid. sermon 3, 7*b*. See Scholem, *Kabbalah*, 165; Wolfson, 'Left Contained in the Right', 37. The kabbalists accentuate the correspondence between the Shekhinah and the exiled nation of Israel by labelling the Shekhinah the supernal Keneset Yisra'el.

64 See Tishby, *Wisdom of the Zohar*, i. 382–5. Some of Landau's parables depicting the exiled Shekhinah seem to be particularly influenced by Cordoverian writings: see Chapter 8.

65 *Derushei hatselaḥ*, sermon 6, 13*b*; sermon 19, 30*b*; sermon 20, 31*a*; sermon 22, 33*a*.

66 Ibid., sermon 20, 31*a*. This parable comprises almost half of the sermon.

67 See Zohar, iii. 114*a*.

68 See *Derushei hatselaḥ*, sermon 6, 13*b*; sermon 22, 33*a*.

69 For a discussion of *Sefer habahir*'s depiction of the Shekhinah as a princess from afar and as a king, see Scholem, *Mystical Shape of the Godhead*, 165, 167–8. The Zohar commonly presents the Shekhinah both as a concealed queen and as a supernal daughter sent to provide for the world below. See Tishby, *Wisdom of the Zohar*, i. 379–80. In *Reshit ḥokhmah*, de Vidas portrays the Shekhinah as an impoverished and exiled king: see 'Sha'ar ha'ahavah', ch. 8: 10 (p. 536). On the general kabbalistic portrayal of the Shekhinah as Malkhut, see n. 57 above.

parables he likens the Shekhinah to an impoverished monarch, dwelling in a distant land where his or her regal nature is obscured.[70] This diminished state, he laments, is the result of Israel's neglect of the commandments.

In contrast to his depictions of the Shekhinah as merciful, Landau, like the kabbalists, who view the Shekhinah as comprised of both *ḥesed* and *din*, also presents her as an aloof regal authority who executes judgement.[71] He accordingly explains that in exile the Shekhinah hides, exhibiting 'a countenance of anger in accordance with the attribute of judgement and the torments of exile. But indeed this judgement is joined with mercy.'[72] Adopting a zoharic idea,[73] he alleges that this manifestation of judgement within the Shekhinah is mitigated, to some extent, in order to enable humans to withstand it.

Drawing on various kabbalistic books,[74] Landau occasionally asserts, however, that, as a result of Israel's sins and the consequent ascendancy of the *kelipot*,[75] the exiled Shekhinah is not a strong force who metes out punishment, but rather resembles an oppressed spouse who suffers along with her children.[76] In one sermon he dramatically describes the Shekhinah as a woman banished by her husband on account of her children's transgressions, lamenting, 'How will Keneset Yisra'el cleanse us, for she was expelled? . . . The Shekhinah was exiled from cleansing the afflictions that we suffer in exile . . . The mother was banished because of our sins.'[77] Now, the former purifier herself requires purification.

70 *Derushei hatselaḥ*, sermon 4, 8*a*, and sermon 6, 12*b*. See also my discussion on pp. 160–1.

71 For a discussion of the dominance of judgement in the Shekhinah, see Scholem, *Mystical Shape of the Godhead*, 186, 189, 196; Tishby, *Wisdom of the Zohar*, i. 372, 375–6.

72 *Derushei hatselaḥ*, sermon 32, 47*a*. Landau alludes to several kabbalistic themes in this passage. According to kabbalah, although the Shekhinah's name is represented by the last letter of the Tetragrammaton, *heh*, which symbolizes divine mercy, this name is pronounced *adonai*, which symbolizes judgement. This dichotomy reflects the kabbalistic notion that in this world the merciful Shekhinah is garbed in the attribute of judgement. Nonetheless, the purpose of the Shekhinah's exile is to protect her people, which is an expression of divine mercy. In accordance with these teachings, Landau, like the kabbalists, asserts that in exile the Shekhinah's divine judgement incorporates divine mercy. Furthermore, although he likens the Shekhinah to a king, he describes the Shekhinah and her acts of judgement in the feminine. This may allude to the kabbalistic notion that in the role of king, the Shekhinah is the executor of *din*, which for the kabbalists is a feminine attribute.

73 On the sweetening of judgement within the Shekhinah, see Zohar, ii. 186*a* and Tishby, *Wisdom of the Zohar*, i. 376.

74 On the kabbalistic portrayal of the attempt of the demonic forces to defeat the exiled Shekhinah, see e.g. Zohar, ii. 219*b*. For a discussion of this kabbalistic theme, see Tishby, *Wisdom of the Zohar*, i. 372, 377–8, 384–5, ii. 511; id., *Doctrine of Evil* (Heb.), 109.

75 He repeatedly states that the multiplication of the *kelipot* 'limits the Shekhinah's footing in this world'. See *Derushei hatselaḥ*, sermon 6, 12*a*, and sermon 34, 48*a*.

76 *Sefer habahir* is the first work that presents the exiled Shekhinah as a rejected woman: see Scholem, *Beginning of Kabbalah* (Heb.), 34. On the Zohar's portrayal of the exiled Shekhinah as a banished woman, see Zohar, iii. 69*a*. For a discussion of this motif in the Zohar, see Tishby, *Wisdom of the Zohar*, i. 383–4.

77 *Derushei hatselaḥ*, sermon 19, 30*b*.

Discussions of the Shekhinah's exile and providence also appear in one of his responsa.[78] Although at first he berates the questioner for asking about this kabbalistic concept, his reply echoes zoharic teachings.[79] Like the Zohar,[80] he explains that before Israel's exile, the Shekhinah, or providence, was primarily bestowed upon Israel, reaching other lands only through the overflow of divine emanation that Israel received. All this is reversed in exile. Currently, divine abundance first flows upon the nations among whom Israel dwells, Israel obtaining only a limited portion thereof.[81] While this description of the Shekhinah's providence is less mythical than those in his sermons, it illustrates that his kabbalistic conception of the Shekhinah penetrated even into his halakhic writings.

Beyond presenting theoretical kabbalistic views of the exiled Shekhinah, in many homilies Landau urges his community to worship in a manner that will facilitate her redemption. He repeatedly criticizes his congregants' prayers for focusing solely on their physical well-being, while ignoring the religious imperative of restoring the divine Shekhinah. He often bewails that no one 'inquires about . . . the exiled Shekhinah', nor is anyone pained by her suffering.[82] Like many kabbalists,[83] Landau further admonishes Israel's indifference, stating that their ongoing sins are responsible for exacerbating the Shekhinah's already wretched condition, causing her 'to sink deeper into the exile each day'.[84] Adopting zoharic language and following a range of kabbalistic works,[85] he regularly implores his community to perform good deeds, fast, pray with tears, and confess their sins on behalf of the Shekhinah.[86] Through these acts, he asserts, Israel will help elevate the forlorn Shekhinah.

Landau's frequent use of kabbalistic motifs concerning the Shekhinah to rebuke Prague Jews, as well as to motivate their mode of worship, attests to his

[78] *NB Tinyana*, 'OḤ', no. 107.

[79] Landau first cites Maimonides' comments on the Shekhinah, which appear in the *Guide of the Perplexed*, i. 25.

[80] See Zohar, iii. 45*b*. Commenting on S. of S. 1: 6, the Zohar remarks, in the voice of the Shekhinah, that 'before, I kept my own vineyard [Israel], and the other vineyards [nations] were kept as a result, but now I keep the other vineyards, so that my own vineyard among them should be kept'. Cited and trans. in Tishby, *Wisdom of the Zohar*, i. 416–17. See also Zohar, i. 84*b*–85*a*. Landau's association of the Shekhinah's exile with the reversal of the flow of divine abundance to Israel and the nations is probably rooted in these and similar kabbalistic teachings.

[81] *NB Tinyana*, 'OḤ', no. 107. Landau offers almost the same explanation in *Derushei hatselaḥ*, sermon 28, 43*a*.

[82] See e.g. *Derushei hatselaḥ*, sermon 4, 8*a*; sermon 9, 17*b*; sermon 21, 32*a*; and sermon 30, 44*a*.

[83] See e.g. de Vidas, *Reshit ḥokhmah*, 'Sha'ar ha'ahavah', 8: 9 (p. 535).

[84] *Derushei hatselaḥ*, sermon 9, 18*b*; sermon 20, 31*a*; sermon 21, 32*a*.

[85] See Zohar, iii. 40*a*.

[86] See *Derushei hatselaḥ*, sermon 3, 7*b*, where he states that the zoharic declaration that 'the Shekhinah will no longer rise' means that it will not arise unaided, but Israel's actions, repentance, and copious tears could assist it. See also sermon 20, 31*b*; sermon 9, 18*a*; sermon 21, 32*a*; sermon 23, 35*b*; sermon 30, 45*a*.

tacit assumption that at least some members of his community were both familiar with and believed in these kabbalistic notions.

Kabbalistic *Kavanot*

Given Landau's espousal of central theurgical tenets, such as the necessity of restoring the Shekhinah, the theurgical efficacy of the commandments, and the importance of having specific mystical intentions during prayer, his alleged criticism of kabbalistic *kavanot* needs to be reassessed. These extra-liturgical aspects of prayer focus on the dynamics within the godhead that are the theurgical result of man's observance of each commandment. While on several occasions Landau strongly repudiates the use of formulaic kabbalistic *kavanot*, a number of sources, including texts from Brody, writings by his Prague students, and other eighteenth-century Prague works, demonstrate that he respected, or at the very least tolerated, both general kabbalistic *kavanot* and even the more esoteric Lurianic *kavanot*.[87] His oft-cited condemnations of their usage must be evaluated in the context of their use by both the Sabbatians and the 'new hasidim'.

Landau's public criticism of *kavanot* is frequently motivated by these movements, which threatened the hegemony of traditional rabbinic culture as well as its curriculum. This is demonstrated by his best-known critiques of the recitation of *kavanot*, which appear in two responsa from 1776 and 1780.[88] In these responsa, he condemns the recitation of the kabbalistic *leshem yiḥud* formula before performing a commandment. The formula focuses on the unification between the last *sefirah*, the Shekhinah (which, as discussed above, is viewed as somewhat alienated from the others), and the sixth *sefirah*, Tiferet (Beauty) or Holy One, blessed be He, induced by man's performance of a commandment.[89] What is less frequently noted, however, is that even in these responsa Landau does not deny the theurgical function of the commandments or criticize the

[87] For an example of a general kabbalistic *kavanah*, see de Vidas, *Reshit ḥokhmah*, 'Sha'ar ha'ahavah', 9: 38 (p. 567); id., 'Sha'ar hakedushah', ch. 16: 31 (pp. 454–5). For a discussion of Lurianic *kavanot*, see Scholem, *Kabbalah*, 75–6, 176–80, 422; Joseph Weiss, *Studies in East European Jewish Mysticism*, 95–125; Krassen, 'Devequt and Faith in Zaddiqim', 248.

[88] See *NB Kama*, 'YD', no. 93 (1776), in which he asserts that this practice was totally unknown in previous generations, and *NB Tinyana*, 'OḤ', no. 107 (1780), in which he adds that this is not to be found in the classic rabbinic works or in the responsa: '[indeed] the early generations that did not know this version were better than those [that did].'

[89] Although this unification theme appears in the Zohar (see Zohar, iii. 83*a*, 109*b*), the notion of focusing on this kabbalistic concept before performing a commandment is first found in the 16th-c. writings of de Vidas and Vital. See de Vidas, *Reshit ḥokhmah*, 'Sha'ar ha'ahavah', 9: 38 (p. 567); id., 'Sha'ar hakedushah', 16: 31 (pp. 454–5); Vital, *Sha'ar hamitsvot*, introd., 2*b*. For a discussion of this formula, see Hallamish, *Kabbalah in Liturgy, Halakhah and Customs* (Heb.), 45–70; Jacobs, *Hasidic Prayer*, 140–3.

concept of *kavanot*.[90] Rather, his words are directed against those who engage in esoteric matters, such as *kavanot*, while abandoning 'the divine Torah and the spring of living waters, the Babylonian and the Palestinian Talmuds'.[91]

To a large extent, Landau's criticism here and elsewhere of the use of *kavanot* and other kabbalistic liturgical formulations is aimed at the 'new hasidim'. Although many scholars, including Moshe Idel, Joseph Weiss, and Rivka Schatz-Uffenheimer, have claimed that the early 'new hasidim' did not employ Lurianic *kavanot*,[92] numerous eighteenth-century hasidic and mitnagedic sources suggest otherwise. For instance, Lurianic *kavanot* are prominent in several important eighteenth-century prayer books used by hasidim, including the *Rashkover sidur*, which incorporates the *kavanot* of Israel Ba'al Shem Tov,[93] and the prayer book of Rabbi Avraham Shimshon of Rashkov, the son of Jacob Joseph of Polonnoye.[94] Moreover, the well-known 1772 anti-hasidic ban promulgated in Brody denounces the hasidim's use of the Lurianic prayer rite with its attendant *kavanot*.[95] Landau's two responsa denouncing the recitation of *kavanot* were written at the height of the hasidic–mitnagedic controversy.[96] Since he was a staunch opponent of the 'new hasidim', this controversy was undoubtedly instrumental in his censure of the use of *kavanot*. In his 1776 responsum on this topic, he even scoffs at these innovators by playing with a phrase from Hosea, asserting that, instead of the 'sinners' (the word used in the original biblical text), the 'hasidim will stumble' in the ways of the Lord.[97]

[90] See e.g. *NB Kama*, 'YD', no. 93.

[91] Ibid. In *Hasidic Prayer*, 140–7, Jacobs describes this responsum as primarily addressing the 'new hasidim'. Piekarz, however, in *Beginning of Hasidism* (Heb.), 336, argues that Landau's criticism here is directed at the uninitiated masses who engaged in kabbalistic matters, and that the hasidim were simply part of this larger group. Although I agree with Piekarz, Landau clearly directs specific critiques, both in this responsum and elsewhere, against the 'new hasidim' and the Sabbatians.

[92] See Joseph Weiss, *Studies in East European Jewish Mysticism and Hasidism*, 95–125; Schatz-Uffenheimer, *Quietistic Elements in Eighteenth-Century Hasidic Thought* (Heb.), 129–47; Idel, 'Perceptions of Kabbalah', 68–76; id., *Hasidism*, 43, 152–4, 169–70. In these sources it is argued that the early hasidim renounced Lurianic *kavanot* and instead emphasized the vocal aspects of prayer. Liebes claims that both the Sabbatians and the hasidim rejected Lurianic *kavanot* because of their ineffectiveness at clearing away 'alien thoughts'. See Liebes, 'Sabbatai Zevi's Attitude towards his own Conversion' (Heb.), 289 n. 148. However, Kallus, in his article 'Relation of the Baal Shem Tov to the Practice of Lurianic *Kavannot*', has shown that R. Israel Ba'al Shem Tov did employ Lurianic *kavanot*.

[93] This prayer book was written in 1755 and published in Koretz in 1797. See Kallus, 'Relation of the Baal Shem Tov to the Practice of Lurianic *Kavannot*', 153 n. 19.

[94] A facsimile of this prayer book was published in Benei Berak in 1995.

[95] See Wilensky, *Hasidim and Mitnagedim* (Heb.), i. 46.

[96] The mitnagedim issued the first three bans against the 'new hasidim' in 1772 and 1781 and around 1780, they purportedly burned the first hasidic book, Jacob Joseph of Polonnoye's *Toledot ya'akov yosef*.

[97] *NB Kama*, 'YD', no. 93. In a play on words Landau substitutes the word *ḥasidim* (pious) for the word *poshim* (sinners), found in the original phrase in Hos. 14: 10. A folk tale relates that in the hasidim's copies of the *Noda biyehudah* they restored the original biblical phrase, replacing *ḥasidim* with

In a gloss in the *Tselaḥ* on *Berakhot*, Landau again denounces the 'new hasidim's' mystical manner of prayer, alluding to their use of *kavanot*. He states that the contemporary hasidim claim to be masters of kabbalah, 'boasting that through their deeds below they know what occurs in the heavens above. Even more absurdly [they assert] that they actually gaze at the supernal realm during their prayers.' He urges his readers to dismiss the hasidim's contention that one needs to pray in accordance with the 'secrets',[98] and instead encourages them to follow a secure path of worship, without directing their prayers to a particular *sefirah*. Even without the use of *kavanot*, he explains, man's prayers automatically cause God to influence the proper *sefirah* through His grace, judgement, and mercy, a reference to these three major aspects of the sefirotic realm.[99] Even in this gloss, Landau does not dismiss the theurgical efficacy of prayer or the validity of *kavanot*, but rather suggests that the latter manner of worship be avoided because of its potential hazards.

Other passages from Landau's writings and those of his students indicate that his criticism of the use of *kavanot* and other mystical liturgical formulations was often aimed at the Sabbatian and Frankist sectarians. The Sabbatians' effect on Landau's public attitude towards mystical prayer is apparent in a description of his repudiation of a particular individual's use of an extra-liturgical kabbalistic formula that also appeared in the Sabbatians' prayer books, recorded in a vivid passage by his disciple Fleckeles.[100] In a Kol Nidrei sermon, Landau himself refers to the Sabbatians' mystical manner of prayer, stating that those who claim to pray according to the mysteries are heretics who have fallen into a deep pit—an allegation that both he and others make against the Sabbatians.[101] One of his responsa criticizing the use of *kavanot* also seems to be directed against the Sabbatians: he bemoans that in his generation people ignore the Talmud, each one proclaiming 'I am the seer.'[102] This disparaging remark probably alludes

poshim. In response, Landau wittily remarked that he transformed the *poshim* into *ḥasidim* (i.e. the sinners into the pious), while the hasidim did exactly the opposite. See Kamelhar, *Mofet hador*, 57 n. 3.

[98] *Tselaḥ*, *Ber.* 28*b*, s.v. *tanu rabanan keshehalah rabi eli'ezer* (pp. 109–10).

[99] Ibid. (p. 110). In *Derushei hatselaḥ*, sermon 25, 40*a*, Landau also intimates that Prague Jews should not concern themselves with esoteric *kavanot*, although here too he does not dismiss them.

[100] Fleckeles, *Teshuvah me'ahavah*, i, no. 1, where he records that Landau refused to allow an individual who recited the *kavanot* to recite a blessing over his exceedingly fine *etrog*. Fleckeles recounts this incident in the context of his repudiation of the Sabbatians and their liturgical innovations based on kabbalah.

[101] *Derushei hatselaḥ*, sermon 26, 41*a* .See also *NB Kama*, 'ḤM', no. 16; *Derushei hatselaḥ*, sermon 25, 40*a*; Landau's approbation for Zahlin's *Hadarat eliyahu*.

[102] *NB Kama*, 'YD', no. 93. Jacobs, in *Hasidic Prayer*, 151, contends that Landau's use of the term 'seer' here is directed against the hasidic claim that the *tsadik* is endowed with special powers to influence the supernal world. Landau's statement, however, that *each one*, not merely the leader, proclaims himself a seer renders Jacob's reading problematic. Landau is probably using this term to refer to Sabbatian prophetic claims.

both to prophetic claims made by the Sabbatians and to their neglect of rabbinic studies, condemnations that he makes in other writings too.[103]

Landau's explicit denunciations of the *kavanot* and opposition to other contemporary mystical liturgical innovations clearly do not tell the whole story. In fact, various circumstances and sources from his years in Brody and Prague show that he respected and even advocated the use of both general kabbalistic *kavanot* and the Lurianic prayer rite. Since members of the Brody *kloiz*, where he lived and studied for thirteen years, prayed according to the Lurianic rite in which *kavanot* are prominently featured, it is likely that he too followed this prayer rite and recited its *kavanot* during his years at the *kloiz*. Moreover, as seen earlier, an approbation that he signed in Brody supports the publication of the *Magid mishnah* commentary, dedicated to popularizing Lurianic kabbalah and *kavanot*. In particular, the approbation extols this commentary for rendering an abstruse text on Lurianic *kavanot*, the *Mishnat ḥasidim*, more accessible to the public. Landau's interest in Lurianic *kavanot* during his Brody years is also manifest in his glosses on the *Peri ets ḥayim*, the classic work of Lurianic *kavanot*.[104] It appears that his intense involvement with Lurianic kabbalah in Brody influenced his attitude towards Lurianic and general kabbalistic *kavanot* throughout his career.

During his Prague tenure, his support for kabbalistic *kavanot* is evident from an array of sources. One of his pupils, Baruch Brandeis, who later became a preacher in Prague, records his teacher's attitude towards *kavanot*. He recounts Landau's criticism that many 'do not know *alef* below but want to know *tav* in the heavens above',[105] and then relates how Landau illustrated the appropriate use of *kavanot*. Building on a cryptic talmudic parable,[106] Landau explains that only the servants of the princess—a common trope for the Shekhinah—who are 'experts in the wisdom of unification'—a catchphrase for *kavanot*—are equipped to bring a specific dish desired by the princess.[107] Here Landau only criticizes the use of *kavanot* by those who lack proficiency in *alef*, i.e. rabbinic texts. However, those who are both knowledgeable in rabbinic studies and 'experts in the wisdom of unification' can theurgically aid the Shekhinah through the use of *kavanot*.

[103] For his criticism of the Sabbatians' neglect of rabbinic texts and their prophetic claims, see *NB Kama*, 'YD', no. 74; *Derushei hatselaḥ*, sermon 32, 47*a*, and sermon 39, 53*b*.

[104] On Landau's involvement with kabbalah during the years he spent at the Brody *kloiz*, see Chapter 4.

[105] Brandeis, *Leshon ḥakhamim*, pt. 1, 'Hilkhot tefilah', 21. On Brandeis, see Chapter 2.

[106] BT *Pes.* 56*a*: 'This is to be compared to a princess who smelled a spicy pudding. If she revealed her desire, she would be disgraced; if she did not reveal it, she would suffer. So her servants began bringing it to her secretly.'

[107] In *Tselaḥ, Pes.* 56*a* (p. 219), Landau cryptically alludes to the kabbalistic interpretation of this parable. On this gloss, see Chapter 6.

Several other overlooked writings from Landau's Prague years also reveal that he tolerated, and possibly advocated, the use of general *kavanot* during his years as chief rabbi. Perhaps most impressively, the *leshem yiḥud* formula appears in most of the *siddurim* published in Prague (in 1757, 1782, 1784, 1804, 1833, 1834, and 1836), during Landau's and his disciples' careers.[108] This formulation is most frequently included in blessings recited on various holidays and during certain ceremonies, particularly before the annulment of vows on the eves of Rosh Hashanah and Yom Kippur as well as before the blessings for the four species and sitting in booths on the Sukkot festival. Remarkably, despite Landau's public opposition to reciting these formulas, he appears to permit, and certainly does not impede, their repeated reprinting in the standard Prague prayer books intended for the community at large. Kabbalistic formulations invoking the Holy One, blessed be He and the Shekhinah are also routinely incorporated into liturgical texts included in the Prague *Tikun nefesh* prayer book.[109] By contributing to this work, published at the height of his Prague career, Landau seems to have endorsed the use of these kabbalistic formulations by members of his community. In 1784 he also gave an approbation for *Or layesharim*, a collection of sermons by the prominent Prague preacher Zerah Eidlitz.[110] Since Eidlitz promotes Lurianic *kavanot* and the use of general *kavanot* in the first homily of this book,[111] Landau's endorsement once again suggests that he approves of the popularization of these kabbalistic prayers.

Notably, a Haggadah was recently discovered that was owned during the late 1780s by Fleckeles, one of the most important transmitters of Landau's teachings and practices. The margins of this Haggadah contain *leshem yiḥud* formulas to be recited before the blessings on the four cups of wine, penned in Fleckeles' hand. Since these marginal glosses were probably written during the late 1780s when Landau was the most influential rabbi in Prague and certainly the most

[108] See e.g. *Maḥzor*, published by Judah Lipmann and his brothers (Prague, 1756 or 1757), i. 125*a*–126*a*; *Maḥzor*, published by Bezalel b. Samuel Fleckeles and Samuel b. Leizer Bahur (Prague, 1782), i. 126*a*, 128*a*–*b*; *Seliḥot*, published by Bokh (Prague, 1784), 58*a* and another edition he published the same year, 102*a*; *Maḥzor*, published by Sebastian Diesbach (Prague, 1804), i. 76*b*–77*a*; *Maḥzor*, published by Moses Landau (Prague, 1833), 1; *Maḥzor*, published by Moses Landau (Prague, 1834), 2*b*; *Maḥzor*, published by Moses Landau (Prague, 1836), ii. 153*b*–154*a*, 158*a*–*b*.

[109] See e.g. *Tikun nefesh*, 23*b*, 28*a*–*b*.

[110] Landau's approbation for *Or layesharim* was given on 30 Nov. 1784.

[111] See Eidlitz, *Or layesharim*, sermon 1, 22. Here Eidlitz endorses the *kavanot* discussed in Ricchi's Lurianic work *Mishnat ḥasidim*. On Landau's approbation for the first volume of this work, see Part II. In this sermon Eidlitz also reiterates that Israel can affect the unification of the Holy One, blessed be He and the Shekhinah through various deeds, particularly through sexual activity performed in holiness. See *Or layesharim*, 11, 13.

influential rabbi for Fleckeles,[112] the latter would not have inserted these kabbalistic formulations had it been against the wishes of his teacher. In fact, it is quite probable that the recitation of the *leshem yiḥud* formula during the Passover seder was Landau's custom as well. However, in *Teshuvah me'ahavah* Fleckeles notes, at least for the public record, that although Landau did not recite the *leshem yiḥud* and other kabbalistic formulas, he did not protest against his congregants' use of these liturgical formulations.[113] These remarks illustrate that, at the very least, Landau did not categorically oppose general *kavanot* and other kabbalistic formulations that members of Prague Jewry had adopted. Had he viewed the recitation of these extra-liturgical prayers as contravening Jewish law, he would surely have protested these practices in his community.

To sum up, Landau's condemnations of the use of *kavanot* are motivated not by a rejection of the *kavanot* per se, but primarily by his repudiation of the Sabbatians and the 'new hasidim', who, he repeatedly asserts, pray according to the mysteries. In fact, as demonstrated, despite his criticism of the use of *kavanot*, several sources indicate that he tolerated and probably advocated the use of both general kabbalistic and Lurianic *kavanot* by those proficient in rabbinic studies.

Notwithstanding his complex attitude towards the *kavanot*, which he both criticizes and accepts, he repeatedly emphasizes the theurgical functions of the commandments. Echoing Ibn Gabbai and numerous other kabbalists, he even challenges Maimonides' conception of the commandments, arguing instead that each detail of the commandments fulfils a need on high. He describes such theurgical notions, some of which appear in ancient rabbinic texts, by using later theosophic terminology. Moreover, like most kabbalists, he frequently singles out the mystical and theurgical efficacy of prayer and Torah study. In particular, in his Prague sermons he accordingly appropriates many kabbalistic motifs in order to urge Prague Jews to consecrate their prayers, Torah study, and repentance to the kabbalistic goal of redeeming the Shekhinah. These findings begin to redress scholarship's unfounded portrayal of Landau's categorical repudiation of mystical prayer, performing the commandments with theurgical intentions, and even the use of general and Lurianic *kavanot*.

[112] Fleckeles seems to have written these marginal glosses between 1784 and 1790. Since this Haggadah was first published in Prague in 1784, this is the earliest possible date for them. A comparison of Fleckeles' earlier and later handwriting indicates that he wrote these glosses during his younger years, probably in his thirties, so they were probably composed during the late 1780s.

[113] Fleckeles, *Teshuvah me'ahavah*, i, no. 90.

Conclusion

THIS STUDY depicts the efflorescence of Prague's rabbinic culture and the mystical character that animated it during the latter half of the eighteenth century. Despite the dramatic political changes imposed on Prague Jews, beginning with Joseph II's Toleranzpatent of 1781, traditional society flourished during Landau's tenure. The Jewish community maintained its independent judiciary system, housed several academies of higher Jewish learning, and was home to over fifty prominent rabbinic figures. Prague's rabbinic scholars produced a wide range of writings, focusing primarily on talmudic, halakhic, and kabbalistic matters. Landau alone wrote several talmudic commentaries, numerous sermons, glosses on kabbalistic treatises, and a two-volume collection of responsa that immediately gained authoritative status.

My research shows the pervasive role that mysticism played in the community, in part thanks to Landau. Notwithstanding his protestations to the contrary, and although he was one of the most influential eighteenth-century halakhists, he was deeply immersed in kabbalah. He incorporated mystical ideas in many of his works and promoted certain kabbalistic practices. His sermons and writings both increased the popularity of various kabbalistic doctrines and rites and built upon the laity's prior knowledge of them. The traditional kabbalistic beliefs and outlook of many Prague Jews persisted during this transitional era, contributing to a spiritual world replete with kabbalistic myths related to God, the demonic, and redemption.

Despite Landau's reservations concerning public kabbalistic discourse, he incorporates mystical teachings in all genres of his Prague writings. His early kabbalistic education, particularly at the Brody *kloiz*, left a lasting impression on him, and he often cites the *kloiz* kabbalists in his later works. Basing his ideas on a teaching of a *kloiz* kabbalist, Landau writes that kabbalah is the key to the inner truth of aggadah and Torah. While residing in the Polish cities of Brody and Yampol, he endorses several kabbalistic books, and, as his rabbinic career evolves, begins to employ kabbalistic teachings regularly, even in public forums. Almost all his Prague sermons and some of his talmudic commentaries are laced with kabbalistic terms such as *nitsotsot*, *gilgul*, and *tikun*, and with allusions to the sefirotic realm. While he often discourages kabbalistic discussion, he sometimes indirectly urges Prague Jews to study kabbalistic concepts by explaining that only those who have studied aggadah and are fluent in the terminology of kabbalah can attain a glimpse of the truth in this world.

Although he asserts that kabbalah should have no influence in the sphere of praxis, Landau observes and advocates some kabbalistic rituals, including the nightly *tikun ḥatsot* vigil as well as numerous ascetic customs espoused by Safed kabbalists. Notwithstanding scholarship's portrayal of Landau and mitnagedic leaders in general, he repeatedly promotes additional theurgical and mystical forms of worship. Among these are his persistent beseeching of Prague Jews to pray, repent, and perform other commandments with the intention of redeeming the Shekhinah and the dispersed divine sparks, as well as his emphasis on the power of the sounds of prayer, joy, and *kavanah* as means of achieving *devekut*. On many occasions, he even supports the use of both general and Lurianic *kavanot*.

Landau's desire to spread kabbalistic tenets and practices was tempered by his reluctance to divulge kabbalistic secrets. His caution was heightened by specific challenges facing Prague's Jewish community. The city was an important centre for Sabbatians and Frankists, many of whom rooted their antinomian practices in kabbalah and simultaneously denounced talmudic study. These sectarians threatened both traditional observance and the stature of rabbinic learning. At the same time, the nascent hasidic movement in eastern Europe was disseminating kabbalistic ideas to individuals who had not mastered talmudic texts, thereby undermining the traditional Ashkenazi curriculum. Secular disciplines, promoted by both the Habsburg state and maskilim, were also beginning to erode talmudic studies. Strikingly, however, Landau reserves his most vituperative attacks for the Sabbatians, expressing his conviction that they present a greater threat to traditional Judaism than either the Habsburg reforms or the maskilim. The centrality of kabbalah for the Sabbatians, Frankists, and new hasidim, and the inroads made by secular studies contributed to the urgency of his call to focus primarily on the Talmud and eschew most other subjects, including kabbalah.

Even as Landau condemns the burgeoning of Sabbatianism, Frankism, and hasidism, he surprisingly advocates many of the same ideals and tenets that they espouse. A salient example is found in his promotion of the goal of *devekut* and the roles of love, fear, and joy in inducing this mystical state—concepts that were central to the 'new hasidim'. His comments on confession are also illustrative of this trend. In a striking echo of both Sabbatian doctrines and teachings of certain 'new hasidim', Landau explains that the 'secret of confession' is the penitent's daring descent into evil in order to redeem the divine fallen sparks. Such similarities between Landau and these other groups are, in part, the result of their common social and geographical origins, as well as their reliance on the same corpus of kabbalistic texts, which they all deemed sacred.

The wide array of kabbalistic sources that Landau and these groups venerate and draw upon stem from eclectic kabbalistic schools. Occasionally, he accentuates kabbalistic motifs and terms that originally derive from a particular kabbalistic school, but more often, he uses diverse kabbalistic teachings in a syncretic manner, intermingling distinct kabbalistic concepts within a single sermon or gloss. He justifies this practice on the basis of his belief, shared with many other kabbalists, that the works of numerous kabbalistic schools all point to a unified Truth. Consequently, his exposition of basic tenets and essential religious themes, such as the nature of the soul, exile, and the supernal realm, are frequently shaped by zoharic, Cordoverian, *musar* and Lurianic doctrines. In his writings on kabbalistic topics, he easily moves between theurgical notions and ecstatic ideals. Echoing ecstatic and Cordoverian kabbalists, he stresses the efficacy of nomian and anomian techniques as avenues to *devekut*, while emphasizing, as do Lurianic kabbalists, the commandments' role in elevating the *nitsotsot*. His particular use of varied kabbalistic paradigms reflects his creative immersion in kabbalah.

Landau's syncretic blend of kabbalistic sources forms part of the larger tapestry of his sermons and commentaries in which he elaborately weaves together a wide range of biblical, rabbinic, kabbalistic and philosophical texts. At times, he uses concepts from one genre of literature in order to reconcile or explain ideas found in completely different genres.[1] His adaptation of Maimonides' legal and philosophical terminology for his own mystical purposes exemplifies this tendency. Landau often reads Maimonides' philosophical writings through the prism of kabbalah, taking exception to Maimonides' teachings only when he cannot reconcile them with his own kabbalistic beliefs. Typical examples are found in his criticism of Maimonides' conception of the sacrifices, in particular, and his view of the purpose of the commandments in general. Landau's mastery and integration of diverse works is attested to by the Brody kabbalist Hayim Zanzer, who asserted that he wove ideas from all available kabbalistic books together with those found in Maimonides' *Guide of the Perplexed*.[2] Landau occasionally even intersperses original kabbalistic interpretations in his remarks on particular rabbinic, philosophic, or kabbalistic teachings. This is especially noticeable in his comments on *devekut*, demonic powers, and the impact of sin.

Eighteenth-century Prague Jewry's familiarity with numerous kabbalistic tropes and works also emerges from his writings. His sermons frequently refer to

[1] See e.g. *Ahavat tsiyon*, sermon 5, 8*a*, where Landau relates a teaching found in the *musar* works to a Maimonidean text, and then reconciles these two texts with a seemingly contradictory talmudic passage.

[2] Jacob Landau, *Divrei yedidot*, 32.

eclectic kabbalistic motifs, such as those relating to the Shekhinah, the sefirotic 'right, left, and centre', and the nefarious *kelipot*, without offering any introductory remarks. In some homilies he employs zoharic, Cordoverian, and Lurianic concepts in order to advance specific normative practices, revealing his assumption that his congregants both knew these ideas and respected these sources.

The Next Generation

Prague's thriving halakhic and kabbalistic culture, however, declined significantly after Landau's death. The process of modernization which began during his lifetime intensified during the last decades of the eighteenth and the first few decades of the nineteenth centuries. Changes in the political status of Prague's Jewish community and the influence of the Enlightenment and state-mandated secular education brought about a steady transformation and secularization of traditional Jewish life. These changes led to the acculturation of numerous Prague Jews and the decreasing commitment of many to traditional religious study and practice.

A striking expression of the rapid cultural transformation in Prague may be seen in Landau's and his son Samuel's divergent reactions to several maskilic innovations. In 1783 Ezekiel Landau harshly censured Mendelssohn's new German Pentateuch translation, which he believed would lead Prague Jews to become knowledgeable in German and then study secular disciplines. Only a few decades later, in 1816, Samuel actually urged Prague Jews to use this German Pentateuch translation as an aid to learn both correct German and Hebrew! Samuel also advanced educational ideals proposed by the maskil Wessely, for instance that parents educate their young children in both Torah and *derekh erets* (secular learning), a programme his father vehemently denounced. Aware of the rapid changes in the currents of Prague Jewry, Samuel tried to accommodate certain secular trends while reinforcing basic traditional values.

Acknowledging Prague Jewry's dwindling knowledge of sacred and Hebrew Jewish texts, Israel Landau, like his brother Samuel, worked to ensure their continued familiarity with both. Employed as a Hebrew printer in Prague, Israel was responsible for publishing an assortment of traditional and maskilic works. In 1798 he wrote *Ḥok leyisra'el* (The Law of Israel), his translation of Maimonides' *Sefer hamitsvot* (Book of the Commandments) into *böhmische Judendeutsch*, a Yiddish dialect spoken by Bohemian Jews. In his introduction he explains that he hopes that this book will enable Prague Jews to become familiar with this central rabbinic work, as many Prague Jews are ignorant of all Hebrew sources.[3] By the turn of the nineteenth century, then, a large number of Prague Jews were no longer proficient in either basic rabbinic Hebrew or classic rabbinic texts.

But the kabbalistic, mythical, and ascetic foundations of Prague's traditional culture did not collapse entirely. In the same year that Israel Landau's *Ḥok leyisra'el* was composed, a standard prayer book was published in Prague that incorporated both kabbalistic liturgical services for Yom Kippur Katan and *tikun shovevim*. In 1794 a separate *tikun shovevim* pamphlet was printed, stating that although this book had been republished in Prague several times during the past few years, there were no longer any copies available for purchase. The popularity of this pamphlet indicates that Prague Jews continued to observe this kabbalistic ritual against demonic sons generated by nocturnal emissions. Indeed, such kabbalistic prayers were included in Prague's prayer books well into the nineteenth century.

Even many of the prayer books and penitential treatises published by Landau's progressive grandson Moses during the 1830s are replete with kabbalistic motifs and prayers. These publications, as well as some of Moses' own writings, refer to the *sefirot* and cite zoharic and Lurianic texts. They also endorse various ascetic Safed practices, such as penitential flagellation and wailing, describe the functions of individual angels, and include the *tikun shovevim* liturgy. Notwithstanding Ezekiel Landau's public denunciations of the use of the kabbalistic *leshem yiḥud* formula, particularly by the unlearned masses, numerous liturgical works published by Moses Landau and other nineteenth-century Prague publishers contain this kabbalistic phrase.

The process of acculturation in Prague was neither linear nor one-dimensional. It often contained and even integrated conflicting, and at times paradoxical, trends. Thus, concurrent with the noticeable decline of basic traditional knowledge and observance in late eighteenth- and early nineteenth-century Prague, kabbalistic rites and traditional customs continued to be practised and preserved. To be sure, the extent to which they were observed is impossible to ascertain. Nonetheless, the significance of this overlooked phenomenon must be noted. The sources suggest that up until a relatively late stage of modernization, during the reigns of the Habsburg emperors Francis II (1792–1835) and Ferdinand V (1835–48), kabbalistic concepts and customs continued to be respected in Prague and disseminated in Prague's liturgy and some of its writings.

Despite the lingering features, the overall trajectory towards the modernization of Prague's traditional Jewish community is clear. By the first decades of the

[3] Israel Landau, *Ḥok leyisra'el*, inside title page.

nineteenth century, the majority of Prague's rabbinic institutions, such as its yeshivas and courts, as well as the level of its traditional scholarship, had declined markedly. A new rabbinic centre arose in nearby Pressburg, in Hungary.[4] Ashkenazi youth, who had previously flocked to Prague to study with Landau, now mostly travelled to Pressburg to attend the yeshiva directed by the leading authority of the next generation of Ashkenazi Jews, Rabbi Moses Sofer (1762–1839), also known as the Hatam Sofer.[5] Whether kabbalah had allowed Prague's traditional society to flourish for longer than it would have otherwise, or whether it accelerated the degeneration of Prague's traditional culture is hard to determine.[6] In either case, by the mid- to late nineteenth century both the knowledge of kabbalistic ideas and kabbalah's importance for Prague Jews had dwindled, alongside the study of all other traditional Jewish disciplines.

The dramatic decline of Prague's traditional Jewish society and culture is best summed up by a reported remark made by the hasidic master Rabbi Simhah Bunem of Przysucha (d. 1827) to his disciple Rabbi Hanoch of Alexander (d. 1870). This exchange, which purportedly occurred only a few decades after Landau's death, is recorded in an introduction to Vital's kabbalistic *Ets ḥayim*. In the course of this conversation, Rabbi Simhah Bunem asserts that he is astounded by the daily deterioration of the state of Judaism in Prague, 'a city acclaimed for its Torah scholars'.[7]

4 Pressburg is now known as Bratislava, the capital of Slovakia.

5 On Moses Sofer, see J. Katz, 'Towards a Biography of the Hatam Sofer', in id., *Divine Law in Human Hands*, 403–3; Kahana, 'Continuity and Change in the Responsa of the Hatam Sofer' (Heb.).

6 Some scholars, such as Scholem, maintain that in general kabbalah plays a subversive role in Jewish society by challenging the basic halakhic framework and emphasis of Judaism. Many other recent scholars of kabbalah, such as Idel, Matt, and Wolfson, disagree.

7 Introduction to the 1960 Tel Aviv edition of Hayim Vital, *Ets ḥayim*, pt. 3 (*Nahar shalom*). On this citation, see also Jacobs, *Hasidic Prayer*, 153.

Bibliography

ARCHIVAL DOCUMENTS

Central Archives for the History of the Jewish People, Jerusalem, on microfilm

HM2/3220: Records of the Prague Jewish court and community

HM2/3577a: Records of the Prague Jewish court and community

Institute of Hebrew Manuscripts and Microfilmed Hebrew Manuscripts, Jerusalem

Abraham Schwadron Collection—letters, commentaries, and approbations of Ezekiel Landau and other Prague rabbis

Heb. 4* 5806: Klaus Synagogue *pinkas*, 1808–65

40869: Sermon of Ezekiel Landau (on microfilm)

30940: Sermon of Ezekiel Landau (on microfilm)

Municipal Archives, Prague

Uncatalogued boxes containing student notes on the teachings of Ezekiel Landau, Meir Fischels (Bumsla), Zerah Eidlitz, and Jonathan Eybeschütz

The National and University Rare Book and Manuscript Collection, Prague

Correspondence between censor Karl Fischer and Eleazar Fleckeles

Records of the censor's daily activities

State Archives, Prague

Cgpubl. 43/186: 1786–95. Ezekiel Landau's letters to the government concerning funds for the elderly

Cgpubl. 43/1789: 1786–95. Ezekiel Landau's letters denying accusations of disturbances in the Jewish community

Cgpubl. 43/351: 1786–95. Samuel Landau's and Eleazar Fleckeles's applications to the Gubernium to become head *jurist*

Cgpubl. [number not available]: 1786–95. Samuel Landau's request to live in his father's apartment

Cgpubl. [number not available]: 1786–95. Fleckeles's request for permission for his son to move to Prague

State Jewish Museum, Prague

MS 83: Prayers offered at Maisel synagogue for Maria Theresa, Francis, and Joseph II

MS 95: *Tsiyun lenefesh ḥayah, beitsah*; a 1791 sermon of Samuel Landau

MS 169: Ezekiel Landau's eulogy for Meir Fischels

MS 330: Ezekiel Landau, *Noda biyehudah*, sections

MS 359: Ezekiel Landau, Talmud commentary

MS 380: Approbation given by Samuel Landau and Eleazar Fleckeles

Concepte (1750–1830) Letters between Habsburg government officials and the Prague Jewish community.

Karlin-Stolin Collection, Jerusalem

MS 241: Landau's letter to Prague judges concerning heretics, 1773

MS 242: Landau's letter to the head of Berlin's Jewish court against Naphtali Herz Wessely

MS 243: Landau's letter to Vienna to pursue Wessely

MS 244: Letter sent to Landau from Nicholsburg concerning Sabbatianism

MS 245: Letter to Landau from Pressburg concerning Sabbatianism

MS 246, 247, 248: Landau, concerning slander against the Talmud

MS 255: Bans issued against the Prague Sabbatians in 1726 and 1800

MS 267: Letter to Landau concerning Sabbatianism

OTHER PRIMARY SOURCES

ANON., *A Dialogue between the Year* 1800 *and the Year* 1801 [Siḥah bein shenat takas uvein shenat taksa; anti-Frankist tract] (Prague, 1800).

ANON., *Divrei no'am* [debate between Jacob Samson of Shepetkova and Ezekiel Landau] (Warsaw, 1892).

ANON., *Ḥemdat yamim*, 2 vols. [Homiletical, ethical, kabbalistic Sabbatian work] (Izmir, 1730–1; repr. Zolkiew, 1763).

ANON., *Eyn mekhtig sheyn mayse* ['A Mightily Beautiful Tale'; a story related to the kabbalist R. Adam Ba'al Shem] (Prague, 1699).

ANON., *Sefer hakaneh*, with commentary *Keneh binah keneh ḥokhmah* [kabbalistic work] by Eleazar ben Abraham Perles-Altschul (Prague, 1610).

ANON., *Ueber die Schädlichkeit der Juden in Böhmen* (Dresden, 1782).

ANON., *Fun tsvay maysim vunderberlikh . . . in tsayten fun R. Yitsḥak Luria* ['Two Miraculous Tales . . . during the Time of Rabbi Isaac Luria'; stories related to Isaac Luria, the Ari] (Prague, 1650).

AARON SIMEON OF COPENHAGEN, *Or hayashar* [collection of expert rabbinic opinions on the validity of the 1766 Cleves *get* (divorce writ)] (Amsterdam, 1769).

ABRABANEL, ISAAC, *Rosh amanah* [on Maimonides' thirteen principles] (Constantinople, 1505; repr. Tel Aviv, 1958).

ALBO, JOSEPH, *Ets shatul: sefer ikarim* [philosophical work] (Frankfurt, 1788).

ALSHEKH, MOSES, *Marot hatsove'ot: perush al nevi'im aḥaronim* [commentary on the Later Prophets] (Zolkiew, 1755).

—— *The Book of Genesis with Translation in Judendeutsch of Moses Alsekh's Commentary* [Sefer bereshit im targum biyehudit ashkenazit shel bi'ur ha'alshekh], trans. Yosef Darmstadt (Karlsruhe, 1770).

ASHKENAZI, ELIJAH BEN ASHER HALEVI, *Sefer hahaḥur* [on Hebrew grammar] (Prague, 1789).

AZIKRI, ELEAZAR, *Sefer ḥaredim hashalem* [spiritual and ascetic manual] (Venice, 1601; repr. Jerusalem, 1990).

AZULAI, ABRAHAM, *Ḥesed le'avraham* [kabbalistic work] (Amsterdam, 1685; repr. Lvov, 1863).

BACHARACH, YA'IR, *Ḥavat ya'ir* [responsa] (Frankfurt, 1699).

BAHYAH IBN PAKUDAH, *Ḥovot halevavot* [ethical work] (Naples, 1489).

BERLIN, SAUL, *Besamim rosh* [responsa falsely claimed to be by R. Asher ben Yehiel, the 'Rosh'] (Berlin, 1793).

Bikurei ha'itim [maskilic literary annual] (Vienna, 1821–32).

BLOCH, ISSACHAR, *Binat yisakhar* [sermons] (Prague, 1785).

BONDI, ABRAHAM, *Zera avraham* [talmudic novellae] (Prague, 1828).

The Book Bahir: An Edition Based on the Earliest Manuscripts [Sefer habahir: al pi kitvei hayad hakedumim] [kabbalistic work], ed. Daniel Abrams (Los Angeles, 1996).

BRANDEIS, BARUCH, *Leshon ḥakhamim* [halakhic novellae] (Prague, 1815).

CHORIN, AARON, *Imrei no'am* [on the *kashrut* of sturgeon] (Prague, 1798).

—— *Shiryon kaskasim* [on the *kashrut* of sturgeon] (Prague, 1799).

CORDOVERO, MOSES, *Or yakar* [commentary on the Zohar], ed. Menahem Z'ev Hasidah (Jerusalem, 1940); ed. Me'ir Elboim, 20 vols. (Jerusalem, 1962–95).

—— *Pardes rimonim* [kabbalistic work] (Krakow, 1591; Munkacz, 1906; repr. Jerusalem, 1962).

—— *Tomer devorah* [kabbalistic ethical treatise] (Venice, 1588).

CRESCAS, HASDAI, *Or adoshem* [philosophical work] (Ferrara, 1555).

DA FANO, MENAHEM AZARIAH, *Gilgulei neshamot* [kabbalistic work on transmigration of souls] (Prague, 1688).

DANZIG, ABRAHAM, *Ḥayei adam* [halakhic work] (Vilna, 1810).

DE LEON, MOSES BEN SHEM TOV, *Sefer hamishkal*, ed. Jochanan H. A. Wijnhoven. Ph.D. diss., Brandeis University, 1964.

—— *Sefer harimon*, ed. Elliot R. Wolfson, *The Book of the Pomegranate: Moses de León's Sefer ha-Rimmon* (Atlanta, 1988).

—— *Shekel hakodesh*, ed. A. W. Greenup (London, 1911).

DE VIDAS, ELIJAH, *Reshit ḥokhmah hashalem* [kabbalistic ethical work] (Venice, 1579).

DEITSCH, JOSEPH, *Divrei yosef* [biblical commentaries, talmudic novellae] (Jerusalem, 1989).

DEUTSCH, DAVID, *Ohel david* [talmudic novellae] (Vienna, 1819).

DOV BAER OF MEZHIRECH, *Magid devarav leya'akov* [hasidic work] (Berdichev, 1808).

EIDLITZ, ZERAH, *Or layesharim* [collection of sermons] (Prague, 1785; repr. Budapest, 1942).

EISENSTADT, MEIR, *Or haganuz* [talmudic novellae] (Fuerth, 1766).

ELIJAH BEN HAYIM HAKOHEN, *Shevilei rakia* [a work on the Jewish calendar and astronomy] (Prague, 1785).

EMDEN, JACOB, *Petaḥ einayim* [polemic against Ezekiel Landau] (Altona, 1756).

—— *Sefer hitabekut* [discusses the Emden–Eybeschütz controversy] (Altona, 1762).

—— *Sefer mitpaḥat sefarim* [work questioning the antiquity of the Zohar] (Altona, 1768; repr. Lvov, 1870).

EMDEN, JACOB, *Shevirat luḥot ha'even* [polemical work against Eybeschütz, particularly responding to Eybeschütz *Luḥot edut*] (Altona, 1756).

—— *Torat hakenaot* [polemical work against Sabbatianism] (Altona, 1752).

EYBESCHÜTZ, JONATHAN, *Luḥot edut* [letters by numerous rabbinic authorities in defence of Eybeschütz during the amulet controversy and Eybeschütz's own defence] (Altona, 1755).

FARISSOL, ABRAHAM, *see* Israel Landau

FLECKELES, ELEAZAR, *Ahavat david* [anti-Frankist tract] (Prague, 1800).

—— *Geist des Judentums*, trans. Meir (Markus) Fischer (Prague, 1813).

—— *Ḥazon lamo'ed* [sermons for the holidays] (Prague, 1824).

—— *Ma'aseh derabi eliezer* [commentary on the Haggadah] (Prague, 1818).

—— *Melekhet hakodesh* [eulogies and essays] (Prague,1812).

—— *Mevaser tov* [sermons] (Prague, 1821).

—— *Nefesh david venefesh ḥayah* [eulogy for his parents] (Prague, 1812).

—— *Olat ḥodesh*, 4 vols. [collection of sermons] (Prague, 1785).

—— *Olat ḥodesh hashelishi* [collection of sermons] (Prague, 1793).

—— *Olat ḥodesh hasheni* [collection of sermons] (Prague, 1786).

—— *Tefilah bishelomah shel malkhut* [prayer for the emperor] (Prague, 1795).

—— *Teshuvah me'ahavah* [responsa], 3 vols. (Prague, 1809, 1815, 1821; repr. Kosice, 1912).

FRIEDLÄNDER, DAVID, 'Sendschreiben an die deutschen Juden', *Hame'asef* (1788), appendix.

GLOGAU, SUSSMANN, *Torah veḥamesh megilot im perush ashkenazi* [German Bible translation] (Prague, 1785).

HANNOVER, NATHAN, *Sha'arei tsiyon* [Lurianic prayer book] (Prague, 1662).

HOESHKE, REUBEN, *Yalkut re'uveni* [kabbalistic anthology] (Prague, 1660).

HOROWITZ, ISAAC HALEVI, *Mishnat halevi* [responsa and novellae], ed. Isaac Raphael (Jerusalem, 1985).

HOROWITZ, ISAIAH, *The Generations of Adam*, trans. and ed. Miles Krassen (Mahwah, 1996).

—— *Shenei luḥot haberit* (*Shelah*) [*musar* work] (Amsterdam, 1648).

HOROWITZ, SHABETAI SHEFTEL, *Nishmat shabetai halevi* [kabbalistic work] (Prague, 1616).

—— *Shefa tal* [kabbalistic work] (Hanau, 1612).

IBN GABBAI, MEIR, *Avodat hakodesh* [kabbalistic work] (Venice, 1567; repr. Jerusalem, 1992).

ISAAC HAKOHEN, *Treatise on the Left Emanation* [Ma'amar al ha'atsilut hasemolit; kabbalistic work], in Gershom Scholem, 'Traditions of R. Jacob and R. Isaac, Sons of R. Jacob Hakohen', *Mada'ei hayahadut*, 2 (1927), 264–93.

ISRAEL MEIR HAKOHEN (HAFETS HAYIM), *Mishnah berurah*, 6 vols. (Warsaw, 1884–1907).

ISSACHAR BER BEN PETAHIAH MOSES, *Imrei binah* [zoharic work] (Prague, 1610).

—— *Mekor ḥokhmah* [zoharic work] (Prague, 1610).

—— *Pitḥei yah* [introduction to the Zohar] (Prague, 1609).

—— *Yesh sakhar* [halakhic work on the Zohar] (Prague, 1609).

JACOB BEN ASHER (BA'AL HATURIM), *Arba'ah turim* (or *Tur*) [halakhic code], 7 vols. (New York, 1959).

JACOB BEN MOSES MOELLIN (MAHARIL), *Sefer maharil: ḥelek halikutim* (Berehovo, 1933; repr. New York, 2005).

JACOB JOSEPH OF POLONNOYE, *Toledot ya'akov yosef* [hasidic teachings organized according to the weekly Torah portions] (Korets, 1780).

JEITTELES, BARUCH, *Emek habakhah* [eulogy for Landau] (Prague, 1793).

—— *Megilat eikhah al mot yeḥezkel* [eulogy for Landau] (Prague, 1793).

—— *Ta'am hamelekh* [commentary on Isaac Nunez Belmonte, *Sha'ar hamelekh*] (Prague, 1801).

JEITTELES, JUDAH, *Benei hane'urim* [biography of his father, Jonas] (Prague, 1821).

—— *Introduction to the Aramaic Language* [Mevo halashon ha'aramit] (Prague, 1813).

JOSEPH HA'EFRATI OF TROPPLOWITZ, *Alon bakhut* [eulogy for Landau] (Prague, 1793).

JOSEPH BEN MEIR TEOMIM, *Peri megadim* [commentary on *Shulḥan arukh*, 'Oraḥ ḥayim] (Berlin, 1771).

JUDAH HEHASID, *Sefer ḥasidim* [ethical compendium] (Jerusalem, 1956).

KADISH, KAYAM, *Ma'amar kadishin* [halakhic novellae] (Prague, 1764).

KARLBURG, JEHUDAH LEIB, *Divrei avel al mot hagaon yeḥezkel landa halevi* [eulogy for Landau] (Offenbach, 1793).

KARO, JOSEPH, *Beit yosef* [commentary on the *Arba'ah turim* by R. Jacob ben Asher] (Jerusalem, 1990–4).

—— *Shulḥan arukh* [halakhic code] (New York, 1959).

KARPELES, ELEAZAR, *Derush lehesped even ha'ot yeḥezkel lemofet* [eulogy for Landau] (Prague, 1793).

KATZ, DAVID BEN JOSEPH, *Pa'amonei zahav* [commentary on Psalms] (Fürth, 1769).

KATZ, REUBEN, *Oneg shabat* [kabbalistic work] (Prague, 1700).

KATZENELLENBOGEN, PINCHAS, *Yesh manḥilin* [autobiography], ed. Issac Dov Feld (Jerusalem, 1986).

KLINGLER, IGNAZ, *Ueber die Unnütz und Schädlichkeit der Jüden im Königreiche Böheim, Mähren und Oesterreich* (Prague, 1782).

KUNITZ, MOSES, *Ben yoḥai* [discusses the teachings of R. Shimon bar Yohai in the Talmud; defends R. Shimon bar Yohai's authorship of the *Zohar*] (Vienna, 1815).

—— *Sefer hamatsref* [responsa], 2 vols. (Vienna, 1820; Prague, 1857).

Lamentations Rabbah (Vilna, 1878).

LANDAU, EZEKIEL, *Ahavat tsiyon* [collection of Prague homilies] (Prague, 1827; repr. Jerusalem, 1966).

—— *Dagul merevavah* [commentary on *Shulḥan arukh*] (Prague, 1794).

—— *Derush hesped* [eulogy for Empress Maria Theresa] (Prague, 1780).

—— *Derush shevaḥ vehoda'ah* [sermon for Emperor Joseph II's military victory at Belgrade] (Prague, 1789).

LANDAU, EZEKIEL, *Derushei hatselaḥ* [collection of Prague homilies] (Warsaw, 1884; photo-offset Jerusalem, 1966).

—— *Doresh letsiyon* [collection of Yampol homilies] (Prague, 1827).

—— 'Eulogy for Isaac Wolf Austerlitz' (Heb.), *Kerem shelomoh*, 7 (1991), 6–8.

—— 'Eulogy for Meir Fischels Bumsla' (Heb.) in Shelomoh Ehrlich (ed.), *Midrash yehonatan* (Bilgoraj, 1933), 52*a*–54*a*.

—— *Herzengefühl Gebet* (Prague, 1791).

—— *Ḥukei ha'ishut* [pamphlet on marital laws, in German] (Prague, 1785).

—— *Igeret shalom* [letter of compromise to halt the Emden–Eybeschütz controversy] (Yampol, 1752).

—— *Krönungslied und Gebet* [prayer for Emperor Leopold II's coronation] (Prague, 1791).

—— 'Letter', *Kovets beit aharon veyisra'el*, 8/1 (1992), 162–5.

—— 'Letter', *Kovets beit aharon veyisra'el*, 8/3 (1993) 123–5.

—— 'Letter', *Kovets beit aharon veyisra'el*, 9/3 (1994), 129–39.

—— *Mareh yeḥezkel* [talmudic glosses, printed with Talmud] (Prague, 1830).

—— *Noda biyehudah* [responsa], *Kama* (Prague, 1776); *Tinyana* (Prague, 1811); repr. Vilna, 1927); Makhon Leyerushalayim edn. (Ashkelon, 1990–2004).

—— *Prayer for the Healing of Maria Theresa* [Gebeth [. . .] um die Wiedergenesung Ihro kais. königl. apostolischen Majestät] (Prague, 1767).

—— *Prayer for Maria Theresa's Good Fortune in War* (German) (Prague, 1756).

—— *Prayer for the Opening of the Normalschule in the Jewish Quarter* (Dankgebet . . . den 2. May 1782 bey der feyerlichen Einsegnung der deutschen Schule in der Judenstadt in Prag) (Prague, 1782).

—— 'Sermon to the First Jewish Recruits to the Austrian Military', *Hame'asef*, 5 (1789), 252–5 (German).

—— *Tselaḥ hashalem* [complete *Tselaḥ* Talmud commentary] (Jerusalem, 1995).

—— *Tsiyun lenefesh ḥayah (Tselaḥ), Beitsah* [Talmud commentary] (Prague, 1799).

—— *Tsiyun lenefesh ḥayah (Tselaḥ), Berakhot* [Talmud commentary] (Prague, 1791).

—— *Tsiyun lenefesh ḥayah (Tselaḥ), Nezikin* [Talmud commentary] (Jerusalem, 1959).

—— *Tsiyun lenefesh ḥayah (Tselaḥ), Pesaḥim* [Talmud commentary] (Prague, 1783).

—— *Tsiyun lenefesh ḥayah (Tselaḥ), Shabat, Eruvin, Yoma, Sukah, Rosh hashanah, Ta'anit, Megilah, Ḥagigah* [Talmud commentary] (Warsaw, 1879).

—— *Tsiyun lenefesh ḥayah (Tselaḥ), Zevaḥim, Menaḥot, Ḥulin* [Talmud commentary] (Warsaw, 1891).

LANDAU, ISRAEL, *Ḥok leyisra'el* [translation of Maimonides' *Sefer hamitsvot* into Judendeutsch] (Prague, 1798).

—— *Igeret orḥot olam* [anthology of Abraham Farissol's *Igeret orḥot olam*, Abraham ibn Ezra's *Yesod morah*, and Maimonides' *Igeret teiman*] (Prague, 1793).

LANDAU, JACOB, *Divrei yedidot* [short biography of Ezekiel Landau], published in *Noda biyehudah, Tinyana* (Prague, 1811); repr. in *Noda biyehudah*, 'Oraḥ ḥayim' (Ashkelon and Netanya, 1994), 31–6.

LANDAU, SAMUEL, *Derush* [eulogy for Koppelmann Porges] (Prague, 1823).

—— 'Eulogy for Isaac Wolf Austerlitz' (Heb.), *Kerem shelomoh*, 7 (1991), 6–8.

—— *Seliḥah be'et hanagaf ḥolerah* [prayer during the cholera epidemic] (Prague, 1832).

—— *Shivat tsiyon* [responsa] (Prague, 1827).

—— *Trauerrede auf den betribten Todesfall Leopold II* (Prague, 1792).

LANDSOFER, JONAH BEN ELIJAH, *Me'il tsedakah* [responsa, and a section on geometry] (Prague, 1757).

'Letters from the Archives of the *Kehilah* of Frankfurt' (Heb.), *Tsefunot*, 2/4 (1990), 105–8.

LEVI, AVIGDOR, *Devar tov* [grammatical work] (Prague, 1783).

—— (ed.), *Letters of Rabbi Moses Dessau* [Igerot rabi mosheh desau] (Vienna, 1794).

LEVISON, MORDECHAI GUMPEL SCHNABER, *Tokhaḥat megulah* [commentary on Ecclesiastes] (Hamburg, 1784).

LOW, ELEAZAR [SHEMEN ROKE'AH], *Sama deḥayei* (Warsaw, 1796).

LUZZATTO, MOSES HAYIM, *Mesilat yesharim* [*musar* work] (Amsterdam, 1740).

MAHARIL, *see* JACOB BEN MOSES MOELLIN

Maḥzor keminhag polin fiham umehrin [festival prayer book] (Sulzbach, 1770–82).

MAIMONIDES, MOSES, *Commentary on the Mishnah*, trans. Yosef Kafah, 3 vols. (Jerusalem, 1963).

—— *Guide of the Perplexed* [Moreh nevukhim], trans. Shlomo Pines (Chicago, 1963).

—— *Letter on Astrology*, in Ralph Lerner and Muhsin Mahdi, *Medieval Political Philosophy* (Glencoe, 1963), 227–37.

—— *Mishneh torah* [code of Jewish law], 14 vols. (Jerusalem, 1975).

—— *Sefer hamitsvot* [Book of the Commandments], trans. Yosef Kafah (Jerusalem, 1971).

MANASSEH BEN ISRAEL, *Vindiciae judaeorum*, trans. into German by Moses Mendelssohn (Berlin, 1782).

Mekhilta derabi yishma'el [HALAKHIC MIDRASH], ed. H. S. Horovitz and I. A. Rabin (Jerusalem, 1970).

MENDELSSOHN, MOSES, *Gesammelte Schriften*, 7 vols., ed. G. B. Mendelssohn (Leipzig, 1843–5).

—— *Jerusalem: Oder, über religiöse Macht und Judenthum* (Berlin, 1783); English edn.: *Jerusalem; or On Religious Power and Judaism*, trans. Allan Arkush (Hanover, 1983).

—— *Netivot hashalom* [German Bible translation, with multi-authored commentary, *Biur*] (Berlin, 1780–3)

Midrash tehilim, (ed. Solomon Buber) [midrash] (Vilna, 1893).

MOSES HAYIM EPHRAIM OF SUDYLKOW, *Degel maḥaneh efrayim* [hasidic teachings organized according to the weekly Torah portions] (repr. Benei Berak, 1969).

MOSES BEN JEKUTHIEL ZALMAN, *Magid mishnah* [commentary on Lurianic work *Mafte'aḥ ha'olamot*] (Zolkiew, 1745).

NAHMANIDES, *Commentary on the Torah*.

—— *Milḥamot hashem*, printed in Romm edn. of the Talmud.

NEUGRÖSCHEL, MATTHATHIAS, *Be'er sheva* (Prague, 1815).

OSTRER, MOSES, *Arugat habosem* [commentary on Song of Songs] (Zolkiew, 1745).

—— *Commentary on the Psalms* [Derush mosheh al tehilim] (repr. New York, 1977).

PEREZ BEN MOSES, *Beit perets* [collection of sermons] (Zolkiew, 1759).

PERLES-ALTSCHUL, ELEAZAR BEN ABRAHAM, *Keneh binah keneh ḥokhmah*, *see* Anon., *Sefer hakaneh*

Pesikta rabati, ed. M. Friedmann [midrashic homilies] (Vienna, 1880; repr. Tel Aviv, 1963).

POLAK, GABRIEL (ed.), *Ben gorni* [articles] (Amsterdam, 1851).

RASHKOVER, SHABETAI, *Siddur* (Koretz, 1797).

RICCHI, RAPHAEL EMMANUEL HAI, *Mishnat ḥasidim* [a work on Lurianic *Kavanot* (extra-liturgical mystical intentions)] (Amsterdam, 1727).

SA'ADIA GAON, *Emunot vede'ot* [philosophy], trans. Yosef Kafah (Jerusalem, 1970).

SASPORTAS, JACOB, *Tsitsat novel tsevi* [collection of letters about Sabbatianism], ed. Isaiah Tishby (Jerusalem, 1954).

SATANOW, ISAAC, *Siftei renanot* [Hebrew grammar] (Berlin, 1773).

SCHICK, BARUKH b. JACOB, *Keneh hamidah* [on geometry and trigonometry] (Prague, 1784).

SCHNABER LEVISON, MORDECHAI GUMPEL, *see* Levison, Mordechai Gimpel Schnaber

Seder shomerim laboker [*seliḥot* prayers] (Prague, 1696).

Sefer yetsirah [early mystical work] (Prague, 1624).

Sefer yetsirah, ed. Ithamar Gruenwald, 'A Preliminary Critical Edition of *Sefer Yezira*', *Israel Oriental Studies*, 1 (1971), 132–77.

SHABETAI BEN MEIR HAKOHEN, *Siftei kohen* (*Shakh*) [commentary on two sections of *Shulḥan arukh*] (Prague, 1660).

SHELAH, *see* HOROWITZ, ISAIAH

SHICK, HAYIM BEN MOSES, *Yad ḥayim* [Hebrew grammar] (Prague, 1759).

SOFER, MOSES (HATAM SOFER), *Derashot ḥatam sofer* [homilies], 3 vols. (New York, 1960).

SPITZ, YOM TOV, *Zikhron elazar* [biography of his grandfather, Eleazar Fleckeles] (Prague, 1827).

Tikun ḥatsot [kabbalistic liturgy for midnight vigil] (Prague, 1767, 1782, 1787).

Tikun nefesh [prayer book] (Prague, 1786; Vienna, 1796; Prague, 1821).

Tikun shivah adar (Prague, 1787).

Tikunei zohar [zoharic work] (Jerusalem, 1948; repr. 1978).

TIRSCH, LEOPOLD, *Grammatica Hebraea* (Prague, 1784).

—— *Handlexikon der Jüdischdeutschen Sprache* (Prague, 1773).

TREBITSCH, ABRAHAM, *Korot ha'itim* [history] (Brno, 1801; repr. Lemberg, 1851).

TRIEBITSCH, ISSACHAR BER, *Goren ha'atad* [eulogy for Ezekiel Landau] (Vienna, 1793).

TSEVI HIRSH OF VAIDOSLAV, *Erets tsevi* [on aggadah] (Prague, 1786).

Tur, *see* JACOB BEN ASHER

VITAL, HAYIM, *Ets ḥayim* [Lurianic work], ed. Meir Poppers (Korets, 1782; Jerusalem, 1910).

—— *Nof ets ḥayim* [Lurianic compendium], ed. Meir Poppers (part published in *Zohar harakia* (Korets, 1785) and part in Vital, *Sefer likutei torah* (Zolkiew, 1775).

—— *Peri ets ḥayim* [Lurianic work] (Dubrovno, 1803).

—— *Sefer hagilgulim* [Lurianic work on reincarnation] (Frankfurt am Main, 1684; Przemysl, 1875).

—— *Sha'ar hagilgulim* [Lurianic work on reincarnation] (Jerusalem, 1863).

—— *Sha'ar hakavanot* [Lurianic work on prayer] (Salonika, 1852; repr. Tel Aviv, 1962).

—— *Sefer halikutim* [compendium of Lurianic teachings], ed. and comp. Benjamin Halevi (Salonika, 1863; repr. Jerusalem, 1913).

—— *Sefer likutei torah* [compendium of Lurianic teachings], ed. Meir Poppers (Zolkiew, 1775; repr. Tel Aviv, 1963).

—— *Sha'ar hamitsvot* [Lurianic explanation of the commandments] (Salonika, 1852).

—— *Sha'ar hapesukim* [Lurianic biblical work] (Salonika, 1863; repr. Tel Aviv, 1962).

—— *Sha'ar ma'amerei rashbi* [Lurianic commentary on zoharic and talmudic passages] (Salonika, 1862; repr. Tel Aviv, 1961).

—— *Sha'ar ru'aḥ hakodesh* [Lurianic meditations] (Jerusalem, 1863).

—— *Sha'arei kedushah* [Lurianic moralizing tract] (Amsterdam, 1715; repr. Benei Berak, 1967).

—— *Shemonah she'arim* [Lurianic work] 1850, 7 vols., ed. Samuel Vital (Jerusalem; rev. edn., Tel Aviv, 1961–4).

WESSELY, NAPHTALI HERZ, *Divrei shalom ve'emet* [maskilic pamphlet defending secular education] (Berlin, 1782).

—— *Ḥokhmat shelomoh* [Hebrew trans. of and commentary on the Wisdom of Solomon] (Berlin, 1780).

—— *Rav tov leveit yisra'el* [pamphlet] (Berlin, 1782).

—— *Yein levanon* [commentary on Mishnah *Avot*] (Berlin, 1775).

WIENER, ISAIAH, *Bigdei yesha* [halakhic work] (Prague, 1777).

WIENER, MOSES, *Nachricht von dem Ursprunge und Fortgange der deutschen jüdischen Hauptschule zu Prag* (Prague, 1785).

WOLFSOHN, AARON, 'Siḥah be'erets haḥayim', *Hame'asef* (1794–7).

Yalkut shimoni [midrashic anthology] (Warsaw, 1878).

ZAHLIN, ELIJAH, *Hadarat eliyahu* [sermons] (Prague, 1785).

ZANZER, HAYIM, *Ne'edar bakodesh* [commentary on Mishnah, *Avot*] (New York, 1962).

Zohar, ed. Reuven Margaliot, 3 vols. (Jerusalem, 1956).

ZUNZ, ARYEH LEIB, *Hespeda yekara deshakhbi* [eulogy for Landau] (Vienna, 1793).

SECONDARY SOURCES

ABELES IGGERS, WILMA (ed.), *The Jews of Bohemia and Moravia: A Historical Reader* (Detroit, 1992).

ABRAMSKY, CHIMEN, 'The Crisis of Authority within European Jewry in the Eighteenth Century', in Siegfried Stein and Raphael Loewe (eds.), *Studies in Jewish Religious and Intellectual History Presented to Alexander Altmann on the Occasion of his Seventieth Birthday* (Alabama, 1979), 13–28.

ADLER, SIMON 'Das älteste Judicial-Protokoll des jüdischen Gemeinde-Archives in Prag 1682', *Jahrbuch der Gesellschaft für Geschichte der Juden in der Čechoslovakischen Republik*, 3 (1931), 217–56.

ALEXANDRIAN, SARANE, *Histoire de la philosophie occulte* (Paris, 1983).

ALTMANN, ALEXANDER, 'Commandments, Reasons for', *Encyclopaedia Judaica* (Jerusalem, 1972), v. 783–9.

—— *Moses Mendelssohn: A Biographical Study* (Philadelphia, 1973).

ANON., *Noda Biyehudah: The History and Life of Ezekiel Halevi Segal Landau* [Noda biyehudah: toledot vekorot ḥayav shel yeḥezkel halevi segal landau] (Benei Berak, 1968).

ANON., *The Wisdom of the Noda Biyehudah* [Ḥokhmat hanoda biyehudah] (Jerusalem, n.d.).

ARNETH, VON, ALFRED, *Geschichte Maria Theresias*, 10 vols. (Vienna, 1863–76).

ASPREY, ROBERT, *Frederick the Great* (New York, 1986).

ASSAF, SIMCHA, *Sources for the History of Jewish Education* [Mekorot letoledot haḥinukh beyisra'el], 4 vols. (Tel Aviv, 1925–43).

AVIVI, YOSEF, *Binyan ari'el* [introduction to the homilies of R. Isaac Luria] (Jerusalem, 1987).

—— *Kabalat hagerah* [introduction to the kabbalah of the Vilna Gaon] (Jerusalem, 1993).

BALABAN, MEIR, *The History of the Frankist Movemement* [Letoledot hatenuah hafrankit] (Tel Aviv, 1934).

BARTAL, ISRAEL, *The Jews of Eastern Europe* 1772–1881 (Philadelphia, 2005).

BEALES, DEREK, 'The False Joseph II', *Historical Journal*, 18 (1975), 467–95.

—— *Joseph II: In the Shadow of Maria Theresa*, 1741–80 (Cambridge, 1987).

—— 'Was Joseph II an Enlightened Despot?', in Ritchie Robertson and Edward Timms (eds.), *The Austrian Enlightenment and its Aftermath*, Austrian Studies 2 (Edinburgh, 1991), 1–21.

BENAYAHU, MEIR, 'The Controversy between Halakhah and Kabbalah' (Heb.), *Daat*, 5 (1981), 61–115.

—— *The Kabbalistic Writings of Hayim Luzzatto* [Kitvei hakabalah shel ramhal] (Jerusalem, 1979).

—— *Shaving on the Intermediate Festival Days* [Tiglaḥat beḥolo shel mo'ed] (Jerusalem, 1995).

BEN-SHLOMO, JOSEPH, 'Moses Cordovero', in Gerschom Scholem (ed.), *Kabbalah* (New York, 1974), 401–4.

—— *The Mystical Theology of Moses Cordovero* [Torat ha'elohut shel r. mosheh cordovero] (Jerusalem, 1965).

BERKOVITZ, JAY, *Rites and Passages: The Beginnings of Modern Jewish Culture in France*, 1650–1860 (Philadelphia, 2004).

—— *The Shaping of Jewish Identity in Nineteenth-Century France* (Detroit, 1989).

—— 'Social and Religious Controls in Pre-Revolutionary France: Rethinking the Beginnings of Modernity', *Jewish History*, 15 (2001), 1–40.

BERNARD, PAUL, *Joseph II* (New York, 1968).

—— 'Joseph II and the Jews: The Origins of the Toleration Patent of 1782', *Austrian History Yearbook*, 4–5 (1968–9), 101–19.

BLANNING, T. C. W., *Joseph II* (London, 1994).

—— *Joseph II and Enlightened Despotism* (London, 1970).

BLOCH, MARC, *Rois thaumaturges: Étude sur le caractère surnaturel attribué à la puissance royale, particulièrement en France et en Angleterre* (London, 1924).

—— *Société féodale* (Paris, 1939).

BLUMENTHAL, DAVID, 'Maimonides: Prayer, Worship and Mysticism', in id. (ed.), *Approaches to Judaism in Medieval Times*, vol. iii (Atlanta, 1988), 1–16.

BOKSER, BEN ZION, *The Maharal: The Mystical Philosophy of Rabbi Judah Loew of Prague* (Northvale, 1994).

BONFIL, ROBERT, 'Halakha, Kabbala, and Society: Some Insights into R. Menahem Azariah Da Fano's Inner World', in I. Twersky and B. Septimus (eds.), *Jewish Thought in the Seventeenth Century* (Cambridge, Mass., 1987), 39–61.

—— *Jewish Life in Renaissance Italy*, trans. Anthony Oldcorn (Berkeley, 1994).

BRAUDEL, FERNAND, 'Histoire et sciences sociales: La Longue durée', *Annales*, 13 (1958), 725–53.

—— *Méditerranée et le monde méditerranéen á l'époque de Philippe II* (Paris, 1949).

BRENNER, MICHAEL, 'Between Haskalah and Kabbalah: Peter Beer's History of Jewish Sects', in Elisheva Carlebach, John Efron, and David Meyers (eds.), *Jewish History and Jewish Memory* (Hanover, 1998), 389–404.

BREUER, EDWARD, *The Limits of Enlightenment: Jews, Germans, and the Eighteenth-Century Study of Scripture* (Cambridge, Mass., 1996).

—— 'Naphtali Herz Wessely and the Cultural Dislocations of an Eighteenth-Century Maskil', in Shmuel Feiner and David Sorkin (eds.), *New Perspectives on the Haskalah* (Oxford, 2001), 27–47

BREUER, MORDECHAI, 'The Early Modern Period', in Michael Meyer (ed.), *German-Jewish History in Modern Times* (New York, 1996), i. 81–260.

BRILL, ALAN, 'The Mystical Path of the Vilna Gaon', *Journal of Jewish Thought and Philosophy*, 3/1 (1993), 131–51.

BRODY, SETH, 'Human Hands Dwell in Heavenly Heights: Contemplative Ascent and Theurgic Power in Thirteenth Century Kabbalah', in R. A. Herrera (ed.), *Mystics of the Book* (New York, 1993), 123–58.

—— 'Human Hands Dwell in Heavenly Heights: Worship and Mystical Experience in Thirteenth Century Kabbalah', Ph.D. diss., University of Pennsylvania, 1991.

BROSCHE, WILFRIED, 'Das Ghetto von Prag', in F. Seibt (ed.), *Die Juden in den böhmischen Ländern* (Munich, 1983), 87–122.

BURIAN, JIRÍ, *Prag die Altstadt/Prague the Old Town* (Prague, 1992).

BURKE, PETER, *The French Historical Revolution* (Worcester, 1990).

BUXBAUM, JOSEPH, 'Introduction: Rabbi Bezalel Ranschburg' (Heb.), in Tsevi Joshua Leitner (ed.), *The Responsa and Novellae of Rabbi Bezalel Ranschburg* [Shut veḥidushei rabi betsalel ranshburg] (Jerusalem, 1980).

—— 'Rabbis Meir and Leib Fischels' (Heb.), *Moriah*, 6/2–4 (1975), 15–17.

CARLEBACH, ELISHEVA, *The Death of Simon Abeles: Jewish–Christian Tension in Seventeenth-Century Prague* (New York, 2001).

—— *Divided Souls: Converts from Judaism in Germany*, 1500–1750 (New Haven, 2001).

—— *The Pursuit of Heresy* (New York, 1990).

CAVALLO, GUGLIELMO, and ROGER CHARTIER (eds.), *A History of Reading in the West* (Amherst, Mass., 1999).

CERMANOVÁ, IVETA, 'Karl Fischer (1757–1844) I: The Life and Intellectual World of a Hebrew Censor', *Judaica Bohemiae*, 42 (2006), 125–77.

—— 'Karl Fischer (1757–1844) II: The Work of a Hebrew Censor', *Judaica Bohemiae*, 43 (2007–8), 5–63.

CERMANOVÁ, IVETA, and JINDŘICH MAREK, *Between the Christian and Jewish Worlds: The Story of a Censor in Hebraicis and a Librarian of the Klementinum, Karl Fischer (1757–1844)* (Czech) (Prague, 2007).

CHARTIER, ROGER, 'Reading Matter and "Popular" Reading: From the Renaissance to the Seventeenth Century', in Gugleilmo Cavallo and Roger Chartier (eds.), *A History of Reading in the West* (Amherst, Mass., 1999), 268–83.

COHEN, M. J., *Jacob Emden: A Man of Controversy* (Philadelphia, 1937).

CRANKSHAW, EDWARD, *Maria Theresa* (London, 1983).

CRAWFORD, T. S., *The History of the Umbrella* (New York, 1970).

DAN, JOSEPH, 'Samael, Lilith, and the Concept of Evil in Early Kabbalah', in Lawrence Fine (ed.), *Essential Papers on Kabbalah* (New York, 1995), 154–78.

DAVIS, JOSEPH, *Yom-Tov Lipmann Heller: Portrait of a Seventeenth-Century Rabbi* (Oxford, 2004).

DEMETZ, PETER, *Prague in Black and Gold* (New York, 1997).

DEUTSCH, GOTTHARD and SCHULIM OCHSER, 'Prague', *Jewish Encyclopedia*, x. 153–64.

DIMITROVSKY, HAIM, 'On the *Pilpul* Style' (Heb.), in Saul Lieberman and Arthur Hyman (eds.), *Salo Wittmayer Baron Jubilee Volume*, vol. iii (Jerusalem, 1974), 176–81.

DINUR, BENZION, *At the Turning of the Generations* [Bemifneh hadorot] (Jerusalem, 1955).

—— 'The Origins of Hasidism and its Social and Messianic Foundations', in Gershon Hundert (ed.), *Essential Papers on Hasidism* (New York, 1991), 159–72

DOKTÓR, JAN, 'Conversions within Shabbatianism', *Kwartalnik Historii Żydów*, 209 (2004), 40–6.

—— 'Jacob Frank und sein messianisches Reich', *Kairos*, 34–5 (1992–3), 218–35.

—— 'Jakub Frank, a Jewish Heresiarch and his Messianic Doctrine', *Acta Poloniae Historica*, 76 (1997), 53–74.

DRÁBEK, ANNA, 'Die Juden in den böhmischen Ländern zur Zeit des Landesfürstlichen Absolutismus', in F. Seibt (ed.), *Die Juden in den böhmischen Ländern* (Munich, 1983), 123–44.

DUBIN, LOIS, *The Port Jews of Habsburg Trieste: Absolutist Politics and Enlightenment Culture* (Stanford, 1999).

DUBNOW, SIMON, *History of Hasidism* [Toledot haḥasidut] (Tel Aviv, 1930–1).

DUKER, ABRAHAM, 'Frankism as a Movement of Polish-Jewish Synthesis', in Béla Király (ed.), *Tolerance and Movements of Religious Dissent in Eastern Europe* (New York, 1975), 133–64.

DURKHEIM, ÉMILE, 'Préface', *Année Sociologique*, 1 (1896), pp. i–vi.

DUSCHINSKY, CHARLES, *The Rabbinate of the Great Synagogue, London, from 1756–1842* (London, 1921).

ELBAUM, JACOB, 'Aspects of Hebrew Ethical Literature in Sixteenth-Century Poland', in Bernard Dov Cooperman (ed.), *Jewish Thought in the Sixteenth Century* (Cambridge, Mass., 1983).

—— *Opening and Withdrawal* [Petiḥut vehistagrut] (Jerusalem, 1990).

—— 'Rabbi Judah Loew of Prague and his Attitude to the Aggadah', *Scripta Hierosolymitana*, 22 (Jerusalem, 1971), 28–47.

—— *Repentance and Self-Flagellation in the Writings of the Sages of Germany and Poland 1348–1648* [Teshuvat halev vekabalat yesurim] (Jerusalem, 1992).

—— 'Trends and Courses in Jewish Speculative and Moralistic Literature in the Germanic Lands and Poland during the Sixteenth Century' (Heb.), Ph.D. diss., Hebrew University, 1977.

ELIAV, MORDECHAI, *Jewish Education in Germany* [Haḥinukh hayehudi begermaniyah] (Jerusalem, 1960).

—— *Jüdische Erziehung in Deutschland im Zeitalter der Aufklärung und der Emanzipation*, rev. edn., ed. Mordechai Eliav, trans. Maike Strobel (Münster, 2001).

ELLENSON, DAVID, *After Emancipation* (Cincinnati, 2004).

—— *Rabbi Esriel Hildesheimer and the Creation of a Modern Jewish Orthodoxy* (Tuscaloosa, 1990).

ETKES, IMMANUEL, *The Ba'al Hashem Tov: Magic, Mysticism, Leadership* [Habesht: magiyah, mistikah, hanhagah] (Jerusalem, 2000).

—— *The Beginning of the Hasidic Movement* [Tenuat haḥasidut bereshitah] (Tel Aviv, 1998).

—— 'Hasidism as a Movement: The First Stage', in Bezalel Safran (ed.), *Hasidism: Continuity or Innovation?* (Cambridge, Mass., 1988), 1–26.

—— *Unique in his Generation* [Yaḥid bedoro] (Jerusalem, 1998).

EVANS, R. J. W., 'The Habsburg Monarchy and Bohemia', in Mark Greengrass (ed.), *Conquest and Coalescence: The Shaping of the State in Early Modern Europe* (London, 1991), 134–54.

—— *Rudolf II and his World* (Oxford, 1973).

FAHN, REUVEN, 'Rabbi Moses Kunitz: A Chapter in the History of Haskalah and Religious Reform' (Heb.), *Reshumot*, 4 (1925), 245–80.

FAIERSTEIN, MORRIS, 'God's Need for the Commandments in Medieval Kabbalah', *Conservative Judaism*, 36 (1982), 45–59.

FEBVRE, LUCIEN, *Destin: Martin Luther* (Paris, 1928).

—— *Problème de l'incroyance au XVIe siècle: La Religion de Rabelais* (Paris, 1942).

FEINER, SHMUEL, 'The Early Haskalah in the Eighteenth Century' (Heb.), *Tarbiz*, 67/2 (1998), 189–240.

—— *Haskalah and History: The Emergence of a Modern Jewish Historical Consciousness* (Oxford, 2002).

—— *The Jewish Enlightenment* (Philadelphia, 2002).

—— and Israel Bartal (eds.), *The Varieties of Haskalah* [Hahaskalah ligevaneiha] (Jerusalem, 2005).

—— and David Sorkin (eds.), *New Perspectives on the Haskalah* (Oxford, 2001).

FIEDLER, JIRÍ, *Jewish Sights of Bohemia and Moravia* (Prague, 1991).

FINE, LAWRENCE, 'The Art of Metoposcopy: A Study in Isaac Luria's Charismatic Knowledge', in id. (ed.), *Essential Papers on Kabbalah* (New York, 1995), 315–37.

—— *Physician of the Soul, Healer of the Cosmos* (Stanford, 2003).

—— 'Purifying the Body in the Name of the Soul: The Problem of the Body in Sixteenth-Century Kabbalah', in Howard Eilberg-Shwartz (ed.), *People of the Body: Jews and Judaism from an Embodied Perspective* (Albany, NY, 1992), 117–42.

—— *Safed Spirituality* (New York, 1984).

FISHMAN, DAVID, *Russia's First Modern Jews: The Jews of Shklov* (New York, 1995).

FLATTO, SHARON, '*Hasidim* and *Mitnaggedim*: Not a World Apart', *Journal of Jewish Thought and Philosophy*, 12/ 2 (Aug. 2003), 99–121.

FRAADE, STEVEN, 'Ascetical Aspects of Ancient Judaism', in Arthur Green (ed.), *Jewish Spirituality from the Bible to the Middle Ages* (New York, 1986), 253–88.

FRAM, EDWARD, *Ideals Face Reality: Jewish Law and Life in Poland, 1550–1655* (Cincinnati, 1997).

FRANKEL, AVRAHAM HAYIM, *Simḥah temimah* [Jewish laws pertaining to the first year of marriage] (Jerusalem, 1986).

FRANKENBERRY, NANCY, and FRANK PENNER (eds.), *Language, Truth, and Religious Belief* (Atlanta, 1999).

FREIMANN, ARON, 'Die hebräischen Druckereien in Prag von 1733–1828', *Soncino-Blätter*, 3 (1929), 113–43.

FRIEDBERG, BERNHARD, *History of Hebrew Printing in the Towns of Central Europe* [Toledot hadefus ha'ivri ba'arim shebe'eiropah hatikhonah] (Antwerp, 1935).

GEERTZ, CLIFFORD, *The Interpretation of Cultures* (New York, 1973).

—— *Local Knowledge*, 3rd edn. (New York, 2000).

GELBER, NATHAN MICHAEL, 'History of the Jews of Brody' (Heb.), in Y. L. Hacohen Maimon (ed.), *Major Jewish Towns* [Arim ve'imahot beyisra'el], 7 vols. (Jerusalem, 1955), vol. vi.

GELMAN, ARYEH LEIB, *The Noda Biyehudah and his Teaching* [Hanoda biyehudah umishnato] (Jerusalem, 1962).

GILLER, PINCHAS, 'Recovering the Sanctity of the Galilee: The Veneration of Sacred Relics in Classical Kabbalah', *Journal of Jewish Thought and Philosophy*, 4/1 (1994), 147–69.

GINSBURG, ELLIOT, *The Sabbath in the Classical Kabbalah* (Albany, NY, 1989).

GINZBURG, CARLO, *The Cheese and the Worms* (Baltimore, 1980).

GINZBURG, SHIMON, *Rabbi Moses Hayim Luzzatto and his Contemporaries* [Rabi mosheh ḥayim luzato uvenei doro], 2 vols. (Tel Aviv, 1937).

GOLD, HUGO (ed.), *Die Juden und Judengemeinden Böhmens in Vergangenheit und Gegenwart* (Brünn, 1934).

GOLDBERG, SYLVIE ANNE, *Crossing the Jabbok: Illness and Death in Ashkenazi Judaism in Sixteenth through Nineteenth-Century Prague*, trans. Carol Cosman (Berkeley, 1996).

GOLDISH, MATT, 'Rabbi Jacob Sasportas: Defender of Torah Authority in an Age of Change', MA thesis, Hebrew University, 1991.

GRAETZ, HEINRICH, 'Ezechiel Landau's Gesuch an Maria Theresia gegen Jonathan Eibeschütz', *Monatsschrift für Geschichte und Wissenschaft des Judenthums*, 26/1 (1877), 17–25.

—— *Geschichte der Juden von den ältesten Zeiten bis auf die Gegenwart*, 11 vols., 3rd edn. (Leipzig, 1890–7); English translation: *History of the Jews*, 6 vols., ed. Bella Löwy (Philadelphia, Pa., 1891–8).

GRAETZ, MICHAEL, 'The Jewish Enlightenment', in Michael Meyer (ed.), *German-Jewish History in Modern Times*, i: *Tradition and Enlightenment* 1600–1780 (New York, 1996), 263–74.

GREEN, ARTHUR, *Keter: The Crown of God in Early Jewish Mysticism* (Princeton, NJ, 1997).

GREENBLATT, RACHEL, 'The Shapes of Memory: Evidence in Stone from the Old Jewish Cemetery in Prague', *Leo Baeck Institute Year Book*, 47 (2002), 43–67.

GREENWALD, JEKUTIEL JUDAH, *Rabbi Jonathan Eybeschütz* [Harav r. yehonatan eibeshuts] (New York, 1954).

GRIES, ZEEV, 'Between History and Literature—The Case of Jewish Preaching', review of Marc Saperstein, *Jewish Preaching* 1200–1800: *An Anthology* (New Haven, 1989), *Journal of Jewish Thought and Philosophy*, 4 (1994), 113–22.

—— 'Between Literature and History: Introductions to a Discussion and Study of *Shivḥei habesht*' (Heb.), *Tura*, 3 (1994), 157–9.

—— *The Book in Early Hasidism* (Heb.) [Sefer, sofer, vesipur bereishit haḥasidut] (Tel Aviv, 1992).

—— *Conduct Literature: Its History and Place in the Life of Beshtian Hasidism* [Sifrut hahanhagot: toldoteihah umekomah beḥayei ḥasidei rabi yisra'el ba'al shem tov] (Jerusalem, 1989).

—— 'The Copying and Printing of Kabbalistic Books as a Source for the Study of Kabbalah' (Heb.), *Maḥanayim*, 6 (1993), 209–11.

HALBERTAL, MOSHE, *Concealment and Revelation: Esotericism in Jewish Thought and its Philosophical Implications* (Princeton, 2007).

—— David Kurzweil, and Avi Sagi (eds.), *On Faith: Studies in the Concept of Faith and its History in the Jewish Tradition* [Al ha'emunah: iyunim bemusag ha'emunah uvetoledotav bamasoret hayehudit] (Jerusalem, 2005).

HALLAMISH, MOSHE, *An Introduction to the Kabbalah*, trans. Ruth Bar-Ilan and Ora Wiskind-Elper (New York, 1999).

—— *Kabbalah in Liturgy, Halakhah and Customs* [Hakabalah batefilah, bahalakhah, uvaminhag] (Ramat Gan, 2000).

HANTSCH, HUGO, *Die Geschichte Österreichs* (Vienna, 1951).

HARRIS, JAY, *How Do We Know This?* (Albany, NY, 1995).

HASSENPFLUG-ELZHOLZ, EILA, *Böhmen und die böhmischen Stände in der Zeit des beginnenden Zentralismus* (Munich, 1982).

HECHT, LOUISE, 'The Clash of Maskilim in Prague in the Early 19th Century: Herz Homberg versus Peter Beer', *Proceedings of the World Congress of Jewish Studies*, 12B (2000), 165–74.

—— *Ein jüdischer Aufklärer in Böhmen: Der Pädagoge und Reformer Peter Beer* (Cologne, 2008).

HERMAN, JAN, 'The Evolution of the Jewish Population of Bohemia and Moravia, 1754–1953', in U .O. Schmelz, P. Glikson, and S. DellaPergola (eds.), *Papers in Jewish Demography* 1973 (Jerusalem, 1977), 255–65.

HESCHEL, ABRAHAM JOSHUA, *The Circle of the Baal Shem Tov*, ed. Samuel Dresner (Chicago, 1985).

—— 'Inspiration in the Middle Ages' (Heb.), in Saul Lieberman (ed.), *Alexander Marx Jubilee Volume*, 2 vols. (Eng. and Heb.) (New York, 1950), 165–207 (Heb. volume).

HESHEL, ISRAEL NATHAN, 'Additional Documents on the Sturgeon Controversy of 1798' (Heb.), *Kovets beit aharon veyisra'el*, 5/59 (1995), 107–18.

—— 'The Opinions of the Rabbinic Leaders of the Generation in their Battle against the Maskil Naphtali Herz Wessely' (Heb.), *Kovets beit aharon veyisra'el*, 8/1 (1993), 149–67; 8/2 (1993), 117–31; 8/3 (1993), 119–33.

HESS, ISRAEL, 'Rabbi Ezekiel Landau and his Position in the History of the Halakhah' (Heb.), MA thesis, Bar-Ilan University, 1979.

HEYD, MICHAEL, 'Protestantism, Enthusiasm and Secularization in the Early Modern Period: Some Preliminary Reflections', in A. Goren et al. (eds.), *Religion, Ideology and Nationalism in Europe and America* (Jerusalem, 1986), 15–27.

—— 'The Reaction to Enthusiasm in the Seventeenth Century: Towards an Integrative Approach', *Journal of Modern History*, 53/2 (June 1981), 258–80.

HILDESHEIMER, MEIR, 'Moses Mendelssohn in Nineteenth-Century Rabbinical Literature', *Proceedings of the American Academy for Jewish Research*, 55 (1988), 79–133.

HIRSCH, SAMSON RAPHAEL, *Die Religion im Bunde mit dem Fortschritt* (Frankfurt, 1854).

HOENSCH, JÖRG, *Geschichte Böhmens* (Munich, 1987).

HOROWITZ, ELLIOT, 'Coffee, Coffeehouses, and the Nocturnal Rituals of Early Modern Jewry', *AJS Review*, 14 (1989), 17–46.

—— 'The Early Eighteenth Century Confronts the Beard: Kabbalah and Jewish Self-Fashioning', *Jewish History*, 8 (1994), 95–115.

—— 'Speaking to the Dead: Cemetery Prayer in Medieval and Early Modern Jewry', *Journal of Jewish Thought and Philosophy*, 8 (1999), 303–17.

HOROWITZ, YEHOSHUA, 'Meir ben Ephraim Fischels', *Encyclopaedia Judaica* (Jerusalem, 1972), vi. 1317.

HUBKA, THOMAS, 'The "Zohar" and the Polish Synagogue: The Practical Influence of a Sacred Text', *Journal of Jewish Thought and Philosophy*, 9 (2000), 173–250.

HUNDERT, GERSHON DAVID, *Jews in Poland–Lithuania in the Eighteenth Century* (Berkeley, 2004).

—— *The Jews in a Polish Private Town* (Baltimore, 1992).

—— (ed.), *Essential Papers in Hasidism: Origins to Present* (New York, 1991).

HUNT, ALAN, *Governance of the Consuming Passions: A History of Sumptuary Law* (New York, 1996).

HUPPERT, GEORGE, 'The Annales Experiment', in Michael Bentley (ed.), *Companion to Historiography* (London, 1997), 873–88.

HUSS, BOAZ, 'Sefer ha-Zohar as a Canonical, Sacred, and Holy Text: Changing Perspectives of the Book of Splendor between the Thirteenth and Eighteenth Centuries', *Journal of Jewish Thought and Philosophy*, 7/2 (1998), 257–307.

HYMAN, PAULA, *The Emancipation of the Jews of Alsace* (New Haven, 1991).

IDEL, MOSHE, *Absorbing Perfections: Kabbalah and Interpretation* (New Haven, 2002).

—— *Ascensions on High in Jewish Mysticism: Pillars, Lines, Ladders* (Budapest, 2005).

—— *Hasidism: Between Ecstasy and Magic* (Albany, NY, 1995).

—— '*Hitbodedut* qua "Concentration" in Ecstatic Kabbalah' (Heb.), *Daat*, 14 (1985), 35–82.

—— *Kabbalah and Eros* (New Haven, 2005).

—— *Kabbalah: New Perspectives* (New Haven, 1988).

—— *Language, Torah, and Hermeneutics in Abraham Abulafia* (Albany, NY, 1989).

—— *Messianic Mystics* (New Haven, 1998).

—— *The Mystical Experience in Abraham Abulafia* (Albany, NY, 1987).

—— 'On the Concept of *Tsimtsum* in Kabbalah and its Research' (Heb.), *Jerusalem Studies in Jewish Thought*, 10 (1992), 59–112.

—— 'On the History of the Interdiction on the Study of Kabbalah before the Age of Forty' (Heb.), *AJS Review*, 5 (1980), 1–20.

—— 'Perceptions of Kabbalah in the Second Half of the Eighteenth Century', *Journal of Jewish Thought and Philosophy*, 1/1 (1991), 55–114.

—— 'Rabbi Abraham Abulafia's Works and Thought' (Heb.), Ph.D. diss., Hebrew University, 1976.

—— *Studies in Ecstatic Kabbalah* (Albany, NY, 1988).

—— 'Universalization and Integration: Two Conceptions of Mystical Union in Jewish Mysticism', in Moshe Idel and Bernard McGinn (eds.), *Mystical Union in Judaism, Christianity, and Islam: An Ecumenical Dialogue* (New York, 1996), 27–57.

INGRAO, CHARLES, *The Habsburg Monarchy* 1618–1815 (Cambridge, 1994).

—— 'The Pragmatic Sanction and the Theresian Succession: A Reevaluation', in William McGill (ed.), *The Habsburg Dominions under Maria Theresa* (Washington, Pa., 1980), 3–18.

—— (ed.), *The State and Society in Early Modern Austria* (West Lafayette, Ind., 1994).

JACOBS, LOUIS, *Hasidic Prayer* (New York, 1973).

KAHANA, DAVID, *History of the Kabbalists, Sabbatians and Hasidim* [Toledot hamekubalim, hashabeta'im vehaḥasidim] (Odessa, 1913).

KAHANA, MAOZ, 'Continuity and Change in the Responsa of the Hatam Sofer' (Heb.), MA thesis, Hebrew University, 2004.

KALLUS, MENACHEM, 'The Relation of the Baal Shem Tov to the Practice of Lurianic *Kavannot* in Light of his Comments on the *Siddur Rashkov*', *Kabbalah*, 2 (1997), 151–67.

KAMELHAR, JEKUTHIEL, *Dor de'ah*, 2 vols. [survey of numerous distinguished eighteenth- and nineteenth-century rabbis] (New York, 1933).

—— *Mofet hador* [hagiographical study of Landau], 2nd rev. edn. (Piotrków, 1934).

KANN, ROBERT, *A History of the Habsburg Empire* 1526–1918 (London, 1974).

—— and David Zdenek, *The Peoples of the Eastern Habsburg Lands*, 1526–1918 (Seattle, 1984).

KAPLAN, LAWRENCE, 'Rationalism and Rabbinic Culture in Sixteenth-Century Eastern Europe: Rabbi Mordecai Jaffe's *Levush Pinat Yikrat*', Ph.D. diss., Harvard University, 1975.

KARNIEL, JOSEPH, *Die Toleranzpolitik Kaiser Josephs II* (Gerlingen, 1986).

KATZ, BEN ZION, *Rabbinate, Hasidism, Haskalah* [Rabanut, ḥasidut, haskalah] (Tel Aviv, 1956).

KATZ, DAVID, 'A Case Study in the Formation of a Super-Rabbi: The Early Years of Rabbi Ezekiel Landau, 1713–1754', Ph.D. diss., University of Maryland, 2004.

KATZ, JACOB, *Divine Law in Human Hands: Case Studies in Halakhic Flexibility* (Jerusalem, 1998).

—— *Exclusiveness and Tolerance* (West Orange, NJ, 1961).

—— *Halakhah and Kabbalah* [Halakhah vekabalah] (Jerusalem, 1986).

—— 'Halakhah and Kabbalah as Competing Disciplines of Study', in Arthur Green (ed.), *Jewish Spirituality*, 2 vols. (New York, 1987), ii. 33–63.

—— *Halakhah in Straits: Obstacles to Orthodoxy at its Inception* [Halakhah bemetsar: mikhsholim al derekh ha'ortodoksiyah behithavutah] (Jerusalem, 1992).

—— 'Kabbalah in the Legal Decisions of R. Joseph Karo' (Heb.), *Daat*, 21 (1988), 85–102.

—— 'Luria's Status as a Halakhic Authority' (Heb.), *Jerusalem Studies in Jewish Thought*, 10 (1992), 259–85.

—— 'On the Question of the Connection between Sabbatianism, Enlightenment, and Reform' (Heb.), in id., *Halakhah in Straits*, 261–78.

—— *Out of the Ghetto* (Cambridge, Mass., 1973; repr. New York, 1988).

—— 'Post-Zoharic Relations between Halakhah and Kabbalah', in B. D. Cooperman (ed.). *Jewish Thought in the Sixteenth-Century* (Cambridge, Mass., 1983), 283–307.

—— *The Shabbes Goy: A Study in Halakhic Flexibility*, trans. Yoel Lerner (Philadelphia, 1989).

—— *Tradition and Crisis*, trans. B. D. Cooperman (New York, 1993).

KERNER, ROBERT, *Bohemia in the Eighteenth Century* (New York, 1969).

KESTENBERG-GLADSTEIN, RUTH, 'Chapters in the History of Czech Jewry' (Heb.), in *Gesher*, 15/2–3 (1969), special issue on the Jews of Czechoslovakia, ed. Z. Kolit, 11–82.

—— 'The House as a Feature of the Feudal-Estate Character of Pre-Emancipation Jewry' (Heb.), *Tarbiz*, 29/2 (1960), 176–90; 29/3 (1960), 282–94.

—— 'The National Character of the Prague Haskalah' (Heb.), *Molad*, 23 (1965), 221–33.

—— *Neuere Geschichte der Juden in den böhmischen Ländern*, vol. i: *Das Zeitalter der Aufklärung*, 1780–1830 (Tübingen, 1969).

—— 'The 1724 Census of the Non-Metropolitan Jews of Bohemia' (Heb.), *Zion*, 9 (1944), 1–26.

KIEVAL, HILLEL, 'Autonomy and Interdependence: The Historical Legacy of Czech Jewry', in David Altshuler (ed.), *The Precious Legacy* (New York, 1983), 47–109.

—— 'Caution's Progress: The Modernization of Jewish Life in Prague, 1780–1830', in Jacob Katz (ed.), *Toward Modernity: The European Jewish Model* (New Brunswick, NJ, 1987), 71–105.

—— 'The Lands Between: The Jews of Bohemia, Moravia, and Slovakia to 1918', in Natalia Berger (ed.), *Where Cultures Meet: The Story of the Jews of Czechoslovakia* (Tel Aviv, 1990), 23–51.

—— *The Making of Czech Jewry* (New York, 1988).

KISCH, GUIDO, 'Die Zensur jüdischer Bücher in Böhmen', *Jahrbuch der Gesellschaft für Geschichte der Juden in der Çechoslovakischen Republik*, 2 (1930), 456–90.

KLEIN, J., 'Zuschrift an Herrn Moses Mendelson in Hamburg', *Literaturblatt des Orients*, 33 (1848), 524–8; 34 (1848), 540–4.

KLEMPERER, GUTMANN, 'The Rabbis of Prague', trans. Charles Klemperer, ed. Guido Kisch, *Historia Judaica*, 12 (1950), 33–66 and 143–52; 13 (1951), 55–82. Trans. of Gutmann Klemperer, 'Das Rabbinat zu Prag seit dem Dahinscheiden des R. Löwe b. Bezalel, gewöhnlich der hohe Rabbi Löw genannt, bis auf unsere Tage (1609–1879)', in Pascheles, *Illustrierter israelitischer Volkskalender* (1881), 121–49; (1882), 124–48; (1883), 118–33; (1884), 85–129.

KLINGER, IGNAZ, *Ueber die Unnütz und Schädlichkeit der Jüden im Königreiche Böheim und Mähren* (Prague, 1782).

—— *Ueber die Unnütz und Schädlichkeit der Jüden im Königreiche Böheim, Mähren und Oesterreich* (Prague, 1782).

KRASSEN, MILES, 'Devequt and Faith in Zaddiqim: The Religious Tracts of Meshullam Feibush Heller of Zbarazh', Ph.D. diss., University of Pennsylvania, 1990.

—— *Uniter of Heaven and Earth: Rabbi Meshullam Feibush Heller of Zbarazh and the Rise of Hasidism in Eastern Galicia* (Albany, NY, 1998).

LAMED, MEIR, 'Ezekiel Ben Judah Landau (his sons)', *Encyclopaedia Judaica* (Jerusalem, 1972), x. 1390–1.

—— 'Fischer', *Encyclopaedia Judaica* (Jerusalem, 1972), vi. 1318.

LAMM, NORMAN, *The Religious Thought of Hasidism: Text and Commentary* (Hoboken, NJ, 1999).

—— *Torah Lishmah: Torah for Torah's Sake in the Works of Rabbi Hayyim of Volozhin and his Contemporaries* (Hoboken, NJ, 1989).

LANDISCH, BOHUMIL, *Praha* (Prague, 1970).

LEFEBVRE, GEORGES, *Grande Peur de* 1789 (Paris, 1932).

LEIMAN, SID Z., 'When a Rabbi Is Accused of Heresy: R. Ezekiel Landau's Attitude Toward R. Jonathan Eibeschuetz in the Emden–Eibeschuetz Controversy', in Jacob Neusner, Ernest Frerichs, and Nahum Sarna (eds.), *From Ancient Israel to Modern Judaism: Essays in Honor of Marvin Fox* (Atlanta, 1989), 179–94.

LEVIN, LEONARD SAMUEL, 'Seeing with Both Eyes: The Intellectual Formation of Ephraim Luntshitz', Ph.D. diss., Jewish Theological Seminary of America, 2002.

LIBERLES, ROBERT, *Religious Conflict in Social Context: The Resurgence of Orthodox Judaism in Frankfurt am Main*, 1838–1877 (Westport, Conn., 1985).

LIEBEN, KOPPELMANN, *Gal-ed* [collection of tombstone inscriptions from Prague's Old Jewish Cemetery] (Prague, 1856).

LIEBEN, SALOMON HUGO, 'Beiträge zur Geschichte der Zensur hebräischer Drucke in Prag', *Soncino-Blätter*, 3 (1929), 51–5.

—— 'Rabbi Eleasar Fleckeles', *Jahrbuch der Jüdisch-Literarischen Gesellschaft*, 10 (1913), 1–33.

—— 'Zur Charakteristik des Verhältnisses zwischen Rabbi Jecheskel Landau und Rabbi Jonathan Eibenschitz', *Jahrbuch des Jüdisch-literarische Gesellschaft*, 1 (1903), 325–6.

LIEBERMAN, HAYIM, *The Tent of Rachel* [Ohel raḥel] (Heb. and Yid.), 3 vols. (New York, 1980–4).

LIEBES, YEHUDA, *The Messianism of Rabbi Jacob Emden and his Connection with Sabbatianism* [Meshiḥiyuto shel rabi ya'akov emden veyaḥaso leshabeta'ut], *Tarbiz*, 49 (1980), 122–65.

—— 'Myth vs. Symbol in the Zohar and in Lurianic Kabbalah' (Heb.), in Havivah Pedayah (ed.), *Myth in Judaism* [Hamitos bayahadut] Eshel Beer Sheva 4 (Jerusalem, 1996), 192–209.

—— 'New Directions in the Study of the Kabbalah' (Heb.), *Pe'amim*, 50 (1992), 150–69.

—— 'New Writings in Sabbatian Kabbalah from the Circle of Rabbi Jonathan Eybeschütz' (Heb.), *Jerusalem Studies in Jewish Thought*, 5 (1986), 191–384.

—— 'Sabbatai Zevi's Attitude towards his own Conversion' (Heb.), *Tsefunot*, 2/17 (1983), 267–307.

—— 'Sabbatian Messianism' (Heb.), *Pe'amim*, 40 (1989), 4–20.

—— *Studies in Jewish Myth and Jewish Messianism*, trans. Batya Stein (Albany, NY, 1993).

—— *Studies in the Zohar*, trans. Arnold Schwartz, Stephanie Nakache, and Penina Peli (Albany, NY, 1993).

—— 'Zohar and Eros' (Heb.), *Alpayim*, 9 (1994), 67–119.

—— 'The Zohar as a Halakhic Book' (Heb.), review of Israel Ta-Shma, *The Halakhic Residue in the Zohar* [Hanigleh shebanistar: leḥeker sheki'ei hahalakhah besefer hazohar] (Tel Aviv, 1995)], *Tarbiz*, 64/4 (1995), 581–605.

LOWENSTEIN, STEVEN, *The Berlin Jewish Community: Enlightenment, Family, and Crisis, 1770–1830* (New York, 1994).

—— 'The Readership of Mendelssohn's Bible Translation', *Hebrew Union College Annual*, 53 (1982), 179–213.

MCCAGG, WILLIAM O., *A History of Habsburg Jews*, 1670–1918 (Bloomington, 1989).

MACARTNEY, C. A., *The Habsburg Empire* 1790–1918 (London, 1968).

—— *Maria Theresa and the House of Austria* (London, 1969).

MAGID, SHAUL, 'Conjugal Union, Mourning and Talmud Torah in R. Isaac Luria's Tikkun Ḥaẓot', *Daat*, 36 (1996), pp. xvii–xliv.

—— 'From Theosophy to Midrash: Lurianic Exegesis and the Garden of Eden', *AJS Review*, 22/1 (1997), 37–75.

MCGILL, WILLIAM, *Maria Theresa* (New York, 1972).

MAHLER, RAPHAEL, *History of the Jewish People* [Divrei yemei yisra'el], 7 vols. (Merhavya, 1952–80).

—— *A History of Modern Jewry* (New York, 1971).

—— *Statistics about Jews in Former Poland* [Yidn in amolikn poyln in likht fun tsifern] (Warsaw, 1958).

MATT, DANIEL, 'The Mystic and the *Mizvot*', in Arthur Green (ed.), *Jewish Spirituality*, 2 vols. (New York, 1986), i. 367–404.

MEROZ, RONIT, 'Faithful Transmission versus Innovation: Luria and his Disciples', in Peter Schäfer and Joseph Dan (eds.), *Gershom Scholem's Major Trends in Jewish Mysticism, 50 Years After* (Tübingen, 1993), 257–74.

—— 'Redemption in Lurianic Teaching' (Heb.), Ph.D. diss., Hebrew University, 1988.

MEVORAKH, BARUKH, 'Jewish Diplomatic Activities to Prevent the Expulsion of Jews from Bohemia and Moravia in 1744–5' (Heb.), *Zion*, 28 (1963), 125–64.

MIKOLETZKY, HANNS LEO, *Österreich: Das grosse 18. Jahrhundert* (Vienna, 1967).

MÖRIKE, EDUARD, *Mozart auf der Reise nach Prag*, ed. Karl Pörnbacher (Stuttgart, 1976).

MUNELES, OTTO, *Bibliographical Survey of Jewish Prague* (Prague, 1952).

—— *Epitaphs from the Ancient Jewish Cemetery of Prague* [Ketuvot mibeit ha'olamin hayehudi he'atik beperag] (Jerusalem, 1988).

—— 'From the Archives of the State Jewish Museum', in *Jewish Studies* (Prague, 1955), 100–7.

NADLER, ALLAN, *The Faith of the Mithnagdim* (Baltimore, 1997).

NADLER, PINHAS (ed.), *Sefer ginzei yehudah* (Brooklyn, NY, 1997).

NALLE, SARA, 'Literacy and Culture in Early Modern Castile', *Past and Present*, 125 (1989), 65–96.

NETTL, PAUL, 'Bemerkungen zur jüdischen Musik- und Theatergeschichte in Böhmen', *Jahrbuch der Gesellschaft für Geschichte der Juden in der Ç.S.R.*, 2 (1930), 491–6.

NEUMARK, DAVID, *Toledot ha'ikarim beyisra'el*, 2 vols. (Odessa, 1913, 1921).

NIGAL, GEDALYAH, 'Sources of *Devekut* in Early Hasidic Literature' (Heb.), *Kiryat sefer*, 46/2–3 (1971), 343–8.

NOSEK, BEDRICH, 'Jewish Hebrew Studies in the Czech Lands in the Pre-Enlightenment and Enlightenment Period', *Judaica Bohemiae*, 27 (1991), 31–44.

PACHTER, MORDECHAI, 'The Book *Reshit ḥokhmah* by Rabbi Elijah de Vidas and its Epitomes' (Heb.), *Kiryat sefer*, 47/4 (1972), 686–710.

—— 'The Concept of Devekut in the Homiletical Ethical Writings of Sixteenth Century Safed', in Isadore Twersky (ed.), *Studies in Medieval Jewish History and Literature*, vol. ii (Cambridge, Mass., 1984), 171–230.

—— 'Homiletic and Ethical Literature of Safed in the Sixteenth Century' (Heb.), Ph.D. diss., Hebrew University, 1976

—— *Milei deshemaya by Rabbi Elazar Azikri* [Milei deshemaya shel r. elazar azikri] (Tel Aviv, 1991).

—— 'The Theory of *Devekut* in the Writings of the Sages of Safed in the Sixteenth Century' (Heb.), *Jerusalem Studies in Jewish Thought*, 2/3 (1982), 1–121.

—— 'Traces of the Influence of Rabbi Elijah de Vidas' *Reshit ḥokhmah* upon the Writings of Rabbi Jacob Joseph of Polonnoye' (Heb.), in J. Dan and J. Hacker (eds.), *Studies in Jewish Mysticism, Philosophy and Ethical Literature Presented to Isaiah Tishby on his Seventy-Fifth Birthday* [Meḥkarim bekabalah, befilosofiyah yehudit, uvesifrut hamusar vehehagut mugashim leyeshiyahu tishbi] (Jerusalem, 1986), 569–91.

PARÍK, ARNO, *The Jewish Town of Prague* (Prague, 1992).

PELLI, MOSHE, *The Age of Haskalah* (Leiden, 1979).

PERLMUTER, MOSHE ARIE, *Rabbi Jonathan Eybeschütz and his Relationship with Sabbatianism* [Rabi yonatan eibeshuts veyaḥaso el hashabeta'ut] (Tel Aviv, 1947).

PICK, ROBERT, *Empress Maria Theresa: The Earlier Years, 1717–1757* (New York, 1966).

PIEKARZ, MENDEL, *The Beginning of Hasidism: Ideological Trends in Derush and Musar Literature* [Bimei tsemiḥat heḥasidut: megamot re'ayoniyot besifrei derush umusar] (Jerusalem, 1978).

—— *The Hasidic Leadership: Authority and Faith in Tsadikim as Reflected in the Hasidic Literature* [Hahanhagah heḥasidit: samkhut ve'emunat tsadikim be'aspekulariyat sifrut heḥasidut] (Jerusalem, 1999).

PLACHT, OTTO, *Lidnatost a spoolčenská skladba českého státu v 16–18 století* (Prague, 1957).

PORTER, ROY, *The Enlightenment* (London, 1990).

—— and Mikulas Teich (eds.), *The Enlightenment in National Context* (Cambridge, 1981).

PRIBRAM, ALFRED (ed.), *Urkunden und Akten zur Geschichte der Juden in Wien*, 2 vols. (Vienna, 1918).

PUTÍK, ALEXANDR, 'The Prague Jewish Community in the Late 17th and Early 18th Centuries', *Judaica Bohemiae*, 35 (1999), 4–140.

—— 'Prague Jews and Judah Hasid: A Study on the Social, Political and Religious History of the Late Seventeenth and Early Eighteenth Centuries', pt. 1: *Judaica Bohemiae*, 38 (2002), 72–105; pt. 2: *Judaica Bohemiae*, 39 (2003), 53–92.

RAPHAEL, ISAAC, 'The Relationship between Rabbi Ezekiel Halevi Landau and Rabbi Isaac Halevi Horowitz' (Heb.), in S. Yisraeli, N. Lamm and I. Raphael (eds.), *Jubilee Volume in Honour of Joseph Dov Halevi Soloveitchik* [Sefer yovel likevod yosef dov halevi solovetsik], 2 vols. (Jerusalem, 1984), ii. 148–52.

RAPOPORT-ALBERT, Ada, 'God and the Zaddik as the Two Focal Points of Hasidic Worship', *History of Religions*, 18/4 (1979), 296–325.

—— (ed.), *Hasidism Reappraised* (London, 1996).

REINER, ELHANAN, 'A Biography of an Agent of Culture: Eleazar Altschul of Prague and his Literary Activity', in Michael Graetz (ed.), *Schöpferische Momente des europäischen Judentums in der frühen Neuzeit* (Heidelberg, 2000), 229–47.

—— 'Wealth, Social Position and the Study of Torah: The Status of the *Kloiz* in East European Jewish Society in the Early Modern Period' (Heb.), *Zion*, 57/3 (1993), 287–328.

ROBINSON, IRA, 'Messianic Prayer Vigils in Jerusalem in the Early Sixteenth Century', *Jewish Quarterly Review*, 72 (1981), 32–42.

ROIDER, KARL (ed.), *Maria Theresa* (Englewood Cliffs, NJ, 1973).

ROSMAN, MOSHE, *Founder of Hasidism: A Quest for the Historical Ba'al Shem Tov* (Berkeley, 1996).

—— 'Innovative Tradition: Jewish Culture in the Polish–Lithuanian Commonwealth', in David Biale (ed.), *Cultures of the Jews* (New York, 2002), 519–70.

—— *The Lords' Jews: Magnate–Jewish Relations in the Polish–Lithuanian Commonwealth during the Eighteenth Century* (Cambridge, Mass., 1990).

—— 'A Prolegomenon to the Study of Jewish Cultural History', *Jewish Studies Internet Journal*, 1 (2002), 109–27.

ROTH, CECIL, 'Sumptuary Laws of the Community of Carpentras', *Jewish Quarterly Review*, 18/4 (1928), 357–83.

RUDERMAN, DAVID, *Jewish Enlightenment in an English Key: Anglo-Jewry's Construction of Modern Jewish Thought* (Princeton, 2000).

—— *Jewish Thought and Scientific Discovery in Early Modern Europe* (New Haven, 1995).

—— *Kabbalah, Magic, and Science: The Cultural Universe of a Sixteenth-Century Jewish Physician* (Cambridge, Mass., 1988).

SACK, BRACHA, 'The Exile of Israel and the Exile of the Shekhinah in *Or yakar* of Rabbi Moses Cordovero' (Heb.), *Jerusalem Studies in Jewish Thought*, 4 (1982), 157–78.

—— 'The Influence of Cordovero on Seventeenth-Century Jewish Thought', in Isadore Twersky and Bernard Septimus (eds.), *Jewish Thought in the Seventeenth Century* (Cambridge, Mass., 1987), 365–79.

—— 'The Influence of *Reshit ḥokhmah* on the Teachings of the Maggid of Mezhirech', in Ada Rapoport-Albert (ed.), *Hasidism Reappraised* (London, 1996), 251–7.

—— *The Kabbalah of Rabbi Moses Cordovero* [Besha'arei hakabalah shel r. mosheh kordovero] (Beer Sheva, 1995).

—— 'Moses Cordovero and Isaac Luria' (Heb.), *Jerusalem Studies in Jewish Thought*, 10 (1992), 311–40.

—— *The Orchard Guard: The Kabbalist Rabbi Shabetai Sheftel Horowitz of Prague* [Shomer hapardes: hamekubal r. shabetai sheftel miprag] (Beer Sheva, 2002).

SADEK, VLADIMÍR, 'La Chronique hébraïque de l'histoire des juifs pragois de la deuxième moitié du 18e siècle', *Judaica Bohemiae*, 1 (1965), 59–68.

SAMET, MOSHE, 'Ezekiel ben Judah Landau', *Encyclopaedia Judaica* (Jerusalem, 1972), x. 1388–90.

—— 'Halakhah and Reform' (Heb.), Ph.D. diss., Hebrew University, 1967.

—— 'Mendelssohn, Wessely, and the Rabbis of their Time' (Heb.), in E. Gilboa, B. Mevorakh, A. Rappaport, and E. Shohet (eds.), *Studies in the History of the Jewish People and the Land of Israel in Memory of Zvi Avneri* [Meḥkarim betoledot am yisra'el ve'erets yisra'el lezekher tsevi avneri], vol. i (Haifa, 1970), 233–57.

—— Review of Ruth Kestenberg-Gladstein, *Neuere Geschichte der Juden in den böhmischen Ländern* (Heb.), *Kiryat sefer*, 47/2 (1972), 273–80.

SAPERSTEIN, MARC, *Decoding the Rabbis: A Thirteenth-Century Commentary on the Aggadah* (Cambridge, Mass., 1980).

—— 'In Praise of an Anti-Jewish Empress', *Shofar*, 6/1 (1987), 20–5.

—— *Jewish Preaching 1200–1800: An Anthology* (New Haven, 1989).

—— 'War and Patriotism in Sermons to Central European Jews 1756–1815', *Leo Baeck Institute Year Book*, 38 (1993), 3–14.

—— *'Your Voice Like a Ram's Horn': Themes and Texts in Traditional Jewish Preaching* (Cincinnati, 1996).

SCHACHTER, JACOB JOSEPH, 'Rabbi Jacob Emden: Life and Major Works', Ph.D. diss., Harvard University, 1988.

SCHALLER, JAROSLAUS, *Kurzgefasste Geschichte der kais. kön. Bücherzensur und Revision im Königreich Böhmen* (Prague, 1796).

SCHATZ-UFFENHEIMER, RIVKA, *Quietistic Elements in Eighteenth-Century Hasidic Thought* [Haḥasidut kemistikah: yesodot kevi'etistiyim bamaḥashavah haḥasidit bame'ah ha-18] (Jerusalem, 1968); published in English as *Hasidism as Mysticism: Quietist Elements in Eighteenth Century Hasidic Thought*, trans. Jonathan Chipman (Princeton, 1993).

SCHECHTER, SOLOMON, 'The Dogmas of Judaism', in id., *Studies in Judaism*, 1st ser. (Philadelphia, 1896), 147–81.

—— 'Safed in the Sixteenth Century', in id., *Studies in Judaism*, 2nd ser. (Philadelphia, 1908), 202–85.

SCHOLEM, GERSHOM, *The Beginning of Kabbalah* [Reshit hakabalah] (Jerusalem, 1948).

—— 'Vehata'alumah be'einah omedet', *Beḥinot bevikoret hasifrut*, 8 (1955), 79–95.

—— 'The Evolution of the Doctrine of the Worlds in the Early Kabbalah' (Heb.), pt. 1, *Tarbiz*, 2/4 (1931), 415–42; pt. 2: *Tarbiz*, 3/1 (1931), 33–66.

—— 'A Frankist Document from Prague', in Saul Lieberman (ed.), *Salo Wittmayer Baron Jubilee Volume*, 3 vols. (Jerusalem, 1974), ii. 787–814.

—— *Kabbalah* (New York, 1974).

—— 'Kabbalah', *Encyclopaedia Judaica* (1972 edn.), x. 489–653.

—— *Major Trends in Jewish Mysticism*, 3rd, rev., edn. (New York, 1974).

—— *The Messianic Idea in Judaism* (New York, 1971).

—— *On the Kabbalah and its Symbolism* (New York, 1965).

—— *On the Mystical Shape of the Godhead* (New York, 1991).

—— *Origins of the Kabbalah*, ed. R. J. Z. Werblowsky (Princeton, 1987).

—— 'The Paradisic Garb of Souls and the Origin of the Concept of *Ḥaluka Derabanan*' (Heb.), *Tarbiz*, 24/3 (1955), 290–306.

—— *Researches in Sabbatianism* [Meḥkarei shabta'ut], ed. Yehuda Liebes (Tel Aviv, 1991).

—— *Sabbatai Sevi: The Mystical Messiah* (Princeton, 1973).

—— *Studies and Texts Concerning the History of Sabbatianism and its Metamorphoses* [Meḥkarim umekorot letoledot hashabta'ut vegilguleiha] (Jerusalem, 1974).

—— 'A Study of the Theory of Transmigration in Kabbalah during the Thirteenth Century' (Heb.), *Tarbiz*, 16 (1945), 135–50.

—— 'Two Letters from Palestine, 1760–4' (Heb.), *Tarbiz*, 25/4 (1956), 429–40.

SCHUDT, JOHANN JAKOB, *Jüdische Merckwürdigkeiten*, 4 vols. (Frankfurt, 1714–18).

SCHUERER, OSKAR, *Prag: Kultur, Kunst, Geschichte* (Munich, 1935).

SCHWEID, ELIEZER, *Judaism and Mysticism According to Gershom Scholem: A Critical Analysis and Programmatic Discussion*, trans. David A. Weiner (Atlanta, 1985).

SEIFERT, JAROSLAV, *Mozart v Praze/Mozart in Prague* (Iowa City, 1985).

SELIGMANN, KURT, *Magic, Supernaturalism, and Religion* (New York, 1948).

SHALEM, SHIMON, *Rabbi Moses Alshekh* [Rabi mosheh alsheikh: leḥeker shitato haparshanit vehashkefotav be'inyanei maḥashavah umusar] (Jerusalem, 1966).

SHERWIN, BYRON L., *Mystical Theology and Social Dissent: The Life and Works of Judah Loew of Prague* (East Brunswick, 1982).

SHMIDMAN, MICHAEL, 'On Maimonides' "Conversion" to Kabbalah', in Isadore Twersky (ed.), *Studies in Medieval Jewish History and Literature*, 3 vols. (Cambridge, Mass., 1979–2000), ii. 375–86.

SHOHAT, RAPHAEL, 'The Vilna Gaon's Commentary on *Mishnat ḥasidim*: The *Mashal* and the *Nimshal* in Lurianic Works' (Heb.), *Kabbalah*, 3 (1998), 265–302.

SHOHET, AZRIEL, *Changing Eras: The Beginning of the Haskalah among German Jewry* [Im ḥilufei tekufot: reshit hahaskalah beyahadut germaniyah] (Jerusalem, 1960).

SILBER, MICHAEL, 'The Historical Experience of German Jewry and its Impact on Haskalah and Reform in Hungary', in Jacob Katz (ed.), *Toward Modernity: The European Jewish Model* (New Brunswick, 1987), 107–57.

SINGER, LUDWIG, 'Zur Geschichte der Toleranzpatente in den Sudetenländern', *Jahrbuch der Gesellschaft für Geschichte der Juden in der Čechoslovakischen Republik*, 5 (1933), 231–311.

SOLOVEITCHIK, HAYM, *Responsa as a Historical Source* [Shut kemakor histori] (Jerusalem, 1990).

SORKIN, DAVID, *The Berlin Haskalah and German Religious Thought* (London, 2000).

—— *Moses Mendelssohn and the Religious Enlightenment* (Berkeley, 1996).

SPERBER, DANIEL, *Customs of Israel: Sources and History* [Minhagei yisra'el: mekorot vetoledot], 8 vols. (Jerusalem, 1998–2007).

STRAUSS, LEO, *Persecution and the Art of Writing* (Illinois, 1952).

SVOBODA, ALOIS, *Prague* (Prague, 1968).

TA-SHMA, ISRAEL, *The Halakhic Residue in the Zohar* [Hanigleh shebanistar: leḥeker sheki'ei hahalakhah besefer hazohar] (Tel Aviv, 1995).

—— 'On the Book 'Pnei Yehoshua' and its Author' (Heb.), in Gershon Bacon, Daniel Sperber, Ahron Gaimani (eds.), *Studies on the History of the Jews of Ashkenaz* [Meḥkarim betoledot yehudei ashkenaz] (Ramat Gan, 2008), 277–86.

THORNDIKE, LYNN, *A History of Magic and Experimental Science*, 8 vols. (New York, 1923–58).

TISHBY, ISAIAH, 'The Confrontation between Lurianic Kabbalah and Cordoverian Kabbalah in the Writings and Life of Rabbi Aaron Berekhiah of Modena' (Heb.), *Zion*, 39 (1974), 8–85.

—— *The Doctrine of Evil and the 'Kelipah' in Lurianic Kabbalah* [Torat hara vehakelipah bekabalat ha'ari]. (Jerusalem, 1984).

—— *The Wisdom of the Zohar*, trans. David Goldstein, 3 vols. (Oxford, 1989).

TWERSKY, ISADORE, 'Law and Spirituality in the Seventeenth Century: A Case Study in R. Yair Hayyim Bacharach', in Isadore Twersky and Bernard Septimus (eds.), *Jewish Thought in the Seventeenth Century* (Cambridge, Mass., 1987), 447–67.

—— 'Religion and Law', in Shlomo Dov Goitein (ed.), *Religion in a Religious Age* (Cambridge, 1984), 69–82.

URBACH, EPHRAIM E., 'Askesis and Suffering in Talmudic and Midrashic Sources' (Heb.), in Salo Wittmayer Baron (ed.), *Yitzhak F. Baer Jubilee Volume* [Sefer hayovel likhvod yitsḥak ber] (Jerusalem, 1960), 48–68.

VAJDA, GEORGES, *L'Amour de Dieu dans la théologie juive du Moyen Age* (Paris, 1957).

VERMAN, MARC, *The Books of Contemplation: Medieval Jewish Mystical Sources* (Albany, NY, 1992).

VILÍMKOVÁ, MILADA, *The Prague Ghetto*, trans. Iris Urwin (Prague, 1990).

VILNAI, ZE'EV, *Holy Tombstones in the Land of Israel* [Matsevot kodesh be'erets yisra'el] (Jerusalem, 1951).

WACHOLDER, BEN-ZION, 'Jacob Frank and the Frankists: Hebrew Zoharic Letters', *Hebrew Union College Annual*, 53 (1982), 265–93.

WALDENBERG, ELIEZER, *Tsits eli'ezer* [responsa], 22 vols. (Jerusalem, 1945–98).

WANGERMANN, ERNST, *The Austrian Achievement 1700–1800* (London, 1973).

WANNIČEK, JOHANN, *Geschichte der prager Haupt-, Trivial- und Mädchenschule der Israeliten* (Prague, 1832).

WEINBERG, YEHIEL YA'AKOV, *Seridei esh* [responsa], 4 vols. (Jerusalem, 1961–9).

WEINGARTEN, R., *The Noda Biyehudah: The Story of Rabbi Yechezkel Landau*, trans. Yaakov Dovid Shulman (New York, 1991).

WEINRYB, BERNARD, *The Jews of Poland* (Philadelphia, 1973).

WEISS, JEROLD, *Zion Hamtzuyenes: A Compilation of Various Materials Relating to the World-Renowned and Illustrious Rabbi Yechezkel Halevi Landau* (Heb.) (Prague, 1993).

WEISS, JOSEPH, *Studies in East European Jewish Mysticism and Hasidism*, ed. David Goldstein (London, 1997).

—— 'A Circle of Pneumatics in Pre-Hasidism', *Journal of Jewish Studies*, 8 (1957), 211–12.

WERBLOWSKY, ZWI R. J., *Joseph Karo: Lawyer and Mystic* (Philadelphia, 1977).

WERSES, SHMUEL, *Haskalah and Sabbatianism: The Story of a Controversy* [Haskalah veshabeta'ut: toledotav shel ma'avak] (Jerusalem, 1988).

—— *Trends and Forms in Haskalah Literature* [Megamot vetsurot besifrut hahaskalah] (Jerusalem, 1990).

WILENSKY, MORDECAI, *Hasidim and Mitnagedim: A Study of the Controversy Between Them in the Years 1772–1815* [Ḥasidim umitnagedim: letoledot hapulmus shebeineihem beshanim 1772–1815], 2 vols. (Jerusalem, 1970).

—— 'The Hostile Phase', in Béla Király (ed.), *Tolerance and Movements of Religious Dissent in Eastern Europe* (New York, 1975), 89–113.

WIND, SOLOMON, 'Ezekiel Landau', in Leo Jung (ed.), *Jewish Leaders* (New York, 1953), 79–98.

—— *Rabbi Ezekiel Landau* [Rabi yeḥezkel landau] (Jerusalem, 1961).

WINTER, EDUARD, *Barock, Absolutismus, und Aufklärung in der Donaumonarchie* (Vienna, 1971).

—— *Ferdinand Kindermann Ritter von Schulstein* (Augsburg, 1926).

—— *Frühaufklärung* (Berlin, 1966).

WODZINSKI, MARCIN, *Haskalah and Hasidism in the Kingdom of Poland* (Oxford, 2005).

WOLFSON, ELLIOT R., *Abraham Abulafia—Kabbalist and Prophet: Hermeneutics, Theosophy, and Theurgy* (Los Angeles, 2000).

—— *Alef, Mem, Tau: Kabbalistic Musings on Time, Truth, and Death* (Berkeley, 2006).

—— *Along the Path: Studies in Kabbalistic Myth, Symbolism, and Hermeneutics* (Albany, NY, 1995).

—— *Circle in the Square* (New York, 1995).

—— 'Circumcision and the Divine Name: A Study in the Transmission of Esoteric Doctrine', *Jewish Quarterly Review*, 78 (1987), 77–112.

—— 'Eunuchs who Keep the Sabbath: Becoming Male and the Ascetic Ideal in Thirteenth- Century Jewish Mysticism', in Jeffrey Jerome Cohen and Bonnie Wheeler (eds.), *Becoming Male in the Middle Ages* (New York, 1997), 151–85.

—— 'From Sealed Book to Open Text: Time, Memory, and Narrativity in Kabbalistic Hermeneutics', in Steven Kepnes (ed.), *Interpreting Judaism in a Postmodern Age* (New York, 1996), 145–78.

—— 'The Influence of Luria on the Shelah' (Heb.), *Jerusalem Studies in Jewish Thought*, 10 (1992), 423–48.

—— *Language, Eros, Being: Kabbalistic Hermeneutics and Poetic Imagination* (New York, 2005).

—— 'Left Contained in the Right: A Study in Zoharic Hermeneutics', *AJS Review*, 11/1 (1986), 27–53.

—— 'Mystical Rationalization of the Commandments in *Sefer ha-Rimmon*', *Hebrew Union College Annual*, 59 (1988), 217–51.

—— 'Mystical–Theurgical Dimensions of Prayer in *Sefer ha-Rimmon*', in David Blumenthal (ed.), *Approaches to Judaism in Medieval Times*, vol. iii (Atlanta, 1988), 41–79.

—— 'Occultation of the Feminine and the Body of Secrecy in Medieval Kabbalah', in Elliot R. Wolfson (ed.), *Rending the Veil: Concealment and Secrecy in the History of Religions* (New York, 1999), 113–54.

—— *Through a Speculum That Shines: Vision and Imagination in Medieval Jewish Mysticism* (Princeton, 1994).

—— 'Walking as a Sacred Duty: Theological Transformation of Social Reality in Early Hasidism', in Ada Rapoport-Albert (ed.), *Hasidism Reappraised* (London, 1996), 180–207.

—— 'Weeping, Death, and Spiritual Ascent in Sixteenth-Century Jewish Mysticism', in John J. Collins and Michael Fishbane (eds.), *Death, Ecstasy, and Other Worldly Journeys* (Albany, NY, 1995), 209–47.

—— (ed.), *The Book of the Pomegranate: Moses de León's Sefer ha-Rimmon* (Atlanta, 1988).

WOLOCH, ISSER, *Eighteenth-Century Europe: Tradition and Progress, 1715–1789* (New York, 1982).

YUVAL, ISRAEL, 'Rishonim and Aharonim, *Antiqui et Moderni*: Periodization and Self-Awareness in Ashkenaz' (Heb.), *Zion*, 57/4 (1992), 369–94.

ŻÁČEK, VÁCLAV, 'Zwei Beiträge zur Geschichte des Frankismus in den böhmischen Ländern', *Jahrbuch der Gesellschaft für Geschichte der Juden in der Čechoslovakischen Republik*, 9 (1938), 358–410.

ZAGORIN, PEREZ, *Ways of Lying: Dissimulation, Persecution, and Conformity in Early Modern Europe* (Cambridge, Mass., 1990).

ZINZ, DAVID LOEB, *Gedulat yonatan* [biography of Jonathan Eybeschütz], 2 vols. (Piotrkow, 1930–4).

Index

Printed and bound by CPI Group (UK) Ltd, Croydon, CR0 4YY

13/04/2025

14656576-0004